THE INTELLIGIBLE WORLD

THE
INTELLIGIBLE WORLD

METAPHYSICS AND VALUE

BY

WILBUR MARSHALL URBAN

STONE PROFESSOR OF PHILOSOPHY
IN DARTMOUTH COLLEGE

GREENWOOD PRESS, PUBLISHERS
WESTPORT, CONNECTICUT

Library of Congress Cataloging in Publication Data

Urban, Wilbur Marshall, 1873-
  The intelligible world.

  Reprint of the 1929 ed. published by G. Allen & Unwin,
London, and Macmillan, New York, in series: Library of
philosophy.
  1. Metaphysics. 2. Values. 3. Philosophy, Modern.
I. Title. II. Series: Library of philosophy.
BD111.U7 1977   110   76-51208
ISBN 0-8371-9437-7

First published in 1929 by George Allen & Unwin Ltd.,
London and The Macmillan Company, New York

Reprinted with the permission of George Allen & Unwin Ltd.

Reprinted from a copy in the collections of the Brooklyn Public Library.

Reprinted in 1977 by Greenwood Press, Inc.

Library of Congress Catalog Card Number   76-51208

ISBN 0-8371-9437-7

Printed in the United States of America

PREFACE

IN the last resort there are only two kinds of philosophies: those that find the world ultimately meaningful and intelligible and those that do not. The present book claims to belong to the first of these, and as such to be a part, however modest, of the Great Tradition in philosophy. That there is such a tradition—that it is continuous and is characterized both by common presuppositions and by a common form—is the underlying thesis of the book. Following an ancient usage, I have given it the name of *philosophia perennis*. From Plato to Hegel this perennial philosophy has been characterized by the notion of an *intelligible* world, in some sense "beyond" the sensible and the phenomenal. Hence the title of the book.

In contrast to this tradition—and often in violent conflict with it—there has always been a party of more or less organized opposition. To this tendency, as it expresses itself to-day, I have given the name of Modernism in philosophy. When the term "modernism" is used, in religion, in morals, in art—and even in science—we are aware, not only of common elements, but also of common presuppositions, which we may call philosophical. Philosophic modernism is from one point of view a new name for old ways of thinking; from another point of view it represents novel forms of thought, starting from novel premises and ending in quite new and startling conclusions. One of the tasks which I have set myself in the present work is to bring to light the common presuppositions, as well as the more important consequences, of those movements of thought which have been typical of the last quarter-century. I can only express the hope that the exposition, and, as I believe, ultimate exposure of these ways of thinking, may be helpful in enabling the reader to come to grips with the fundamental, spiritual, and philosophical issues of our time.

It can have escaped none but the most unobserving that a strong reaction has set in against these tendencies of the last quarter-century. This means, according to the second thesis of the book, that we are gradually discovering the inherent unintelligibility of philosophic modernism and the necessity of a return to the main insights of perennial philosophy. This return has, I believe, actually been going on for some time. For one thing, the interpretation of "science" to which modernism had parasitically attached itself has been rendered obsolete by important developments within science itself. In the second place, the consequences for life and knowledge—including science itself—which follow from the premises of modernism, have issued in a veritable *reductio ad absurdum*, a sort of philosophical nonsense of which we are gradually becoming aware. It is now possible to see, I think, that philosophy has reached an *impasse*, and must in a very real sense do its first works over again.

The Great Tradition, as I have characterized it, is represented in present-day philosophy largely, if not wholly, by Idealism. In so far, therefore, as fundamental issues are concerned, the present work is dominantly idealistic in tendency. This does not mean, however, that it is idealistic in any sectarian sense; in fact, it is one of the main contentions of the book that traditional philosophy has been "beyond realism and idealism" in the modern meaning of these terms. It cannot be denied that to modern Idealism chiefly belongs the glory of keeping alive both the spirit and the insights of this tradition, and of none of the merit for this loyalty would one care to rob it. On the other hand, I believe it to be of the utmost importance to recognize that this modern opposition between realism and idealism is not—and has never been—the fundamental issue in philosophy, and also that the very truths for which Idealism has stood are not bound up with particular epistemological theories. At certain points I have found it necessary to take issue with positions often identified with Idealism. This does not mean any serious disagreement with its fundamental intentions. It has been said that no sane philosophy has ever been exclusively realistic or idealistic. My own belief is that the great philosophers have, in an important sense, always been above the battle.

The key to the understanding of the entire book is to be found in the sub-title *Metaphysics and Value*, and it is in connection with the working out of the relations of "value" to "reality" that the more original features of the book—such as they are—are to be found. Few will be disposed to deny, I think, that this is the key-problem of our age. In our attempts to solve it we have, I believe, reached a point at which we may see certain things with sufficient clearness. The ultimate inseparability of value and reality is now almost axiomatic; to attempt to divorce them can issue only in unintelligibility. This thesis is maintained throughout the book. It is, moreover, the insight embodied in this thesis, and in general the development of our thinking on value problems, that enables us both to see the unintelligibility of modernism and to reinterpret traditional philosophy in terms of present-day thought. From this point of view traditional metaphysics is seen to be throughout a value-charged scheme of thought, and as such must be understood and evaluated. It represents the "natural metaphysic of the human mind," a natural bent of the intellect which it is impossible to unbend.

Something may be said with advantage about the divisions of the book. The positive portion of the argument is found in Part II. In this second part I have sought to restate in modern form what I consider to be irrefutable in the Great Tradition. The fundamental notions or categories of this "natural metaphysic" have been examined both in their separate significance and in their systematic relations. For this constructive portion of the task Part I constitutes the indispensable preliminary. In addition to the development of the contrast between the Great Tradition and Modernism in the first chapter it was necessary also to go into certain present-day controversies concerning the nature and presuppositions of philosophic thought, the nature and function of logic, and finally, concerning the relation of value-theory to philosophy in general. Whatever value these studies may be found to have in themselves, their primary object is to provide the background for philosophical reconstruction, or, better perhaps, to furnish the philosophic idiom in which these ancient truths may now be most adequately expressed.

My indebtedness to others has been sufficiently acknowledged in the body of the text. If I should single out any recent writers for special mention, it would, of course, be the German *axiologists*, especially Rickert. Although greatly influenced by them in the earlier phases of my studies in value-theory, in recent years I have developed my position wholly independently— largely in critical reaction against modernist tendencies in England and America. I find, however, a gratifying confirmation of my own ways of thinking in the notable return to metaphysics—through value-theory—so characteristic of much of present-day German philosophy. I have found further confirmation in two important books —Mr. Wyndham Lewis's *Time and Western Man* and Professor Eddington's *The Nature of the Physical World*—both of which came into my hands only after the present book had gone to press. Those familiar with these books will understand how helpful the former would have been in my exposition of modernism in philosophy, and how gladly I would have made use of the latter, not only in connection with my discussion of such questions as "degradation and value," but also in my treatment of more general philosophical topics such as the relation of value and reality. In conclusion, I wish to express my thanks to Professor J. H. Muirhead for his very kind interest in the work, and for valuable criticisms and suggestions.

WILBUR M. URBAN

HANOVER, NEW HAMPSHIRE
February 1929

CONTENTS

PART I

TRADITION AND MODERNISM IN PHILOSOPHY

PART II

THE RETURN TO PERENNIAL PHILOSOPHY

PART I

TRADITION AND MODERNISM IN PHILOSOPHY

CHAPTER I

THE GREAT TRADITION AND MODERNISM
IN PHILOSOPHY

It is a positive achievement for a philosopher to be orthodox, provided his orthodoxy is philosophic.

HENRY JONES, *The Philosophy of Lotze*, p. 12

He who desires something new desires something old, only he desires it in a different way.

ALIOTTA, *The Idealistic Reaction Against Science*, p. 225

I

IN his *Alciphron, or The Minute Philosopher*, Bishop Berkeley draws the picture of a type of thinker which, borrowing a term from Cicero, he describes as the "minute philosopher." The minute philosophers, according to Crito, are "a sort of sect which diminish all the most valuable things, the thoughts, views, and hopes of men; all the knowledge, notions, and theories of the mind they reduce to sense; human nature they contract and degrade to the narrow, low standard of animal life and assign us only a small pittance of time instead of immortality."

The thinkers of this way, Berkeley holds, "have taken a direct contrary course to all the great philosophers of former ages, who made it their endeavour to raise and refine human kind, and remove it as far as possible from the brute; to moderate and subdue men's appetites; to remind them of the dignity of their nature; to awaken and improve their superior faculties, and direct them to the noblest objects; to possess men's minds with a high sense of the Divinity, of the Supreme Good, and of the Immortality of the Soul."

For this latter type of thinkers, to whom Berkeley confesses his own allegiance, he has no special name. But, borrowing a phrase from Sir Thomas Browne, they are to be described, perhaps, as those who have "a sense for the magnalities." These are the magnanimous philosophers who, while not "swallowing things in the gross," as Alciphron, in his defence of those who consider things minutely, charges, nevertheless

insist upon seeing things in the large; who, while not dis-
daining analysis, always recognize its limits and understand
fully the difference between explaining things and explaining
them away.

To this magnanimous tradition "the great philosophers of
former ages" have, as Berkeley rightly insists, all belonged.
It is characteristic of them that they have been essentially
human—"all too human," perhaps, in the minds of many;
but, if so, they are secure in the consciousness that they have not
reduced, contracted, and degraded, but, precisely because it is
human so to do, have sought to see things under the aspect
of eternity. In the words of a representative of the Great
Tradition to-day, they have seen in philosophy but an attempt
to develop "in the form of reflection what every living creature
at least is doing one way or another, between birth and death."
If in this attempt they "put the central things in the centre
and take as their standard what man recognizes as value when
his life is fullest and his soul at its highest stretch," it is because
this also is what every human being is doing, if not in every
hour of the pilgrimage from birth to death, at least in all the
hours and moments that have supreme significance.

This is doubtless to make philosophy "edifying"; and even
Hegel, who belonged to the magnanimous philosophers, tells
us that philosophy must guard itself against trying to be
edifying. But, if truth is edifying, there is no reason why we
should guard ourselves against that result. If it should turn
out to be true, as Leibniz said, that "in general there is nothing
more true than happiness, and nothing more happy and
pleasant than truth," he would be a churl, indeed, who would
insist upon defining truth so narrowly as to make it unpleasant,
and on conceiving philosophy in such a fashion that it could
not by any possibility be edifying. In any case, to build up,
and not to tear down, has always been of the essence of the
magnanimous tradition. *Lebensweisheit* has always been part of
philosophy, and one can scarcely conceive of a wisdom that
is of life which should be wholly life-denying.

This is, I repeat, the great, the magnanimous tradition in
philosophy. To this tradition the Platos, the Aristotles, the
St. Augustines and the St. Thomases, the Fichtes and the
Hegels have belonged. What constitutes this great tradition,

this *philosophia perennis*, we need not now inquire. The restatement and reinterpretation of this great tradition is, indeed, in one sense the objective of our entire study. It may be we shall find that, as it has been said, "the spiritual character of reality has never been doubted by any of the great philosophers; the difficulty has been to express this belief adequately." It may be that all the great philosophies embody an immitigable scale of values; that they represent the normal and fundamental way of viewing the world; that, as there is one *philosophia perennis*, so there is one fundamental system that underlies all minor differences of expression. It may be that that which is central in perennial philosophy from Plato to Hegel is the logical priority in human experience, theoretical, moral, æsthetic, and religious, of an Idea, of an order of perfection, which goes beyond and supplements the fragmentariness of our time experiences, under whatever name this may be known —the Good, Reason, God, as in ancient philosophy, or the infinite, the *causa sui*, the absolute in modern philosophy. All these things may be true, and I believe them to be true, but they are not what concern us at the present moment. I am rather interested in the *spirit* of the Great Tradition, and wish rather to emphasize certain outstanding characteristics, certain qualities of mind and heart, that distinguish this tradition from much of modern thought and the magnanimous from the minute philosophers.

There are undoubtedly such qualities, qualities that have uniformly characterized the magnanimous philosophers. One of these is a certain absence of scruple, a certain lack of inhibitions, a certain willingness to acknowledge as supremely significant and supremely real that which is found when "life *is* fullest and the soul at its highest stretch." As this search for reality has seemed to them the most human of all quests, so they have not hesitated to remain human in the method of the quest. As they have not scrupled to conceive their problem as one of the entire man, so they have not hesitated to use all their capacities and powers in the prosecution of the research magnificent. Penetrating thought, hair-splitting distinctions, dialectical skill, mathematical thought—all the mechanics of intellect have been employed, but also the intuitions of genius. Poetry and mythology, pathos and irony, mystical insight, even to visions and ecstasy—all the powers of creative imagination and emotion have been drafted into the service of the one supreme end. It is this large-mindedness, the absence of those scruples that mark the minute philosopher, that make the greatest philosophers also the greatest humanists of the race.

These qualities follow from the premises of the Great Tradition. The inseparability of the highest value from the most truly real has been at once the venture of faith and the "axiom of intelligibility" of the greatest thinkers. *Ens est unum, verum, bonum*—from Plato to Hegel the deliberate and reiterated identification of being and value has been the hidden spring of traditional thought, and from this spring has welled up all the effort, as well as all the effortless insights and realizations, which make up the treasure of historic philosophy.

Of all this effort—and of the faith or insight that vitalized it—what, it may well be asked, remains? Certain systems ancient and modern, mournful monuments to the audacity and egotism of speculative man? This is one way of viewing the products of the Great Tradition; but that would be sadly to misconceive the nature of philosophy and its function in the history of human culture. Not one of these ancient doctrines but can be in certain respects refuted and surpassed dialectically. Nevertheless, they conserve in themselves something as eternal as the great works of classic art. There is in them that which escapes all refutation. Rather do they seem to be like those edifices in the grand style of which the fundamental lines remain, even when certain parts have fallen.

It is these fundamental lines which, as I believe, are perennial, because they belong to the natural movement of the human spirit as such. They express normal and fundamental ways of seeing the world, and that which has veritable value in them is not so much the actual objectives which their constructors have either foreseen or attained as the unconscious foundations on which they have built and the inevitable method with which they have proceeded in their work. When the barriers of the sects have fallen there remains a *philosophia perennis* which is not so much a conscious construction of the pure intellect of the individual as the inevitable expression of the typical spirituality of the human soul.

II

Man's perennial speculations about the future of his own institutions and activities are among the most interesting and enlightening preoccupations of the human intelligence. The irreligion of the future, the passing of philosophy, are the favourite topics of the silly seasons of philosophic journalism. Recently, however, we have become rather more circumspect and sophisticated. Rarely now do we hear of some inevitable law, according to which religion gives place to metaphysics and the latter to science. The sophisticated modern no longer envisages a future without philosophy, but rather a futuristic philosophy. He talks, not of the "passing," but of the "changing concept" of philosophy.

There is what may properly be called "modernism" in philosophy. The thinkers of this way have, like the minute philosophers, the modernists of Berkeley's day, taken a direct contrary course to the great philosophers of former ages. Their modernism, we shall see, consists in challenging the premises of the Great Tradition; the "changing concept of philosophy" they preach involves the abandonment of the presuppositions and ideals of perennial philosophy. The way of thinking we have chosen to designate by this name is many-coloured, the philosophical tendencies it embraces varied enough, and in many respects mutually opposed; but underneath all the variations and oppositions there are certain common elements and tendencies which show them all to be products of that Time-Spirit which we understand if we cannot define. Both the sources and the principles of these novel tendencies in philosophy will engage our attention presently. We shall understand them all the better, however, if we examine those general tendencies in culture to which the name "modernism" has been given and with which these movements in philosophy are closely connected.

Modernism in art and religion, in politics and philosophy, in all the manifestations of culture, is as familiar as it is puzzling. Whatever difficulties we may have in defining it, we have none in appreciating its spirit. We know, for one thing, that it is the product, directly or indirectly, of modern science and the scientific spirit. Having begun by asserting the autonomy of science as against more original and elemental forms of the human spirit, the modern has ended by giving a privileged position to this latest and most unstable of its manifestations. Fundamentalism, whether in religion, in art, or in politics, however pathetically crude its gestures, is first of all and primarily an assertion of their own autonomy, of their own values and their own truths. Whatever else it is, it is the assertion of the "limits of science" in the household of the Spirit.

Modernism in religion is, in one aspect at least, the result of an unscrupulous and uncritical application of science to religion. History turns the absolutes of religion into the relatives of an evolutionary process, and psychology and biology reduce religious faith to a mere instinct in the service of life. In art, modernism is, in principle, the same thing. In the pictorial arts, Impressionism and Post-Impressionism alike are the result of a deliberate application of science and intellect to form and colour—mistakenly applied in many cases we may think, but none the less deliberately. Here, too, absolutes have everywhere given place to relatives, beauty to effectiveness, and truth to impressionism and expressionism, the complete subjectivism of art reflecting itself in the denial of all standards of æsthetic value. Not otherwise is it in the spheres of morals and politics, in which the deliberate turning of intellect and science on "instinct" has driven out all certainties and left only relativism and opportunism. All the "instincts" basal to community and State are analysed away, and in the most modern psychology the denial of instinct itself, the plain man's idiom for standard values, is the startling outcome of a movement which was inevitable.

But this is only one side of the picture. It is the other side that makes the attitude called modernism so puzzling and so interesting. Scarcely had the scientific spirit begun to celebrate its triumph in these other spheres of human culture and experience when modernism entered into science itself, and novel tendencies in this field threatened to change the whole picture. The modern spirit is nothing if not sophisticated. The very movement which began with a relentless application of intellect to the deepest initiatives of the human spirit comes full circle in a conception of science according to which its own concepts and laws themselves have no ultimate validity, but are merely useful instruments for the control of phenomena in the interests of life.

Modernism, as distinguished from the modern spirit and modern thought in the broader sense of the term, is an essentially novel form of the Time-Spirit. The key to this novelty lies in the equivocal character of the concept of science itself. The rake's progress of modernism has been swift and certain. Starting with the assertion of the autonomy of science, its divorce from wisdom and the moral and spiritual values, the acknowledgment of which is implied in all wisdom, it has ended in a philosophy of illusionism which includes science itself. Few scientists quite dare any longer to look truth full in the face, and truth and reason are terms almost lost from the vocabulary of the other forms of the human spirit. Of the modern spirit it has been well said:

> It feels that knowledge is the only good,
>   Yet fears that science may confound it quite,
> Changing what yesterday seemed logical,
>   To something different and bitter overnight.

It is this confounding of knowledge by "science"—is it not?— this something different and bitter, that has entered into our logic, that affords the key to the understanding of the whole modern spirit, and this sophistication regarding knowledge and science itself leads to very definite consequences. A certain mysticism becomes, as Simmel says, the necessary characteristic of every first-rate modern mind. In art one modernist tendency follows another, and impressionism with its scientific bias gives place to a reaction against all externality and objectivity in art, to an expressionism the very heart of which is illusionism. In science it leads to a pan-illusionism, to a philosophy of "as—if," which leaves nothing but the flux of sensation as belonging to the real.

This super-sophistication—even regarding knowledge and science itself—has certain further characteristics which definitely mark the spirit we call modernism. Not the least of these is one which we can describe no better than as the desire and tendency to transcend every limit. "Here," says Ferrero, "we have the great problem with which contemporary thought is confronted. Everything seems to totter to its fall around man, who, by transcending every limit, even the reality of the world, has become too powerful."[1] Transcendence of all natural limits, the natural law in society and politics, the norms of thought in logic and philosophy, all those "obstructions" to "creative thinking," is in one form or another the motive of all phases of modernism. "Human, all too human," is the scornful epithet applied to the natural metaphysic of the human spirit, and the abandonment of "the human scale" is considered the condition of world wisdom.

This abandonment of the human scale is, perhaps, the most striking, if not the most fundamental, character of our modern civilization. In our buildings and in our industry, our institutions and our arts, it is everywhere patent. Yet we are still unaware, I imagine, how completely it has also entered into the world of the spirit, how completely it has marked the products of our culture. That there should be some limits to the transvaluation of values, some truth *a priori* in knowledge, in morals, and in art—some limits within which intelligible thought moves—is simply another way of saying that human thought, to be significant and intelligible, must have a human scale. To deny all such limits, to deny all essential structure and system—as modernism in its most clairvoyant moments does—is simply to deny the human scale in thinking. That this very denial of the human scale and all it implies is frequently done in the name of humanism itself should not surprise us; it simply serves to show the widespread ignorance in the modern world of what the genuinely human is.

With this disdain of all limits, this fear of the past and its prejudices, come *Futurism* and the futuristic fallacy. Ideas are no longer disproved; they are simply superseded by new ideas. The latest is the truest, and time refutes everything. The classical, it has been said, is reality purified by time. But for the genuine modernist time purifies nothing, for in the eternal flux there is nothing there to purify. Everything is refuted, for it is the very fundamental character of everything that it becomes something other than it is. To reality itself is assigned the breathless task of keeping up with the idiosyncrasies of time, and the mere "creative accumulation"

[1] G. Ferrero, *Europe's Fateful Hour*—an excellent picture of modernism in its many aspects.

of these idiosyncrasies is hailed as the progress of reality itself.

With this super-sophistication and futurism there appears finally an element in modernism for which I am at a loss to find an adequate term. I can describe it in no other way than as an attempt to combine the incompatible. The profound contradictions in modern civilization and culture lie open to every eye—nowhere so patently, perhaps, as in the idea of progress around which all its thinking has revolved, and in which it has sought to embody its highest aspirations and values. So vaguely is progress conceived that it may with little difficulty "include both peace and war, justice and violence, steam-ploughs and Lewis-guns, Pasteur serum and Melinite." And indeed, if there are no limits to creative thought, if the doors of the future are completely open, both for life and for thought, why should we not seek to combine the incompatibles? As a matter of fact it is taken by many as a sign of greatness. At our level, it may be said, the inclusion of an element of contradiction seems to be a sign of reality and largeness rather than of error.

Such an attitude may easily create the illusion of magnanimity of spirit. But it *is* an illusion. It bears a superficial resemblance, indeed, to a similar attitude on the part of the magnanimous philosophers for whom the premises of the Great Tradition afforded a justification. But on the premises of modernism it can mean but decadence. A philosophy that assumes total ultimate coherence, the absolute, may allow itself many liberties. To attempt to transcend contradictions, to combine apparent incompatibles, is a sign of vigour and large-mindedness. But a philosophy that denies these assumptions can attempt such things only at the risk of intellectual and moral decadence.

III

It must be observed that by philosophic modernism I understand not any single one of the distinctively modern movements of thought, such as Pragmatism, Intuitionism, or the New Realism, but rather certain features common to them all and certain novel ideas which seem to follow from them. Philosophic modernism is the abandonment of the axioms and presuppositions of traditional thought, and it does not hesitate, in extreme cases, to see in traditional thought simply a gigantic *rationalization*. The idea of a "changing concept" of philosophy is accordingly, as we have said, a conspicuous feature of all these movements. Philosophic reconstruction is the goal of all their efforts. There is sufficient uncertainty as to the precise nature and direction of the change, but that there must be a change no self-respecting modern is in doubt. In this respect philosophy but shares the equivocal and paradoxical character of modern culture itself, and mirrors in one way or another all the moods which we have found distinctive of the modern spirit.

There are, however, certain points in which these proposed reconstructions of philosophy all agree and at which the essentials of modernism come to light. The "meeting of extremes" in modern thought has developed points of agreement which cut across and transcend the traditional divisions in philosophy. All agree, for one thing, in contracting and degrading the field of philosophy itself. All agree in denying the premises and postulates of traditional philosophy, and, like the minute philosophers of Berkeley's time, degrade philosophy to a mere pittance of its former self.

In certain quarters, in the most modern realisms and naturalisms, the humanistic premises of the Great Tradition are challenged and the province of philosophy narrowed down to a method of analysis that makes of it merely an appendix to science. The ancient postulate of perennial philosophy—the inseparability of value and reality—is *psychologized* into the demand that reality must satisfy us; the denial of the necessity of this demand is followed by the exclusion from philosophy of most of its traditional problems and " the raising to the dignity of philosophy many trivial and often foolish questions," marking their propounders as the "minute philosophers" of the modern world. In other quarters the denial of the humanistic premises of the Great Tradition takes the form of the denial of the ancient goal of philosophy, the *ens realissimum*, and philosophy is "contracted and degraded" to the mere service of ephemeral interests and ends. Not only is the great postulate of traditional philosophy psychologized into the demand that reality must satisfy us, but reality consists only in that satisfaction, and truth itself is metamorphosed into a means of satisfaction of desire or an instrument of control. In still other quarters, finally, the denial of these same premises leads to a challenge of the entire natural metaphysic of the human mind, the natural bent of the intellect; and to turn our back upon intellect is said to be the highest wisdom. Philosophy itself, the love of wisdom, becomes a non-rational intuition of life.

All these proposed "reconstructions" of philosophy represent, in one way or another, a radical change in the conception of the nature and objective of philosophy. Proposals of such a character demand of us that we shall examine with care the concept of philosophy as it has uniformly been held by the Great Tradition. Part of our problem—and an important part —must, as is indeed inevitable in books on philosophy, become the question of the nature and objective of philosophy. For the moment we shall confine our interest to the nature of these proposed reconstructions and the common element which is the motive of them all.

The changes in the objective of philosophy proposed by modernism represent then, not so much merely a contraction of the field of philosophy as a transvaluation of all philosophical values, the denial of the very premises of metaphysical thought, an inhibition of its deepest initiatives. Nor is this at all surprising; for all these forms of modernism, each in its own way, contract, if not degrade, the human reason to a mere pittance of its former self.

Each in its own way I say, for the ways are different. The contraction resulting from the merely instrumental view of mind needs no comment. For new realism the logical reason appears to be supreme, but it is only apparently so. Reduced to the form of merely logical analysis, the results of that analysis are a logical atomism which excludes from the realm of reason a large part of that which has uniformly been assigned to it. Even those forms of modern thought which seek metaphysical truth outside the ways of reason and would have us turn our backs upon it, presuppose this same contraction of reason.

Now, when we seek the common source of all these attitudes

we find it in the biological or evolutionary conception of mind. It is from this that all the sophistication, as well as all the violence of the modernist spirit, arises. To this is due the abandonment of the "human scale," the desire to transcend every limit, and to combine the incompatible in a freedom of creative thought which knows no limits and acknowledges no laws.

A fundamental characteristic of the "modern" man is, as Paul Rosenfeld says (he is writing of the music of the moderns, especially of that of Bloch), "his lately gotten sense of the tininess of the human element in the race, the enormity of the animal past." For the typical modern the primeval forest, with its thick spawning life, its ferocious beasts, its brutish phallic-worshipping humanity, is still here. Before him there lie the hundreds and hundreds of years of development necessary to make a sapient creature of him. That the moderns write as those who feel this goes without saying. That it is also the "hinterland" of the typically modern thinking in philosophy is what I wish to emphasize here. This conception of mind as *merely* something "in the making" underlies all the typically modernistic conceptions of philosophy, all the proposed "reconstructions" that we are about to examine. It is the source of all its negations, of all its paradoxical and sophistical affirmations.

IV

Modern thought, then, is nothing if not sophisticated. A profound scepticism lies in the heart even of those who deny scepticism with their lips. Not, be it understood, merely the scepticism of a Voltaire, engendered by the strife of opinion, but the deeper scepticism that comes from understanding. Nowadays one does not so much refute a philosopher as explain him.

One of the impressive things about the present situation in philosophy is the fact that, precisely at the moment when modernism in its various forms proposes to turn its back on traditional thought, the continuity of that tradition is most adequately recognized and its principles most completely formulated. Let us examine this sophistication—"new learning about philosophy," as Nietzsche calls it—in one or two of its most important phases. There is, first, the sophistication about the metaphysical instinct itself, and, secondly, regarding the strife of systems as it appears in philosophy.

The metaphysical *nisus*, the "ontological instinct," owes its perennial character to its relation to the vital instinct, of which it is, perhaps, in one sense the highest sublimation. The great philosophers have always recognized, consciously or unconsciously, this relation and the obligation it entails. The unity of the vital instinct and the instinct for knowledge is always assumed by traditional thought. The assumption of this unity, or in more philosophical terms, of the inseparability of value and reality, is the driving force of the natural metaphysic of the human mind.

Such is the belief of traditional thought, and in the light of that belief the whole movement of the natural metaphysic of the human mind can alone be understood. But what if this were not the case? What if the two were at war with each other, and the natural metaphysic but a "rationalization" to protect the life-instinct from knowledge? But let us hear this sophistication as it finds expression in the words of a typical modernist.

The vital instinct and the instinct for knowledge, "far from being the allies that popular thought proclaims them to be, are," according to M. Jules de Gaultier, "really at secret war with each other." The vital instinct, he holds, expresses itself in myth. "When," he continues, "the instinct for knowledge awakes in some sceptic, if it cannot be suppressed it must be answered, and now occurs a curious inversion of the rôles. The vital instinct disguises itself as the instinct for knowledge, and, if unable to save the old myth, promptly invents another." Such an invention, he holds, is the entire conception of knowledge from Plato to Kant. The identification of the *ens realissimum* with the *summum bonum* is such a myth, and Kant's account of the practical reason is but the same myth in a more subtle form.[1]

Such, with all the variations made possible by a sophisticated

---

[1] Jules de Gaultier, *De Kant à Nietzsche*. In this and in his other works, more especially *La Fiction Universelle*, one finds what is, perhaps, the most consistent development of "modernism" in its philosophical form.

psychology, is the modernist's account of traditional thought. Speculative philosophy, with its traditional problems and traditional form, is a species of myth-making. Its source is a latent animism. Its supposed rational structures and systems are, in the psychological slang of the day, but "rationalizations," with which the human spirit must, perhaps, clothe and protect itself if it is to continue to live, but from which it must, like lowlier forms of life, in turn set itself free. Is it any wonder that *philosophia perennis*, that great reason-myth, shows a constant structure and a constant form?

"How unfailingly," writes Nietzsche, "the most diverse philosophers always fill in again a definite fundamental scheme. . . . Under an invisible spell they always revolve once more in the same orbit, however independent of each other they may feel themselves; . . . with their critical or systematic wills something within them leads them, something impels them in definite order, the one after the other—to wit, the innate methodology and relationship of their ideas." But this continuity of the Great Tradition, which even those who challenge it more and more recognize, is easily understood. "The wonderful family resemblance of all Indian, Greek, and German philosophizing is easily enough explained. . . . Their thinking is, in fact, far less a discovery than a recognizing, a remembering, a return, and a homecoming to a far-off, ancient common household: philosophizing is so far a kind of atavism of the highest order."[1]

Such extreme sophistication and a-logism are, indeed, not to be attributed to every form of modernism, but something of it at least is to be found in all those ways of thinking we have been examining. It is, in fact, a necessary consequence of the contraction and degradation of the human reason that characterizes them all. Of the essential sophistry, not to say perversity, of this sophistication, the developments of this book will, it is hoped, constitute a proof. In this invisible spell that compels thought to revolve continually in the same orbit, this irresistible attraction which continually brings the intellect back to its natural movement, we shall hope to find, not a form of atavism, but rather the essential form of intelligible discourse itself. Here we are concerned wholly with the

[1] F. Nietzsche, *Beyond Good and Evil*.

modernist's interpretation of traditional thought, and of the "wonderful" continuity which underlies all its differences.

The very continuity of the Great Tradition, which even those who challenge it more and more recognize, is, as we have seen, only too well understood. No less sophisticated is the modern attitude towards the oppositions in philosophy which its equivocal character has generated. Philosophy is perennial, but so are its problems and solutions. We become aware, not only of an inborn systematic affinity of philosophical concepts, but of a certain fundamental scheme of possible philosophical positions, of great contrasting concepts and ideas which, like great crags, remain untouched by the waters of time and the passing generations, of great dualities and oppositions which spring from dualities and oppositions of the human spirit. Philosophy may, indeed, be a pantheon of great thoughts; yet are not these thoughts, great as they are, but the crystallizations of perennially opposing temperaments or of necessary social values?

It is in an atmosphere such as this that the modern thinker faces the challenge of *philosophia perennis*. It is in this form that the grand divisions of philosophical thought become the preoccupations of the modern. The "strife of systems" bulks large in the discussions of the present. The oppositions of naturalism and spiritualism, of monism and pluralism, of intellectualism and voluntarism, claim our attention; but for the modern thinker the problem becomes concentrated in the opposition of Idealism and Realism.

The growing struggle between these two positions has been the outstanding feature of the intellectual life of the last hundred and fifty years. It has absorbed all the energy and attention of the philosophers, and as a result they have had little time left for the genuine problems of traditional thought. A change in attitude towards this great opposition is, however, a characteristic note of present-day thought. From the most varied quarters one hears the belief expressed, as in the words of Mr. Russell, that "the issue between realists and their opponents is not a fundamental one." With such a view one may well agree. It has never been a fundamental issue in traditional thought, and "no sane philosophy has ever been exclusively realistic or idealistic." It is, however, with the distinctively modernistic attitude towards this opposition that I am here concerned, for it is precisely in this attitude that one of the characteristic notes of modernity makes itself heard.

The first reaction to this continued opposition is, indeed, one of complete scepticism. Yet in face of the real earnestness of the problems which it implies the irony of history passes us by. Our sceptical smile gives place to understanding, and we become sceptical of scepticism itself. In an age when survival becomes so nearly identical with truth and reality itself, the mere persistence of this opposition, the struggle for existence between philosophical creeds and systems, tends to take on a new meaning. Here, again, a sophisticated psychology with its doctrine of fundamental types, with its slang of extravert and introvert, of tender-minded and tough-minded, seems to come to the help of the modern.

Are they not extraordinarily naïve who suppose that there must be one type of philosophy? Is there not, as the poet Schiller says, a psychological antagonism among men, an antagonism which, "just because it is radical and rooted in the innate constitution, robs not only the poet and the artist of the possibility of making a universal appeal, although this is his task; but which also makes it impossible for the philosopher, in spite of every effort, to be universally convincing, although this, it has seemed, is involved in the very idea of philosophy?" Reality, it is felt, can hardly be as simple as many of the philosophers have supposed it, if varying and even opposing points of view are necessary to express it. Does not the very persistence of these oppositions argue a more than ephemeral significance, and is it not probable that a pragmatic attitude towards these oppositions is the highest philosophical wisdom? Is it surprising that out of the bitter scepticism and irony of our situation we should try to extract some sweetness, and that under the divisions and sects of philosophy we should seek a sort of sentimental catholicity?

This super-sophistication of modern thought is excellently expressed in a conception of the nature and function of philosophy developed by Paulhan. In an address before a philosophical conference in France, M. Paulhan, a modern of the modernists, offered the following suggestive interpretation of philosophy. The actual *lutte philosophique* and the *division des croyances* are inevitable and necessary characteristics of philosophy. The struggle for existence and division of labour among our philosophical creeds are necessary consequences of the practical and social character of philosophy. Each one of the main parties, chief faiths, has its own particular work to do; it represents a tendency useful and even necessary to society. Opposition in society of diverse needs and different tendencies, when translated into the world of ideas, takes, for instance, among other forms, the appearance of the struggles of materialism and spiritualism, realism and idealism. In a social organism well constituted these different tendencies would not, perhaps, be more irreconcilable than eating and breathing in a physiological organism. But man is apparently condemned, perhaps irremediably, to this struggle.

The rôle which he ascribes to the enlightened thinker, in the premises, is curious and not wholly enviable. These dualities, divisions, themselves become, of course, a chief problem of his philosophy. He sees clearly enough, on the one hand, that if humanity is to live such division of beliefs is necessary. He must, if he is to be a philosopher, in the ancient and honourable sense at least, accord to each a relative and partial truth. On the other hand, can truth be divided between parties any more than the child of Solomon's famous judgment?

Perhaps, however, a still further division of labour is possible. May there not be certain spirits, outside all parties, who seek to comprehend the essential nature of the tendency in each of them, as well as the system of ideas, images, and desires that nourish it? Such men will know that the actual social world could not live and endure if their transcendent ideas should nourish all spirits, but that is scarcely a danger that we have to fear. They will conclude that the great oppositions in philosophy, between realism and idealism, materialism and spiritualism, are in a sense eternal. They will even see that it is desirable, at a given time or for a given nation, for one tendency to have dominance over the other. If despite these facts they construct a system of the world, which may be necessary to them as to other spirits, they will know that in all these points it can be only transitory and must remain imperfect and incomplete. "It is vain," M. Paulhan adds, "to expect such a view to be accepted by the many, but what it lacks in vital appeal and immediate efficacy it will have gained in intellectual truth, in purity and *hauteur*."

The note of modernity in the foregoing is undeniable. The idea itself is by no means new, although the way of expressing it is ultra-sophisticated. Greater thinkers than M. Paulhan have seen in these grand divisions of belief the necessary conditions of life and its interpretation, although they have never found their meaning in merely pragmatic psychological and sociological conceptions. The idea that duality and opposition are part of the conditions necessary for philosophic truth is as old as philosophy, and it was Hegel himself who said that all philosophies have been necessary. The Great Tradition in philosophy, as we shall ourselves try to show, has always been above these oppositions, and has sought to find truth in a higher synthesis. This has been a characteristic of all the magnanimous philosophers. But the modern attitude, as we have sketched it, is quite a different matter. It is, in the sphere of philosophy, but a symptom of that impressionism and eclecticism, that willingness to combine the incompatible, which spells decadence. Bound up as it is in the modern spirit in general with the illusions of futurism, in the sphere of philosophy it implies and expresses that denial of all finality, that abandonment of the ontological point of view, which is the deepest note, as it is also the common element, in modernistic philosophies. To this further phase of modernism, the phase in which its opposition to all traditional thought is most fundamental, we must now turn.

V

The difference between traditional and modernistic conceptions of philosophy may best be indicated in terms of the figures in which the objective of philosophy is envisaged. For the older conception being or reality was said to be the goal of true knowledge. Men spoke of the "pathway to reality," of an ultimate goal, to which a predetermined path of reason inevitably leads. Philosophy is a well-trodden path to the *ens realissimum* and the *summum bonum*, and but puts in the form of reflection what everyone is doing, in one way or another, from birth to death. For the modern conception, on the other hand, the nature and function of philosophy are far differently envisaged. Ultimate reality, "true being," is essentially an illusion. It is rather like the pot of gold in the fable which the father told his sons was buried in the ancestral field. There was no such pot to reward the labour of the hopeful youths, but they attained their end notwithstanding, for the very incessant digging produced bumper crops and the father's promise was fulfilled. The *ens realissimum* is such a fruitful illusion.

Curiously enough the denial of this humanistic premise of the Great Tradition is made in the name of humanism itself. This distinctive note of modernism is sounded by many who otherwise think in the main within the bounds of that tradition. No more than in the case of poetry, we are told, can philosophy hope for finality. Life is perpetually at war with thought, and the forms of reflective thought are made only to be broken, all goals are set only to be surpassed. The only absolute truth is that there is no such truth. It is at this point that our sophistication regarding human knowledge, the impulse to transcend all limits, the abandonment of the human scale, in thought as well as in life, reaches its climax. It is here that futurism not only has its roots, but also reaches its most characteristic expression. For the natural metaphysic of the human mind is essentially the application of the principle of the human scale to thought, and its abandonment involves the complete denial of that scale.

Now, whether this denial of the humanistic premises of traditional thought is itself a kind of humanism is perhaps a matter of words. Nietzsche, at least, was in no doubt. For him the ontological instinct was essentially "human—all too human"; and of his own inhumanity to man, in denying it, he was fully conscious. Be that as it may, two things are evident. We have come here to the ultimate issue between traditional and modern thought. In the second place it seems fairly obvious that the tendencies in modernism must ultimately eventuate in this denial.

It is not my purpose to argue for the traditional conception of philosophy here. One of the tasks of the next chapter will be to show that the presupposition of an ultimate reality, of an *ens realissimum*, is a necessary presupposition of intelligible thought and its communication. Moreover, the purpose of this introductory chapter is descriptive rather than polemical, our chief object being to contrast the philosophies of modernism with the Great Tradition, and to point out the ultimate sources of their divergence. From this point of view the chief point of interest is the *complete break* with traditional thought, the complete transvaluation of all metaphysical values which it involves.

That the reconstruction of philosophy proposed by modernism should go to the length of a complete transvaluation of its very objective is in itself doubtful wisdom. There is no way of defining philosophy except in terms of its history, and nothing is clearer from that history than that the ontological motive is alike its constant driving force and its constant justification. Much more impressive than this change in objective is the novel conception of philosophy which this transvaluation of its objective, this denial of its historic premises, permits the more modern thinker to contemplate.

"We must become accustomed," says a recent writer, "to the idea of the universe as a Wandering Jew. The future of philosophy belongs to the naked demand of reason for a beyond anything given, to the idea of the all of things as inherently unfinished, a progress having no term, either finite or infinite." We might, perhaps, become accustomed to such an idea—we can become accustomed to anything. But of the philosophy to which such a future belongs certainly the least said the better. We may conceivably become accustomed to such an idea— the possibilities of sophistication appear to be without limit; it seems possible for the modern to carry the principle of fiction, fruitful illusion, to the length of making *that* for which the illusion is fruitful *itself* an illusion—in short, to making illusion the fundamental principle of reality itself. But to call such an idea a philosophical idea goes beyond the permissible. Philosophy must be intelligible or it is nothing. To speak of a demand of *reason* for something which by its very nature is irrational, to speak of progress without that which alone can give the concept of progress any meaning, is to talk an unintelligible language. But is not that what modernism in its more consistent moods asks us to do?

VI

The reconstructions of philosophy typical of modernism involve, we have seen, a rather complete transvaluation of the chief philosophical values; it is not surprising that they should also involve a changing conception of truth. The nature of truth is, in fact, the problem which above all others is diagnostic for modernism in general. Modernism we have found to be highly equivocal. Starting with its assumption of the autonomy of science, and with the privileged position of its conceptions of truth, it was forced ultimately to face the problem of the truth of science itself. From this confrontation it drew back humbled if not abased. To say with Poincaré that scientific concepts and formulas are not true, but that they are convenient, is to open up a way of thought the end of which is not yet in sight.

It is not my purpose to consider here the problem of truth as such; we shall have occasion to enter into more detail in later connections, especially in the chapter on logic. Our chief interest is rather to see the transformations in our notion that have followed necessarily from the premises of modernism, more especially the consequences for our conceptions of the *truth of philosophy*.

"With the best of intentions," wrote Paul Carus, "William James put truth on trial." It was not so much William James as the whole movement of modern naturalism speaking, in only one of its voices, through him. For him truth survived its trial. What he did not see, but others have seen, is that truth, in any intelligible sense, has not survived, that we have to do here with an entire revaluation of the value of truth itself, necessitated by the premises of modernism, by naturalistic evolutionism and the biological conception of the mind. The line between truth and fiction really disappears and we have a pan-fictionism. Truth is denatured, and instead of the problem of truth and falsity we have simply a problem of degrees of value among fictions, as Gaultier makes clear.[1]

It is to Vaihinger in Germany (and to Gaultier in France, perhaps) that we are chiefly indebted for revealing to us the

[1] See in this connection Jules de Gaultier, *La Fiction Universelle* (especially the last two chapters).

true inwardness of the premises of our thinking. Both develop a doctrine of *fiction universelle*. Vaihinger, in pointing out the instrumental value of "untrue" concepts, merely carries out to its logical conclusion that which was implicit in a genetic logic. The value of concepts is to be determined by their purpose, but when we seek to find out what end or purpose is in his thinking we find these to be a fiction also. The serpent devours its own tail. True, Vaihinger makes assumptions which the pragmatist would call absolutistic. By speaking of "untrue" concepts, and by characterizing them as fictions, he implicitly assumes an absolute criterion of truth, and must admit, although he may not like it, an independent realm of absolute validity, and hence the possibility of concepts that "represent" the world or demand universal acknowledgment. Vaihinger pleads for a new evaluation of concepts, which according to his characterization are untrue, while the pragmatist pleads for a new conception of truth which would not permit of such characterization. But what difference does it make? What difference—whether we define truth narrowly and admit to our world as value that which is untrue; or change our concept of truth so that we may call that value truth? The essential sophistication and sophistry are the same.

It is this sophistication and sophistry that are at once the cause and the widespread effect of this process by which truth has gradually been "denatured." No criticism of knowledge, it is said, can destroy knowledge, no theory of its nature can prove that reality is unknowable. This is undoubtedly true. But certain theories of knowledge, while not destroying it, can denature it, can take all the value out of it. That is what any merely biological and evolutionary conception of intelligence inevitably does.

The subtle effect of this process on our conceptions of knowledge and truth in general has already been indicated; it remains to consider its influence on our conceptions of philosophy. Now the modern is sophisticated regarding science, but he is a super-sophisticate when it comes to philosophy. The idea of philosophy as a gigantic "rationalization," of the oppositions of the philosophers as the expressions of merely psychological types, leads naturally to the denial of the "truth" of philosophy or to the development of notions of truth as subtle and sophisticated as these ideas out of which they spring. We find certain representatives of modernism saying: "The category of truth is, perhaps, not exactly applicable to philosophy, but rather the category of value, that is to say oi the importance of the spiritual direction manifested in the works of the philosophers." Or, in the words of John Dewey, philosophy deals with meanings and values rather than with truth.[1]

There is nothing, perhaps, which indicates more clearly the point to which modernism has brought us than this contrast of meaning and value with truth. Now, that philosophy does deal with the meanings and values of existences rather than with existence abstracted from meaning and value, is, indeed, true and one of the main contentions of this entire study. But the inference that this interpretation of meanings and values cannot have *truth* as its objective, can follow only from a most imperfect conception of both meaning and truth, and still more from an inadequate notion of the relation of meaning and truth to the more ultimate concept of value. In any case, this denial of the category of truth to philosophy is but a phase of that general transvaluation of all philosophical values inherent in the very premises of modernism. The same ways of thinking that would have us accustom ourselves to the idea of the universe as a Wandering Jew would also have us get used to the futility of a philosophical activity deprived of the only objective that makes it in any way intelligible. It suffices to record here that some consciousness of the situation I have been describing is gradually making itself felt. Certainly the suspicion is everywhere gaining ground that there is something suicidal in such ways of thinking; it is with the realization of this fact that the return to perennial philosophy must begin.

VII

"He who desires something new desires something old, only he desires it in a new way." "It is a positive achievement for a philosopher to be orthodox, provided his orthodoxy is

[1] "The Rôle of Philosophy in the History of Civilization," *Proceedings of the Sixth International Congress of Philosophy*, 1926.

philosophic." With these two quotations I began this chapter. Some development of what I consider to be their significance in this context may, perhaps, fittingly bring this chapter to a close.

The desire for something new in philosophy is sincere and significant. It is not wholly an expression of that vulgar illusion of modernity that whatever comes next must be better. It springs, as we have tried to indicate, from genuine exigencies of the present situation. That in seeking the new, the modernist in philosophy, as elsewhere, succeeds often merely in reviving some partial and fragmentary aspect of ancient truth, is nothing to his discredit; the discredit, if any, attaches solely to his failure to recognize the fact. It is but part of that unseen fate that drives human thought along a certain fundamental scheme of possible philosophical positions. For in truth what we really desire is something old. For true philosophy, like everything genuine and elemental, is, if not a kind of atavism, at least a search for the true homeland of the soul.

But while we really desire old things, we also desire to say them in a new way. New ways of expressing old truths is the condition of the vitality of these truths. If we have a distinctively modern idiom, as we most certainly have, we must think and speak in that idiom. The deeper one lives himself into the great philosophies, ancient and modern, the more he becomes convinced, I think, that philosophic truth is almost wholly a matter of adequate expression. With respect to the more fundamental problems and their solutions at least, what we call progress and development is in large part development of our *media* of expression. If there is any ancient truth that is irrefutable, it is so largely because it can be, and demands to be, expressed in modern form. Even more important is the fact that if there is a modern thought-idiom, and there certainly is, we must use that idiom, for that is the only language the modern now understands.

Tradition in philosophy is no literal repetition of dead concepts any more than tradition in the life of the State is a literal repetition of precepts and laws, or in religion of dogma and scriptures. Tradition is life and movement and perpetual reinterpretation. That which is permanent in it is, above all, an abiding sense of direction. To seize a tradition, as thus understood, it is above all necessary to live oneself into it; to continue it creatively, not to contemplate it; to follow and prolong it, not to arrest it under the pretext of being faithful to it. It is, accordingly, not a paradox to say that the way back to the Great Tradition must be through modernism.

But this truth in no way conflicts with the truth of that other quotation in which I have sought to crystallize the spirit of this chapter. It is, I believe, a positive achievement for a philosopher to be orthodox—to be within the spirit of the Great Tradition—provided his orthodoxy is philosophic. That which is permanent in tradition, we have said, is an abiding sense of direction. Now it is the loss of this sense of direction, of the genuine problems and significant objectives of philosophy, that we have deplored in many forms of modernism. To keep this sense of direction, as it is the chief *desideratum*, is also the highest achievement of the modern thinker. There is no inherent reason why there should not be orthodoxy—straight thinking— in philosophy. There is every reason to believe that there should be.

I need not repeat here the points at which I have conceived the typical modern tendencies to have taken a direct contrary course to all the great philosophers. That which I hope to show is that in doing so they have lost their way and have become ultimately unintelligible. There is what we may call the *a priori* of an intelligible world, and in turning their backs upon the "innate metaphysic of the human mind" they have abandoned the conditions of essential intelligibility. To be philosophically orthodox is to understand and acknowledge those fundamental forms of reflective thinking without which intelligible communication and interpretation are impossible.

Yet in all this, it cannot be denied, the sincere thinker may easily think to find a great insincerity—or at least a funda- mental contradiction—the same difficulty in philosophy that faces all the historic and traditional activities of man. Tradition is life, movement, perpetual reinterpretation. Yes, but at what point does reinterpretation become new creation? At what point, for instance, does free construction of the law become new legislation? At what point does free interpretation of dogma in religion become its denial? At what point in philo- sophy does saying old things in a new way become the saying of entirely novel things? In short, are we not faced with a dilemma that is ultimately insoluble? Either the denial of all novelty and development, or else the frank acceptance of absolute novelty, the abandonment of all finality in philosophy— the essence of the modernist position.

The question here raised is fundamental and as difficult as fundamental. It involves all the questions of progress and system in philosophy, questions that it is worth while considering only when they can be considered adequately. Here is certainly not the place to anticipate the details of later discussions. Some things can, however, be said in the most general terms. And we may at least indicate our general attitude towards the problem.

The idea of the possibility of knowledge that is *wholly* new is a common and characteristic feature of modernist positions. Our familiarity with what seem to us to be complete novelties in the sphere of scientific knowledge predisposes us to the idea of the possibility of such novelties in all spheres of the human spirit. Now, as to this supposed novelty in science, there is reason to think that it is often greatly misunderstood if not grossly exaggerated. Change in scientific concepts themselves seems to be in inverse ratio to their fundamental character. Men have, for instance, spoken successively of the conservation of matter, of force, and of energy. The first two are now found to be untrue—not even capable of intelligible expression. But the significant element in them all—*conservation*—persists, and has seemed to have, as Balfour says, a kind of intuitive certainty more or less independent of empirical fact. Be that as it may, there is a difference between the accumulation of fact and the interpretation of fact, as also between "science" and other spheres of the human spirit, which is too often overlooked. We speak of creative thought, fertile thinking, and it is assumed, *without thinking*, that invention and novelty mean the same thing, and are equally possible in all these spheres. This is far from being the case, and such novelty, if possible, would be the destruction of all genuine knowledge.

For let us consider the concept of a knowledge that shall be wholly new, that, as it has been expressed, shall "change the very structure of our knowledge out of all recognition." Such a change could not possibly be progress in knowledge. It would be complete self-alienation, that kind of change of which the poet wrote when he said:

> I changed myself to renew myself
> And lost myself. . . .

This will sound dogmatic—and cannot, perhaps, sound other-wise than dogmatic at this stage of our discussion. Let us, then, for the moment abandon argument and content ourselves with a mere statement of the attitude that has emerged from the reflections of this chapter and which shall guide the reflections of the chapters to come. I know no better way of expressing it than by an adaptation to our own purpose of some charming words of Anatole France.

An admirer of M. France had complimented him upon his scientific knowledge and the wisdom of his judgments on these questions. "My dear sir," M. France replied, "the important thing, perhaps, is not my scientific attainments, which are slight, but rather the effect of modern discoveries on a mind formed by prolonged commerce with the charming, subtle, humane authors of our country. I have tried to say as well as possible of the things I have learned and seen in my own time what those fine minds of old would have said if they had seen and learned the same things." Orientation towards the fine minds of all time is, I believe, the secret of wisdom in philosophy no less than in the world of humane letters. For it is this fineness and largeness of mind—the magnanimity that puts the central things in the centre and which takes as its standard that which man recognizes as truth when life is at its fullest and his soul is at its highest stretch—it is this and this alone that is the final place of understanding. For, in the long run, it is human nature as a whole that passes judgment, not only upon every attempt to improve it, but upon every pretence to know it and to understand it.

CHAPTER II

THE PREJUDICES OF THE PHILOSOPHER: THE PHILOSOPHICAL HINTERLAND

Having kept a sharp eye upon the philosophers and having read between their lines long enough, I now say to myself that the greater part of conscious thinking must be counted among the instinctive functions, and it is so even in the case of philosophical thinking; one has here to learn anew, as one learned about heredity and innateness.

NIETZSCHE

Es bleibt der Philosoph von wert für alle Zeiten:
Er findet stets auf's neu die selbstverständlichkeiten.
OTTO ERICH HARTLEBEN

I

THE *Vorurteile der Philosophen,* of which Nietzsche makes so much, are facts to be reckoned with. "In philosophy," it has been said, "ethical neutrality has been seldom sought and hardly ever achieved. Men have remembered their wishes and have judged philosophies in relation to their wishes." To recognize this is ordinarily to condemn it. It is assumed without question, especially by those who claim to be "genuinely inspired by the scientific spirit," not only that such neutrality is desirable, but that it can actually be achieved. Is it that those whom the so-called scientific spirit has inspired are especially childlike, as Nietzsche thinks?— that they do not feel scientific preconceptions to be prejudices, and that they think freedom from prejudice to be really possible? It matters not. The discouraging thing is not the actual inability of the scientifically inspired philosopher to achieve neutrality; it is rather that he has not yet learned, as all the great philosophers have learned, that such neutrality is impossible, and that he still preserves the prejudice that it would be desirable if it could be attained. This is the last prejudice that all genuine philosophizing must overcome.

Philosophy, it is true, is supposed to be presuppositionless, and in a sense, of course, this is true. It is possible, we have seen, to define philosophy only by an inductive study of its own material, and such a study makes it abundantly clear that freedom of thought is the very principle of its life. From Xenophanes to Nietzsche this is the one thing that philosophers have in common. Criticism of first prejudices might be written as the sub-title of that extraordinary history. Yet closer examination shows that this is only relatively so. The *de omnibus dubitandum* remains an ideal which even the wariest of thinkers find it difficult to apply.

Completely radical, in the first place, this attempt rarely is. It is seldom sought and never fully achieved. As a rule knowledge is sought which shall be independent of some *single* presupposition, that shall rise above some *particular* prejudice or assumption. Now it is the belief in divine powers or traditional moral values; again it is the belief in the validity of the immediate impressions of the world of sense, or in the exclusive value of reason. It is at best only piecemeal that the ideal is realized. *Universality* of doubt remains largely a philosophical affectation.

More than this, the doubt itself is never absolute. The ideal of doubt rests usually upon an ineradicable faith. Thus it is that the great monuments of philosophic doubt—the confessions or meditations of an Augustine or an Anselm, of a Pascal or a Descartes—even of a Tolstoy or a Nietszche—fail to produce completely the illusion of reality. In all of them there are hidden reserves, even make-believes, that show them to be nearer to art than to reality. One feels that the issue never really was in doubt—that in every *dubito* there is an element of artistic convention—that the doubt itself is but a cloak for a transparent certainty.

Yet with all these limitations there is, nevertheless, something about this ideal of philosophy that distinguishes it sharply from the ideals of common sense and science. "Philosophy," says Croce, "has for its object what really is and must justify itself fully, neither admitting a presupposition nor allowing any presupposition to exist." Such an objective, were it possible of achievement, which it is not, would make of philosophy the supreme instance of human self-deception. It is rather because philosophy admits its presuppositions and acknowledges their necessity that it is the supreme instance of freedom of thought. The so-called free thought of science has distinct limitations. It seeks only ethical neutrality. It refuses to be the handmaid of religion or morals, and in its new-found intellectual righteousness it becomes prejudiced against them, as sources of truth. Science tries to forget men's wishes. True philosophy not only remembers them but tries to understand them. "Freedom itself," says Renouvier, "is the first truth in the world of knowledge." It is, indeed, a presupposition of which even the determinist avails himself when he elects to make determinism his first principle. Only he involves himself in a contradiction which the genuinely free thinker avoids. The free-thinkers of the future will not, as Nietzsche says, like their brothers of the past, simply exchange one prejudice for another, but will be those who acknowledge and accept their own prejudices.

Philosophy is the one field of thought in which presuppositions are admitted and values acknowledged. In this deeper sense, then, absolute freedom from prejudices is the distinguishing mark of philosophy. If not a completely realizable goal it is at least that which determines its direction. The autonomy of philosophy lies in this very fact—that, in principle at least, it has overcome the last prejudices of common sense and science alike. But this very autonomy brings with it certain obligations. The very right and duty of philosophical thought to pursue its objective with a greater degree of independence than is possible in other spheres of knowledge, bring with them the duty to recognize its own prejudices and presuppositions. More than this, it involves the obligation to distinguish clearly between those prejudices which are individual and racial, and the still more fundamental presuppositions that condition all philosophizing as such.

It is just this enlightened consciousness that, in a sense, is the ideal of modernistic philosophy. Nietzsche's *Die Vorurteile der Philosophen* is in one respect the quintessence of this modernism. In art, we are told, certain obstinate ways of seeing things prevent us from appreciating what the "artists of the future" seek to express. Certain "very obstinate prejudices," we are told, stand in the way of our understanding the new concepts of space and time involved in the theory of relativity or the new conceptions of the infinite. Similar prejudices stand in the way of what is called the New Logic, and as the new this, that, and the other appear on the stage axioms and postulates gradually pass into prejudices—until at last full circle is reached and truth and reality themselves become prejudices.

Unearthing of prejudices and prepossessions is thus the most joyous part of that gay science to which the unscrupulous empiricism of modernism has given birth. Naturally modernistic philosophy is in its element. Nietzsche discloses the "characteristic prejudice by which the metaphysicians of all time may be recognized." Bergson unearths the hidden prejudices of all traditional philosophy, disclosing that natural bent of the intellect which we must all now learn to unbend. The new realists find traditional philosophy vitiated by a whole complex of "philosophical errors" which have their roots in the speculative dogma itself. All unite, however, as we have seen, in considering the traditional concept of philosophy itself a prejudice. Now, all this is well enough in its way, but such "freedom of thought" involves a corresponding responsibility, and in these matters we moderns display an irresponsibility that is regrettable. For one thing, we are extraordinarily free with question-begging epithets. With an unbelievable light-heartedness, permanent presuppositions are turned into "gratuitous assumptions" and "sheer mistakes," and enduring postulates are airily turned into plain prejudices.

We have already seen how deep this strikes—into the very conception of philosophy itself. Perennial problems are eliminated as arising out of racial prejudice, and under the caption "Problems of Philosophy" the ancient discipline is narrowed down to certain technical questions in which the individual thinker happens to be especially interested. Reconstructions of philosophy are proposed which in the face of the plain story of the human spirit substitute definitions which embody individual and ephemeral interests. Philosophy must in a very real sense do its first works over again. And this requirement, as we have seen, goes deep, even to the conception of the nature and objective of philosophy itself. For the prejudices and gratuitous assumptions with which the modernist charges perennial philosophy are all inextricably bound up with a conception of the objective of philosophy which, he holds, is itself a prejudice; the changing conception of philosophy on which the modernists are working is itself to be the result of the removal of these prejudices. Philosophy, we have said, is the one field in human thought in which presuppositions are admitted and values acknowledged. We may, with Nietzsche, call these the prejudices of the philosophers if we will, but, if we do, we must recognize that these are the prejudices of the philosopher *qua* philosopher, and that without them no philosophizing can take place. To an examination of these "prejudices" we shall now turn.

II

A certain philosopher recently undertook the paradox of "A Defence of Prejudice." The point of his contention was that what appear prejudices are often really not prejudices in the dyslogistic sense of the word, but rather judgments well validated by experience, including thought, the grounds for which have, however, fallen into the background. The hinterland of common sense and philosophy alike is, then, not a jungle of irrational emotions and passions, but a world of reason—in the sense at least in which the "magnanimous philosophers" use that term.

Whatever may be said of common sense, this is certainly true of philosophy. The philosopher must, indeed, as we have seen, confess to his peculiar prejudices as an individual—prejudices which determine the very questions he shall ask and to a degree his answers. Part of his highest wisdom is to recognize that "my judgment is *my* judgment." Again, no philosopher can wholly escape the prejudices of his time and his race. To try to divest himself wholly of the pack that he carries on his back is to write himself down as either a knave or a fool. Prejudices of this kind we have, in principle at least, no difficulty in distinguishing and discounting. But deeper than all these are certain fundamental presuppositions, certain "prejudices of the philosopher" *qua* philosopher, original valuations which are not expressions of either individual or race, but of the "typical spirituality" of humanity. From these prejudices and presuppositions the philosopher cannot free himself without transcending his own skin. Nietzsche tried it, and the horrid cries of pain that accompanied the process are the scandal of the century.

Prejudices of individual and race, I repeat, we have no difficulty in distinguishing and discounting. Any sympathetic study of the philosophical systems of individuals—and, indeed, of the philosophical attitudes of entire centuries and peoples— always brings us at last to certain ultimate valuations or systems of valuation, themselves without proof. It goes without saying that this is true in the fields of appreciation and practice, of ethics and æsthetics, but it is also more or less true in the realm of scientific logical principles. A Plato may not have been able to think outside the bounds of certain space conceptions, but the modern mathematician and philosopher can. A modern finds it hard to think without the concepts of evolution and progress, but a Plato could, and we may conceivably be able to do so again.

Such, then, are the prejudices—the *Grundurteile*, as they have been called—that underlie the world views of great individuals, dominate whole peoples, and give colour to the thinking of entire cycles of human life. But are there not *Grundurteile* of a wholly different kind? Are there not *Vorurteile*, typical prejudices by which the metaphysicians of all time can be recognized and without which metaphysics itself is impossible? Are there not certain ideas, postulates, outside the bounds of which it is not possible to think consistently—much less speak intelligibly? If so—and I certainly think there are such—they would no longer be prejudices in any dyslogistic sense of the word, but necessary presuppositions. Such would, indeed, constitute a "natural bent of the intellect" which it would, perhaps, be very amusing, but also very futile, to try to unbend.

The conviction that there is such a natural bent that cannot really be unbent is a deathless element in all traditional philosophy. It is not surprising, therefore, that throughout the history of thought attempts have constantly been made to find a means of distinguishing between prejudices and necessary presuppositions, attempts which have been registered in the history of the concept of the *a priori*. The attempt to strengthen the objective validity of at least some of the elements of our knowledge, by seeking to show that in the very assumption of their impossibility there is a contradiction, is in itself a temptation which thought never has been, and probably never will be, able to resist. The "blessed certainty that two and two make four" is blessed by reason of the mere fact of certainty, however trivial from some points of view the fact itself may be. But even more tempting is the possibility it seems to offer of an ultimate criterion of intelligible philosophical discourse. The principle of self-refutation has always been the favourite method of distinguishing between prejudices and necessary presuppositions. It may almost be said to be the typical philosophical method.

It cannot be denied that in many quarters this method has fallen into disrepute, not wholly undeserved. It has not always been treated understandingly either by those who have used it or those who have criticized it. For one thing, according to Nietzsche, it has never occurred to the wariest of the philosophers to apply it to their own ultimate prejudices; and its employment has ended, as in the case of Kant, the much advertised All-destroyer, merely in "erecting into postulates his moral prejudices." The wariest of the philosophers have found it difficult to distinguish between that which is inconceivable and that which is unimaginable, and to call a thing unthinkable has often been but a euphemistic way of saying that it is intolerable. Yet despite this criticism —much of it deserved—it remains true that *internal consistency*, properly understood, must remain the ultimate touchstone of all thought. Indeed, we cannot proceed a step in our thinking without acknowledging that which, for internal reasons, we regard as the inevitable way of interpreting experience. There are no fundamental truths of experience for which I can give any reasons which are not, in part at least, *a priori*; reason being here defined in that large-minded way which thinks of it in terms of an internal necessity which my consciousness makes manifest in various ways.

The very general use of the principle of self-refutation in philosophic thought is itself significant. The sceptic, the agnostic, the relativist have all at different times been silenced by its crushing and damnatory logic. With it the idealist has refuted the realist and the realist the idealist. In one way or another it is the last argument that both employ. And in this the instinct of both is profoundly right, for such argument is essentially an *argumentum ad hominem*, and in ultimate matters this is, as Lowes Dickinson says, "the only argument possible and, indeed, the only one in which anyone much believes." But this character of the argument has not always been wholly understood, nor the real significance of the inferences drawn from it. Rightly used, and with a proper understanding of its nature, this type of argument does, I believe, serve its end, and does enable us to establish certain presuppositions of all thinking which are above the differences of the schools. Let us try, therefore, to get to the heart of the argument.

Taken as a characteristic device of formal logic, as a means of establishing abstract logical axioms, the method of self-refutation suffers under a genuine disability which the slightest logical acumen serves to make clear. The sceptic, for instance, is said to refute himself when he asserts with conviction that there is no knowledge. And he certainly does. But this self-refutation is immediately applied by the unwary not to the sceptic, where it rightly belongs, but to the abstract proposition which he enunciates, where it does not belong.

It will be worth our while to examine this a little more closely. Whoever claims that there is no valid knowledge, in this very claim expresses a "case" of knowledge for which he presupposes objective validity. So far he contradicts or refutes himself. X makes the assumption A, that he possesses no valid knowledge. This has as its consequence merely that X himself can have no valid knowledge of this assumption A, for if he had this knowledge he would possess in it a case of valid knowledge. It is not the assumption A (that X possesses no valid knowledge) that contains a contradiction, but rather a further assumption B (namely, that X possesses a valid knowledge of A). From this contradiction there follows as a consequence, however, not the falsity of A, but merely the falsity of B. To repeat, when one claims to know that he knows nothing, he contradicts himself of course, but one may not, therefore, conclude that he knows anything, but only that this which he claims to know he does not know. And how can it be otherwise, since from the principle of contradiction, viewed as a principle of abstract logic, only "analytical" propositions can be inferred? The proposition that we possess objectively valid knowledge is, however, obviously of a synthetic character.

Now, the importance of this conclusion is immensely more far-reaching than appears at first sight. It by no means follows from this criticism of the principle of self-refutation that it does not do its work, but merely that it does not do a kind of work it was never intended to do. The precise character of the work it may legitimately be expected to perform this entire chapter is intended to show in detail. In general, it may be said that it *is one of the determining principles of intelligible philosophical discourse.* It is concerned with those presuppositions which the thinker cannot deny without making himself unintelligible, the values, logical and a-logical, that must be acknowledged if communication from mind to mind is to be possible. The possibility of intelligible communication is the ultimate postulate of all thought, all knowledge. It itself cannot be explained, but is the presupposition of all knowledge and science. As applied to our particular problem, the prejudices or premises of traditional thought, we may hope by means of this principle to distinguish prejudices from necessary presuppositions.[1]

The task of this chapter is to make just this distinction and to determine the necessary presuppositions of intelligible philosophical discourse. A word on the use of this term *presupposition*, as well as of certain other terms, such as assumption, postulate, axiom—often used interchangeably with it—is necessary if the positions of this chapter are to be entirely clear.

I have taken "presupposition" to start with as the most colourless term to describe the more general conditions of intelligible discourse. A presupposition becomes an *assumption* when it is more or less consciously acknowledged as such a condition.

---

[1] One of the outstanding characteristics of modernist thought is its loss of the sense for intelligibility. This characteristic will be developed more fully in Chapters V and VI; here I wish merely to call attention to but one aspect of it— namely, the loss of the sense for *implicational argument*. From Plato to Hegel this has been one of the chief marks of philosophic method, and it was one of Kant's chief merits to set this entire type of thinking in high relief. The principle of self-refutation is only one aspect of this general method. One of the chief characteristics of modernism is, as we saw in the preceding chapter, its readiness to combine incompatibles. I am at a loss to understand this except, perhaps, that in this matter radical empiricism has been a loose master, having accustomed us to the idea that whatever goes contrary to the natural prejudices of thought is likely to have the greater probability.

Thus the presupposition of all meaningful discourse—that truth is better than error—becomes the explicit assumption of any intelligible logic. Now, an assumption becomes a *postulate* when, as the term indicates, it takes the form of a demand. Such demand is made, however, only when that which is demanded may conceivably be denied. Thus in philosophy, notably in Kant, a postulate is a demand for that which may be doubted, but which yet seems necessary to the solution of a self-evident problem, as in the case of the postulates of the practical reason. An *axiom* cannot be completely distinguished from a postulate, as may be seen by the modern tendency to treat axioms as postulates. It can be defined no more accurately than as an established principle in any art or science which is accepted as self-evident.

Throughout philosophical as well as ordinary discourse these terms are often used interchangeably, as evidenced by the fact that they are defined more or less in terms of each other. We shall attempt to keep the foregoing distinctions in mind, although the task is not always easy, since many thinkers with whom we shall be dealing do not always make them. But anything like pedantry in this connection is not desirable, for what we are really concerned with is the distinction of necessary presuppositions from prejudices. Whether these presuppositions should be called assumptions, postulates, or axioms, while often an important question in a specific context, is one which so far as the general argument is concerned may be left undetermined. That which characterizes them all is that they are acknowledged in some way, and to some degree, as necessary conditions of intelligible thought, and thus as distinguishable from prejudgments in the sense of prejudices.[1]

III

Now, there are three "well-nigh invariable beliefs," certainly necessary presuppositions of intelligible communication,

---

[1] When quoting from other writers I shall take pains to indicate by quotation marks that it is *their* use of the terms "assumption," "postulate," "axiom," as the case may be.

namely, that *I exist and others like me, inhabiting a world.*[1] Of these presuppositions there is not, nor will there ever be, any empirical proof nor disproof. Not being results of, but implied in, experience, they are "intangible by its vicissitudes." They are not the outcome of reflection and communication, but their co-implications. Kant found them only presuppositions of action, but when we realize that thought involves that form of action which we call communication, we see that they are the presuppositions of thought also.

Such objects, or *Gegenstände*, are, in the first place at least, not so much objects of *knowledge*, in any narrow or sectarian sense of that word, as objects of *acknowledgment*. As such they are not so much entities as values and validities. They are objects the validity of which must be acknowledged if intelligible communication is to be possible. This acknowledgment cannot be the distinguishing character of any particular philosophy, as, for instance, of idealism, as is often supposed. For the distinction between idealism and realism is one that is made *only within a field of discourse which, in order to be intelligible, has already acknowledged them.* They are beyond the distinction of realism and idealism. The term "idealism" should be reserved for that form of thought which denies the ultimacy of the "world" and gives us only self or selves; "realism" for that form which denies selves and their communication as ultimate. Intelligible discourse implies all three.

These presuppositions are, then, intangible by the vicissitudes of experience, because they are its complications. They are accordingly, in the proper sense of the term, *a priori*. For "that is *a priori* which is true, no matter what." The concept of the *a priori*, like that of self-refutation, has suffered from grave misunderstandings. Whatever is *a priori* is necessary, but we have misconstrued the relation of this necessity to mind. *A priori* truth is necessary as opposed to contingent, but not as opposed to voluntary. What is *a priori* is necessary truth, not because it compels the mind's acceptance, as does sensation, but precisely because it does not. It is that which is acknowledged and involves all the freedom of acknowledgment.

[1] These are both beliefs and presuppositions. I call them presuppositions here because their *acknowledgment* is the necessary condition of intelligible communication. The nature of acknowledgment is treated fully in Chapter IV, pp. 146–7.

But this freedom is only from *external* compulsion, not from those compulsions arising out of the conditions of intelligible communication.[1]

Intelligible communication, with all its co-implications (as they have been developed), is, then, the necessary presupposition of all philosophy of whatever kind. These co-implications cannot be prejudices, for in denying them one refutes himself —that is, if he intends to communicate any intelligible meaning in his denial.

Needless to say, traditional philosophy makes these "assumptions." But the "prejudices" of this philosophy do not stop here. That I exist, and others like me inhabiting a world, are assumptions that in a very real sense are pre-philosophical. It is rather in the presupposition of a "world"—that presupposition which, while implied in, yet goes beyond, the experience of the subjects communicating with each other —that the distinctively philosophical "prejudices" appear. The presupposition of a "world" is as such pre-philosophical. We cannot carry on even the most ordinary discourse, the most ordinary communication from mind to mind, without acknowledging this presupposition. We cannot tell each other anything about ourselves or our fellows without implying something about the world of which we are a part. But while such discourse about the world is unavoidable it is also unavoidably vague. The term "world" is indefinite, and as soon as we seek to make it definite the most fundamental of all philosophical problems appears.

One thing we are bound to recognize at the outset. While philosophical discourse always implies the "world" as its ultimate subject, the world cannot become the subject of such discourse without an element of paradox. When we use the term "world" in its widest unqualified sense, we believe that in some way we grasp the sum-total of all things and all happenings when in truth we are grasping only a part. We believe that we are talking about the all-of-reality when we

---

[1] In formulating this conception of the *a priori*, a notion which will be made use of throughout the ensuing chapters, I have been greatly aided by the suggestive treatment of the subject by C. I. Lewis in his article "The Pragmatic Conception of the *A Priori*," *The Journal of Philosophy, Psychology, and Scientific Methods*, vol. xx, No. 7.

actually, for the most part, think and express something quite other—namely, a limited whole, a part of a larger unknown, which, to the extent that it is unknown, is unlimited. The reason for this is that we do not seem to be able to ask intelligible questions about that which is not limited in some way; we cannot apply predicates or epithets to that which is unlimited.

What can be the meaning of this paradox? Perhaps only that we are in some way in possession of a formula which permits us to relate the unknown to the known, so that the unknown becomes part of the unity of the world. Certainly this is the belief that constitutes the driving force of traditional philosophy, as we shall see. Be that as it may, we are for the moment interested merely in this paradox and its meaning for our present context.

Now, the idea of totality involved in the notion or presupposition of a "world" is implied in all our discourse. We make a moral judgment on a particular situation, and we say in justification, "*such* is the world," or a scientific judgment, and in that judgment is implied that the world is governed by universal causation, or that the world of "nature" is uniform. We apply concepts of evolution or progress to the "world," to totalities, and we even venture to say that the world is good or bad. Now, it is entirely conceivable that in every case we shall find that these predicates apply only to the world in some limited sense—only to limited wholes. In fact, a large part of our education consists in learning what things we must not say about reality as a whole. The point is, however, that we were *seeking*—and are *always* seeking—to find things that we may say about reality as a whole; and we feel that there must be something to say about it, otherwise the predicates we apply to the limited wholes lose something of their meaning and validity. It is this belief that something may be said about the world in the unlimited sense, about *being* in its most universal extent, that constitutes the driving force of metaphysics.

It is in connection with the presupposition of a world, in this metaphysical sense, that all the distinctively philosophical "prejudices" appear. Traditional philosophy postulates not only *a* world, but that it is an *intelligible* world. *Ens est unum,*

verum, bonum—in this "axiom of intelligibility," as it has sometimes been called—the prejudices of the metaphysicians of all
time are summed up. In applying to being in the unqualified
sense these attributes of unity, truth, and goodness, or value,
a distinction is inevitably made between these predicates and
those which apply only to limited wholes, and it is the significance of this distinction that is of first importance. In the
following sections we shall consider in their order these three
"prejudices"—the prejudice in favour of totality, the prejudice
in favour of meaning and value, the prejudice in favour of
reality, or of an *ens realissimum*. The proper interpretation of
these three prejudices or presuppositions is our first task, for
it is precisely their denial that constitutes the essence of
modernism in philosophy.

IV

The philosopher may be described as one who has a
specially developed sense or organ for the totality of things.
In general men are concerned with particulars—the demands
of practical life see to this. These objects of human interest
may be large or small, our daily bread or a dogma of religion,
a love adventure or the discovery of a law of chemistry, but
they remain particulars. The philosopher, on the other hand,
always has—naturally, of course, in different degrees, and never
completely—a sense for the totality of things. In so far as he
is productive he seeks to translate this feeling into concepts.
He need not, indeed, be always speaking of the "whole," and,
in fact, those philosophers who do so become singularly tire-
some. "Cannot we live as though we always loved?" asks
Maeterlinck. Can we not think as though we were always
conscious of totality? Perhaps. But the only time to talk about
either, as true lovers and true lovers of wisdom alike know,
is in those supreme moments of realization in which insight
can alone find adequate expression. But in the genuine philosopher the sense of totality is always there.

This is the philosopher's sense for and acknowledgment
of the "world" which is one of the co-implicates or presuppositions of intelligible communication. Yet precisely this

sense for totality the typical modern does not hesitate to call a prejudice, and the perennial attempt to give expression to this sense of unity the fallacy of speculative dogma. As though there could be intelligible philosophical discourse without assuming it! There are, doubtless, things we must learn not to say about reality, but we shall always have something to say about reality as a whole, and when we cease to say it we cease to philosophize. Even if the ultimate metaphysical principle is sought in plurality itself, if what we say about reality is that it is *not* one, even then this discontinuity, this unrelatedness of things, becomes the characteristic of things, and tends to be elevated into a principle of unification, of reality as a whole. The prejudice in favour of totality is, accordingly, one of those prejudices which, through application of the principle of self-refutation, shows itself to be no prejudice but a necessary presupposition. As well ask a philosopher to whistle and smile at the same time as to philosophize and make no judgments upon reality as a whole.

It is of the utmost importance to make the significance of this "prejudice in favour of totality" perfectly clear. With it the entire question of system in philosophy is ultimately bound up, the ideal of systematic thought being for modernist philosophers, in the main, a prejudice.

In the first place the idea of the whole, the concept of totality, has many meanings, and it by no means follows that, because the assumption of totality is a necessary presupposition of intelligible thought, some of these conceptions may not be false. C. S. Peirce distinguishes some forty different adjectives characterizing as many different kinds of wholes which have been distinguished in philosophic thought. Collective composite, essential, integrate whole, mathematical, logical, and metaphysical wholes—such are some of the distinctions thought has found itself compelled to make.[1] It is entirely conceivable that while reality must be postulated as a totality if there is to be intelligible discourse, *it does not at all follow that it is a whole in certain of the senses in which that totality has been assumed.* Let us examine some of the meanings

[1] See article on "The Whole (and Parts)," *Baldwin's Dictionary of Philosophy and Psychology.*

of the "whole" as they form the subject of dispute in present-day philosophy.

First of all, as James says, the world is at least *one subject of discourse*. And he considers it an odd fact that many monists consider a great victory scored when pluralists say that the universe is many. "The universe, they chuckle; his speech bewrayeth him. He stands confessed of monism out of his own mouth." "Well," so he continues, "let things be one in so far forth! You can fling such a word as universe at the whole collection of them, but what matters it? It still remains to be ascertained whether they are one in any further or more valuable sense."[1]

But really a great deal more is involved in the idea of a world as one subject of discourse than at first appears. For it must be *intelligible* discourse, and it is precisely this that requires that it shall be conceived as one in a further and more valuable sense.

The world as subject of intelligible discourse must be a whole in one further sense at least—as a *logical* whole. For intelligible discourse is logical discourse whatever it may be besides, and logical discourse is directed by the ideal of unity. Now, logic understands by unity, or the whole, the concept of necessary thought synthesis. There is more to intelligibility, as we shall see, than logical coherence, but such coherence must at least be there. Now, it must be admitted that the world need not be exhausted as the subject of logical discourse. It is precisely the position of the various forms of a-logism that it is not. But in so far as it becomes an object of intelligible discourse it must be capable of logical synthesis. Even those who fall back on intuition, and non-logical or æsthetic language as a means of communication of that intuition, have already justified both the intuition and the means of communication by showing their place in a *logically* intelligible whole.

But unity in still another and more valuable sense is, I think, implied by intelligible discourse. This we shall describe as metaphysical unity, "metaphysical" being used in its proper and legitimate sense.

The concept of totality first acquires significance in metaphysical reflection through the presence of certain charac-

[1] *Pragmatism*, pp. 133 ff.

teristics in addition to the logical. If one speaks of logical unity or coherence it does not at all mean that metaphysical validity is forthwith included. In the concept of categorical or methodological unity the meaning of the metaphysical whole is not yet reached. From the Ionians to Bergson metaphysical unity has always consisted in the application of some *quality* or character to the world as a whole. To apprehend it metaphysically is first of all to apprehend it as a totality, and secondly to characterize that totality.

Now, it is our position that, *if* the "world" enters into our thought as an object of intelligible discourse, it *must* be conceived as a totality in this sense also. The object of talking about the "world" at all is to discover and communicate its nature and meaning. Even if we say the world is not a unity, it is a plurality, a chaos, we have still said something about it as a whole. We have given it a characteristic from which consequences and meanings flow. If we say that all is change, that duration is the deepest character of reality, we have given a privileged position to some aspect of experience and applied it to the world as a whole.

The attribution of some quality or character to the world as a whole is, then, the further condition of intelligible discourse about the world. Something must be given a privileged position—"dominant unity," to make use of an expression of Leibniz. We may, perhaps, contrast this kind of unity with the logical by calling it *axiological*. Eucken has the same distinction in mind when he speaks of the "no-ological standpoint" and contrasts no-ological unity with logical unity. Such dominant unity involves selection, and in so far involves distinctions of meaning and value. The essential notion in this conception of unity is that of the *ens realissimum*.

This distinction between *logical* and *axiological*, or dominant, unity will be of the utmost importance throughout the coming discussions. For one thing, it marks the difference between the position we shall develop and that form of logical monism that identifies metaphysical unity with logical unity. The latter notion is the basis or presupposition of only one type of philosophy; the former, if our argument is sound, the presupposition of any philosophy whatever. It is a distinction which we shall also find crucial for our interpretation of philosophic system and of the relation of logic to philosophy in general. Let us seek, therefore, to make this idea of axiological totality somewhat clearer.

We have seen that totality is the necessary presupposition of intelligible philosophical discourse. We cannot, however, form an idea of an existing universe or totality without an element of paradox. Every existing totality is, after all, necessarily a partial totality, for it is only to partial totalities that predicates can be intelligibly applied. It follows, therefore, that no totality of existing things, however inclusive we may make it, can exhaust the philosophical notion of the "universe." This is true also of the whole in the sense of logical totality. For such a whole excludes, by definition, the alogical, in the sense, of course, of any elements that may be intractable to logic, but even more significantly in the sense of those values that transcend logic (the values of logic being only one type of values). Any concept of totality that shall satisfy the demands of philosophy and philosophical discourse must, accordingly, be one that includes the meaning and value of things as well as the things themselves and any merely logical unity of things. This is what I mean by axiological unity.

We may say, then, that the problem of a world-whole, in order to be solvable at all, must be turned from a merely existential or logical problem into an axiological problem. In other words, the totality of the real world, in the sense of the existent world, consists in something that is more than existence. It seems clear, also, that in such an axiological totality the principle of order will be one that arises necessarily out of the essential nature of value as such, and that, in the last analysis, a system of philosophy must be a system of values. All this will be developed fully in a later chapter.[1] Here we shall content ourselves with pointing out that such a unity must be a "dominant unity" in Leibniz's sense, in the sense, namely, that a "privileged position" is given to something— to an *ens realissimum*, and the principle of order becomes one of axiological dominance rather than of logical co-ordination.

But to return to the main point of this discussion—totality in some sense is the necessary presupposition of philosophical activity and of intelligible philosophical discourse. Many

[1] Chapter XIII.

concepts of totality may contain prejudices, but the notion itself cannot properly be called a prejudice. It is of the utmost importance to make the necessity of this presupposition entirely clear. It may help us if in this connection we consider a certain alternative to this position which recognizes, at least partially, the irrefutable character of this presupposition.

It is the idea of many that wholeness may be sought at the end rather than at the beginning of things, that the philosopher may still be a philosopher and make unity the *terminus ad quem* rather than the *terminus a quo* of thought and endeavour. Thus certain moderns even glory in the thought of a forcible imposition of order on a disorderly world, and find in philosophy scarcely more than an exciting adventure.

Need it be said that such an idea is unintelligible when we try to think it out? One way of saying this is that it involves an ultimate dualism, a discord in the universe. But the charge of dualism no longer terrifies, perhaps because we have heard it so often that we have lost the sense of its true import. It is quite another thing, however, to say that such an idea is nonsense.[1] But that is what it really is. For if the universe is made the subject of discourse, the question is not what it *was*, nor what it *will be*, but what it *is*. If the universe is chaotic now, any order we may impose upon it does not make it less chaotic in its essence, but even more so. For each new order we may create is itself a product of history, and thus becomes part of the historical temporal reality. As such it but adds to the variety and multiplicity of the world. The absolutizing of the historical and temporal categories finds its extreme consequence in the idea that "every increase of rationality is necessarily accompanied by a corresponding increase of historical chaos."

In ultimate metaphysical judgments, past, present, and future cannot be thus separated from each other. To say that the universe is chaotic in its essence now but may become orderly involves the same kind of contradiction—the same essential unintelligibility—as if one should say there has been progress but there is no progress now. If there is no progress now there never has been any *real* progress; for, as we shall

---

[1] The term *nonsense* is used throughout in the philosophical sense of the "unmeaning," or *non-sense*.

see later, an intelligible concept of progress can be formed only within a system of values that embraces the whole. Judgments of this type are judgments of totality or they are nothing at all.

The failure to recognize these obvious—I had almost said self-evident—things arises alike from a misunderstanding of the philosophical judgment of totality and of the nature of philosophical intelligibility. It is, perhaps, natural to suppose that judgments of totality are but extensions of the generalizations of common sense and science, hasty or careful as the case may be. Nothing is further from the truth. The metaphysical judgment of totality differs *in toto* from the general proposition of logic. If I say all is God, all is matter, the world is my idea, all is rational or beautiful, such judgments express not a universality abstracted from the things, but rather the expression in the form of concepts of our sense of totality. Many of the predicates we thus use may represent things that we must learn not to say about the world, but something we must say about it if the world is to have communicable meaning. *Ens est unum*—being must be one in this metaphysical sense, for without this unity the application of all other predicates would be meaningless. The philosophical judgment of totality, as thus understood, is not the end but the beginning of philosophical intelligibility.

V

This, then, is the significance of the sense for totality characteristic of the philosopher. It is the lasting merit of the Kantian philosophy, despite its errors, to have made this finally clear. The ultimate object of our thought is not abstract being unrelated to meaning and value, but meaning and value itself of which being is a form. Thought is not oriented towards absolute being, but towards absolutely valid values. The world in its totality, the "universe," is an "Idea," but an idea without which intelligible communication and interpretation are impossible. In other words, deeper than the "prejudice" in favour of totality is the prejudice in favour of meaning; the world is judged as totality precisely because without totality meaning is impossible.

This postulate—that the world necessarily has a meaning—is a constant element in traditional philosophy. Precisely this postulate, however, the modernist continually turns into a prejudice. To ask after the meaning of the world is, according to Vaihinger, a question which has no meaning, and he quotes the phrase of Schiller: "Know thou that the noble mind reads greatness into life, does not seek it there." Taken as an abstract proposition, this has a specious appearance of truth. But this appearance arises only if we separate structure and function in thought and knowledge, only if we divorce things which no man may, without unintelligibility, put asunder. It is, to be sure, a prejudice to seek in the universe such meanings as can come only by putting them there, but to read greatness and meaning into life unless we assume some greatness and meaning to be there, is the height of sophistication and inanity.

The denial of meaning in the world is one of those denials which ultimately refute themselves. An application of this ancient principle of self-refutation has recently been made by Prince Troubetzkoy in a vivid and telling way.[1] With true Russian frankness he admits that human life, as it merely unfolds before our eyes, reveals no meaning whatsoever. It is a meaningless circle, a movement from death unto death, attended throughout by suffering, and suffering, too, without apparent meaning or aim. The life of man in the modern State does not alter these conditions, but rather intensifies them. It repeats them in a more disastrous form and on a more extended scale. Nor does nature reveal anything different. We receive an overwhelming impression of a reign of nonsense, of no-meaning, an impression which becomes appalling in virtue of the suffering involved. Progress is an illusion, since every advance inevitably returns to the point of departure and ends in death.

Yet that a meaningless world is not the final truth is clearly indicated, he believes, by the fact that we consciously recognize its nonsense and condemn it as evil. The discovery of nonsense in the world would not have been possible to us unless we were aware of a meaning in life which we perceive to be contradicted by the senseless spectacle before us. Were we

---

[1] Prince Eugene Troubetzkoy, "The Reign of Nonsense in the World, in the State, and in Human Life," *The Hibbert Journal*, vol. xvi, p. 117 ff.

merely the victims of the vicious circle of existence we would neither recognize it as vicious nor lament our condition as victims. But we recognize its viciousness, we do lament our condition, and this clearly proves the presence of some element in our nature which is above the reign of nonsense and opposed to it. Let us, then, follow up the clue afforded by this attitude of condemnation in which we view the senseless revolutions of the natural world. May it not be that man, "in becoming the *judge* of a natural world, declares himself at the same time the prophet of a better"?

I am not concerned here with this particular form of an ancient argument. For my own part I do not admit with the pessimist that human life, as it unfolds before our eyes, reveals no meaning—that it is a meaningless circle, a movement merely from death unto death, without apparent meaning or aim. What I do hold is that, *even if this were the case,* the logic of this ancient argument is unanswerable. He who says there is no meaning in the world is asserting a self-refuting proposition in the sense in which we have defined the term. For the very values in terms of which he condemns the world as meaning-less are already in the world in some sense. He who says we do not find meaning in the world but put it there is talking nonsense. For we are in the world and our meanings are already part of that world. In what sense we may say that these meanings and values are "in the world" is, indeed, one of the root problems of philosophy, as we shall see later. Enough for our present purpose that they are there, and he who denies it has in that very denial assumed them to be there. If he did not acknowledge meaning there would be no point in its denial, for the question would not be raised at all. One thing we may assert unhesitatingly: when it is said that the mind reads meaning into the world, does not find it there, such a statement can only mean, if it has meaning at all, the world in some narrow and "prejudiced" conception of the world. Otherwise the proposition is nonsense.

In all this impression of nonsense and its condemnation as evil we are then, we must admit with Troubetzkoy, taking but a partial point of view. Our time experience, which we follow in the aforesaid estimate of reality, is "unilateral," and needs to be supplemented and crossed by another line of

inquiry. When we free ourselves from the temporal prejudice
—the belief that meaning can be found in the time-process
alone—and seek it in a timeless order of values which alone
gives the time-process significance, we shall find the real source
of our condemnation and the inspiration of our hope. With
all this I agree, and recognize in the problem of the relation
of meaning and value to time the root question of philosophy.
With this question we shall attempt to deal in its proper place.[1]
Here I wish merely to emphasize the character of this argument
from self-refutation, as deathless as it is ageless.

VI

He who says that the assumptions of totality and meaning
in philosophy are prejudices writes himself down, it should
now be abundantly clear, as one who has not yet learned to
distinguish between prejudices and necessary presuppositions.
Prejudgments, in one sense of the word, they certainly are,
but only in the sense that they are primal judgments, *Grundurteile*, without which all interpretation and communication are
impossible. The objects of these judgments cannot be said to
exist in any intelligible sense of that word, but they must be
acknowledged if any judgments of existence are to be either
valid or even intelligible.[2]

The nature of meaning, "the meaning of meaning," has
become one of the central problems of present-day philosophical discussion. The symposiums upon this most subtle
and sublimated question are in no sense the result of accident,
but were the predestined goal of the discussions initiated by
the developments of modernism. The inability of pragmatist,
idealist, and new realist to make themselves intelligible to
each other on this question is one of the most enlightening
features of this discussion. The ludicrous effect of the attempts
to apply so-called "scientific method" to an idea that is
beyond all science is one of the few rewards for conscientious

---

[1] See Chapter VII, especially Section VI.

[2] The meaning of "exist" will be developed in later sections of this chapter.
Here our point is merely that objects of "acknowledgment" are elements in the
interpretation of our world even if they do not "exist" in the world.

following of the debate. With certain of these specific problems in connection with meaning we shall be concerned in other connections.[1] Here we are interested only in the great outlines of our general problem. One thing emerges from all this debate with a certain definiteness. *Back of the concept of meaning lies the concept of value, and the two concepts cannot be separated.* Following the thread of our thought we are led still more deeply into the hinterland of philosophical prejudice—from the prejudice in favour of meaning to the prejudice in favour of value.

"The direct acceptance of things as having significance *and* value is," it is held by the modern idealist, "the characteristic mark of idealism as found in the great systems."[2] It is my contention that it is the premise of the entire Great Tradition, and that this tradition is above the opposition of realism and idealism. "The identity of value and reality" is, indeed, "the great venture to which idealism is committed," but it is the venture also to which all thinking which follows the natural bent of the intellect is committed, for the intellect is oriented towards value. The prejudice in favour of value, if it be a prejudice, is a prejudice of all philosophizing on the grand scale.

"It is contradictory to separate value and reality," the modern idealist continues, and since the "axiom" of the identity of the two underlies all valid philosophizing, idealism, which rests upon this axiom, must be maintained. Whether idealism, in any exclusive sense of the word, results from the acceptance of this axiom, remains to be seen. The modern idealist is assuredly right in insisting that only contradiction results from its denial. "Whoever contends against it is," as Royce loved to say, "already its victim." "He is undertaking to determine by his own rational ideals what the real world genuinely is, how it ought to be conceived. By virtue of this very reasoning he confesses that the question, 'How ought I to conceive the real?' is logically prior to the question, What is the real itself? . . . the ought is prior in nature to the real; or the proposition, I ought to think so, is prior to

---

[1] Especially Chapter V.

[2] J. E. Creighton, "Two Types of Idealism," *Philosophical Review*, vol. xxvi, No. 5.

the proposition, this is so."[1] So sure of the finality of this argument from self-refutation is Royce that he is "fond of hearing men formulate a condemnation of idealism. The more definitely they formulate their condemnation the more explicitly do they define their world as an expression of their own ideal regarding the way in which it is rational to think the world. Their voice is the voice of idealism, however they may attempt to disguise it."

Final the argument certainly is, in so far at least as the inseparability of value and reality is concerned. That must be clear, I think, to anyone who has come to understand the nature of the argument from self-refutation. This validity is, of course, denied. But its apparent cogency is recognized even by those who ultimately seek to escape it. The argument has even been dignified by one of its opponents by the name of the "Value-centric Predicament." The predicament, or apparent predicament, in which the human mind finds itself, according to Spaulding, is precisely this confession which, Royce maintains, the realist "by virtue of his very reasoning" must make, that the question, 'How ought I to conceive the real?' is prior to the question, 'What is the real itself?' In other words, in the very moment that he denies the ideal of knowledge of the idealist he does so by virtue of his assertion of another ideal, in which the prejudice in favour of value is equally necessarily implied. Can this prejudice, and the predicament it causes, be escaped, as Spaulding believes?[2]

The development of the "value-centric" predicament out of the much-discussed ego-centric predicament is itself an interesting commentary upon the most recent developments of philosophic thought. It is now generally recognized, at least by modern idealists, that the nerve of modern idealism is not to be found in the ego-centric predicament, and that to continue to exploit this is to labour dead issues. The formula, "the world is my idea," is after all merely an illegitimate inference from the axiom of the identity of value and reality, and can be abandoned without affecting the essence of idealism in the least. If there is any axiom of thought from which idealistic inferences are to be drawn it is rather that the

---

[1] J. Royce, *Lectures on Modern Idealism*, p. 237.
[2] E. G. Spaulding, *The New Rationalism*, 1918, pp. 206 ff.

separation of value and reality is contradictory. It is this more fundamental predicament that Spaulding denies.

Now, there is one way of describing this situation which is little less than caricature. According to certain clever, though superficial, thinkers, there is "one judgment" which, according to traditional philosophy, everyone is supposed to make—namely, that "the universe must satisfy us." Having accepted this judgment as true, the task of philosophy is to discover what kind of a universe will satisfy us. When this has been done philosophy has merely to add the footnote: "The universe, ultimate reality, has such and such a character." Now, such a judgment, it is held, is pure prejudice, "an assumption philosophy is by no means compelled to make." Reality must satisfy us? Who says that we must find a complete satisfaction for all our needs? Besides, every endeavour to represent a complete satisfaction always involves a certain selection from among our needs, a selection the justification of which is indemonstrable, and into which of necessity prejudices individual and racial are bound to enter. Surely this, then, is an assumption philosophy is by no means compelled to make. One may hold the pious opinion that the universe must satisfy us, but who would venture to say that the opposite involves a contradiction?

But this is merely a caricature of the view we are considering and need not detain us over-long. The value-centric predicament, if there be one, is far different. For, let us suppose we accept the standpoint of "ethical neutrality" as represented by those who have drawn this caricature—the standpoint, let us say, which finds its classical expression in the famous maxim of Spinoza: "*Neque ridere, neque flere, nec deterstari, sed intelligere.*" Even, then, we have acknowledged a value. Our philosophy is shot through with a pathos all its own. We may avoid the prejudices, the moral evaluations involved in smiling, detesting, or lamenting reality, but how shall we avoid the valuation involved in their repression? How shall we avoid the prejudice involved in the exclusive evaluation of truth? It is here, in the very denial of the postulate of value, that he who denies refutes himself.

But this predicament is, Spaulding insists, no predicament. It is true, he admits, that after I have eliminated all values there is still the value of truth which I desire and acknowledge, and this can never be eliminated. But from this relation we cannot infer the dependence of truth upon that value. But is not this to miss the point of the whole argument? Is it not to misinterpret the nature of the argument from self-refutation as we have come to understand it? The argument is not that the truth of a judgment depends upon my desire for the truth. To argue thus would be to fall back upon that assumption which, as we have seen, "we are not compelled to make." More than one modernist has not hesitated, with Nietzsche, to speak of the prejudice in favour of truth. It does not mean even that the truth of a judgment depends upon the acknowledgment of an over-individual demand. It is, rather, that the very distinctions between truth and falsity, between appearance and reality themselves, depend upon certain ideals or norms of truth and reality. Every judgment that something exists presupposes the meaning of it as true. It is because meaning lies above all being, and because meaning is inseparable from value, that the value-centric predicament cannot be escaped.

All this will become clearer when we consider the prejudice in favour of reality itself in the following section, and still more when we take up the question of logical values in the next chapter. We may, however, with advantage anticipate one point by way of illustration. If, for instance, with the realist, I take the independence of the object of knowledge as the criterion of the real, and of *bona-fide* logic as the ultimate science of the real, I have already thereby acknowledged independence as a value. Otherwise my distinction between genuine knowledge and *bona-fide* logic, as contrasted with other knowledge and other logics, is meaningless. Similarly, if I take as my criterion of genuine knowledge, and therefore as the axiom of logic, coherence, I have thereby equally acknowledged coherence as an ultimate value.

It must be evident, I think, that the "prejudice" in favour of value, and the predicament occasioned by it, are a prejudice and a predicament that cannot be escaped. They are inherent in the philosophical attitude as such. If we admit the concept of logical values, and, as we shall see in the following chapter, that concept cannot be escaped, certain logical values must be acknowledged if there is to be "meaning," if there is to be intelligible communication.

VII

The essence of the Great Tradition is the recognition, consciously or unconsciously, that intellect is oriented towards significance and value. This is the natural bent of the human reason, and in following this natural metaphysic the great ideas of perennial philosophy have been developed. It is of the utmost importance that this orientation of intellect towards value should be understood. Moreover, it is only by understanding this that we shall also understand the last and most fundamental presupposition of traditional thought—the prejudice in favour of ultimate reality or of an *ens realissimum*. It is, we saw, the denial of this "prejudice" that constitutes one of the distinctive notes of modernism. It is in a sense, therefore, to the examination of this, the philosophical prejudice *par excellence*, that the discussions of this entire chapter have all been leading up.

The ideal of a *real world* that constitutes the goal of thought, one to which a well-trodden path leads, is, as we have seen, a constant presupposition of traditional thought. We may call it the *ontological prejudice*. It is, of course, obvious that this prejudice is bound up with the other so-called prejudices in favour of totality and of meaning and value. Together they all form part of that inborn system of concepts, or philosophical errors if you will, which form the structural elements of perennial philosophy. But this ideal represents assumptions or postulates which many modernists feel philosophy is by no means compelled to make. This is felt to be pre-eminently the case in regard to the ontological prejudice. For one thing, a genetic study of the intellect itself may show us how relative and wholly pragmatic our conceptions of reality are. It may show us that there is no reason, except that of a very obstinate prejudice, why the meaning of knowledge should not lie wholly in activity and not in fruition, why the universe should not ultimately be "unfinished," and why the ontological prejudice itself should not be completely abandoned. On the other hand, others point out that an impartial examination of "objects," *Gegenstände* in the broadest sense of the word, may make it clear to us that the object of knowledge is not necessarily existence or "reality," and that, therefore, the idea of reality as the exclusive goal of thought or knowledge may easily be a prejudice. In general, this prejudice in favour of reality, while, perhaps, part of the natural bent of the intellect, and as such an idea that has acquired the sanctity of the centuries, is, nevertheless, one that a more sophisticated understanding enables us to transcend.

It is for reasons such as these that the problem of the nature and meaning of the *ontological predicates* has attained such importance in recent philosophical discussion. It is because of a certain impartial attitude, resulting alike from genetic and pragmatic motives and from purely phenomenological analysis, that a revaluation of the traditional ontological "prejudice" has been characteristic of so much of modernist thought. Let us examine this attitude more closely.

The prejudice in favour of an ultimate reality is, as I have said, closely bound up with the prejudice in favour of totality. The same compulsion makes us seek both unity and the *ens realissimum*. Accordingly, when we speak of the real world we naturally think that "totality" and "reality" are interchangeable terms, that the real world and the universe are the same. But this is precisely what the modern mind finds itself compelled to deny, and the denial rests upon the recognition of certain facts which all must admit in principle, however differently they may be interpreted.

Everything that *is*, we should naturally argue, exists, and everything that exists must be real. Little reflection is necessary, however, to make us realize that this cannot be quite as it appears. The predicate "real" has inevitably the meaning of suggesting a contrast with something unreal, which, however we may understand that term, must, nevertheless, fall within the universe, which by hypothesis included everything. Thus the real world contains less than the universe, and from the impartial point of view preoccupation with *this* world must inevitably involve a prejudice. It is this prejudice, the prejudice in favour of existence, of actuality or of reality, whatever terms we may use, that we must seek first to understand.

To the ordinary mind the very idea that the preference for the real is a prejudice must seem but a paradox, and with that judgment the present writer must agree. It is a paradox, moreover, of which the consequences, when thought out, can lead only to complete self-refutation and unintelligibility. A way out of this paradox must be found for modern thought, otherwise it will find itself in a complete *impasse*. But first let us see the element of truth in this prejudiceless attitude of modernism.

The impartial attitude is well illustrated by an interesting discussion of Meinong in which he examines what he calls the "natural prejudice in favour of the actual." A natural prejudice in favour of existing objects (*Vorurteil zu Gunsten des Wircklichen*) has, he holds, led us to ignore the importance for thought and knowledge of objects that merely subsist, that do not and cannot have existence. There is, he holds, unquestionably, knowledge of that which does not exist—and very important knowledge too, e.g. in mathematics. It is, indeed, chiefly owing to this prejudice—which identifies all being with existence—that epistemological idealism (mentalism) has arisen, and with it the impossible conception of existence for mind. There is unquestionably knowledge of the non-existent, as in mathematics, and since something known does not exist outside us, it must exist in our minds as thought. Were our knowledge wholly of existents, such a conception as that of mentalism could never have arisen. How far Meinong carries his impartiality is well known. Among the *Gegenstände* in the universe are not only various objects of "assumption," such as objects of imagination, but also impossible objects. All these *are* in the broadest sense of the term, *subsist* in the universe.

To this it is, indeed, possible to object that we ought not to say that the objects of mathematics do not exist but only subsist, or that we ought not to ascribe to impossible objects any kind of being at all. But such objections only serve to bring out the point we had in mind in using this illustration. The only point of view from which one may insist on the existence of mathematical objects is on the basis of the acknowledgment of their meaning and importance. To say that we ought not to ascribe being to objects of the imagination or impossible objects means that we do not acknowledge their meaning and importance. From a wholly impartial point of view all are in the universe in some sense. In any case, different meanings of reality are admitted, and any identification of reality with one of these meanings, as, for example, the *actual*, involves a prejudice.

Next to the prejudice in favour of the actual and the sensible, that which has the widest influence, perhaps, is the prejudice in favour of the "permanent." Indeed, the prejudice in favour of the sensible is "natural" only in the sense that it exists easily side by side with other evaluations equally primal. Physical science and moral reflection alike contribute their share to disabusing common sense of its prejudice in favour of the sensible, and it is not difficult to get the plain man to acknowledge the existence or reality in some sense of moral principles and scientific law. "Deep down somewhere," writes Mr. Frederick Soddy, "the ultimate test of reality appears to be the law of conservation. Does the soul exist? If so, it must be immortal. Is matter real or a mere impression of the mind? It cannot be created or destroyed, and therefore has an existence apart from the mind. Lastly, has energy a specific existence? Or is it merely a convenient abstraction? Energy is conserved like matter, and therefore obeys the test of objective existence . . ."[1]

Yet to the typical modernists this is also pure prejudice. "I believe this to be a sheer mistake," writes Mr. Bertrand Russell. "The persistent particles of mathematical physics," he continues, "I regard as logical constructions, symbolic fictions, enabling us to express compendiously very complicated assemblages of fact."[2] Mr. R. B. Perry subsumes this "prejudice" under one of the most serious speculative errors of thought, namely, that tendency "to apply to reality as a whole certain concepts of science which satisfy thought's peculiar bias for identity and permanence."[3]

It is not necessary for our present purposes to enter into

---

[1] Frederick Soddy, *Matter and Energy* (Home University Library), p. 41.
[2] Bertrand Russell, *Mysticism and Logic*, p. 128.
[3] R. B. Perry, *Present Philosophical Tendencies*.

this particular debate. Nor is it necessary to emphasize the transvaluation of all natural metaphysical values involved in a dictum such as that of Bergson's, "to be is to change." That the "prejudice in favour of the permanent" is wholly a prejudice, and that it arises wholly out of a peculiar bias of science, we may well doubt. If there is bias here we shall find it rather bound up ultimately with the very conditions of intelligible philosophical discourse. Enough for the moment to note these two completely contrasting definitions of the real, and the fact that each is, from the standpoint of the opposing point of view, held to involve a prejudice.

We are concerned here merely with enumerating certain different and contrasting definitions of the real, all of which from one point of view or another are considered to involve prejudices. Of such contrasting definitions, conceptions which have played important parts in the history of philosophic thought, I will note only two more, but these again of great significance. These are the conceptions of the real as *that which is related*, and of the real as *that which is independent of relations*.

The importance of these two conceptions or definitions of the real lies in the fact that, unlike those already examined, they purport to be, not merely natural and instinctive conceptions or intuitions, but logical conceptions or definitions. In the case of both, logic is assumed to be the "ultimate science of that which is," and that which logic seems to demand as the nature of the real is what reality ultimately is. In both cases, moreover, the protagonists of these two conceptions, the idealistic and realistic logics respectively, appeal to the principle of self-refutation, of intelligibility, as their ultimate argument. For each the opposite conception involves a self-contradiction. In the following chapter we shall examine these two "logics" in connection with the entire question of the nature and rôle of logic in philosophy. Here we have merely to record the fact of these two contrasting definitions of the real, and the further fact that both have been reached in the attempt to get beyond certain instinctive prejudices. That each position involves an element of prejudice is claimed by its adversary. As Royce, for instance, claims that the realist's position can be maintained only by an appeal to natural instinctive and social motives, so Holt and others insist that the idealist makes his point by appeal to extra-logical motives. Both, I believe, are right, and the reasons for my belief I shall develop in the next chapter. For my part, I can scarcely doubt that the exclusive identification of the meaning of reality with one of these conceptions involves a prejudice. Otherwise philosophical discussion would not have, for the past one hundred and fifty years, revolved so continually about this question—a discussion which has given rise to "an almost agonized question whether some standpoint in philosophy cannot be found which will do away for ever with the unfruitful controversy which idealism and realism feel obliged to carry on regarding the meaning of reality." Just what that element of prejudice is we may leave undetermined until we have gone into the nature of logic itself, and into the question of its power by itself to determine the nature of reality.

In any case, our problem here is merely that of attempting to understand the impartial attitude towards the ontological predicates. From this point of view it seems clear that some element of prejudice does enter into all of these metaphysical positions. The different and often contrasting definitions of the real which we have examined seem to indicate this. If, therefore, impartiality here means nothing more than the abandonment of particular ontological prejudices—in other words, the prejudices of the sectarians in philosophy—it can only be welcome to the magnanimous philosopher. But radical modernism often means a great deal more than this. It involves in many cases the abandonment of the whole idea of finality and the acceptance of an ideal of philosophical activity without goal and without end—the denial of the entire notion of an *ens realissimum*. In so far as it means the latter, it involves a transvaluation of all metaphysical values which it is impossible for the human mind really to conceive, much less to carry out. It is of the utmost importance, therefore, to distinguish if possible between *ontological prejudices* and the *presupposition of ultimate reality as such*.

We may, perhaps, begin this task best by again considering one of these particular prejudices, the *prejudice in favour of the actual*. This prejudice finds its expression in the identification of the two concepts of "reality" and "existence," for the actual is equivalent to existence, and existence is equated with position in space and time. Now, who that recognizes the great world of objects that have value for knowledge and meaning for life, but which are "non-existent" objects in the sense defined, does not find it a vulgar prejudice to deny these objects reality because they do not *exist* in the sense defined? When faced with this situation the philosopher may take either one of two possible courses. He may follow what he is pleased to call the "persistent usage of common sense" and continue to treat reality and existence as synonymous, or he may follow what has been the practice of the main body of philosophical tradition and distinguish between them. In the former case he will find himself, I think, in a very serious predicament; in the latter case he will be compelled to make precisely the distinction between the particular ontological prejudices and the presupposition of reality *überhaupt* for which we have been contending.

Let us consider the first alternative. Suppose the philosopher takes the terms "existence" and "reality" as synonymous. He will then find himself compelled either to exclude from the world of reality innumerable objects of human experience, the acknowledgment of the reality of which is the condition of intelligible discourse; or acknowledging them as real—and still continuing to identify reality with existence—to apply the term "existence" to them. In the first case, while he may, perhaps, be said to follow common sense in one of its moods, he will certainly find himself out of harmony with all that is characteristic of the *sensus communis* on what I may describe as its higher levels of spiritual communication. For nothing is more certain, I think, than that there are many "things" which the plain man feels to be real, but which also belong to a "transcendental, ideal" world, in the sense that they cannot be defined in terms of space and time, and are communicable only in a non-spatial and non-temporal idiom.[1]

---

[1] In his admirable work, *The Ways of Knowing*, Professor W. P. Montague says in a note on page 295: "In view of the universal and persistent usage of common sense, according to which reality and existence are treated as synonymous, it seems to me inadvisable to differentiate between them, as some authors have done, by restricting the term 'existence' to the concrete things which alone can be said to occupy positions," I doubt whether this is the deliverance of

If, however, he retains these objects as *real*, he must then apply the predicate "existence" to them. In this case, the difficulties are of another order. He will inevitably so broaden the meaning of the word "exist" as to render it unfit for the specific contexts for which it was made and in which it is primarily and properly usable.[1]

This dilemma is, I think, inescapable for anyone who persists in identifying the notion of reality with that of existence. It is a predicament everywhere present in modern thought, and gives rise to the most extraordinary forms of sophistication, some of which we shall presently examine. But the philosopher is under no compulsion to treat existence and reality as synonymous. Following the main line of traditional thought, he may recognize that the category of existence by itself—bare or mere existence—is not adequate for the purposes of philosophy, for the very good reason that it is not adequate for the purpose of intelligible human discourse. He will, indeed, realize that this identification is the result of a natural prejudice—in favour of the actual—but one which the genesis of that prejudice enables us both to understand and to transcend.

I have indicated the difficulties which arise when one makes reality synonymous with the actual. Similar difficulties attend the identification of reality with any of the particular ontological prejudices, such as, for instance, the prejudice in favour of the permanent, or the prejudice in favour of the changing. Each represents the relative aspects of the real, and each receives its own special emphasis in different moods, but to make any one of them absolute is to exclude other meanings of reality, the acknowledgment of which is necessary for intelligible human discourse. It was the recognition of just this situation, of the element of prejudice in all the varied and contrasting definitions of the real, which led to the impartial attitude in modernism—and ultimately to the abandonment of the ontological standpoint as such, or the ideal of the *ens realissimum*. With this we are brought back to the main problem of this discussion.

___

common sense, and the reasons for this view will appear in the chapter on "Space, Time, and Value." In any case, I doubt whether we can make our ontological meanings intelligible without this distinction.

[1] This point is further discussed in Chapter IV, pp. 150 ff.

I have already said that the denial of this presupposition is a pure paradox, and one, moreover, the consequences of which, when thought out, can lead only to self-refutation and complete unintelligibility; that a way out of this paradox must be found, otherwise modern thought will find itself in a complete *impasse*. I shall now attempt to make clear what seems to me to be the only way out, namely, the recognition of the *value character* of the predicate of reality. But first let us see the element of paradox and of self-refutation in the notion.

Now it is doubtless, as we have seen, a prejudice that leads us to identify "reality" exclusively with the actual or the existent. It is similarly a prejudice that leads the Platonist to identify reality exclusively with changeless essences. Both arise out of exclusive and morbid evaluations of one aspect of reality. I may well charge a thinker with a prejudice in favour of any such exclusive concept of reality—in favour of the sensible, the permanent, the related, or what not—but to charge him with a prejudice in favour of reality as against unreality would seem to be an inanity possible only to a philosopher at his wits' end. If I seek to overcome his prejudice in favour of merely existing objects I thereby assume, unless I am guilty of just this inanity, that the non-existent objects are real in some sense. If I seek, as Bergson does, to overcome his prejudice in favour of the permanent and unchanging, I thereby assume that the changing is the ultimately real. And so on throughout the entire range of possible definitions of the real. In short, the concept of ultimate reality, with its correlative unreality, is not merely a practical concept, and as such, from the point of view of impartial theory, a prejudice or an illusion. It is rather the *a priori* of intelligible thought and of meaningful discourse.

Is this merely verbal dialectic? It will doubtless appear so to some. If so, it simply means that intelligible philosophic thought is ultimately dialectic. Certainly it has all the cogency of any valid application of the argument from self-refutation. Assuming a world of rational, intelligible discourse, the presupposition of ultimate reality is part of that world. The proposition which denies that reality does not refute itself, but he who makes the proposition refutes himself if thereby he means to convey an intelligible meaning. The nature of the argument is indicated by the eternal protest of the human spirit against all those sophisticated philosophies which propose the inanity of interest in the unreal, especially those which speak of valuable objects that are unreal and of illusions that are "valuable as essence but valueless as reality."

The sophistication of modernist thought, which we have found to be its most constant character, reaches its highest perversity at this point, and vitiates many forms of modern philosophy. "The world of universals," says Russell, "is delightful to all those who love perfection more than life." In this there is, perhaps, an element of "private endearment," and it would, indeed, be a prejudice to identify reality wholly with this world, but surely it is sheer perversity to say that interest in this aspect of being is merely "an affinity which the human mind may develop for certain provinces of essence." Their value presupposes their reality. To say, with Vaihinger, that it is precisely the tragedy of thought that the most valuable things have no value as reality would be, indeed, to enunciate the perfection of tragedy if it were not rather the perfection of nonsense. Yet it is just such meaningless collocations of words that one finds everywhere in modernist philosophy; it is one phase of a general *impasse* in thought to which it has been slowly but surely coming.

But this is not all. If the preceding argument is sound further consequences follow from it, as important as they are obvious. The so-called prejudice in favour of reality is, indeed, no prejudice, as we have seen, but a necessary presupposition of intelligible discourse. The ideal of an *ens realissimum* can never be eliminated from philosophical activity without making that activity wholly meaningless. But this ideal is itself intelligible only when it is realized that value and reality are inseparable concepts. The value character of the ontological predicates follows necessarily. The recognition that the very givenness of objects and their existence involves valuation is, as Münsterberg has said, the first step towards a general theory of value; but it is equally true that it is the first step towards any satisfactory theory of the ontological predicates.

The question, "What is the real?" we now recognize is a futile question if being is abstracted from value. If we identify reality with being in the widest sense, we can answer the question only by saying that the real is everything. Reality, being, in this sense, is, indeed, the most ultimate category of thought, but it is also the most meaningless. In order to give any meaning to our ontological predicates it becomes necessary for us to make within the general category of being certain distinctions, between appearance and reality, between reality and unreality, and between different kinds of being. When we judge anything to be real or unreal we are not opposing a general class of unreal things to real things, but are comparing one particular reality with another, from which it ought to be, but in a certain judgment has not been, distinguished. But this demand for distinction is meaningless except as it presupposes distinctions of value and their acknowledgment. To separate reality from value becomes contradictory. It is at this point that the intrinsic relation of value to reality appears. For an ultimate reflection reality and value must be identical (or at least inseparably related), since the highest object of reflection is just the full ground and meaning of our judgments of reality. It is here, also, that we see why none of the traditional philosophies has been without the notion of degrees of reality in some form, why the notion of an *ens realissimum*, or of "metaphysical perfection," as Leibniz calls it, is part of the inherent structure of traditional thought.

The futility of trying to answer the question, "What is the real?" if being is abstracted from value, is increasingly recognized in modern thought. The impartiality of modernism, of which we have spoken, is partly a recognition of this fact. This has found expression recently in a suggestive and interesting argument for what is called Ontological Liberalism.[1]

This ontological liberalism is the outgrowth of that other line of thought which we have described as the genetic account of the ontological predicates. The argument up to a point is not notably different from that of the preceding pages. The attempt is made, and I think successfully, to show that every judgment of reality is a valuation, and that every definition of reality is from the point of view of some purpose. The consequences drawn lead to pure relativism. By some it is

---

[1] I am indebted for this term to Professor C. J. Ducasse, whose very suggestive article, "A Liberalistic View of Truth," appeared in the *Philosophical Review*, vol. xxxiv, No. 6.

thought to be entirely hopeless to bring any order or system into our ontological predicates. Others would say, one conception of the real is true from one point of view, another from another, but which is the more true or more real they would say, as James said of the ontological predicates of common sense, science, and metaphysics, God only knows. It is this very *value-character* of the ontological predicates, as thus interpreted, that leads to relativism and ultimately to the denial of all finality to philosophy.

Now, this ontological liberalism—which is, in any case, better and more understanding than ontological dogmatism—is true up to a point. But what is overlooked is that, if we accept the value-character of the theoretical, the value-character of the ontological predicates, precisely that fact—that they are values —implies their relation in a scale or system of values. The relativism of this point of view is based wholly, of course, on the assumption of the purely biological and psychological conception of values and the doctrine of subjectivism which results. Our own interpretation of the ontological predicates and their value-character must wait upon our study of the nature of value and its relation to existence and reality. Here we may simply note that there is another form of this ontological liberalism, that connected with the thought of Hegel, that does not involve relativism in this purely humanistic, psychological sense.

It is the imperishable merit of Hegel that he finds the organon of philosophy in the history of the concepts of reality and truth. To him we owe the realization of the fact that the ontological predicates are meanings that depend for their meaning on acknowledgment of values. His statement, for instance, that philosophic knowledge depends for its starting-point on the acknowledgment, *Anerkennen*, of the different forms of truth and reality in the perceptual, æsthetic, ethical, and logical consciousness is a complete expression of this liberalism. Hegel, it is true, never recognized the value-character of the ontological predicates explicitly, but his whole doctrine of degrees of reality presupposed it. It is clear that for him—and, indeed, for all traditional thought—reality, in the metaphysical sense, was not to be identified with any of the particular definitions of reality as determined by the specific ontological prejudices. It can be found only in some "dialectical" combination or system of them all—as we should say nowadays—of values and validities. Any solution of the ontological problem must be, as Hegel saw, dialectical in the broadest sense of the term.

For every one of these prejudices and definitions of the real has a basis deep down somewhere in the processes of intelligible thought and its communication. Hegel's entire treatment of the problem rests upon the recognition of this fact, and, as I think, on the recognition of the value-character of all ontological distinctions. The "absolute idea" as he uses it is precisely the idea of reason as the system of meanings and values.

But while it was Hegel's merit to develop this organon, the fundamental insight upon which his developments proceed is as old as traditional philosophy itself. It is ordinarily supposed that the objective of perennial philosophy is pure being, i.e. being abstracted from value. I regard this as a profound and serious error, and one which the entire history of philosophy refutes. The great philosophers, it is true, have often thought of their philosophies as systems of existences or entities. In reality they have been much more systematic interpretations of meanings and values. For one thing, none of these philosophies has been without the conception of different orders of being and degrees of reality. Indeed, it will be one of our later tasks to show that in all the great philosophers the order of being, the scale of values—in short, the principle of system—has been fundamentally the same. However that may be, the principle of degrees of reality is present in all, and for none is being without hierarchical order.

It is true that the ontological instinct has often misconceived itself, or at least expressed itself in faulty and inadequate terms. Plato, for instance, while recognizing value as the last and highest object of "science" *in principle*—even when speaking of the good or value as above or beyond all existence—forthwith turns value itself into a transcendent entity. For St. Thomas *bonum et ens sunt idem*, yet he continually treats being as prior because it is the first object of the intellect (in time) and the whole concept of value becomes secondary and adjectival. Substance becomes that which exists in and for itself. Yet, despite these apparent objections to our thesis, it will be found,

I think, that the true inwardness of perennial philosophy is to be found in the principle of the value-character of the theoretical. The inseparability of value and reality is consciously or unconsciously assumed by every thinker to whom the principle of an *ens realissimum* is a fundamental presupposition of intelligible thought. In any case, it is only in this direction that any escape is to be found from the paradoxes to which modernism, with its extremes of ontological liberalism and licence, has brought us. The fuller development of this position is in part the substance of the chapters to come.

VIII

Traditional philosophy, as we said, is for the modernist a bundle of prejudices, a tissue of philosophical errors. The presuppositions with which the magnanimous philosophers have come to the interpretation of reality are held to be gratuitous assumptions which philosophy is by no means compelled to make. To these primary assumptions—of totality, meaning, value, and ultimate reality—others are added which it will be our province to examine on later occasions. Thus there are, it is held, "three errors which have perpetually played into one another, and have begotten certain well-nigh inveterate habits of philosophical thought"—the errors of "speculative dogma," with its idea of ultimate substance or cause, the error of pseudo-simplicity, and the error of indefinite potentiality. They are said to be characteristic of all substance and activistic philosophies.[1] All these so-called errors have entered into the very structure of the Great Tradition, and must be taken into account as we develop the main features of that tradition. Here we are interested merely in evaluating the primary prejudices or assumptions, and we will close this chapter with a summary of our conclusions.

It is our contention, in the first place, that, properly understood, these so-called prejudices are not prejudices, but presuppositions or assumptions that philosophy is compelled to make. Prejudices, we have fully recognized, enter into many of the formulations of these assumptions. We may demand a

---

[1] See R. B. Perry, *Present Philosophical Tendencies*, pp. 64 ff.

unity, a meaning, a satisfaction in the universe which we have no right to demand. We may say things about the all of reality which we must learn not to say. Prejudices may enter into our definition of the real which beget exclusive and dogmatic systems. But criticism of these prejudices is possible, and when the work of criticism is done there remain these ultimate presuppositions that cannot be eliminated.

These compulsions of philosophy are not *logical* in the abstract sense of the word. The postulates of totality, meaning, and value are above all logics in this sense, as they are above all ontologies. Logic itself, as we shall learn in the next chapter, however logic be conceived, itself presupposes the acknowledgment of these meanings and values. It is, indeed, to logic the philosopher appeals in order to transcend his prejudices, but logic is itself not presuppositionless, a fact which is one of the first things that an enlightened philosophy must learn. No; the compulsions of philosophy with which we are here concerned are rather the necessary conditions of philosophical intelligibility as such.

These compulsions cannot accordingly be associated with any particular school of philosophic thought. They have, indeed, been specifically acknowledged by the great idealisms, past and present. It is natural that modern idealists should identify them with idealism and draw the necessary exclusive inferences. Of none of the credit for its faithfulness to the Great Tradition should modern idealism be denied, but the fact remains that these premises of the Great Tradition are prior to, and above all, distinctions of epistemological idealism and realism. This I hope to make abundantly clear in our study of the logics of these two positions in the next chapter. It is enough to say that they are compulsions acknowledged alike by Plato and Aristotle, by St. Anselm and St. Thomas, by Leibniz and Hegel.

Philosophy is compelled to make these assumptions because without them there can be no intelligibility. The objective of philosophy is an intelligible world, the interpretation and communication of the meaning of our experience. Now, it is always possible abstractly to deny that the world need be intelligible. That there is a "world," and that it necessarily has meaning, are assumptions or postulates that we may call prejudices if we choose. But no one can deny the obligation of being intelligible. That cannot by any stretch of modern paradox be called a prejudice. No philosopher can deny these presuppositions without refuting himself, and thus as a philosopher becoming unintelligible.

The study in detail of the meaning and conditions of philosophical intelligibility will engage our attention as we seek to develop the specific conceptions by means of which traditional thought has sought to achieve such intelligibility. Here we shall content ourselves with calling attention to a point without which this chapter would be incomplete. It is that *intelligible communication itself is one of the presuppositions of philosophical activity as such*, or rather the ultimate presupposition.

I have constantly insisted upon the principle of self-refutation properly understood, as the final means of distinguishing between prejudices and necessary presuppositions. Now, there is no such thing as self-refutation in a solipsistic world. A proposition does not refute itself; nor does a thinker really refute himself, except as it is assumed that he seeks to convey an intelligible meaning. The assumption of intelligible communication as a necessary presupposition of philosophy is often conceived to be part of the idealistic philosophy alone. Nothing could be farther from the truth. Intelligible communication is presupposed by idealist and realist alike, and the only argument to which either in the last analysis can appeal to substantiate either his realism or his idealism is, as we shall see, an *argumentum ad hominem*. Communication is, moreover, not itself an object of knowledge and explanation, but is rather assumed in all knowledge and explanation.

There are many, indeed, who refuse to accept this position as it has been assumed by traditional thought. But they are forced to accept it when it is presented in other terms. We must all "play the game" of thought, whether we be realists or idealists. Without mutual acknowledgment of certain presuppositions we must give up the game. It is, moreover, a fact that if we do not accept knowledge and thinking as a serious moral occupation of man, in which logic is the morality of that thinking, knowledge itself degenerates into play. Even as play it is, however, never a game of solitaire.

The social character of all thinking is, to be sure, the first step in the understanding of the fundamental character of the category of communication in philosophy. But it is a mistake to exaggerate that aspect. It was, for instance, a distinct disservice to philosophy when Royce, under the influence of the psychologism of his time, tended to confuse problems of description with problems of validity. His over-emphasis of the social and the psychological but retarded the development of his brilliant treatment of communication in his later book, *The Problem of Christianity*.

The whole tendency to reduce communication and meaning to scientific terms is due to a gross misunderstanding. "There is no interchange between one and another in the scientific meaning of the term," and the problem of intercourse is *the* problem of philosophy. Even when certain realists speak of the overlapping of minds, communication is not explained in any scientific causal way, but rather in a logical way, through a doctrine of relations. In either case the whole thing involves a vicious circle. It makes of communication a part of existence or being while the ontological predicates and distinctions themselves presuppose communication. It is precisely this reduction to unintelligibility of the whole category of communication that a philosophy of validity and values seeks to avoid.

To acknowledge these truths is, however, to see at once the larger significance of this entire chapter. The philosopher, as an ironical poet tells us in the quotation at the head of this chapter, remains of value in all ages, if for no other reason than that he constantly rediscovers the *Selbstverständlichkeiten*. The measure of culture, Emerson somewhere says, is the things taken for granted. The continuity of culture depends, however, on constantly rediscovering these things anew. It is not different with philosophy, itself at once the condition and the highest sublimation of any culture. The things that must be taken for granted, the values, logical and a-logical, that must be acknowledged if there is to be intelligible thought and its communication—these have always been and must for ever be part of the preoccupation of the genuine philosopher. For the true lover of wisdom the irony of poet and scientist alike is but cause for quiet and judicious mirth. He knows that they are his brothers, and that when knowledge rises to wisdom, discourse to understanding, they must all acknowledge the same things.

CHAPTER III

"GENUINE KNOWLEDGE" AND "*BONÂ-FIDE* LOGIC"
LOGIC, VALUE, AND REALITY

Logik ist die Moral des Denkens.

HERBART

The Spirit of logic is love and the spirit of value is logic.

BOSANQUET

I

THE belief that logic is in some sense the "essence of philosophy" is as old as conscious philosophy itself. It rests upon a fundamental preference (or shall we say prejudice?) of the human spirit, one of those unavoidable valuations which it is extraordinarily difficult for the mind to overcome. That mind is higher than body, reason higher than sense, that reason is godlike, and that reason and reality are ultimately one—these are durable connections of ideas, to dissociate which means turning one's back upon the natural bent of thinking itself.

Against the keenest and most extravagant forms of this rationalism there has always been, it is true, a standing protest. A morbid evaluation of intellect has been charged against it. Feeling, intuition, and instinct have set up rival claims. Scepticism and a-logism celebrate temporary triumphs. But the victories are temporary, for they are possible only by calling on logic itself. They claim to go beyond intelligence, but can do so only by calling on intelligence to justify them, and from this vicious circle they can find no exit except by some *tour de force* that thrusts the intelligence outside itself by an arbitrary act of will. A-logism, the appeal to instinct, feeling, intuition, life, or what not, is an essentially extra-philosophical standpoint. Such an appeal is always possible; it has always been made and always will be. But the appeal is to values that are non-philosophical.

It is, for instance, often affirmed that genuine knowledge is attained only by sensation, intuition, the ineffable vision of the mystic, or what not other a-logical processes. But these affirmations and their corresponding negations are themselves not the outcome of such processes, but of conceptual thinking the structure of which is logical. These judgments, moreover, however contradictory in themselves, always involve the acknowledgment of the universal character and absolute validity of the concepts they employ. Through them it is always possible to distinguish the logical form of knowledge, as represented by such affirmations, from the other forms, and the logical form of reflection is established as the essentially and fundamentally philosophical form.

It is reasonably safe, then, to say that philosophy, to be philosophy, must be "intellectualistic." The prejudice in favour of logic is no prejudice but a necessary presupposition of intelligible thought. In any case, this assumption is one of the premises of the Great Tradition. Ever since thought has become conscious of its own "natural movement" it has called that movement logic.

II

But when we have said this we have said about all that can be definitely said. In some sense logic must be ultimate. Yes, but in what sense? Logic is to be the means of getting beyond the prejudices of the philosophers; but what, pray, are the prejudices of logic? Logic is the essence of philosophy; but, we may well ask, "Which logic?"

These questions cannot but strike the uninitiated with a shock, yet a little reflection shows that they are very much in place. It is, first of all, just the charge that logic, with its exclusive claims, is based upon a prejudice that constitutes the position of anti-intellectualism in general. "Why," asks Nietzsche, "should an irrefutable assumption (upon which all logic, or rather all logics, rest) necessarily be true?" This question, he continues, "may exasperate the logicians, who limit the things according to the limitations they find in themselves, but I have long since declared war on this logicians' optimism." Behind all logic, he holds, and its apparent neutrality, there are certain valuations—for example, that the distinct is of more value than the indistinct, appearance of less value than the truth. Valuations of this sort, with all their regulative importance for us, can, he holds, be only *Vorgrund* valuations. Moreover, it is, according to him, precisely the "poorest proved assumption in the world"—namely, that truth is more valuable than appearance—that constitutes the basis of all logic. It is really nothing more than a disguised moral prejudice.

This heresy of the *enfant terrible* of modernism we need not take too seriously. From his general position, however, that logic has certain *Vorurteile*, there can be no dissent. *Grundurteile* there are, which underlie all logic, that can never be proved but only assumed, "logical values" which can be but acknowledged. The validity of the appeal to logic as a means of overcoming the prejudices of the philosophers depends entirely upon our estimation of the prejudices and presuppositions of logic itself.

But the situation is further complicated. This appeal to logic raises the further question: What logic? But surely this is absurdity, it will be said. Is there not but one genuine, *bonâ-fide* logic? This logic may itself have its prejudices or presuppositions, but they at least are ultimate and absolute. Yet just this, also, the experienced thinker finds it necessary to question. Paradoxical as it may sound, logic, at least as the term is employed by the philosopher, is precisely the one discipline which is not neutral. In a recent article Professor Montague distinguishes at least four different logics: it is, according to him, due to the fundamentally different assumptions underlying these logics that fundamentally different interpretations of reality result. We are familiar enough with the expressions, "pragmatist logic," "realist's logic," "idealist's logic." Whether they are really different logics or merely different theories of logic is immaterial. It is sufficient that they are not neutral—that they all, as we shall presently see, have fundamentally different assumptions, that the idealist, realist, pragmatist, as the case may be, reproduces the ontological prejudices of his own particular attitude as the postulates of logic *überhaupt*.

Logic may, indeed, in a sense, be the essence of philosophy, but, if so, the problem of philosophy is not simplified but further complicated. The appeal to logic as the means of overcoming the prejudices of the philosophers is but an appeal from prejudice to prejudice. The appeal to logic as a means of overcoming the oppositions of philosophers created by these prejudices is merely to push the problem a step further back, for these very oppositions are repeated in our conceptions of logic itself. It is for these very reasons that the battle-ground of philosophy to-day is logic. It is for this very reason that the prejudices of epistemological realism and idealism have been identified with the postulates of logic itself, at least by these sectarians in philosophy, that the logical problem itself became central and the war in this field war to the knife. On the other hand, it is precisely because these prejudices, and others like them, are recognized for the prejudices they are, that logic itself has been abandoned by many for a-logical approaches to reality.

The battle-ground of philosophy to-day is logic. By this I mean, not only the fact that the question of the nature and principles of logic as a "science" is still unsettled, but also the still more fundamental question of its relation to knowledge, to philosophy, and to life. Precisely because there are these different conceptions of logic, even these "different logics," because each party in the dispute appeals to some idea or ideal of "genuine knowledge" and "*bonâ-fide* logic," the true inwardness of the battle becomes evident. It is, to be sure, over the nature of knowledge that men dispute, but the dispute always turns upon the question what is genuine knowledge, and that is a question which turns on values that can be acknowledged but never proved. It is over the nature of logic that logicians dispute, but in it is always involved the question of *bonâ-fide* logic, and the question of good faith always involves the question of sincerity and of values which again can be acknowledged but never proved. In other words, it is becoming increasingly evident that the ultimate problem of logic is a problem of values, and that the question of the place of logic in knowledge in general and in philosophical knowledge in particular depends upon a solution of this problem.

III

This enlightenment, this sophistication regarding logic, is, however, one of the chief characteristics of modernism. The changing conception of philosophy, the digging under the very foundations of thinking, the turning of axioms into postulates and postulates into prejudices, presupposes reconstructions of logic itself. The daring of the modern mind is nowhere so completely shown as in what it is willing to do with logic.

All forms of modernism agree, of course, in their indictment of the "old logic." It is true that, as Mr. Russell has said, since the seventeenth century all vigorous minds have been engaged upon the task of logical reconstruction, of extending the field of logic and of transcending the limits of formal and traditional logic as it is called. But the "new logics" are in a sense ultra-modern and arise out of conditions, scientific and cultural, that are comparatively recent. This attack on traditional logic is in part an affair of logic itself, but it involves also an attack on the fundamental presuppositions and forms of traditional thought, and it is with this aspect of the question that we are ultimately chiefly concerned.

The modern logics, or, perhaps better, modern conceptions of logic, are the so-called monistic or idealistic logic, the atomistic logic of the new realism, the instrumental logic of pragmatism, and the a-logism of intuitionism. The principles and postulates of these different logics will engage our attention in later sections of this chapter. Here we wish to emphasize solely their common opposition to traditional thought and its interpretation of the nature and function of logic.[1]

---

[1] In his *Budget of Paradoxes* De Morgan makes merry over a book by a certain Justin Brenan, published in 1830 and entitled *Old and New Logic Contrasted*, the sub-title of which announces that it will elucidate for ordinary comprehension how Lord Bacon delivered the human mind from its two thousand years' enslavement under Aristotle. Now, it is freeing of the mind that the newest logics still have as their primary object. The author of the tract referred to connects the old logic with the indecencies of the classical writers and the new logic with the new moral purity. The authors of the new logics of the present have not made the matter a moral issue in this sense, but they have not hesitated to connect the old logic with every sort of infirmity of the human mind and with all the prejudices of traditional thought. The old story, says De Morgan, "about Aristotle having one logic to trammel us and Bacon another to free us is always laughed at by those who know either Aristotle or Bacon." Of ignorance either of Aristotle or Bacon the modern logicians would be the last to be accused. Yet that the magic powers of the new logic have been greatly exaggerated who can doubt? My own view is that a more ultimate evaluation of this period of logic will show its chief significance to be in a definite expansion of the science of logic without abandonment of its character as a formal discipline distinct from epistemology. This is, in a sense, the thesis of this chapter.

The "new logics" are all part of a general movement to free the mind from certain ancient prejudices by which it has been desperately possessed, part of that changing conception of philosophy which all forms of modernism envisage. Traditional thought is bound up with a traditional conception of the nature and function of knowledge. Modernistic philosophies imply novel views of logic. Now, it is only from this general point of view—of the relation of logic to philosophy and metaphysics—that the problem of the nature and function of objective of logic is to be studied. We shall not be concerned very much either with the details of logic as a "science," nor with the specific positions of the new logics as they appear in the course of the discussion. Any criticism of these positions should be construed neither as a wholesale denial of their truth nor as a refusal to recognize their value for general philosophy. In so far as such criticisms enter into our study, they do so only as they bear on the ultimate question of the nature of logic and its relations to problems of reality and value, only in so far as they bear on the question of the relation of logic to the fundamental presuppositions of philosophic thought.

A reinstatement of what I conceive to be the traditional view of logic, but in a more modern form, it may frankly be said at the outset, is the ultimate objective of this chapter. To the question, "What is logic?" we shall answer that it is a normative science, a science of those absolute values that must be acknowledged if intelligible communication is to be possible. The development of this thesis will involve the question whether logic is a "science" of the laws of thought or of laws of being, the question of the relation of the assumptions of logic to the more ultimate presuppositions of intelligible thought and its communication, and finally the question of the relation of logic to language, as the medium through which all communication, logical or other than logical, is alone possible.

The examination we propose will, then, include two parts. In the first place, we shall undertake an examination of the prejudices or presuppositions of logic as such, as opposed to a-logical points of view; and, secondly, an examination of the specific prejudices of the specific logics, more particularly the two fundamental logics of realism and idealism. The real problem of logic, from this point of view, is not, then, the formulation of a presuppositionless logic, but rather the determination of those general presuppositions which any logic as such must acknowledge, those absolute values that are above all ontology and all ontological prejudices.

IV

"I have long declared war," cries Nietzsche, "against this logicians' optimism." By this optimism he understands, we have seen, the rationalist's faith, based upon the prejudice that truth is more valuable than appearance, or, more fundamentally, that the instinct for knowledge and the vital instinct are one.

This war on logical optimism is one of the characteristic notes of modernism. Both the optimism it attacks and the pessimism that is the motive of the attack are natural products of the modern world. By studying these two attitudes towards logic, together with a third which may be described as logical meliorism, we shall have the necessary background against which to see the fundamental problems around which modern logical discussion revolves.

Logical optimism says *ratio est capabilis*, capable of apprehending reality as it is. In the extreme form of panlogism, reason and being are identical. That such a judgment involves an element of faith goes without saying. The *Grundurteil*, *ratio est capabilis*, has no meaning except in the light of some ideal as to what knowledge ought to be. From this general point of view, and for the moment it is indifferent whether that ideal be found in the criterion of non-contradiction or coherence, or, as in the case of the atomistic logic, in the ultimate simples of analysis; in either case it is assumed that logic is the ultimate "science of whatever is," that it has the power to determine what is the real, and that its values, whether the values of connection or of simplicity and transparency, are ultimate values and constitute the ideal of genuine knowledge.

Logical optimism is based upon a value judgment—upon the acknowledgment of what genuine knowledge ought to be.

But just this ideal of knowledge the logical pessimist refuses to acknowledge. The eternal charge against rationalism is accordingly this: The intellect, reason, has a natural bent towards analysis and abstraction. This is what it wants and therefore what it finds. But, having determined what it wants, it is not, therefore, justified in adding the footnote, "That is what reality ultimately is." We can do so only by a prior exclusive evaluation of the intellect which begs the whole question.

Logical pessimism springs from a fundamental and, at bottom, no less indisputable valuation. It also is determined by an ideal of what genuine knowledge should be. The logical pessimist does not, in the first place, accept the ideal of clearness and distinctness as the ideal of genuine knowledge. He frankly says that mere simplicity, transparency as the logician understands it, leaves him cold. He goes farther, and insists that the more transparent the world of logical connections and forms becomes, the more opaque and impenetrable, in another sense, it appears. It gains these qualities by a progressive loss of essential intelligibility. And with this pessimism there are not lacking, we shall see, scientists who are in agreement.

The ideal of knowledge which underlies this logical pessimism has been expressed most vividly by Bergson when, in arguing that we should turn our backs upon the natural bent of the intellect towards logic, he says: "What such a metaphysic (of intuition or direct penetration) will lose in utility and rigour it will recover again in depth and extension of meaning."[1] In other words, as other passages make clear, the clearness and distinctness, the ease of apprehension, which the stable and immovable forms of mathematics and logic assure us, is for him not the ideal of knowledge.

In contrast to the two preceding attitudes towards logic we may distinguish a third which, for lack of a better name, we may describe as logical meliorism. Vaihinger, in contrasting these two attitudes of logical optimism and logical pessimism, describes a third as *logischer Criticismus*, and characterizes it as one which, coldly and without prejudice, investigates the instrument of thought. With the logical pessimist

[1] *Introduction to Metaphysics.*

the critical logician emancipates himself from the childish superstition of the unlimited power and validity of thought, and with the logical optimist he holds fast to the belief in the final practical reality of thought and being.[1]

To this attitude in the main, although not necessarily in its pragmatic form, as represented by Vaihinger, the deeper forms of modern thought would probably confess their allegiance. "It will probably be agreed" (says Kemp-Smith in his inaugural lecture) "that the most important and fruitful of the changes that have taken place in the philosophical disciplines since the eighteenth century has been the growing recognition that logical analysis and dialectic, however indispensable, can play only a subordinate part in the problems traditionally assigned to philosophy."[2] In so far as the traditional problems have been kept in mind this is undoubtedly true. When philosophy has been identified with technical logic it has been only, as we have seen, by "jettisoning most of the cargo of the good ship Philosophy."

Now, what does this attitude mean? If it means anything, it must signify primarily that the logical values *par excellence*, the values of clearness and distinctness, of simplicity and transparency, of necessary connections, are not recognized as the exclusive ideals and values of reason. Logical meliorism means, of course, the perfection of the logical instrument—the means by which these values are worked out, but it means much more, the evaluation of these values themselves as but parts or aspects of a larger ideal of intelligibility and truth. It represents the development of a larger conception of reason in which reason *is* the system of values, a larger conception of truth in which the objectivity of reason involves not merely the correctness of logic, but the validity which has its source in something deeper than logic.

To choose between these three general attitudes towards logic is no part of our present purpose. The object we have had in mind is rather to show that *any* attitude towards logic, any conception whatever of its nature and function, involves an evaluation. They all involve certain ideals of knowledge

---

[1] *The Philosophy of "As If,"* Introduction.
[2] "The Present Situation in Philosophy," *The Philosophical Review*, January 1920, p. 23.

which are extra-logical in the narrow sense of the word. Neutral logic, in the sense that it is without any presuppositions whatever, is, as Nietzsche rightly saw, a pure illusion. But even more important is the fact that the general presuppositions of logic are above the differences of the particular logics. The prejudice in favour of reality—that reality is more valuable than appearance; the prejudice in favour of meaning, even if expressed merely in the form that the distinct is more valuable than the indistinct, the defined than the undefined; the prejudice in favour of totality—that the connected is more valuable than the unconnected; and finally that which underlies them all, the prejudice in favour of value, the orientation of the intellect towards value, however narrowly the value may be conceived: all these are shared by any logic, as they are shared by any philosophy whatsoever. The denial of these means not another logic but the opposite of logic.

Neutral logic, in the sense that it is without these general prejudices or presuppositions, is impossible. The reason for this is that, whatever else logic is, it is the necessary form of intelligible communication, and such communication has necessarily these presuppositions. But there are other prejudices —those which characterize the specific or sectarian logics— concerning the necessity of which we cannot be so certain. Is the axiom of independence, with its doctrine of externality of relations, the condition of a *bonâ-fide* logic? Or is coherence, with its doctrine of internality of relations, the necessary condition of genuine logic? Need it be said that with these questions we have reached the very heart of the problem of logic? For each of these logics, it is apparent, involves not merely an acknowledgment of values which any logic must acknowledge to be logic; it includes also an ontological prejudice as part of logic itself. In so doing both imply a certain theory of the nature of reality and of the relation of logic to the real. To this problem we must now turn.

V

The entire question of the nature of logic, of its function in knowledge and the material or objects with which logic deals, is now before us. On just this question of the definition of logic, we shall not be surprised to find, there is the greatest variety of opinion, and in the very definitions the prejudices of particular philosophical attitudes are repeated. Before we can undertake to consider this ultimate problem we must first examine the particular logics and the specific ontological prejudices that underlie them. It is the importation into logic itself of these particular prejudices that creates the various logics which add to the turmoil of modern philosophical thought.

This idea of a plurality of logics, properly understood, is not, we found, a paradox. The expressions—pragmatist's, idealist's, realist's logic—everyone understands perfectly. At this point we shall content ourselves with examining the idealistic and realistic logics, which the upholders of each maintain to be identical with logic as such. Thus far we have considered the general prejudices or presuppositions of any logic whatsoever. Now, we shall examine the specific prejudices of the specific logics.

"Every idealistic theory of the world," says Pringle-Pattison, "has as its ultimate premise a logically unsupported judgment of value—a judgment which affirms an end of intrinsic worth and accepts thereby a standard of unconditional obligation." The same may be said of every realistic theory of the world. It is of the utmost importance that we should see what these *Grundurteile* are.

The logically unsupported judgment of value of the idealist is precisely the ideal of genuine knowledge which underlies all his thinking. For him genuine knowledge is always knowledge of the whole. The idealist acknowledges, it is true, the fundamental presuppositions of all philosophy, the postulate of meaning, of the inseparability of value and reality, but that which determines his logic most definitely is his emphasis upon the postulate of totality. *Meaning and value are themselves functions of unity and totality.* So far so good. This is merely a special case of the general principle that no logic is neutral, that any logic, as logic, presupposes values that must be acknowledged. But the idealistic logic does not stop here. It claims, on the one hand, to be able to demonstrate the impossibility of the opposite of this conception of knowledge. It claims also, since it is assumed that logic is "the ultimate science of being," that demonstration of the ultimate nature of "genuine" knowledge involves demonstration of the nature of reality.

For this general position, as is well known, there is a form of argument consisting of a peculiarly subtle application of the principle of self-contradiction. Every effort to deny knowledge of the whole involves, it is held, such knowledge of the whole, every effort to deny an absolute experience involves the assertion of such experience.

The nature of this argument is not always understood either by those who make it or those who criticize it. It is essentially an *argumentum ad hominem*—an appeal, not to any "fact" outside human discourse, but rather to an ideal of "genuine knowledge," to a value which, it is assumed, must be acknowledged if such discourse is to be intelligible. That reality must be *one* to be genuinely known is a proposition that can only be acknowledged but never proved. If we insist on separating fact and truth from value, nothing can force this acknowledgment from us.

This *argumentum ad hominem* is even more obvious in the case of the second part of the argument—regarding the relation of knowledge and logic to reality. In our examination of the idealistic definitions of reality in the preceding chapter we found them determined by the assumption that logic is the ultimate science of being, and that what logic seems to demand as the nature of the real is what reality ultimately is. The definition of reality depends upon our conception of genuine knowledge—as organized experience or logical stability. Refuse to acknowledge this evaluation and the entire argument falls to the ground.[1]

---

[1] Both Royce and Bosanquet make this perfectly clear. "The question, Is there an absolutely organized experience?" says Royce, "is equivalent to the question, Is there an absolute reality? You cannot first say there is a reality now unknown to us mortals and then go on to ask whether there is an experience to which such reality is presented. The terms 'reality' and 'organized experience' are correlative terms. The one can only be defined as the object, the content of the other. Drop either and the other vanishes. Make one a bare ideal and the other becomes equally such. If the organized experience is a bare and ideal possibility, then the reality is mere seeming. If what I ought to experience and should experience, were I not ignorant, remains only a possibility, then there is no absolute reality, but only possibility in the universe, apart from your passing

It is now perfectly clear, I think, that the idealistic logic has as its ultimate premise a logically unsupported judgment of value and accepts thereby a standard of unconditional obligation. It is perfectly clear, also, that this judgment of value is precisely the ontological prejudice which we examined in the preceding chapter. In other words, this logic identifies the presuppositions of a particular logic with the postulates of logic *überhaupt*. It is also clear how an entire reconstruction or reinterpretation of logic flows from this initial assumption. This is chiefly seen in the cardinal principle of the monistic logic, namely, that the object of the judgment is always the whole of reality, or that the unit of logic is the implicative system. The reconstruction of the traditional law of identity and the doctrine of the concrete universal are the principal consequences of this principle. With the details of this logic, or interpretation of logic, we are here not concerned. Whether the idealistic conception of the judgment of identity arises, as the analytical atomistic logician maintains, out of the confusion of two senses of the judgment of identity, or lies deeper in something which such criticism wholly misses, we may for the present leave undetermined. Whether the concept of the concrete universal is, as these same critics maintain, a contradiction in terms, or the necessary form of all intelligibility, is a question we may also leave for another occasion. That which interests us here is the much more fundamental point, namely, that the "idealistic" logic, with all its details, presupposes an ideal of genuine knowledge, including a logically unsupported judgment of value, and that this ideal involves also an ontological prejudice as to the ultimate nature of reality.

It is, to be sure, natural to identify this prejudice in favour of reality as a logical whole with the presupposition of totality

feelings and mine. Our actual issue then is, Does a real world ultimately exist at all?" (*The Conception of God*, pp. 35 f.).

It may be brought out still more clearly by another statement of the argument. "The driving force of idealism, as I understand it," says Bosanquet, "is not furnished by the question how mind and reality can meet in knowledge, but by the theory of logical stability which makes it plain that nothing can fulfil the conditions of self-existence except by possessing the unity that belongs to mind." Here obviously, again, the whole argument depends upon the acknowledgment of an ideal of genuine knowledge as involving the absolute value of "logical stability," and also of the identity of reality with this value. Refuse to acknowledge either of these and the whole argument falls to the ground.

which, as we have seen, is a necessary presupposition of philosophical discourse. If such an identification were necessary, monistic logic with its conception of reality would necessarily follow. For, as we have seen, the prejudice in favour of totality is one of the necessary presuppositions of intelligible discourse, one that cannot be denied without self-refutation. But it is precisely at this point that the greatest care must be exercised. It was for this reason partly that we were at great pains to distinguish between two different conceptions of totality. It is not wholly easy to make this distinction clear, but it must be made if there is not to be complete confusion throughout our entire discussion.

The distinction between logical and axiological, between logical and metaphysical totality, was forced upon us by the facts of philosophic discourse. That distinction may be further illuminated by reference to our present problem. The postulate of a coherent whole of reality as the ultimate postulate of logic presupposes a whole which must itself have value and validity on some other grounds than logical, if the parts of the whole are to have value through logical relation to the whole. Now, this value of the connected whole must either be simply acknowledged, "mystically" as it were, without reasons; or, if there are any reasons they must be of the nature of showing the place of the value of the connected whole in a larger system of values. In other words, the value of logical connection cannot be identical with value as such, but only *a* value among other values.

This, then, is my thesis. Any philosophy whatsoever presupposes totality in the axiological sense of a system of values. But the identification of totality in this axiological sense, with logical totality, is merely the prejudice or presupposition of one type of logic. The logical values of necessary connection are part of a system of values but only a part, and the axiological whole which any philosophy presupposes is not exhausted in this type of unity or totality. It includes other values in its system not necessarily reducible to logical connection, although there can be no expression of these values except in logical form. This distinction will prove to be of the utmost importance at various points in the following discussions, more particularly in determining our notions as to the nature of philosophical system. A narrowly intellectualistic conception of truth, out of harmony with our natural conceptions and with the deepest intentions of traditional philosophy, seems unavoidable on a purely logical conception of totality and has consequences for philosophy which are far-reaching. Of these the most baleful, as we shall see, is the tendency to reduce many of the most fundamental categories of metaphysical thought to appearance. Substance, causation, purpose are found to contain much that is irrelevant to the character of logical system, with the result that they are abandoned in favour of purely logical connections. Philosophical system becomes solely the fixation of experience in concepts and the relation of these concepts according to their logical connections, with the result that the autonomy of values is sacrificed and all other values subordinated to the logical.

Realistic logicians never tire of advancing the foregoing criticisms against the idealists and their logic, nor of pointing out that the ultimate premise of this logic is precisely the logically unsupported judgment of value we have described. But they sometimes overlook the fact that they are in a similar case, that their own logic has a similar unsupported premise upon which it must fall back.

The realist in criticizing the idealist is fain to make much of his own good faith. Part of his good faith consists in the fact that he keeps faith with the beliefs of common sense and takes science at its "face value." In contrast with the speculative logic of the idealist he never tires of insisting upon the fact that his is the *bonâ-fide* logic. This in itself should make us wary. Quite apart from the fact that this is an *argumentum ad hominem* which may or may not be cogent, it is clear that in saying these things valuations are already involved. Without considering the very difficult question of what the "face value" of science really is, an appeal to that value *is* an appeal to value. When he describes his logic as the *bonâ-fide* logic, the case is already prejudiced by an assumption as to what true knowledge and ultimate reality really are.

The unsupported valuation upon which all realism and its logic ultimately rest was well stated by Herbart. "The leading principle of all logic and metaphysics," he writes, "first

established by the Eleatics, is that Being is absolutely simple."
Modern realism, with its atomistic logic, tells us the same thing
in many and much more technical words. In order to have any
genuine knowledge, in order that any entity may be known,
it must be unmodifiable in its essential nature by entering
into relations with other entities, primarily the "knower."

Attempts have been made to support this "leading principle"
by arguments, and these arguments, as in the case of idealism,
take the form of the argument from self-refutation. It would
be idle to canvass the various forms in which this argument
has been presented, an argument familiar to every reader of
present-day philosophy. I will recall in this connection only
one, and that principally because it displays so egregiously
the essential point for which I am contending. It is the argument of E. G. Spaulding that any *bonâ-fide* logic presupposes
the acknowledgment of this judgment or affirmation.[1]

You cannot, it is argued, refuse to admit the axiom or
postulate of independence, or, in other words, that relations
make no difference to the things related, without self-contradiction. For you presuppose, at least tacitly, that in one case,
namely, your present assertion, the two terms related, your
assertion and that which it denotes, are not thereby and there-
with modified. Self-refutation is no less involved in the proposition that a relation implies an underlying, transcendent whole
of which the terms are manifestations; for herewith it is equally
tacitly assumed that both terms and relations can be known
without being modified by the knowledge.

Thus it is argued, precisely as in the case of the idealistic
logic, that any denial of this axiom really presupposes it. Nor
is the argument in its essential nature any different from the
principle of self-refutation employed in the earlier argument.
It is essentially an *argumentum ad hominem*. For it is further
argued that the postulate of independence, the externality
of relations to the things related, is the very condition
of there being such a thing as genuine knowledge or *bonâ-
fide* logic. Here again, as in the preceding case, we must
insist that the proposition that terms are modifiable by the
relations that relate them does not refute itself. The enunciator

---

[1] "The Logical Structure of Self-Refuting Systems," *The Philosophical Review*,
vol. xix, Nos. 3 and 6.

of the proposition may refute himself, but only in case he acknowledges the ideal of genuine knowledge presupposed; and only in case he admits also that logic determines the nature of the real, and that logical argument may determine the nature of the relation of a proposition to the reality it represents.

The final appeal of the realist, as Meinong, for instance, makes quite clear, is always that the thesis of his opponent is *widersinnig*. But for any proposition to be *widersinnig*, *Sinn* (meaning) must be acknowledged, and in this case the meaning is precisely the meaning of "genuine knowledge" which was to be demonstrated. The circle is the same as in the case of the idealist, and the situation to which it leads precisely the same. For either the value of independence must be merely acknowledged as a matter of belief or of "animal faith," or, if there are any reasons to be given, they must be of the nature of determining the place of this value of independence in a larger system of values. Just as the realist can always charge the idealist with an appeal to extra-logical motives, so, with no less justification, can the idealist make the same charge.

It is now perfectly clear, I think, that the realistic logic also has as its ultimate premise a logically unsupported judgment of value, and also identifies the presuppositions of a particular logic with the presuppositions of logic *überhaupt*. It is also clear that an entire reconstruction or reinterpretation of logic flows from this initial assumption. This is principally seen in the cardinal principle of the realistic logic, that the object of the judgment is always a simple entity, and in the doctrine of externality of relations that results. Here, too, the reconstruction of the traditional law of identity and the doctrine of reality as ultimately neutral entities or abstract universals are the chief consequences of this principle. Here again we are not primarily concerned with the details of this logic. That which interests us *here* is the main point, namely, that the ideal of genuine knowledge, or *bonâ-fide* logic embodied in the realistic logic, is itself a logically unsupported judgment of value, and that it includes a prejudice—an ontological prejudice—which is not the necessary assumption of logic as such.

The examination of one point of detail in this logic may, however, make the point clearer. I refer to the doctrine of the nature of definition. "The vice of all latter-day philosophy, by which I mean idealism," writes Holt, "is to try to define the simpler entities of being in terms of the more complex aggregates, wills, minds, experiences. Unless one will define laws in terms of government, carbon in terms of trees, and mathematical points in terms of dodecahedrons, one must not attempt to define severally the component elements that we experience in terms of experience, of consciousness or mind."[1] This is the doctrine of the irreversible character of definition. All definition, it is assumed, proceeds from the complex to the simple, never the reverse. It is at this point, perhaps, that the hypnotism of the atomistic logic, of which Lord Haldane speaks, is strongest. And yet this irreversible character of definition is not an "axiom," not even a necessary postulate, of knowledge. It is a prejudice of but one type of logic, and one bound up with a specific metaphysic, as, indeed, Herbart was both intelligent enough to see and frank enough to admit.

The importance of our reference here to this particular detail of the realistic logic is that it forms the basis for the most fundamental attack on the fundamentals of traditional philosophy. It is by appeal to this atomistic logic that the entire attack on natural language, more particularly the traditional language of metaphysics, has been justified. It is by appeal to this logic that all genuine philosophic concepts have been turned into "pseudo-simples" and the entire structure of traditional thought reduced to a complex of "philosophical errors." Both of these consequences of the atomistic logic will be examined more fully later. Here we wish merely to emphasize the presumption of this atomistic logic, the presumption, namely, that this sectarian logic is identical with logic as such, a presumption all the more gratuitous for the reason that it rarely realizes, to say nothing of acknowledges, the metaphysical prejudice on which the entire structure is raised.

VI

The conclusions to be drawn from this examination of the two fundamental logics are far-reaching in their consequences. We might, for instance, infer that, as both realism and idealism

[1] E. B. Holt, *The Concept of Consciousness*, pp. 78 ff.

identify the "axioms" of logic with their own ontological prejudices and presuppositions, there is no solution of their perennial opposition by means of logic as they understand it. Each is powerless, as Royce recognizes, to convince the other. Furthermore, that the only way of transcending this opposition, if there be a way, is by a change of *venue* from fact to value. That is by a recognition on the part of both idealism and realism that their so-called axioms are not facts but values, and as such, perhaps, not mutually exclusive.

That is, indeed, an inference which I myself have drawn in an article in which the main lines of the argument are suggested.[1] It is also a position which is maintained implicitly or explicitly throughout the developments of this book. But this is only an incidental suggestion and not the main point to be emphasized here. That point is rather this—and this also has far-reaching consequences—namely, *the essentially unneutral character of these two logics.* The recognition of this fact immediately suggests the question whether conceptions of logic which are thus unneutral, which contain these ontological prejudices in their very structure, can represent the true nature of logic; whether, in fact, a conception of logic is not possible which transcends this opposition?

Is there, then, we may well ask, no conception of logic which is neutral? Is there no justification for the idea, almost as old as thought itself, that we must all be logical when we think—when we, so to speak, "play the game"—quite irrespective of our attitudes towards logic, optimistic or pessimistic, our theories of logic whether idealistic or realistic? Certainly this idea was inherent in the traditional conception of logic which defined it as the science of the laws of thought. May it not be that it is precisely the so-called "reforms" of logic that have made it unneutral? May it not be true, after all, that the old conception of logic as normative rather than ontological is sound, that it is the science of the norms or principles that must be acknowledged if intelligible thought and its communication is to be possible?

Such at least is the conception of logic I propose to maintain. It is the object of this chapter to restate the traditional conception of logic in a more modern form. We may, perhaps, best

[1] "Beyond Realism and Idealism," *The Philosophical Review*, vol. xxvii, No. 1.

begin our task by asking whether there are any points on which all conceptions, all definitions, of logic agree; whether, in other words, there is not a *minimum* of agreement, divergence from which means not logic but the denial of logic.

I think it may be said that all logicians are at one in the idea that the fundamental laws of logic are the most universal truths—that is, are the conditions that every judgment which makes a truth claim must meet. But there is also agreement in the idea that these conditions are not sufficient but merely necessary. The logical first principles, identity and contradiction, are then negative criteria for every judgment as such, but never positive criteria.

This, I think, may be taken as a true statement regarding all forms of thought with the exception of extreme logical pessimism and a-logism. Even in those cases where the attack on traditional logic goes so deep as to make the laws of thought, particularly the law of identity, fictions, it is still necessary fiction, without which coherent thought and intelligible communication are impossible. But all are agreed that these fundamental laws, while necessary, are not sufficient; and it is out of this feeling that the attempted reforms of logic have arisen. Each of the "new logics," in its own way, has tried to make logic not only necessary but sufficient, and in attempting to do so it has inevitably identified logic with epistemology and ultimately with ontology—with the resulting strife of logics. For myself, I cannot escape the conclusion that on these premises strife is inevitable; but let us first examine the premises of the ontological logics.

"Logic," says Mr. E. B. Holt, "is not the science of correct thinking but of what is." Truth and falsity apply not to judgments and beliefs, says Mr. Russell, but to their objects. Now, this definition of logic as the science of what is, is capable of two interpretations. On the one interpretation of being, the widest possible, being includes all things, all *Gegenstände*, real or unreal, possible or impossible. On the other interpretation, "what is" includes only that which falls under reality as distinguished from the unreal. Now I think it can be shown that according to our interpretation of being this definition of logic is either meaningless or lacks the universal character claimed for it.

Let us examine the first interpretation. Logic is the universal science of whatever is, of all things, real or unreal, possible or impossible. The logical laws do, indeed, hold of the real and unreal, but do they hold of impossible objects? This may, indeed, be allowed for the mathematically impossible, but scarcely for the logically impossible. For this impossible is precisely the contradictory of logic and is excluded by definition. Perhaps, it will be said, these impossible objects are not "things," not part of what is. But the meaninglessness of this answer is apparent; for how do we decide whether anything is a "thing" or not? Here we have no other criterion except that a thing is that which fulfils the demand of logic. We move in a circle, for we have already presupposed the concept of logic and cannot carry it back for definition to the concept of entities or things.

This kind of neutrality, accordingly, that defines logic as the science of whatever is, of being defined in the broadest sense, is meaningless. The other interpretation of being escapes this difficulty, but it does so only by sacrificing universality and neutrality. It frankly limits the field of logic to but one part of the larger field of *Gegenstände*. "Logic, I should maintain," says Mr. Russell, "must no more admit a unicorn than zoology can, for logic is concerned with the real world just as truly as zoology, though with its more abstract and general features." This, Professor Hoernlé remarks, "we shall agree, is common sense, and when common sense can quote the high authority of mathematical logic it is time for philosophers to sit up and take notice." It is time to take notice, I agree, but what we should particularly notice is that logic so defined is not neutral and never can be. The logician who so conceives his science should be the last to claim neutrality for it; for such a definition of logic does not merely contain the prejudice in favour of reality in the sense that it is, as we have seen, involved in all thought. It frankly makes a specific definition of reality the postulate of logic *überhaupt*.[1]

Bosanquet, I am glad to find, takes a similar position. He expresses regret that he cannot follow Russell and Hoernlé in thus limiting the field of logic. The judgment, for instance, which excludes worlds of imagination from the world of logic is "simply *ex parte*" and "rests throughout on the assumption

[1] See Chapter II, pp. 169 ff.

that our real world of fact is the one reality."[1] In other words, he recognizes precisely what we have been maintaining—namely, that such a definition of the field of logic involves an ontological prejudice. Yet, curiously enough, he does not recognize that a similar difficulty inheres in *any* ontological logic—even his own. If he defines logic as the ultimate science of whatever is, he too must give an *ex-parte* definition of the real, or else fall back on the first and broader interpretation of being which we have characterized as "meaningless." If we take being in this broader sense—of whatever is, whatever is the case (including Hamlets, unicorns, or what not)—the only significant meaning we can possibly give to the proposition that logic is the ultimate science of whatever is, is that it is the structural form of whatever we can intelligibly express, whatever be our universe of discourse. Logic can give us the form of intelligible discourse, but never by itself determine its intelligibility. It can give us the scaffolding of an intelligible world, but can never by itself determine the ultimate character of that world But if this is so, we have denied the ontological character of logic.

It is considerations such as these, I suppose, that have led Meinong to insist upon the traditional definition of logic as the science of the laws of thought. In any case, he is the one "logical" and coherent thinker among the moderns on this point. He sees clearly enough that he must make and keep a fundamental distinction between logic and *Gegenstandstheorie*—a distinction which many others have allowed to disappear. If he does this, however, he must keep to the old definition of logic as the science of the laws of thought.

But the significance of these considerations is still more far-reaching. Realization of the difficulties involved in either interpretation of the definition of logic as the science of "what is" will inevitably lead to a reinstatement of this traditional view of logic and its function. My own opinion is that a final evaluation of the logical development of this period will show its chief result to be in a definite expansion of the content of the science of logic, while still retaining its character as a "formal" discipline distinct from epistemology. In other words, it will recognize the ontological prejudices that necessarily

[1] *The Meeting of Extremes in Modern Philosophy*, p. 39.

underlie these different logics. It will be seen that logic is not the science of whatever is, but the science of correct thinking; that logic is above and beyond all ontologies whether realistic or idealistic, and that the claims of any logic, new or old, to determine by itself the nature of being must be denied.

VII

Considerations such as these inevitably incline one, I repeat, to a reconsideration of the old conception of logic as a normative science, as *die Moral des Denkens*, to use a significant phrase of Herbart's. Indeed, it is only as so defined that we can find any point upon which logicians are generally agreed. All are one, we have seen, in the idea that the laws of thought are the most fundamental truths, that they are the conditions that any judgment which makes a truth claim must meet, norms which all must acknowledge who would think correctly. Starting with this point of agreement we may, perhaps, find the road to a genuine and significant neutrality. Neutral our "logics" are not, as we have seen. Each sectarian logic presupposes an ideal of knowledge which the other logics do not acknowledge. The idea that *these* are neutral is an illusion. But this situation does not exclude the possibility that there might be a conception of logic which would be neutral in the significant sense that it would embody values that any logic *qua* logic must acknowledge. To the development of such a conception we now turn.

"Logic is ethics," says Mr. Charles Peirce, thereby in principle accepting the challenge of Nietzsche that the most fundamental principles of logic are moral prejudices. While not ready to go the full length of this assertion, perhaps, pragmatists in general are agreed that, to be significant, logic must deal with meanings, and, as any serious examination of "meanings" soon shows, meanings presuppose values. The fundamental notion that truth is a value makes values the objective of logic.

On this subject, at least, pragmatism must be admitted to be extraordinarily clear-sighted and consistent. It sees clearly the illusoriness of the ideal of logical neutrality if logic is defined as the science of the real. But it is with practical reality and material truth alone that the pragmatist is concerned, and he readily accepts the consequences. Indeed, he presents us with a dilemma that is worthy of careful consideration. Either we must accept formalism in logic and abandon meaning, or renounce formalism and frankly accept human prejudices and presuppositions. Choosing the latter, he does not try to disinfect the logical instrument, because frankly he does not believe that it can be disinfected and does not think it desirable to do so if we could.

On one very important point, at least, the pragmatist is fundamentally sound. The only possible alternative to the conception of logic as the science of being or reality is the conception of logic as a science of meanings and values. The only point at issue is that between the pragmatist and the absolutist, whether the recognition of this general truth commits one to a frank acceptance of "humanism" in logic as the pragmatist understands it, or whether such a view is compatible with a conception of absolute norms and values. The premises of the Great Tradition are humanistic in the larger, magnanimous sense of the word, yet the assumption of absolute values is the essence of that tradition. Let us examine these two points of view.

The pragmatist's logic, we have seen, frankly disclaims neutrality. It does so because it recognizes the dilemma in which the logician finds himself. Either formalism without meaning, or meaning with a frank acceptance of prejudices and presuppositions. The realist or idealist may refuse to accept the dilemma, may repudiate the existence of prejudices and primal valuations; but every time he denies them he affirms them; every time he insists upon an ideal of genuine knowledge or *bonâ-fide* logic he condemns himself out of his own mouth.

So far the pragmatist's position is unimpeachable. No one understands the hinterland of logic better than he. In this respect he has all the wariness in which Nietzsche finds most of the philosophers fail. But, like Nietzsche, to whom he owes so much, he is himself under the dominance of a prejudice— a prejudice, moreover, which not only itself involves a popular and probably ephemeral valuation, but one which makes it impossible ultimately to distinguish at all between prejudice and necessary presupposition. I refer to the "biological prejudice," with its accompanying "psychologism." Under the influence of this prejudice, moreover, he finds himself inevitably drawn back into a "naturalism" which, when logically thought out, lands him again in all the ontological prejudices of realism.

This "biological" prejudice, as I have called it, is that which, perhaps, gives modernism in philosophy its chief colouring. The entire movement of pragmatic and genetic logic is a development of this biological prejudice; but it is in Nietzsche—to whose daring conceptions, we are now beginning to see, a large part of modernism owes its inspiration—that this conception owes its first formulation as well as its most rigorous application. The logical values themselves—nay, even the prejudgment that underlies all logic, namely, that truth is more valuable than appearance—owe not only their origin, but whatever validity they may have, to their instrumental relation to life. The determining rôle which the merely biological conception of mind plays in modernistic thought in general, both in its more general attitudes and in specific philosophies, has been made clear in a preceding chapter. Here we are interested solely in the rôle it has played in one of the typically modernistic reconstructions of logic. Here again, as in the case of our discussion of the idealistic and realistic logic, we are concerned not so much with details as with principles. In the case of the pragmatist's logic, as in the others, it is the interpretation of the laws of thought, more particularly of identity, that brings out the point most clearly.

The extreme consequence of this way of thinking is the doctrine of logical fictions. Nietzsche, for instance, is constantly repeating that the forms of logic rest on fictions. "*Logik*" is for him "*eine konsequente Zeichenschrift auf Grund der durchgeführten Voraussetzung dass es identische Fälle giebt,*" and so "*ist das Logische nur möglich in Folge eines Grundirrtums. Dass es gleiche dinge, gleiche Fälle giebt, ist die Grundfiktion, schon beim Urteil, dann beim Schliessen.*"[1] Parmenides said we do not think that which is not—and on this rests the identity of logic and ontology. We are now at the other end of things and say rather, what can be thought must surely and necessarily be a fiction. But what does this mean when it is thought out? If the principles

[1] Quoted from Vaihinger, *The Philosophy of "As If,"* 1924, pp. 348 ff.

of logic are but fictions in the service of life, then the biological conception of life built up by logical thought is itself a fiction; and one, we may add, of a singularly unintelligible kind.

The biological prejudice consists, then, in narrowing the conception of life to its biological meaning, when the very essence of the philosophical meaning of life is, as Simmel brilliantly shows, to transcend life in this sense.[1] My point here, however, is that the biological prejudice in logic simply lands the thinker in all the ontological prejudices of naturalism and realism, or in some *Willensmetaphysik* that is essentially ontological.

Now, this psycho-biological point of view—with its sceptical relativism in logic—cannot be refuted in case its advocates refuse to recognize the authority of the laws of thought and the absolute values that they presuppose and embody. In reality there can be no argument with those who repudiate them, for there is no stable platform of argument. But he who does acknowledge them can, at least, point out how his opponents contradict themselves at every step. Relativism, and the biological conception of mind with which it is bound up, assume, at least, the truth of its account of mind and thought, and this truth can be assumed only in case the mind we are talking about is identical with itself throughout our account of it. Again, if the law of contradiction were not absolute, this relativism would be both true and false, and consequently neither true nor false. In other words, the ultimate laws of thought have the peculiar character of being involved in their very denial, and thus of automatically maintaining themselves against every attack. Reason cannot commit suicide. The old logic is the foundation of all logic, and is assumed even by those who attempt to overthrow it.

This theory of logical fictions, while the extreme and perhaps only consistent consequence of the biological prejudice, is, to be sure, not the only one actually drawn. The theory of truth, or, better, of truths, as "practical values," of "axioms as postulates," the best-working hypotheses available for the satisfaction of needs, is a half-way position which many pragmatists feel that they can occupy with satisfaction to themselves if not to others. The "process of falsification," necessarily involved in logic for a Nietzsche or a Bergson, may seemingly be avoided.

[1] G. Simmel, *Lebensanschauung*, chapter i.

But only apparently, I think. It remains at best but a clumsy statement of a half truth. The half-way position of pragmatism is admissible only on the basis of an obscure although no less genuine ontology. Truth cannot be reduced to a merely practical postulate unless we are prepared to admit that reality itself is no more than a practical postulate of an absolute self-realizing, creative will. Such a *Willensmetaphysik* may be difficult to make intelligible, but it is a metaphysic none the less. One does not get rid of absolutes by making life or will absolute.

The pragmatist's logic, or the pragmatic conception of logic, contains no answers to our problems, neither to the problem presented by the prejudices of the different logics, nor to the more fundamental problem of the rôle of logic in philosophic thought. Yet the pragmatist's logic contains an important element of truth, even if it is only a half truth. The dilemma in which logic finds itself, according to the pragmatist —either formalism without meaning or meaning with a frank acceptance of prejudices and presuppositions—is a genuine one. The only alternative to the acceptance of the theory of logic as the ultimate science of the real, with all the non-neutrality which that involves, is the conception of logic as the science of meanings and values. The situation is this: Logic is *die Moral des Denkens*. It involves the negative element of the control of thought through the acknowledgment of laws and norms. It involves the positive element of the acknowledgment of ultimate meanings and values which give these norms their validity. If these values are but human prejudices, then logic is wholly human in the relativistic sense. If they are the necessary conditions of intelligible communication, then they are also human, but human only in the larger magnanimous sense of the Great Tradition, in which human and absolute are not wholly incompatible terms. To the development of this conception of logic as a "science" of absolute values or validities we shall now turn.

VIII

The concept of "logical values," and of logic as a science of absolute values, has become central in present-day philosophy. It is most adequately presented, perhaps, in the thesis of Rickert, that logic is *Wertwissenschaft*. The full development of this conception is not to be found in the earlier editions of his famous book, *Der Gegenstand der Erkentniss*, but only in the last edition. As finally formulated it presents a view which, although at first sight highly paradoxical, is, nevertheless, at least one of the most significant movements of modern thought.

The meaning of this thesis is briefly this: Every judgment of existence or truth presupposes an over-individual *Sollen* or ought, the acknowledgment of which is necessary to give meaning to the judgment. This *Sollen* presupposes values and these "logical values" are neither existent nor subsistent, but merely valid. Thus far we have merely that form of the Neo-Kantian "philosophy of validity," with which we are familiar when the name of Rickert is mentioned.

It is, however, the conception of logic developed on this basis in which we are interested. Rickert opposes both the psychological and ontological conceptions of logic and makes it the ultimate value science. According to this view, logic deals neither with existents, physical or mental, nor with subsistents, but rather with the problem as to what values must be acknowledged in case *any* answers to the question what is or is not, what is true or not true, shall have any meaning whatever. But this "meaning" itself is, as he says, a "non-existent" meaning. It is not even subsistent in any intelligible sense—as, for instance, universals are subsistent. Of it it can merely be said that it is valid. Logic itself, when really understood, is above all the prejudices of the ontological point of view, all those necessarily involved in defining it as "the science of what is."[1]

This line of thought may be stated in somewhat different words. However much the sciences that deal with existents or subsistents differ from each other, according to material or method, they always have one thing in common: all seek to establish what is and how it is. This we may call their ontological character: *das Seiende* is their problem. Objective logic, on the other hand, never inquires after this, and in so far stands above all the sciences of being. The problem of logic is rather

[1] *Der Gegenstand der Erkentniss*, 4th and 5th editions, 1921, chapter iv, especially sections 3, 4, and 5.

the values that must be valid in case answers to these questions
—of the sciences—as to what is or is true, shall have a meaning.
Logic is above all ontology because the meanings of truth and
existence cannot themselves be either true or existent.

That some such position is the inevitable outcome of the
line of argument we have been pursuing seems evident, whether
we accept Rickert's form of statement or not. That such a
view of the nature of logic, if tenable, would vitally affect our
view of the relation of logic to philosophy in general, of the
sense in which logic is "the essence of philosophy," seems
equally clear. Logic, as a science of values above all ontologies and all ontological prejudices, might again become what
it has ceased to be—a neutral discipline which should interpret
and reconcile the oppositions in philosophy that arise out of
these prejudices. It might also point the way to a conception
of logic, and of its relation to truth and reality, which would
do full justice to the ultimate intentions of traditional thought.

Such is, indeed, a consummation devoutly to be wished.
But is not this whole conception of logic as a normative or
value science essentially paradoxical? Can an intelligible conception of the relation of logic to reality be formed on such
a theory of logic? To many such a conception seems, indeed,
wholly paradoxical. For one thing, against the concept of
"logical values" itself, it is urged that such a widening of the
customary and "proper" meaning of the word "value" is objectionable both linguistically and practically, and can lead only
to confusion. Much more fundamental is an objection to the
conception of "non-existent meanings and values"—in other
words, to the paradox felt by the idealistic and realistic logics
alike, to the idea of logic as a science which has as its
material anything else than the real. But let us examine these
objections.

This paradox has been felt by many realists, and the feeling
has found expression notably in the criticisms of Holt and
Lossky. As against those who argue that being is not the fundamental category, Holt answers that the fundamental category
of logic must be simple and include all entities. Those who say
that being perceived, being thought, being willed are more
fundamental, overlook the fact that these are complexes sus-

ceptible of logical analysis, and into what are they analysable if not neutral entities? The same would hold, of course, of "being valued," or the category of value. To this part of the argument the answer is, of course, immediate and simple. Perception, thought, will, even valuing, are, as psychological processes, perhaps complexes, and susceptible of analysis into simpler entities. But not the meanings and values which are the objectives of these processes. Validity and value are themselves not entities, except in the wholly meaningless sense that any object of thought has being. Truth and error, reality and unreality, Holt admits, are opposed categories and presuppose distinctions of meaning and value, but being has no opposed category and must, therefore, be fundamental and all-embracing.[1] But this means nothing, as we have seen. If the logician believes that there is any solution of the problem of knowledge here, he "is as ignorant of the real problems of philosophy as the sanguine digger for gold who unearths the precious metal everywhere." The assumption, finally, that the fundamental category of logic must be simple, may or may not be true. But if it is, it is still, as we have seen, but the assumption of a *value* that can only be acknowledged and never proved. That genuine knowledge must be a knowledge of simples is a proposition that can, in the last analysis, be established only by an *argumentum ad hominem*, in which case the "value-character of the theoretical" is obvious.

But the paradox in this conception of logic has also been felt by idealists no less than realists. Thus Croce takes up the problem in his article, "The Task of Logic,"[2] in which he wages an equally bitter polemic against the conception of logic as a science of values and validities, and reasserts the conception of logic as the ultimate science of being.

He understands, to be sure, the reasons for "recourse to the term value" on the part not only of logic but of the other philosophical sciences. "We believe," he says, "that they have been forced to this because Empiricism has outwitted them, and has unlawfully possessed itself of the names 'reality' and 'fact,' in order to bestow them on her classificatory conceptions

---

[1] E. B. Holt, *loc. cit.*, pp. 20 ff.

[2] *Encyclopædia of the Philosophical Sciences* (edited by W. Windelband and A. Ruge), vol. i.

and abstractions which are, as a matter of fact, unrealities. It is as though an honest man were obliged to change his name because it had fallen into disrepute through the criminal behaviour of a member of the family. The 'value' which is the object of logic is logical reality and fact itself; it is value and norm intrinsically as existing and working. It is now high time for the real logic to claim her own again; nor does she owe any consideration to the empiricists and positivists. Concessions in this direction, although merely verbal, would be a serious mistake. Let logic once more assert her claim to firm facts and cease to content herself—whether out of pride or modesty—with anything so unsubstantial as values."

Now, all this eloquence is not without its plausibility. There is also not a little cleverness in these observations regarding some of the motives which have led to "recourse to the term value" in the definition of logic. Nevertheless, I cannot but feel that the plausibility is only apparent. As to the "change of name," one can, indeed, reply that it may be thoroughly justified if it prevents misunderstandings, and this the new conception of logic certainly does. Again, the unsubstantial character of values can be urged only by one who has not realized the ultimate character of the value concept, that the term "substance" itself is ultimately a value concept. What Croce is protesting against is the separation of value and validity from being, and in this protest he is undoubtedly right. But to make that protest it is not necessary to identify logic with being and the science of logic with the science of being. Croce, indeed, admits this by implication when he says: "The value which is the object of philosophical logic is logical reality and fact itself." By thus qualifying reality as logical reality he implies a realm of meanings and values above ontology.

These objections to the view of logic here proposed may, perhaps, for the sake of getting on with the argument at least, be assumed to be met. That our answers really remove the appearance of paradox in the conception is probably more than we have a right to expect. The problem cannot be satisfactorily solved, if it is to be solved at all, until we have seen it in the wider setting of a general theory of value—until we have taken up the question of the nature of value and validity and of the relation of value to reality. The "value-character of the theoretical" can be understood only in the light of these more comprehensive considerations.

These will constitute the topics of the following chapter. Even at this point, however, something may be said, and, indeed, must be said, on the question of the relation of logic to reality. Can, we asked, an intelligible concept of the relation of logic to reality be formed on such a theory of logic?

In thus defining logic as above all ontology we do not, of course, deny a relation of logic to reality. That would be to deny a relation of logic to truth; for truth is in some sense at least an agreement of thought with reality, in the terms of traditional philosophy *adæquatio intellectus et rei*. Every treatise ever written on logic is dominated by some theory of the nature of truth. Such theory is, to be sure, often merely implicit, but in some form or another it is always there. And since truth is always agreement of thought with thing, some conception of the nature of reality and being is implied. That which we insist on here is merely that, if logic is to be the ultimate science, is to be neutral in the sense we have understood that term, it must not be bound up with any particular ontological prejudice and with the concept of truth *it* implies.

So far as the relation of logic to truth is concerned we shall content ourselves here with saying that, although logic implies a conception of truth as adequacy of thought to thing, it is not within the power of logic to define that relation. Logic always finds itself in difficulties when it attempts to define truth. Logic, *by itself*, can claim nothing more than right thinking, right reasoning, law, universality, but not truth. Its final word is purity, pure reason, and this can never be fully equated with truth. For whence, after all, comes the demand for truth—as represented by right reasoning in logic? Certainly from something beyond logic. It is the moral element, or, better expressed, value, that first brings in the element of truth. Truth is the objective of logic, but the nature of truth is not, as we shall see, exhausted in this relation to logic.

Again, in refusing to identify logic with the science of being in the most ultimate sense, we do not abstract from all reference to being and reality. It is only from such reference as results, as in the case of the realists' and idealists' logics, in identifying the prejudices of their particular logics with the presuppositions of logic *überhaupt*. Logical propositions give us the form, the scaffolding of an intelligible world. "Of themselves they treat of nothing." They presuppose that terms have meaning and that propositions have sense, but they have no power to determine that meaning and that sense. Their meaning and sense are their connection with the world, and this connection can never itself be the material of logic.

Such abstraction of logic from "material" reality and truth does not, moreover, make it formal in any invidious sense. It still leaves logic with a reference to thought and its ideals and values, and these are related to reality. When this reference, together with the problem of validity and reality it involves, is examined under the conditions of philosophic insight which a true understanding of the relation of value and validity to reality gives, what we call formal logical thinking itself gains a vitally spiritual significance.

This, however, is the problem of the next chapter. Here I wish merely to make my general point by a brief comment on the "laws of thought" and their relation to reality.

Everything turns, as we have seen throughout this discussion, on the nature of the laws of thought and of their relation to "reality." The validity of these logical forms has such ultimate significance for us, is so completely the condition of intelligible discourse, that it is difficult, if not impossible, to imagine the world otherwise than as really conditioned by them. Their validity is not confined to the fact that, once conceived and fixed in definition, they demand general and compulsory assent from every mind. It also includes the idea that they are the conditions of any intelligible world. The "existence," the "reality" of an intelligible world, is inseparable from intelligible expression, communication of it, unless it be conceived to be merely the object of some individual mystical incommunicable insight. But the recognition of this fact does not necessarily involve the illusory idea that these logical forms yield an interpretation of the whole nature of the real. Truth and reality are presupposed by them, but not completely determined.

IX

I have described this view of logic as *Die Moral des Denkens*, as a normative science, as one of the most significant tendencies in recent thought. But if it be new, it is new only in the sense that it says very old things in a new way. It is, I am convinced, the true inwardness of the traditional view of logic. From Aristotle until the most recent reconstructions of logic, logic has always been conceived, if not in so many words at least in principle, as concerned with the principles of right reasoning. Its central problem has always been the classification of arguments, so that all those that are bad are thrown into one division and all those that are good into another. This, at least, logic always is, whatever more it may be held to be in a special philosophy. It is precisely because logic is first of all this that it is also ultimately a way to reality and truth. If we do not accept knowing and thinking as a serious occupation of man—if they are not in their very nature oriented towards value—they must of necessity degenerate into mere games. Even then, as mere play, they are never games of solitaire. Intelligible communication is always assumed, either implicitly or explicitly, as the necessary presupposition of logic.

The realization of this fact immediately brings with it the recognition of two other facts which raise problems of great importance. The first of these is the question of the relation of logic to language. If the presupposition of logic is intelligible communication, then logic, whatever else it may be, is perfected language, is the technique of intelligibility. Any complete divorce of logic from natural language must lead to unintelligibility. The second question is that with which this chapter opened—the sense, if any, in which logic is the essence of philosophy. If logic is the technique of intelligibility and of intelligible communication, what is the relation of philosophical intelligibility to logical form?

The influence of language on philosophy is, as we are coming more and more to realize, profound. "Philosophers as a rule," writes Mr. Russell, "believe themselves free from linguistic forms, but most of them seem to be mistaken in this belief." Now, whether most philosophers do or do not believe themselves to be thus free, they certainly ought not to, despite what

Mr. Russell says. If philosophy and logic were entirely divorced from language, they would cease to communicate intelligible meanings. This entire tendency to depreciate language in modern thought is an interesting phenomenon. We have on the one hand the tendency of students of linguistics to free language from logic, and a similar tendency on the part of logicians to separate logic from language. He who is interested in speech as a medium of communication in the broadest sense scorns the idea of speech as logical, and he who is interested in logic as a special science would free logic entirely from grammar and syntax. Logic curses that in language which literature blesses, and contrariwise. This dispute over language is of interest to the philosopher also, because it is the key to the understanding of the two chief tendencies of modernism, that alike of those who would make logic the whole of philosophy, and of those who would have philosophy turn its back on logic. It is the source of the attack of both upon the *natural metaphysic* of the human mind, that metaphysic which the whole of traditional philosophy embodies.

The "new logic" deplores the tendencies of language as regards both vocabulary and syntax, its chief object of attack being, of course, the so-called subject-predicate logic with its substance—attribute metaphysic. The primal function of language, the naming of things, is the source of an all-pervasive error of "pseudo-simplicity."[1] We suppose, for instance, that there is a certain more or less persistent being called Socrates, because the same name is applied to a series of occurrences which we are led to regard as appearances of this one being. As language becomes more abstract, new entities enter into our thought, those represented by abstract words, the universals. Many of these abstract words, at least, do not stand for single entities, but the tendency of language is to assume that they do, and a logic that trusts to language in any degree is likely to lead to the verbalism of a false metaphysic.

The influence of syntax is, perhaps, even more vicious. Almost any proposition can be put into a form in which it has a subject and a predicate connected by a copula. It is natural to infer that every "fact" has a corresponding form and

[1] B. Russell, article entitled "Logical Atomism," in *Contemporary British Philosophers*, vol. i, pp. 367 ff.

consists in the possession of a quality by a substance. This subject-predicate logic leads to many metaphysical consequences, among the most important of which is the philosophical notion that logic demands a self-identical substance as the subject of intelligible discourse, and ultimately to the philosophical error of speculative dogma—the prejudice in favour of an ultimate substance and ultimate cause. Needless to say this is the logical source of the whole modern attack on the traditional concepts of intelligible substance and intelligible causality.

In view of these considerations, the ideal of the new logic is to operate wholly with symbols rather than with words. Exact thinking demands a special language, not only because ordinary language is "too clumsy for the nice distinctions necessary to precise thought," but also because our language itself is irreparably infected with error. Being but "the cries of the forests corrupted and complicated by arrogant anthropoid apes," it is unfitted to express the true nature of being.

Now, one need not deny the necessity of a constant *critique* of language, or that the criticism exercised by this new logic has had valuable results, in order to feel the essential wrongness of this position. Something surely is out of order here. A conception of logic that necessarily eventuates in the abandonment of the natural language of communication must have something fatally wrong with it. It is one of the most important tasks of modern thought to find out precisely what that is. Certainly the assumptions underlying this entire attitude cannot but give one furiously to think.

A completely satisfactory answer to the problems here raised would involve a consideration of the entire question of the *philosophy of language*—a question which is coming to be recognized more and more as fundamental to science and metaphysics alike. This is not the place for such far-reaching investigations, but even without them something may be said with a degree of certainty. Surely this entire proposal to free logic from language, and the attack on traditional logic to which it leads, are based on certain assumptions which turn out, on examination, to be a monstrous begging of the entire question at issue.

As regards language in general, the assumption is made first of all that, because new symbols and new idioms have been created for certain special purposes, the utility and validity of these latter necessarily involve the exclusion or abandonment of the earlier forms of communication. Science is language well made, but because it is well made for certain purposes it is immediately argued that it supersedes and invalidates all earlier forms of communication. It is difficult to see why anyone should entertain so obviously gratuitous an assumption until we bring to light a still more basal assumption underlying the entire point of view. This is that natural language is infected with error, embodies a primitive mythology which, as Nietzsche complains, all our effort can only with difficulty remove. In other words, our language is not "moulded on reality" and must, therefore, be abandoned for an artificial one that is so made.

Such are the general assumptions underlying the position we are examining. We shall presently see that they beg the whole question which a philosophy of language has to solve. But first let us see how these assumptions are applied to the specific question of the relation of logic to language. Here it is assumed that because a certain specific logical calculus has been devised to deal with certain types of external quantitative relations, this new calculus necessarily involves the invalidation and supersession of the type of logic which deals with the more universal relation of predication. This assumption is evidently but a special case of the assumption regarding language, for traditional logic—the type of logic that deals with the more universal relation of predication—is that which has been developed from natural language. The *petitio principii* in this assumption is evident, for in arguing that the special logic invalidates the more original and more general it assumes that the latter is moulded on reality and the former is not— which is precisely the question at issue.[1]

[1] An admirable statement of the same position, made from a somewhat different standpoint, seems to me worth quoting. Speaking of this attack on Aristotelean logic made by the New Logic, Professor Montague writes (*Ways of Knowing*, p. 84): "When a man writes an arithmetic, he cannot be criticized for not writing an algebra. And when a man writes a treatise on the relations common to all forms of statement, he should hardly be blamed for not treating of relations peculiar to some forms of statement. The fact that when A is west of B and B is west of C, then A will be west of C, is interesting and important, but it in no way conflicts with the fact that 'west of B' is as much a predicate

This *petitio principii* is rather naïvely expressed by Wittgenstein when he writes: "Russell's merit is to have shown that the apparent logical form of the proposition need not necessarily be its real form." *Real* in what sense? How is one to determine what is the real form of the proposition without determining the purpose and meaning of the proposition, and how is that to be determined without involving the entire question of the relation of language to reality? As a matter of fact, in attempting to substitute for the *apparent* form of the logical proposition, namely, that of the subject-predicate relation, another type of relation, as determined by a calculus devised for relations of quantity, the assumption is made that reality is only of the type to which this form corresponds— and that is, of course, the whole question at issue.

The point at issue here may be well illustrated by the endless debate waged by the monistic and atomistic logics over the *real* structure of propositions. The atomistic logic claims that logic deals always with propositions that are relational in structure and thus always analysable into simpler components. Thus, in the proposition, "John is mortal," James may be substituted for John without changing the meaning of the remainder of the proposition. Against this the monistic logic maintains the opposing thesis, based largely on the usages of language and the principle of context, that a proposition is an indivisible unity, such that if any of it is changed the whole meaning is changed. What are we to make of such a flat contradiction as this? Surely it can be resolved only by recognizing that the opponents have different notions of reality in mind and that the issue is nowhere actually joined. It is clear for one thing, I think, that the dispute turns partly at least on the meaning of that *meaning* which one theory says is unchanged and another says is changed. In some propositions there may, perhaps, be substitution in the subject without changing the meaning of the remainder of the proposition,

---

of A as 'red' is a predicate of 'rose.' That the latter is a simple quality and the former a spatial relation does not affect their common similarity of inhering as predicates in their subject." He then continues: "Whether or not the Aristotelean *metaphysics* is properly chargeable with neglecting the types of external quantitative relationship which modern science finds fruitful, it does not seem to me that the Aristotelean *logic* is impugned either in its intrinsic validity or in its status of logical priority to any more specific logic of relations."

but in others it certainly is not so. Change, for instance, the proposition, "John is noble," into the proposition, "This building is noble." Surely the meaning of the predicate "noble" is changed. We are in quite different universes of discourse. It is possible to say that the remainder of the proposition is unchanged only by ignoring completely one of its most important aspects, namely, allusiveness or connotation. This is, of course, what the atomistic logic does, for meaning is here understood only in the denotative sense. On the other hand, it is this very allusiveness of terms, which for the other logic alone expresses the internal relatedness of things in the real world, which is for it the inmost character of reality.

The purpose of the introduction of this dispute over the real nature of the logical proposition was not to take sides in the dispute, but rather to show how the whole question of the relation of logic to reality is begged. This *petitio principii* is, moreover, when one comes to examine it closely, but a special form of the more general fallacy involved in all ontological logics. These logics, we found, define their subject as the science of the real in its most universal aspects, and then proceed to determine what is genuine or *bonâ-fide* logic in terms of some antecedent prejudice as to the nature of the real. The charge that our natural logic is not moulded on the real simply begs the whole question as to the nature of the real.

But let us return, now, to the primary question of the relation of logic to language. The entire proposal to divorce logic from language is based on the assumption that our natural language is not moulded on reality. The same charge is made by thinkers who have totally different notions as to the nature of the real— by a Russell or a Wittgenstein on the one hand, and by a Bergson on the other—a fact which seems to suggest an antecedent prejudice in both cases. Be that as it may, the same general assumption as to the nature of language is made, namely, that it is something external, artificial, attached to objects, "ill-fitting clothes," as Wittgenstein expresses it. In both cases it is assumed that a language which is merely "the cries of the forests, corrupted and complicated by arrogant anthropoid apes," cannot conceivably be anything but a practical instrument of adaptation to environment, and cannot therefore "correspond to reality."

This neo-nominalism, as we shall call it, is the deepest root of modernism in all its forms. It is, to be sure, but the old nominalism put in terms of a merely biological or behaviouristic conception of the mind, and, like all nominalism, it begs at the beginning the very question which a philosophy of language has to solve. It assumes that language is something external to the real, whereas, as a matter of fact, language is the *very condition of there being any significant reality whatever*. Any event or object that is more than a mere diffused consciousness has language as one of its necessary conditions. In this sense language creates reality—in the only intelligible sense of the word "real." He who talks at all must be a realist. Realism, as opposed to nominalism, is the condition of any intelligible communication whatsoever, and such communication is the presupposition of any philosophy whatsoever. No one doubts that some *critique* of our natural language is necessary, but the reality created for us by language cannot be condemned out of hand as unreal or illusion without begging the entire question of a philosophy of language. As the postulate of the potentiality of logical form in natural language is the condition of any intelligible logic, so the presupposition of reality is the necessary postulate of any intelligible language.[1]

The principle I have been insisting upon here may be stated in the following general form. Logic is reflected thought; but all that is reflected presupposes the spontaneous. The reflected cannot negate the spontaneous on which it rests; it can only clarify it and determine its true direction. If logic is the morality of thinking, then for logic to seek to free itself wholly from the linguistic forms in which human thought and discourse express themselves spontaneously is a highly immoral proceeding. If logic is the technique of intelligibility—the science of the conditions of intelligible discourse, of those values which must be acknowledged if the very distinctions between the real and the unreal, the true and the false, are to have any ultimately intelligible meaning whatsoever—then surely for logic to negate the fundamental linguistic forms in

---

[1] The recent work of Ogden and Richards, *The Meaning of Meaning*—the latest contribution to the philosophy of language in English—while valuable in many ways, is in its fundamentals just such a monstrous begging of the question throughout.

which this discourse primarily expresses itself can mean only that logic ceases in the end to express anything truly significant.

It is not surprising that a completely consistent carrying out of this ideal of the divorce of logic from natural language has led some at least to the conclusion that we can neither ask nor answer intelligibly questions about anything that we really care very much about. And yet just this *paralysis of speech* is the inevitable consequence of this neo-nominalism that underlies modernistic logics. Now, I think I can understand how, under the influence of some prejudice as to the nature of the real, one can deny these necessary assumptions of both language and logic. But I confess my complete inability to understand the mentality of those who can entertain a conception of logic as the essence of philosophy, and then entertain also a conception of logic that compels them to call almost everything that philosophy has hitherto sought to express inexpressible, and which relegates almost all the significant things in the natural language of metaphysics to the realm of the mystical and unintelligible. It is one thing to say that intelligible speech must be logical; it is quite another thing so to define logic as to make a large part of our speech say nothing.[1]

The condition of intelligible communication is, indeed, logical form. Such form is so woven into our speech, and even into the play of our ideas, that it is impossible to utter a phrase, or to call to mind images of the past or future experience, without throwing them into the forms which we call logical. To say that a fact is not of logical form is to say that no significant

[1] It is sometimes difficult to realize just how far this curious mentality has really gone. Some protagonists of the "new logic" have actually persuaded themselves that "our mental nature has so changed" that, while Aristotle, Leonardo da Vinci, and even Newton and Huxley, would all have understood each other perfectly, anything like an understanding between minds such as these and those of the modernist type, such as Bertrand Russell, Einstein, *et al.*, could now be attained only with the greatest difficulty. "Natural science," we are told, "at its present height of development, does not any longer know what to do with the old categories of language. . . . If our language was at the same state of development as our science all the old categories would be abandoned. We would have then a language in the making that only a small part of mankind could understand." Now, this is by no means so funny as it sounds. Many moderns find themselves in the embarrassing position of being unable to translate their latest intuitions into the normal speech of man. It is not surprising that in their embarrassment they should take refuge in a wholesale condemnation of all that men have hitherto thought and said. Unfortunately it never occurs to them to examine their own assumptions.

assertion can be made about it; is to say that it is not a fact. Such a "fact" is placed beyond the reach of thought or intelligible expression of thought. But this truth, important as it is, has as its reverse side another truth, no less important and no less inevitable—namely, that an intelligible logic is one that must be interwoven with our natural language. To free logic wholly from linguistic form is really to say that logic is not the necessary form of significant expression, for by the very divorce of logic from language many things that are capable of significant expression in language are placed outside logic, and many questions which language can both intelligibly ask and intelligibly answer are *ipso facto* excluded from it.[1]

X

The theory of the relation of logic to natural communication here developed gives us the key, I think, to the answer to our second question, the sense in which logic may be said to be the "essence of philosophy." The true sense, and the only sense, in which it may be said to be such, is that it is the *Moral des Denkens*—the morality of intelligible communication.

This may be seen first of all in the rôle of definition in intelligible discourse. Definition is universally recognized as one of the chief chapters in logic, and theories of definition are, therefore, more or less diagnostic of our general theories of the nature and function of logic. Now, definition, with its universally acknowledged obligation to clearness and definiteness,

---

[1] In the volume entitled *Mind* (London, 1927, by various authors), Professor F. A. Lindemann asks the question, whether it "can be maintained that an alternative to our ordinary logic is unthinkable?" He answers that "the attack upon the citadel will indubitably be launched; whether it will prove successful the future alone can tell. For more than a hundred generations defences have been subconsciously prepared. The most important, perhaps, is language. . . . Aristotelean logic is enshrined in the structure of the sentence, the temporal indefinable in the conjugation of the verb. *The symbolism of the mathematician alone has remained free. No other, probably, can usefully devote itself to the problem*" (italics mine). In this last sentence is the whole sum and substance of my contention. As the symbolism of mathematics alone can usefully devote itself to the problem at all, so by that very fact are the limits of the enterprise determined. Except as an extension of the symbolism of mathematics, an alternative to our ordinary logic (so far as human communication in general is concerned) is, I rather fancy, unthinkable.

indicates at once the relation of logic to intelligible communication and to philosophy.

It is, first of all, only when ambiguity is felt that logic presses upon us the necessity and obligation of definition. The natural indefiniteness and fluency of language are actually the first law of communication. But this natural fluency must never reach the point of ambiguity. The law of identity, which ambiguity violates, must be acknowledged as the necessary condition of intelligible communication. In a sense all definition is verbal, the distinction between verbal and real definition being relative. In a sense all definition is "stipulated" —in the sense, namely, that it rests upon purposes and values that must be acknowledged. But there is another sense in which this is not quite the case. There is a sense—and a very important sense—in which there is what is called the "proper" meaning of a term, in which the distinction between verbal and real definition is a valid one. It is admitted by everyone that to stipulate a meaning of a term that diverges too completely from the "customary" meaning is not convenient. But what is often not realized is that there comes a point at which such variation ceases to be merely inconvenient and unpragmatic; it becomes unintelligible. It leads to a *contradictio in adjecto,* in which intrinsic incompatibility between the subject and predicate of the defining proposition destroys the meaning by an implicit denial.[1]

The function of definition as here suggested is, I think, diagnostic of the function of logic in general. As with the function of naming things, so with the function of relating them, with syntax, the principle that reflected thought presupposes the spontaneous, and cannot deny it in any absolute sense without ultimate unintelligibility, holds good. No doctrine of relations that turns into appearance or illusion the fundamental relational categories of substance and attribute and cause and effect can ultimately escape creating a complete chasm between logic and normal communication of meanings.

The function of logic in general has been suggestively

---

[1] This point will be discussed at length in Chapter V, in which the conditions of philosophical intelligibility and the nature of the philosophical idiom will be gone into fully. Here I will merely note that the notion of the *proper* meaning of a term has a definite and intelligible meaning which it is important to retain.

likened to the rôle of natural selection in the process of biological evolution. Instead of being the creative thing, in this case the truth-creating thing, logic, like natural selection, is merely the occasional determinant and the directing function in thought. Misleading though the figure may easily become if pressed too far, it has this value, that it emphasizes the view of the nature and function of logic on which various logics alone can agree—namely, that while the fundamental laws of logic are the necessary conditions which every judgment that makes the claim to truth must meet, they are not the sufficient conditions. Otherwise expressed, whatever else intelligible discourse may be, it is not intelligible unless the elements of that discourse are related by logical connections. Whatever else an intelligible world may be, it is not intelligible unless the concepts in which that world is conceived are related logically. To present in language anything whatever that contradicts logic may be "as impossible as in geometry to present by its co-ordinates a figure that contradicts the laws of space, or to give the co-ordinates of a point that does not exist." But it does not follow that we may not present in language things that have other conditions of intelligibility and intelligible communication besides those of logic. This is the whole sum and substance of my contention.

But all this is but a way of leading up to our final problem, that of the relation of logic to philosophy and metaphysics—the problem set us by the criticism which modernist logics pass upon the fundamental categories of our natural language, and therefore upon the natural metaphysic that is bound up with it; and, above all, the problem set by the two chief tendencies in philosophical modernism—of those who would make logic the whole of philosophy and of those who would have philosophy turn its back on logic. For it is, after all, these questions that have been chiefly at issue throughout our discussion.

The details of this question will be taken up at many points in the following chapters. Here we shall merely formulate the general principle which emerges from our present study. We found that because a special calculus of relations has been developed in logic for certain specific purposes, it does not follow that the more universal logic of predication has been either excluded or superseded. Similarly, I see no good reason why, because for the special purposes of the mathematical sciences a new idiom has been made, the more fundamental idiom of metaphysics should hereby be superseded. The necessity of such a position can be argued only by one who has already assumed the right of reflective thought to negate the spontaneous activity of mind which it presupposes—the right of a special logic, devised for special purposes, to extrude or supersede the more fundamental categories.

Now it is on the assumption of this conflict of the reflective with the spontaneous that the two distinctively modernist theories of the relation of logic to philosophy or metaphysics are based. For the one, logic, in the narrow and specialized sense of the term, is the whole thing, and the chief function of philosophy is the negation of the spontaneous activity of the mind; for the other, the spontaneous and intuitive is the whole thing, and the essence of philosophy consists in turning our backs on logic. It seems certain that neither of these extreme positions can be right. It seems equally certain that, if the conception of logic here developed is valid, neither is necessary.

Logical analysis and dialectic are indispensable in philosophy, but, however indispensable, they can play only a subordinate part in the solution of the problems traditionally assigned to philosophy. Their indispensable character has already been shown. Whatever else philosophy and metaphysic may be, they are intelligible expression of meanings, and we cannot express ourselves intelligibly except in logical form. On the other hand, by its very nature, logic is subordinate. By this I mean that intelligibility, as determined by logical form, is only *one* of the conditions of philosophical intelligibility, as reason, in the sense of logical analysis and dialectic, is one aspect of a larger conception of reason. "Dialectic," says Bergson, "is necessary to put intuition to the proof, necessary also that intuition should break itself up into concepts and so be propagated to other men. But all it does, often enough, is to develop the result of that intuition that transcends it." To the general principle embodied in this statement I see no reason to take serious exception. It is in its essentials the view of the relation of logic to philosophy that I have been attempting to develop. The sharp contrast of intuition with dialectic involves, to be sure, further consideration.[1] Here I will merely note that this is also the essential position of traditional philosophy. No representative of the Great Tradition has been without some doctrine of intuition. On the other hand, none has separated intuition wholly from intelligence and reason. Intuition does not negate intellect and logic, but is rather its culmination and fulfilment. For them all, generally speaking, knowledge begins with the natural light of intelligence, confused and darkened though it may be. To become definite and expressible this knowledge must become discursive, break itself up into concepts. Only so can certitude pass into evidence; only so can this natural light be communicated from man to man. But dialectic is not the end of knowledge any more than it is the beginning. It passes on to intuitive understanding and insight, which, indeed, transcend it.

For none of them has intuition ever been anything else than intelligence and intellect oriented towards the good. Even in its lowest, biological form, intellect is, for Aristotle and St. Thomas, turned towards the good unconsciously. To this extent the intellect is practical. Reason in the narrower sense arises out of the necessity of making distinctions—still, however, in the pursuit of rational good. It is at this stage that the intellect sometimes loses its natural direction, and turns its back on the spontaneous thought, on the initiatives on which it lives. It is only when it transcends the discursive, through intuition of essence, of metaphysical perfection, that it knows its real nature and its ultimate end.

"The spirit of logic is love and the spirit of value is logic." This, if rightly interpreted, is, I agree with Bosanquet, the essence of the Great Tradition. But it must be rightly interpreted. The spirit of logic is love, but this can be true only in case the intellect, with its logic, is actually oriented towards the good or value. One cannot love space or matter. If the intellect and logic were really directed towards these, as some maintain, we should all be misologists. Nor can one really love "simples" and neutral entities; although, it must be confessed, a highly sophisticated liking for them can be cultivated, as

[1] See Chapter V, pp. 184 ff.

for many other forms of mental caviare. If the intellect were really exclusively bent in their direction we should all make superhuman efforts to unbend it. Neither can one love merely logically consistent wholes, although a *nisus* towards totality is an element in love as it is in life. If the intellect were exclusively oriented towards logical consistency in this sense, disorientation would be the goal of all. The spirit of value cannot be logic, if logic is identified with this alone.

But the intellect is not exclusively directed towards any of these things, relatively significant and valid though they may all be. What the intellect can love—and he who forgets that there is an *amor intellectus* has forgotten the first premises of philosophy—is truth alone, and truth is as unlovable as it is ultimately meaningless, unless it is connected with the "good." *Ens est unum, verum, bonum.* Deny this major premise of the Great Tradition—and its denial, in one way or another, is precisely the root of all distinctively modernist philosophies, and a-logism is not only our natural refuge but the predestined goal of all our thinking.

A modern interpretation of this ancient axiom is the subject of the next chapter.

CHAPTER IV

METAPHYSICS AND VALUE THEORY

For you have often been told that the essential Form of the Good is the highest object of science, and that this essence, by blending with just things and all other created objects, renders them useful and advantageous. . . .

Then admit that in like manner the objects of knowledge not only derive from the Good the gift of being known, but are further endowed by it with a real and essential existence; though the Good, far from being identical with real existence, transcends it in dignity and power.

PLATO, *The Republic*, Book VI

The recognition that givenness of the objects and their existence involves valuation seems to me the first step towards a theory of values.

HUGO MÜNSTERBERG

Die Metaphysik macht es sich zur Aufgabe die gesamte Welt, in der es Wirkliches und Werthaftes giebt, einheitlich zu deuten.

RICKERT, *System der Philosophie*, p. 138

I

FOR one who has really lived through the thinking of the modern world the "problems of value" have become the central problems of philosophy as it presents itself to-day. "In the last resort," says Mr. Belfort Bax, "all problems of metaphysics may be said to resolve themselves into questions of value—I do not mean of practical value, in the sense in which the pragmatists might use the term, but of value in the sense of relative position and importance of each element in the complete system of consciousness." When it is recognized that "the question of the relation of the world of values to the world of reality is the principal question of theoretical philosophy," "that the question of values is at the centre of any conceivable philosophy," we have but an explicit and conscious acknowledgment of a long series of changes that mark off definitively from immediately preceding epochs the philosophy of the present day.[1]

[1] F. C. S. Schiller, in his article on "Value" in the *Encyclopædia of Ethics and Religion*, speaks of value as "the last of the great philosophical topics to have received recognition," and of its "discovery" as "probably the greatest philosophical achievement of the nineteenth century," as "still one of the growing points of philosophy and one which seems likely to overshadow other interests."

In a very real sense, of course, problems of value have always been the central problems. If reality or true being has always been the traditional goal of reflection, it is because it has always been assumed, tacitly or explicitly, that reality and value are ultimately one, or at least inseparable. This has been the "premise" of the Great Tradition because it is the natural metaphysic of the human mind. We find reality intolerable without raising it to the sphere of value, but we find it equally difficult to think value without its implying some kind of reality and without giving it some form of being. If, then, the centre of gravity of philosophical thought has recently been consciously moving from being to value, it is merely because that which has hitherto been tacitly assumed is now explicitly acknowledged.

But the perennial character of these problems should not blind us to the extraordinary change which the definite and conscious recognition of their central character has brought about. It is scarcely an exaggeration to say that it has altered the entire philosophical perspective. It is not merely, for instance, that every treatise on philosophy now has its specific chapters on values, not merely that idealism is being rewritten in an almost new language. It is rather, still more, that we have come to recognize that *"we miss the true inwardness of the epistemological problem itself unless we realize that it is but part of the problem of values at large."* That which has finally marked this definite change in perspective is precisely the concept of intellectual and logical values with which we became familiar in the last chapter. The "recognition that the givenness of objects and their existence itself involves valuation," provides a background against which, for the first time, the true inwardness of the philosophical problem can be seen.

It does not detract in the least from the novelty nor from the importance of this insight that it is saying a very old thing in a new way. In a sense it means but the restoration of the original, and in its essentials imperishable, insight of Plato— namely, that "value is the highest and last object of science," and that it is "from value that objects derive the gift of being known," and, finally, that value, "far from being identical with actuality or existence, transcends it in dignity and power." But these old sayings of Plato were hard sayings. Did he not himself admit in the *Republic* that value or the good was the most difficult object of "science"? If modern philosophy can, as I believe, say these things in a new way, in such a way, moreover, as to make that which is difficult—even paradoxical —in the ancients the commonplaces of the moderns, that in itself is no mean accomplishment. It is the use of the modern idiom of values, as I shall hope to show, that makes possible reinterpretation of the Great Tradition to modern thought. But we must first learn that idiom.

II

"Value" is a very popular word just now, and for that reason, as Mr. E. B. Holt has said, "the theme of no end of current philosophical vagarizing." But to see in it, as he does, merely "a sort of psychological synonym for the good" is to miss the reason for its popularity and for its central place in modern thought. A statistician of words, one of those, for instance, who think to determine the mind of a poet by the frequency of his use of certain words, might easily find a clue to the soul of our epoch in our constant use of the word "value." For not only the fact that the word itself is in every mouth, but, even more, the exigencies that have forced us to coin the new word, are symptomatic of our epoch. Back of this "glib use of the lingo of values," as one writer has rather contemptuously expressed it, there has, indeed, often been much vagarizing and no little poverty of real thought, but the mere fact of the almost universal use of the idiom is itself a significant sign. It may be said to express the entire cultural and philosophical situation.

No one at all alive to the present situation can fail to be aware of the fact that the implicit assumption of the meaning, significance, and value of our civilization, of our scientific, economic, and industrial "rationalism," is being questioned on all sides. "Culture is the measure of things taken for granted," and when the things, the goods, taken for granted are questioned, revaluation follows. This revaluation of all values, which we may think of as either originated or merely epitomized by Nietzsche, the protagonist of all modernism, reached its culmination in the questioning of the entire concept of progress in which our culture expressed itself, and of the entire scale or system on which that progress was predicated.

All this is, of course, platitudinous. The important point

for us is that, with the problem of revaluation of values, attention itself is shifted from "facts" to values. The driving force of thought is, so to speak, no longer merely ontological but rather axiological. This change in the general cultural situation was also reflected in changes in the scientific situation. Even Nietzsche's deepest thought was given, not so much to the revaluation of moral and cultural values in the narrower sense, as to the revaluation of science and logic. The disintegrating effect of intellect on instinct was driven home not merely by the constantly increasing effect of a mechanical and scientific civilization, but also by the evolutionary biological thinking of the day. It was not long before this questioning of cultural values led to a revaluation of science itself, the determining element in our culture.

All this is, again, an old story, and has already been told in our account of the philosophy of modernism in the first chapter. That which needs to be emphasized here is that modernism, by the very conditions of its origin, must be, so to speak, obsessed by the problem of value. The modern man is constantly protesting his belief in values, but we have a deep-seated feeling that he is protesting overmuch. "The values are there," he insists, but he has a curious reluctance or inability to say just *how* they are there, or *where* it is they are. The situation I am trying to depict has been expressed in many ways, in many books and articles, but nowhere, perhaps, more clearly, or, indeed, naïvely, than in a recent popular article.[1] I choose it as my example largely for its naïve pathos and its charming incoherence.

The argument in this case, as, indeed, is customary, starts with the assumption that science and intellect have demolished the structure with which our values have been bound up. "Gone—clean gone—is the necessary rational basis for that whole magnificent scheme of thought which has dominated the Western world for over a thousand years, that comprehensive scheme of theology and philosophy, etc. . . . But— and a most important but! the realities or values by which that construction had life—they are found to persist."

"The values are there," we are told. ". . . Even the complete mechanist cannot escape them . . . he must acknowledge that

[1] Julian Huxley, "Will Science Destroy Religion?" *Harpers' Magazine*, April 1926.

the ecstasy of beauty, the overpowering awe that sometimes seizes upon reflection and the rapture of love, are facts that have utmost value for men." The values are there. "We find, moreover, that some values are higher than others—there is a scale of values. Some are ends in themselves and some only means to ends, and the higher among them, by universal consent, are the values of truth, beauty, love, and goodness."

"Science, in taking stock of the world, is brought up against the existence of values, and must then acknowledge that certain attributes of man possess the highest values known, and it is in this way that science is brought back to humanism. . . . The search for truth for its own sake, irrespective of apparent value; the realization of the existence of value as apparent facts; and then the adjustment of mental knowledge and of the control born of that knowledge, to the value-charged scheme of human thought—that is the new humanism."

Thus for the modern man—in the words of Münsterberg— "through the world of things shimmered first weakly, then ever more clearly, the world of values." This world of values is there; but how is it there? These values, and their reality, it is admitted, "have been uniformly connected with the traditional idealistic and spiritualistic theories of the world." There are those who now "feel the need to transfer them" to what they call "the more solid foundations of realism and naturalism." Can this be done? Can it be done without turning them into a realm of imagination or of useful fictions? There are those who hold that in order to be "enjoyed" values do not have to be connected with existence at all. Their character as values is to be immediately objective, their very being is to be enjoyed. To mistake them for existences is to suffer illusion. Can such extremes of sophistication be more than an interesting gesture? Surely the new humanism has its problems. In any case, the problem of value must, it is evident, be central in any philosophy that moves within the circle of present-day ideas. One thing has emerged with certainty out of the turmoil of present-day discussions. It is no longer possible merely to write a chapter on value at the end of a philosophical treatise. If the problem of values is to be introduced significantly at all it must be introduced at the beginning. This involves a problem of metaphysics, as difficult as it is ultimate.

III

The problem of value is, then—evidently Plato was right—the most difficult task of all human "science." Unless, forsooth, it is not a problem of human science at all!

To many philosophers, it is true, there seems to be no special problem here. "The question of value," writes Creighton, "has never seemed to me to be a special 'problem' capable of special treatment and solution." In a sense this is doubtless true. All the great philosophies have been value philosophies, and the "axiom" of the inseparability of value and reality, the ultimate "premise" of the Great Tradition, has as its consequence the inseparability of axiological and ontological questions. But in another sense it is a special problem—so special, in fact, that for it the modern philosophic consciousness has found it necessary to create a new term, namely, Axiology. In one sense, Axiology, or the theory of value *eo nomine*, may be merely a collective name for a group of problems, psychological, epistemological, and ontological. In another sense, it expresses an entirely new situation in philosophy. It focuses the entire group of problems into one—the *metaphysical status of values.*

A serious difficulty in the way of the solution of the value problem is the widespread ambiguity in the use of the word "value." The question of definition has accordingly bulked large in modern discussions. This is not merely the result of the popularity of the word and the vagarizing that has accompanied that popularity. Ambiguities there have been in plenty, and verbal definition, here as elsewhere, is the condition of intelligible discourse.[1] But the problem really lies much deeper. The values, we say, are there, *but the question of how they are there is already predetermined to a large extent by our definitions of what these values are.* What is it we are talking about when

[1] Space will not permit me to consider in detail the different meanings of value (there are, according to Dewey, at least six different meanings), or the heroic efforts that have been made to clear up this confusion. I shall have to confine myself to two fundamental issues which are determinative for our entire discussion. These issues are in a sense the old question of the extension and intension of the terms we are using, questions as to how broad we may properly make our term, and how much of meaning or intension that term shall carry. As it presents itself to us in this context, it is the question of how value is to be defined if the term is to be adequate for its uses in modern philosophical discourse as we have just described it.

we speak of values? The various conceptions of value *assume* that they are *real* definitions.

Much discussion has revolved around the question of the narrower and broader use of the term "value." Shall we confine value to the so-called a-logical values of utility, goodness, beauty, or shall it be extended to include the logical or theoretical values of existence, truth, etc.? Against this broader concept it has been urged that it is not the customary and proper meaning, and is, therefore, objectionable both linguistically and practically and can lead only to confusion. In a sense, of course, all definition is stipulated, and whether we shall use the term "value" in the narrower or broader sense is a matter of our own choice. And yet the broader use may be inconvenient. Its necessity will be made clear in a later connection. Here I will simply insist that the broader use has established itself in the value idiom, and is always implied in modern discussions of the value problem.

Of much more immediate concern is the question of intension; and here the issues are much more complicated. Shall value be limited to instrumental value or utility and the term "value" denied to experiences of intrinsic value such as the æsthetic—as by Pragmatism? Or is all value ultimately intrinsic? Shall value be defined as a psychological character, or in a more cosmological objective way? Shall it be defined in relational terms, either psycho-biological or cosmological, or is it ultimately indefinable, an indefinable quality or essence; or indefinable, perhaps, in the sense that all ultimate categories are indefinable, as are being or existence themselves?

Elsewhere[1] I have gone into this entire question of definition in detail. Here I must confine myself to reaching conclusions on certain points which are fundamental for all that follows.

We find the idea of value everywhere defined so as to mean a quality of anything that satisfies a need or evokes a feeling of pleasure. There is still a widespread prejudice which persists in seeing in value merely a sort of psychological synonym for the good. In a sense this prejudice is natural. The first and

---

[1] *Valuation : Its Nature and Laws*; but more adequately in "Value and Existence," *The Journal of Philosophy*, vol. xiii. A recent discussion of this entire question will be found in my article in *Philosophy To-day* (The Open Court Publishing Co., 1928).

most immediate condition, both of the origin and development of ideas and judgments of value, lies obviously in human desire and feeling, wish and volition, and ultimately in the impulses and instincts and tendencies which they presuppose. The psycho-biological definition (and ultimately foundation) of values, accordingly, appears to many to be the most natural. It appears to them also as primary and, one might even say, of absolute significance. Every assertion of value, it is immediately evident, is at least dependent on the experiences of the affective-volitional life. It is these that not only determine the "existence" of values in the world, but also, in so far as they condition their existence, justify their claim to immediate validity.

The psychological definitions thus seem to tell—in principle at least—the whole story. It is not necessary to enter into the details of that story; they have been told over and over again. What interests us here is rather the main theme of which these details are the developments. Now, so far as the principle involved is concerned, it is rather generally recognized that an account of values in merely psychological terms does not tell the whole story. It is also generally recognized that definitions of value in these terms, whether analytical or genetic, are really circular in character.

Why, it is asked, should fulfilment of desire or interest be a good? Why should pleasure confer a value? In all such definitions valuableness is already assumed as an intrinsic quality of pleasure or of fulfilment. The circularity of the definition appears, moreover, in still another way. The value of an object consists, it is said, in its satisfaction of desire, or, broadly, fulfilment of interest. But it is always possible to raise further questions which show conclusively that the value concept is already presupposed. Is the interest itself worthy of being satisfied? Is the object worthy of being of interest? In other words, the assumption of intrinsic value somewhere requires us to find the essence of value in something other than the terms of this definition.

It is not strange, therefore, that definitions in psychological terms have often shifted to more objective biological formulas. Back of desire and feeling lie certain biological tendencies or instincts presupposed by desire and its satisfaction. So that

value becomes, in the words of Orestano, "a biological phenomenon appearing in psychological form." But the circularity
of such definitions is, if anything, even more evident than in
the former case.

The genealogy of values finds its expression in the definition
that values are adaptations to environment, relations between
organism and environment that emerge as evolution runs its
course. The deduction of value from concepts of adaptation
is, however, generally recognized as circular. Adaptation can
scarcely be thought without some concept, however vague, of
end or purpose, and end or purpose presupposes value, not
value end and purpose. Moreover, the problem here is not
merely that of the meaning and nature of value, but also of
the meaning of degrees of value, of more and less. If we say
that one thing is better than another because it is more highly
developed, we must first assume that development is necessarily improvement, i.e. that there is always greater value in
a thing in proportion to its development. This may, indeed,
be so, but, if so, it involves an *a priori* relation between value
and development which can only be acknowledged.

The recognition of the circular character of both of these
forms of definition is so entirely a commonplace of present-day
thought—not only of technical philosophy, but of ordinary
culture—that it need not be insisted upon here. Much more
important is the recognition of the fact that part of the meaning
of value is its validity—its worthiness to be—and that this
cannot be reduced to existential terms.

This situation may be expressed in several ways. It is clear
that it does not follow that if we know what goes on in consciousness when we value we necessarily know the nature of
value. It is also clear that, for a theory of value that involves
also the question of the validity, or worthiness to be, of objects,
a psycho-genetic account of the origin of value is wholly
irrelevant and can afford no decisive criterion. But reflections
such as these really go much deeper than this. Our charge
of circularity has been directed against only one form of
relational definitions of value. But it also holds in principle
against *any definition which is in its essence a reduction of value to
non-value terms, against any relational definition.*

There are those who recognize fully the circular character

of the psycho-genetic definitions, but who hope to escape these difficulties by resorting to more objective and cosmological conceptions. Value is defined as the fulfilment of any tendency whatsoever,[1] not merely the fulfilment of interest nor the relation of a sentient organism to its environment. It is conceived to be a relation of harmony, or teleological dependence of parts of the universe on each other. But here again the argument is no less circular. The deduction of value from concepts of adaptation or teleological dependence is clearly circular. On the other hand, the concept of harmony presupposes a whole which must itself have value on some other ground if the parts are to have value through relation to the whole. It is doubtful, however, whether we can say of the whole of reality that it has value any more than we can say of the whole of matter that it is heavy.

It may, indeed, be argued that tendency is a purely factual category, and that, in defining value as the fulfilment of any tendency whatsoever, we escape the circular character of other relational definitions. Now, I am willing to admit, for the sake of the argument, although I do not believe it, the purely factual, value-free character of "tendency." But that still does not save the definition from being circular. For to say that the furthering of a tendency is to that tendency a good is to imply that furthering or fulfilment is in itself a good; and why, after all, should it be so? I think there can be no doubt that this definition gets its meaning only from the assumption that fulfilment is better than non-fulfilment; and just as little doubt that this assumption can be questioned. In any case, value is assumed, the value relation "better than" being already assumed in the definition.

To this it is answered: "Good is no doubt a different notion from fulfilment, and therefore appears to contain something not authorized in the content of the latter notion. But that is because good or value is the relation between the fulfilment (or furthering) and the tendency, a relation uniquely and sufficiently determined by the two."[2] I am not able to see that this answer meets the difficulty. The relation between

---

[1] W. N. Sheldon, "An Empirical Definition of Value," *Journal of Philosophy, Psychology, etc.*, vol. xi, No. 5.

This is Professor Sheldon's reply to the above criticism of his definition and as made by the present writer. *Op. cit.*, p. 122.

tendency and its furthering or fulfilment is doubtless unique, but that it sufficiently determines the notion good must be denied. It appears to do so only because the "value" notion is already imported into the relation—in the assumption that fulfilment is better than non-fulfilment. Without this the equating of the relation with "good" is meaningless. That the later stages of becoming are better than the first can never be more than a groundless pronouncement.

I have laboured these purely logical points perhaps unduly. But I have done so for two important reasons. It is, in the first place, one of the few points on which the collective consciousness has come to a large measure of agreement. There are few of us who do not now see that value is a logically primitive concept, and cannot be deduced from, nor defined in terms of, anything else. In the second place, this concept of the ultimately indefinable character of value is of absolutely fundamental significance when we come to the ontological problems of value. If, for instance, it is found impossible to reduce value to any form of "being," but that the reverse reduction is possible, we should have consequences of the utmost importance for general philosophy.

With an objective or cosmological view of value I have as such no quarrel. It is my own view as it is the view of perennial philosophy. For Aristotle, and even more clearly for St. Thomas, every created thing has its own good, which it seeks to realize consciously or unconsciously. Value, I shall hold, is part of the nature of anything. The idea that any objects are value-free, except as a result of a wilful or purposeful abstraction, is to my mind an untenable conception. The question here is, however, merely one of definition—and of the possibility of reduction of value to existential, non-value terms. This is what must be denied. The assumption of all these definitions is that value is a complex derivative, and can be reduced to simple entities or relations of such entities. The category of being valued, like the category of being perceived or being willed, is, perhaps, such a complex, capable of being analysed and in the process of analysis of being defined. But the category of being valued is not the category of value. The latter is a logically primitive concept, and as such indefinable.

To this idea of the indefinability of value many objections have been made. It is said—and in a sense with truth—that *all* definition is circular. However and wherever we start in human discourse, we must start with a set of words which are undefined, because by assumption we have no more words with which to define them. Precisely. In criticizing these definitions as circular I am certainly not asking of those that make them the impossible; nor do I deny their right to define value as so and so for their particular purposes. In a sense every definition is a postulate. All I ask is that those who make these definitions of value should recognize their circular character—that when value is defined for a certain purpose, value is already presupposed in that purpose and acknowledged in any attempt to define it.

Finally, to say that ultimate values, i.e. the good, the beautiful, and the true, are ultimately indefinable is to say that they are "individual" concepts, and that their nature cannot be apprehended by such general propositions as form the material of natural science, more specifically in this case biological or psychological science. There is no higher genus to which to ascribe them as a species or as examples. There are no simples into which they may, as complexes, be analysed. There are no valuable objects which may be considered as completely representative of these ultimate values in the sense that in logic certain particulars are said to be representative of a class. All of which means—to go back to the more general question of the rôle of the value idiom in present-day philosophy—that if we are to do justice to the problems of value, we must not prejudice our solutions of these problems by premature and narrow definitions, which by the very character they ascribe to value beg all the questions at issue.[1]

---

[1] The indefinability of value means merely that we have to do here with one of the ultimate and underivable concepts with which we think or understand the world, and it shares this lack, if one wishes so to call it, with other concepts, such as being, existence, and reality. Its indefinability means, therefore, no objection to its use in philosophy any more than in the case of these other ultimate and inescapable concepts. To use the word in philosophy we have merely to make quite clear what we understand when we use the word. This takes place through showing its relations to meaning and existence.

IV

The limitations of the purely psychological and biological approaches to values soon disclosed themselves to all who attempted to think the problem through. The recognition of the circularity of all definitions in these terms—and, therefore, of the logically primitive character of value—forced new problems and new issues into the foreground. The contrast of "judgments of value" with "judgments of fact," as it found philosophical expression, first of all in Lotze and Ritschl, and ultimately in the entire *axiological* standpoint, was made primarily in the interest of the assertion of this *autonomy* of values. All these men were saying, in one way or another, *the values are there*—independently of our scientific and theoretical judgments about the world. But to say that they are there implies that they are known, that the process of valuation is in some sense and in some degree noetic. An epistemological problem thus trod close on the heels of the psychological problem; it was, indeed, implicit in the psychological approach itself.

The consciousness of this problem registered itself in the doctrine of the value judgment, and the dispute over the value judgment is one of the most enlightening, as it is also one of the most confused, chapters in modern philosophy. Into the details of this debate I shall not enter here.[1] I shall confine myself to two points of importance for the general argument of this chapter. The first point concerns the denial, on the part of some, of a specific value judgment, in the sense that it is distinguishable from the ordinary judgment of fact or truth.

In a sense, of course, no one would deny that there are value judgments. Many of our judgments are mixed—made up of factual and value judgments—and the logical form is the same in both cases. If I say the mountain is high and beautiful the character of beautiful is predicated in precisely the same form as that of high. To say that there are value *judgments* is simply to say that it is impossible to express

---

[1] A fuller treatment of this entire subject is to be found in an article, "The Knowledge of Value and the Value Judgment," *The Journal of Philosophy, etc.*, vol. xiii, No. 25; and also in an article, "Value, Logic, and Reality," *Proceedings of the Sixth International Congress of Philosophy*, 1927.

anything intelligibly without logical form. The real question at issue is rather whether the manifest difference between the two predicates involves sufficient difference between the two types of predication to merit the distinction between judgments of value and judgments of fact.

It is said that what we call a judgment of value is either a mere expression of feeling (and, therefore, not really a judgment), or else it is actually a judgment of truth or fact. In a sense, also, this is true. We cannot make any judgment about anything which is not "the case." If we say that the mountain is beautiful, this is, if we are dealing with judgments at all, as much "the case" as if we say it is high. The contrast between value and fact has meaning only if "fact" be understood in some narrower sense of the term. We are evidently not using fact in the impartial sense of logic, nor being in the impartial sense of our earlier discussion of the ontological predicates. We are clearly using these terms in some *ex-parte* sense, in a sense involving some ontological prejudice.[1]

The real question at issue is then, I repeat, the nature and the extent of difference of the two types of predication. Now, "value" is predicated of an object by means of the same verbal form as quality is predicated, but there seems to be a very real difference in the mode of predication not brought out by the verbal form. When we predicate value of anything we pass from the mere concept of quality or essence to a certain *bearing* which this essence has on existence. It is "worth existing" or "ought to be." In other words, in a predicate such as noble or beautiful there is, in addition to its essence, this unique relation to being. Now, it is undoubtedly this double character of the value judgment, this unique bearing on existence, that constitutes the *differentia* of the value judgment. It is this *differentia*, also, that makes value and the value predicate the most difficult object of science. For (to put it quite bluntly) how can there be a judgment of fact which is not of fact; how can there be a judgment of truth or being which is not a judgment of existence or essence, but of oughtness?

The most impressive way in which this objection has been stated is the assertion that the value judgment is a logical monstrosity. Take, it is said, the value judgment in its usual form. A is as it should be, or, negatively, A is as it should not be. Apparently it is a judgment because it seems to assure us by implication of a specific A. That an existential judgment is presupposed in so-called value judgments is beyond doubt, but one must not confuse the conditions with the conditioned. Such confusion can only result in a logical monstrosity. It is best seen in the negative form. For if A exists, it is already as it should be, for it cannot be otherwise. But the positive form is no better. A is as it should be. If this form escapes contradiction it falls into tautology, for if A is, it is already as it should be.

From this argument is drawn the conclusion that the so-called value judgment is not a judgment in any "proper" sense, but merely an expression of feeling. In my examination of this argument elsewhere[1] I have admitted that the conclusion is perfectly valid if value be conceived as a quality. Qualities inhere in objects, since it is the quality that makes the object precisely what it is; the judgment of quality presupposes that the thing is not other than it is. Make value equivalent to ought to be, and call this oughtness a quality, and the contradiction is complete. It has, indeed, been argued that this contradiction holds only if value be conceived as a "natural" quality. For myself I am unable to make any such distinctions in qualities. A quality is natural or it is no quality at all. What seems to be meant here—at least, it is the only meaning that I can give to the distinction—is that value is a sort of tertiary quality, not natural in the sense that the primary and secondary qualities are. In that case value becomes but a psychological character which an object acquires through its relations to the interests of a subject, and there is then no point in calling it a quality; we should call it rather the "expression of feeling," which in that case it really is.

We seem, then, to have come to this point in our argument: either the so-called value judgment is no judgment at all, but merely an expression of feeling; or else value as it is cognized in the value judgment is not a quality in any sense, but is rather, as I have described it in other connections, an *objective*, or a unique form of objectivity. To bring out the grounds

[1] "Value and Existence," *Journal of Philosophy, Psychology, etc.*, vol. xiii, No. 17.

for this position it will be necessary to analyse the act of judgment itself more fully.

Judgment is too often conceived as merely the bringing together of a subject and a predicate in a relation. But a deeper analysis always discloses a more fundamental "reflexive act" that recognizes or acknowledges "that it is so." Truth and existence are acknowledged in *this* act, and we express this fact by saying that these predicates are not adjectival but attributive. Now, in the so-called value judgment we have a similar situation. Deeper than the mere bringing together of subject and predicate is the act that acknowledges "that it ought to be," or "is worthy to be." This meaning, ought to be, this unique bearing on existence, *is an object solely of acknowledgment.* In the judgments, this mountain is beautiful, this character is noble, there is the bringing together of subject and predicate precisely as in any judgment, and in so far value judgments are the material of logic. But the *meaning* of the predicate, its connection with reality, is *different* from that in other types of judgment. When I say that the mountain is beautiful or the character is noble, part at least of the implication of that judgment is that I acknowledge that it is worthy to be, that it is as it ought to be.

The point I am trying to make is really very simple. We have already seen that, despite similarity of verbal form, the predication of value to an object is different from the adjectival predication of a quality. We now see that it is also different from the attributive predication of existence. Although like the latter, in that it includes the element of acknowledgment, it differs from it in that it attributes, not *being* in the sense either of existence or subsistence, but *worthiness to be.* This difference is of such character and degree as to have required, and in my mind to have merited, novelties in terminology. This oughtness, or worthiness to be, has been called validity, a *dignitative* (Meinong), or, in my terms, the "value objective." Space will not permit me to rehearse here the arguments for my own position. For the purposes I have in mind here it is not necessary. The name is of secondary importance if the fact itself is recognized. For it is precisely this fact—this difference which we have been pointing out—which determines to a large degree the more ultimate question of the relation of value to being.

This leads me to the second point of importance for the general argument of this chapter. As I pointed out, the doctrine of the value judgment expressed the growing consciousness of the objectivity of value; it registered the sense that the values are *there* independently of our scientific and theoretical judgments about the world. But for the philosopher it is not sufficient merely to assert that the values are there; he must also be able to say where they are and how they are there. It is evident that the whole problem of the ontological status of value is already involved in the problem of the value judgment. This problem we shall take up specifically in a later section. Here we shall confine ourselves to the problem of objectivity merely as it is related to the problem of knowledge of values.

In the analysis of the value judgment it was pointed out that deeper than the mere bringing together of subject and predicate is the reflexive act that *acknowledges* that it "ought to be," that it is "worthy to be," and that the unique relation to being that constitutes the essence of value is *an object solely of acknowledgment*. It is now necessary to make clear what is meant by this statement. By the use of the term "acknowledgment" (*Anerkennen*) it is intended to bring out two aspects of the unique character of value. In the first place, while valuation is noetic, this noetic character is not describable as any kind of perception, intuition, or apprehension of a *quale*, but only as the recognition of, or assent to, a form of objectivity. In the second place, the status of this objectivity is not describable in terms of ontological predicates, such as existence or subsistence, but only in terms of a validity. In the case of value *its being is its validity*. Values are there, but in quite a different sense from that in which objects either of perception or of conception are there—in the sense, namely, that their acknowledgment (mutual acknowledgment, as we shall see) is the necessary condition of all intelligible communication— even, as we have already seen, of the communication of the meanings of the ontological predicates themselves. In this sense value is above all ontology.[1]

[1] It is not surprising that the value concept should have introduced great perplexity among the "realists" and have led to greatly divergent theories. Shall we, with some, hold that value is merely a psychological character which

K

The introduction of the term "acknowledgment" at this point affords the proper occasion for making clearer the meaning of a concept we have already used and one which will become increasingly important throughout the coming discussions. Its use raises certain questions which must be definitely settled at this stage of our study.

Both the necessity and the significance of the term can be best shown, I think, by the consideration of certain questions which arise in connection with our position that value is ultimately indefinable. When terms are indefinable we may always indicate, it is said, that for which they stand by "pointing." Thus we may be asked to *point* to what we *mean* by the term "value." In such a demand it is assumed that just as we can point to the object or *quale* red, itself indefinable, so we can point to similar cases of value. Nothing can, to my mind at least, be further from the truth than such an analogy. When, for instance, Sidgwick asks what it is that alone is good or intrinsically valuable, and finds it wholly and alone in a pleasurable state of consciousness, he assumes that good is something we can find, point to, like a sensation or a sense *quale*. It is, of course, nothing of the sort. It is not an *entity* to be pointed to; it is a *meaning* to be acknowledged. That character of value, that something is worthy to be, or ought to be (what I have ventured to call an objective), is something that can only be acknowledged. The identification of value with a pleasurable state of consciousness, for instance, is intelligible only in case that meaning is acknowledged by those who experience the meaning of the good, which notoriously it is not.

an object acquires only by a relation to the liking or disliking of a sentient subject; or, with others, that it is an indefinable that attaches to existents in much the same way as natural qualities such as a colour? Or shall we hold, with still another group, that values are qualities that attach only to essences rather than existences, either physical or psychical; that their being is to be enjoyed, and that to mistake them for existences is to suffer illusion? It is fortunately not necessary for our purposes to enter into this interminable debate among the realists, which, after all, has significance largely, if not wholly, within the special circle of ideas in which their thinking moves. It is enough to point out here that all these difficulties, largely artificial in character, arise out of the false assumption that value is a quality, and out of the failure to recognize the intrinsic difference in the two types of predication. With this assumption it becomes necessary to ascribe to value some kind of being and the perplexities we have noted become inevitable.

Such acknowledgment, it is said, however, is a hybrid construction—a fusion of mere emotional expression and judgment, of feeling and knowledge. Valuation, though not independent of knowledge, is other than knowledge. I cannot understand how anyone can say this. Knowledge, in any intelligible sense of the word, is impossible without *acknowledgment*, acknowledgment of the values presupposed in any distinction between the true and the false, the real and the apparent. But it is equally true that there is no acknowledgment without knowledge in some sense of the object or objective acknowledged. These two theses of *Axiology* are equally incontestable.

V

We have been considering the epistemological problem of value in that form in which it has chiefly presented itself in the ordinary discussions of value—namely, in the form of the question of the subjectivity or objectivity of values. But this problem was to appear at still another point, even more significant—namely, the question of the valuational character of cognition, "the value character of the theoretical."

Thus far the question was chiefly that of the objectivity or validity of what are called the *a-logical* values, the useful, the good, and the beautiful. In fact, for most thinkers the term "value" had meant merely these. But it was not long before truth was spoken of as a value and the term "logical values" entered into the discussion. It is at this point that the question of the narrower and broader use of the term arises. In a sense, of course, no one would deny that truth and existence are values. The unexpressed assumption of all logic is that truth is better than untruth, the postulate of all science and philosophy, that reality is of more value than appearance. This is simply a part of the general fact of the orientation of intellect towards value, the value-centric predicament of our earlier discussion. But that is not the real question at issue. It is not whether truth and existence *have* value, but whether they *are* values. The real question is the relation of logical validity to value.

As thought went more and more deeply into this problem it became ever more apparent that so-called a-logical values could not be separated from the logical. The two hang together, and if they do not, they "will hang separately." It became clear that if value is a logically primitive concept, so also is validity. Not only do the concepts of truth and reality, if they are to have any meaning, presuppose that truth is better than error, reality better than unreality—in other words, that such distinctions are value distinctions—but truth and reality themselves are values to be acknowledged, rather than existents or even subsistents to be merely apprehended. In short, philosophy began to talk of the "value character of the theoretical." In addition to saying that valuation is noetic it also said that cognition is valuational.

This conclusion forced itself on modern thought in the following way. Even from the psycho-biological point of view truth must be considered as a form of value. For is not knowledge itself, on this view, a form of adaptation? Any merely naturalistic validation of values (and as we have seen, the psycho-biological point of view always assumes their validity) goes back ultimately to life, to the original complex or organic forces and tendencies which, in their totality, we call life. In this manifold of tendencies called life, the element of knowledge is present, but from the naturalistic point of view it plays only a subordinate rôle. It is only one tendency among other tendencies, represents only one instrumental value among other values, and has not yet developed autonomy. From this point of view it is completely in the service of the all-powerful biological life and its purposes. This service *is* its validity and its sole validity. But precisely here we see that the circle evident in all merely biological definitions of value is *a fortiori* present when we consider the values of knowledge. For if knowledge, and the logical values upon the acknowledgment of which knowledge rests, get their significance solely through their "teleological" relation to "life," surely life itself must get its significance from absolute values which it embodies or realizes, or knowledge itself loses all genuine significance, ceases to be genuine knowledge or *bonâ-fide* logic in any sense of those terms. It was precisely this situation we had in mind in our examination of the pragmatist's logic and of the pan-fictionism in which any merely psycho-biological conception of knowledge and its values must issue. This circle in Vaihinger's thinking is one which only a theory of absolute values can escape.

These things are so entirely the commonplaces of competent philosophic thought that one is almost ashamed of going into them again. In any case, this value character of the transcendental element in knowledge is at once the key to the entire axiological position in modern value theory and the clue to the relation of value to reality as it determines metaphysical thought. When one has once grasped the fact that every judgment, even the existential, involves the acknowledgment of a value, he can scarcely dare any longer to speak of values as mere matters of feeling or belief. Nor will he be disposed again to reduce value and validity to existence, as all the existential definitions do. It may not be easy to reduce existence and truth to value, but it is certainly true, as Cyril Walker says,[1] that it is much easier to reduce existence to value than value to existence. But this problem opens up the entire question of the ontological status of values—the third general problem of our study.

VI

The prejudice which sees in values merely psychological facts among other facts has, we have now seen, been largely eliminated by reflection on the two epistemological problems— and by recognizing as a consequence the transcendent element in valuation and the value character of the transcendental element in cognition.

With this has disappeared also another prejudice, even more deeply intrenched—namely, the limitation of value to the "good" in the narrow moral sense, or more generally the limitation of value to the a-logical. So long as this association of ideas remained intact, Plato's saying, that the objects of knowledge "derive from the good the gift of being known," could be nothing but a hard saying and one unintelligible to the modern mind.

This moral prejudice is, to be sure, one that dies hard.

[1] *The Construction of the World in Terms of Fact and Value*, chap. iii.

Yet, however deeply intrenched, it must be recognized that it is wholly modern in origin—due largely in fact to the Kantian distinction between the theoretical and practical reason. In any case, it is in complete opposition to the entire movement of traditional thought. The complete "identification of metaphysical perfection with moral good," which Leibniz, for instance, warns us against, is one which none of the great thinkers has ever made. *Ens* is for them *unum, verum, bonum.* This is the presupposition of all their thinking, but *bonum* as thus understood was never merely moral and always implied a perfection of a metaphysical character.

With the elimination of these two prejudices our mind is now free to approach the central and ultimate problem of value, the *ontological.* We already know in a general way what that problem is. The somewhat lyrical protest of the modern consciousness, that *the values are there*, presents the entire problem in a naïve way. But the philosopher wants to know *how* they are there. We are here using ontological predicates, and we simply must know whether we are using them aright. Do values exist, or are they merely subsistent essences to which reality must not be attributed? Or is neither of these terms applicable? Is not their validity their only objectivity? Finally, we have seen that the only intelligible use of the predicates "real" and "unreal" involves the value character of these predicates. How shall we at the same time say that reality is a value and that values are real? Such are the questions as they appear in the technical jargon of the day. But back of these technical questions lie issues of the first importance for modern thought. The relation of value to being—the ontological status of values—we are not surprised to find, is the ultimate question to which all philosophers, realists and idealists alike, are driven.

Do values exist? The answers are varied and contradictory enough. "Yes, emphatically," is one answer. "Yes, they exist if they are felt. Just as much as gravitation, pressure, collisions exist." On the other hand, just as emphatically, the assertion of the existence of values is said to be a nonsense. To ask whether values exist appears to Rickert, for instance, to be a sort of *pons asinorum* of philosophical thought.

The scandal of such a conflict of opinion is to my mind

equalled only by its needlessness. For the conflict owes its origin largely, if not solely, to equivocal meanings of the term "existence," arising from those ontological prejudices which we have considered in an earlier chapter. For it is entirely clear that if we take existence in the sense of the broadest definition we must, of course, say that value exists, as does everything else in the world of logical discourse. But our statement is just as meaningless as it is true. On the other hand, if we take existence in the narrower sense, as modern thinking seems to demand, value cannot exist. The feeling of value exists. The qualities valued subsist, as does also the relation of value for a subject. But value as such neither exists nor subsists: it is simply valid.

But let us be entirely clear in this matter. There is, indeed, a certain justification for our speaking of values as existing. There can be no practical harm in saying that values exist when we really mean that certain feelings, desires, or sentiments exist. Or we may take existence in the broader sense and say that values exist, but they exist only for persons or for will—have, as it is sometimes phrased, "imperative existence." We may even say that it is not fair to ask whether values are relative to human feeling or are objectively real; they are both. When the social nature of valuation is considered the alternative between objectivity and relativity to human feeling is unsound. All this is true enough; but it is evidently another question that is here at issue. Can we, with a proper sense of the meanings of the terms, speak of validity itself as existing? We cannot, I think, without eviscerating the plain meaning of existence. And if, philosophically, we can scarcely say that value and its validity exist, there is just as little reason for saying that they subsist. At most we can mean that the qualities valued subsist, or the relation between value and the subject—the "value for the subject"—subsists. Value itself is merely valid. *That is* its objectivity.[1]

It is by ways of thinking such as these that many are forced to the view that value and validity are above all ontology. With a special form of this argument, as it applies to "logical

[1] A fuller discussion of this problem is to be found in my article, "Ontological Problems of Value," *The Journal of Philosophy, etc.*, vol. xiv, No. 12.

values," we have already become familiar in the preceding chapter. That such a view involves a certain element of paradox and is difficult to state intelligibly we found to be the contention of its critics. both realistic and idealistic. The same paradox is held to be inherent in the doctrine in its more general form. We shall undertake a detailed examination of these criticisms in the following section. Here we shall content ourselves with merely recognizing the difficulty which such a line of thought seems to involve. Rickert, who, perhaps, has followed out this way of thinking more consistently than anyone else, apparently feels the full force of the paradox. He recognizes that "it is the custom of philosophy to call any last principle upon which philosophy comes, reality" (*Realität*). From the beginning the absolute is conceptually identified with the real. The word "real," when thus used, is, however, always used with "a certain emphasis." "It is identified with the highest, deepest, inmost, most essential, or other superlatives, beyond which nothing more is thinkable." To say, then, that the absolute value is merely valid and not real seems to contain a contradiction in terms. We might choose for it, perhaps, the term *Wert-Realität*. Nevertheless, Rickert continues to insist that clear thinking will not permit this and is content to leave the antinomy as it is. Yet the antinomy simply cannot be left in this form. Against this internal contradiction the spirit of man must, it would seem, for ever strive. To separate value and reality is ultimately contradictory, and makes all our thinking and its communication ultimately unintelligible. Some solution of this antinomy must be found, and we shall now make an attempt to solve it.[1]

[1] It is, perhaps, desirable at this point to make clear the divergence of my own position from that of Rickert on this point, for the reason that divergence here results in still greater difference on the question of the nature of metaphysics later to be considered.

The line of argument here presented (developed first by Rickert in *Die Gegenstand der Erkenntniss*, and further elaborated in his *System der Philosophie*, 1921) leads him to assert the unreality of value and to speak of it as *ein Irreales*. This position results from his identification of "existence" with "reality," already discussed and criticized in an earlier chapter. As a result of this he is led to define metaphysics, not as the science of reality as a totality, but rather as one which has as its object the search for a higher totality which shall combine real existence and unreal values. Now, I agree that metaphysics is not a science of real being in the sense that it is concerned with "value-free" existences. It has as its object "die gesamte Welt, in der Wirkliches und Werthaftes giebt, einheitlich

VII

The status of value is, indeed, pre-eminently the problem of philosophy as it presents itself to-day. But in recognizing this fact "we do not," as it has been well said, "evade metaphysics." Nor do we "issue in a new era of thought for which questions of being appear juvenile simply because we have learned to talk about values *in abstracto*." In other words, it may be that the attempt to make the category of value more ultimate than that of being, far from being a solution of all our philosophical problems, may, in fact, turn out to be an attempt to avoid them by means of a very patent and vicious abstraction. This criticism of the philosophy of validity is so common, and has in it so important an element of truth, as to require a very careful examination. As a result of such examination we may be able to express our own view of the relation of value to being more intelligibly.

Now, that many who hold the view here criticized have sought thereby to evade metaphysics is probably true. It is certainly not the object of the present writer, for whom the metaphysical or ontological point of view, properly interpreted, is not only the essence of traditional philosophy, but the very position which value philosophy is to enable us to interpret. Be that as it may, it is so understood by many of its critics, and it is necessary to consider their criticisms with the greatest care.

The entire conception that there is something, *validity*, which is different from existence and set over against it as validity and value, seems to many to contain a nonsense. Would it not be simply a nothing and the concept of validity a thing that is not? For if I set validity over against existence, do I not make of this non-being? What meaning or value can be attributed to that which is not? Are we not in a world of fictions? Must not everything that we think or acknowledge itself have being? Either validity belongs in the sphere of the irrational, the ungraspable, beyond thought, in which case it does not belong to the sphere of philosophical investigation;

zu deuten." But we are not justified in calling value "unreal," or in defining metaphysics as a combination of real and unreal. The issue here may seem to be merely verbal, one of definition, but certainly much more than that is involved.

or it shows itself to be being, as identical with being, and any theory of value and validity is a theory of being.

The issue has been well stated by Lossky in his book *The Intuitive Basis of Knowledge*, in which he attacks this position as it has been formulated by Rickert. "Rickert says that the object which we oppose to the judging subject is nothing, an 'ought' which *is* not, but has timeless validity. Yet is there intelligible meaning in saying that anything can be valid and at the same time not be? Contradiction seems to be involved in this line of thought: and for our part we turn to the realistic conception of being which instinctively guides us in science and practical activity."[1] Here speaks the "ontological" instinct, to be sure, but does it speak with wisdom? If Lossky thus turns "instinctively" to the naïvely realistic conception of being, he must either be frankly instinctive in his procedure, with all the "confused knowledge" that instinct involves, or else he must define his realistic conception. If he does the former, we have nothing to say to him. Life solves no philosophical problems and certainly instinct no epistemological ones. If he chooses to define the real, he must either say the real is everything, or else he must choose among the various meanings of the real. If he does the former, his answer is meaningless; if the latter, it involves an *ex-parte* definition involving one of the ontological "prejudices." But such *ex-parte* definition can only be justified by an appeal to value that must be acknowledged, precisely the "ought" of which the philosophy of validity speaks. This circle, I hold, is absolutely inescapable. It can be broken through only by the *tour de force* of an appeal to instinct or intuition.

But it is far from clear that there is no intelligible meaning in saying that a thing can at the same time be valid and not "exist." In the first place it may be remarked that to set validity over against existence is not to negate it. Difference from being does not mean absolute nothing. Kant has certainly made us aware that besides the affirmative and negative judgments there is also a *limitative*, and that this constitutes no unconditional negation, but rather only the denial of particular affirmations. A judgment of this type serves rather to disclose the possibility of an infinite manifold of positive

---

[1] *The Intuitive Basis of Knowledge*, 1919, pp. 246 ff.

determinations. To distinguish validity from being, to set it in contrast to being, means merely to disclose a sphere the peculiar character of which is not completely characterized by its determination as being.

There is, then, no necessary contradiction involved in this line of thought. But there is also a positive meaning in the concept of validity as contrasted with being. Every affirmation of being or existence takes place from a particular point of view, involves the acknowledgment of a particular order and a particular kind of validity. In the frame of this order, however it may be developed and thought, every affirmation of existence or non-existence takes a particular place, and this place is validity. In truth, the case for validity is often made impossible by the very form in which the alternative is presented by its critics.

Would not—so the question runs—would not a validity and value which are different from being and set over against it simply be a nothing? But such a question is unreal, for the very test of that which is existent or non-existent, real or unreal, is precisely an acknowledgment of the validity of the judgment. In this respect the alternative here presented is not unlike the much more popular and famous alternative of freedom and determinism. We say that it is impossible that we should choose indifferently between two motives, for even then the stronger motive must prevail. But, as one can see with only a moderate expenditure of logical acumen, such a question is unreal, for there is no other test for the stronger motive except the fact that we choose it. In like manner there is no other test between the existent and the non-existent, between being and non-being, than the fact that we acknowledge the validity of the distinction.

All this may be admitted—*must*, in fact, be admitted, I think, by anyone who cares to think things through. It is intelligible to say that a thing may be valid, and at the same time not be, in any of the definable senses of being. Yet the position fails to bring entire conviction, and in a sense this lack of conviction is justified. The language of validity is a valuable idiom—nay, an indispensable idiom—but it is a highly sophisticated language and may easily lend itself to sophistry. The realm of validity is a highly rarefied atmosphere. It is necessary to be able to breathe this atmosphere, but neither plain man nor philosopher can remain long in it. In the end we must all talk ontological language.

The plain man, for instance, simply cannot use the language of validity. Renan observes that if we tell the simple to live by aspiration after truth and beauty, these terms would have no meaning to them. "Tell them to love God, not to offend God, and they will understand you perfectly. God, Providence, Soul—good old words, rather heavy, but expressive and respectable, which science will perhaps explain, but will never replace to advantage." Nor is the philosopher in the long run likely to find this language any more satisfactory. While using the term "validity," and finding himself compelled to use it, he will, nevertheless, feel tempted to add, with Professor J. A. Smith, "a term I do not like." Other philosophers have shared this dislike. Thus Royce, speaking of this very language and the point of view involved, asks: "The truth is, indeed, valid, but is it only valid? The forms are eternal, but are they only forms? The universal truths are true, but are they only universal? The moral order is genuine, but is it only an order? The concept of God is a necessary and valid idea, but is it only an idea?" For him the thought is intolerable—this indeterminateness. Can we really tolerate this view of reality as final? His answer is, "We cannot."[1]

This lack of finality does seem to inhere in the "standpoint of validity" as it is sometimes stated. If it belonged to it necessarily, this last state of philosophy would, indeed, be worse than its first. But there are ways of stating it which, far from being an attempt to avoid metaphysics, lead necessarily to it. Let us, then, attempt to state it again.

That value and validity "are no strangers to being," to use a suggestive phrase of Windelband, is now evident. The problem is whether we shall leave the relation between them

[1] Ruggiero also speaks thus of this lack of finality : "Value is a neutral concept oscillating between thought and being. Because of its neutral character, explanation of value is supposed to solve the problem of the relation between thought and being. But how are we to solve it? Since the neo-Kantians are unable to see in the categories anything except the simple fact of value, they have already exhausted its source. . . . They must, therefore, search for it in psychology and biology, and end in finding themselves in a position on which their own starting-point is a considerable advance." (*Modern Philosophy*, pp. 73–80.)

indeterminate, or whether, abhorring this lack of finality and following a natural bent of the intellect, we shall turn value and validity themselves into existences. We may do this, but if we do it, there remains nothing for us, we are told, but to give them some sort of *psychical* existence. "The systematic examination of the different fields of validity leads back to the valuing soul." In this case we seem faced with the alternative either of a return to the merely psychological account of values, or of resorting to a transcendental psychology with its concept of an over-individual subject. In either case we are back again in precisely those ontological prejudices which it was one of the chief objects of the doctrine of validity to overcome.

But do we need to turn these forms of validity back into existences? We need not, for the very reason that they have never been strangers to being; they have never, except by processes of abstraction, been separate from existence. The perceptual object, the æsthetic object, the historical happening, the moral act—what are these objects when the value element is abstracted? Things do not, indeed, have to be beautiful and good in order to "exist" in the narrow and abstract sense of that word employed by science. But things do have to be in relations of value, as well as in other types of relations, to be things in the full sense of our experiencing them as things. Certainly value never exists in isolation and we do not avoid metaphysics by talking of values *in abstracto*. Value has meaning only in connection with things, and validity has meaning only in connection with the communication of persons. But it makes a great difference whether we think of objects existing in their own right and incidentally possessing value, or think of their value as the very essence of their reality. If the latter view is adopted—and it is the only view possible if we are not content to identify reality with some particular ontological prejudice—we shall cease to contrast judgments of reality with value judgments in any absolute sense. Nor shall we separate ontological from axiological problems, for on this view the only truly ontological judgments are the axiological.

This notion—that the meaning and value of things is the very essence of their reality—represents not only the natural orientation of the human mind, but the true inwardness of traditional philosophy. Yet even when these things are realized, it is extremely difficult, if not impossible, to escape the feeling of an opposition between value and something which is not a value but which may possess it. A certain bent of our intellect, not the natural bent but one acquired as a habit, makes us think that there is something neither good nor bad, and making it good or bad is a value which thinking has the power to add. Value, then, becomes a predicate as opposed to the predicate of existence.

The point that is chiefly overlooked by those who would separate an independently existing object from its meaning and value is that the reality and unreality of objects in any purely empirical sense are as much the product of the activity of thought as the "value" of objects. The question, What is the real? we have found to be a futile question if being is abstracted from value.[1] In other words, the reality or unreality of objects will have to be called subjective, and, conversely, the value of objects must be admitted to be objective, in any sense that their reality is said to be objective, if, indeed, their being and their value are not in some sense the same thing. It may still be asserted that values are subjective and contingent, in the sense that they are valid only as the conditions of the world which the human mind knows, which is the object of its acknowledgment and communication. But, since nothing can be categorically affirmed or denied of any other world, the assertion is not so much true or false as meaningless. It is only within the world of human discourse and communication that any of these conceptions and distinctions have any meaning. Communication is the ultimate presupposition of any philosophy, and is above the distinction of idealism and realism. In such a world—the only intelligible world—the inseparability of value and reality is axiomatic.

Nevertheless, it is still not easy to keep this fundamental insight clear. The opposition between existence and value is the final and most persistent form in which dualism asserts itself. It was doubtless this fact which led ancient philosophy, despite its basal principle, *ens est unum, verum, bonum,* nevertheless in practice to treat value as secondary and as an attribute of existence. This dualism of fact and value is, it is

[1] In Chapter II, pp. 74 ff.

sometimes said, insoluble; the fact that value and validity are
no strangers to being, and yet opposed, is the final antinomy of
thought which, in the nature of the case, must remain unresolved. According to Windelband it is the "sacred mystery,"
marking the limits of our nature and of our knowledge.

Now, I have no desire to minimize the real mysteries either
of our nature or of our knowledge. Mysteries there are aplenty,
and without acknowledging them, without, indeed, a certain
"trenching on the mystical," there is no intelligible communication of our ordinary experience, still less of fundamental
metaphysical insights. On the other hand, there is no need to
magnify unduly the mystery of this relation of value to reality.
Let us see, then, what can be made of this most persistent of all
dualisms, this final paradox of philosophical thought.

We have seen that value and being, while no strangers to
each other, are not identical for thought and knowledge. For
all willing—and thought is a form of willing—the duality of
value and existence is an indispensable condition. If fact and
value were identical there would be no will and no event.
The innermost meaning of time is the inalienable difference
between what is and what ought to be. If there are any points
where these two come together, where they fuse in one experience—and I think there are—we can know them only by
trenching on the mystical, and can communicate our knowledge only in figures and symbol. That there are such moments
of insight is not only the constant deliverance of the general
consciousness of mankind, but also the steadfast faith of the
Great Tradition in philosophy. But while this identity is not
attainable for thought, the "axiom" of the inseparability of
value and reality is thus attainable. We have repeatedly seen
that to make any intelligible distinctions between the real and
the unreal—still more to communicate such distinctions—
presupposes mutual acknowledgment of values. In the very
conception of reality itself—of the "real thing" as contrasted
with the unreal—we experience, as Bosanquet says, not only
the positive quality of absoluteness, but also that this positive
quality *is* value. Not value, be it understood, as a mere
addendum to something which of its own nature is without
value, but value as of the very substance and essence of the
thing. It is at this point, also, that we realize that *the philosophy*

*of value is not a way to avoid metaphysics, but necessarily passes over
into metaphysics, when the nature of metaphysics is properly understood.*[1]

This is the main contention of this entire chapter. The
justification of this position will be the task of the remaining
paragraphs, its development in detail the programme of
discussions to come. The way opened up by this conception
of the relation of value to reality is, indeed, the path which
many of the "new idealisms" have followed—those of whom
I said earlier that they have been rewritten in an almost
wholly new language. It is, therefore, pertinent to ask whether
such a metaphysical position is necessarily idealistic in the
epistemological sense—and thus one of the sectarian views in
philosophy, one determined by an antecedent ontological
prejudice. To such a question our answer must be a decided
negative. The idea that value is not an addendum, but part
of the nature of the perceptual, the æsthetic, or the historical
object, may, to be sure, be based on the theory that reality
of any kind arises from an act of mind, and, since mind is
essentially purposive and as such oriented towards the good,
reality, as the creation of mind, will necessarily embody value.

[1] The line of thought which underlies this position has been so well stated
by Ernest Troeltsch that I cannot deny myself the pleasure of a quotation here.
In an account of the pilgrim's progress of his own thinking he gives a vivid
description of his own wrestling with the problem of value and validity. Although
principally concerned with its bearing on the philosophy of religion, his statement
of the problem, and the outcome of his own thinking as he presents it, are so
universal in their implications, and so nearly a picture of the stages through
which thought has generally gone, that they have more than ordinary significance.
For a time, he tells us, the merely psychological and phenomenological point
of view concerning value was sufficiently satisfying; but only for a time. Eucken's
metaphysical psychology was also for a time helpful, but could not long satisfy.
There was nothing for it but to sink himself in the anti-psychological theory of
validity of Rickert and Windelband. As over against the merely psychological-
biological point of view this was a means of clarification and rescue. But the
tendency of neo-Kantianism to make all objectivity a product of the subject,
and the transformation of reality into constructs of the subject, he found "the
opposite of every natural sense of reality." Here also something must be out of
order. With this the entire mass of ideas was set in motion again. The philosophy
of value and validity must somewhere be a transition to a metaphysics that must
be developed from it. The movement of his thought, as he confesses, is still in
process of becoming. That his present thinking, like that of so many who have
gone through the processes here depicted, is in the direction of the old form.
as represented by Leibniz and Hegel, is of secondary interest. The significant
thing is that the philosophy of value and validity leads back to metaphysics
(Ernst Troeltsch, in *Philosophie, der Gegenwart in Selbstdarstellungen*, vol. ii).

But it need not necessarily be based on this assumption. All that is necessary is to assume the priority of communication to *any* philosophy, whether idealistic or realistic, for intelligible communication presupposes this relation of value to reality. Any philosophy must, however, make this assumption. Communication cannot be explained by science, for it is assumed in the very nature and activity of science itself. It is precisely the characteristic of the position here developed that it is above realism and idealism in the epistemological sense, and it is for this reason that it has been the position of traditional philosophy which itself transcends this modern distinction.

VIII

To some readers of this chapter the technical aspects of the preceding discussion of the problems of value will seem too extended; to others they may well seem not extended enough. To the former I must say that this much, at least, was absolutely necessary if the further developments of the chapter are to be understood. To the latter I can but hold out the hope that further problems will be resolved in the chapters to come. One thing, at least, has, I think, emerged beyond question from this study—the centrality of the value problem in modern philosophy. Let us now turn to the significance of that central rôle.

This significance is both general and special. The general results of this change in the philosophical centre of gravity are making themselves felt everywhere in a gradual change in the conception of the nature and function of philosophy itself. The special significance is to be found in the gradual recognition that the problem of knowledge is itself essentially a value problem, and with the recognition of this fact the further realization that in a sense "ontology is a roundabout way of solving value problems," that the great systems of philosophy are value systems. This special significance we have already considered in the chapter on logic; the general significance will be the main theme of the chapters that are to follow.

One after another we shall take up the historic problems

of space and time, of origin and destiny and their traditional solutions. We shall examine the systematic structure of traditional thought and seek to reinterpret it in terms of this central conception. The remainder of this chapter will be devoted to a fuller statement of the general significance of this position and a defence of it against current criticism.[1]

It was a significant, if inadequate, expression of this point of view when Lotze, in the concluding chapter of his *Metaphysik*, says: "The true beginning of Metaphysics lies in Ethics." "I admit," he goes on to say, "that the expression is not exact: but I still feel certain of being on the right track, when I seek in that which should be the ground of that which is." Lotze rightly felt that the expression was not exact. Such an abandonment or modification of the exclusively ontological point of view was possible only with the recognition of "logical values" and of the value character of the theoretical.

But Lotze was at least certain that he was on the right track, and if our interpretation of the inevitable development of modern thought is sound, History has been most kind to him. Not only is it the path which a large part of the more critical philosophy has taken since Lotze's day; it is also, as I believe, gradually showing itself to be the only way out of the incoherence of modernism and the only way back to the perennial truths of traditional thought.

To say—even in Lotze's inadequate way—that the beginning of metaphysics lies in ethics, involves, to be sure, a quite different idea of metaphysics from that which has constituted the bogy of so much of modern thought. The notion of metaphysics as an unnatural movement of thought to an object beyond all experience, implies the notion that the

---

[1] The use of the terms "special" and "general" in this description suggests a similar distinction made in Einstein's theory of relativity. The analogy is not wholly accidental and by no means as far-fetched as it may seem. The similarity lies in the fact that the theory of value and validity, first developed in the attempt to solve the special problem of knowledge, finds a wider application in the solution of more general ontological or metaphysical questions. The change in the centre of gravity of thought which makes value and validity more ultimate than existence, involves profound reinterpretations of the entire "natural metaphysic of the human mind." It does not make this traditional metaphysic invalid, any more than the theory of relativity makes the Newtonian physics untrue. It reinterpets it.

intellect is directed towards pure being abstracted from value, whereas the natural metaphysic of the human mind has always been oriented towards value. Metaphysics is simply the systematic interpretation of experience with all its implications. The implications of experience are not to be described, in any condemnatory sense at least, as beyond experience, although doubtless the result of metaphysical analysis and interpretation is to show the impossibility of identifying experience with data abstracted from the transcendent values that give them meaning. The implications of experience itself include precisely those absolute values and validities which must be acknowledged if intelligible communication of our experience is to be possible. Lotze himself put this truth in memorable words when he said: "The apodeictic character of experience itself can be ascribed only to the good (value). Everything depends upon the fact that an ought is there that sets the play of thoughts, of ground, cause, purpose, etc., in movement." [1] Precisely this movement of thought constitutes metaphysics. Precisely this movement constitutes, as we shall see, the traditional form of philosophic intelligibility and of an intelligible world.

The revolutionary character of the line of thought expressed in the last sentences, as, indeed, in the entire value point of view in philosophy, must to a degree at least be admitted. So also a certain paradoxical element which is naturally very generally felt. So conceived, philosophy would, it is said, lose all scientific character. Philosophy is the work of the theoretical intellect or it is nothing. After all, values themselves must go back to a theoretical foundation. Unless they are to be mere subjective opinion, moonshine, they must rest upon propositions about reality, the truth of which must be independent of our valuations. Thus speaks "common sense," in this case through the mouth of Wundt, than whom, perhaps, common sense has no better spokesman. [2]

---

[1] *Metaphysik* (1841), pp. 374 ff. In the *Logik* (1874) also, p. 843, we find Lotze saying: "Wie der Anfang der Metaphysik, so liegt auch der der Logik in der Ethik, und zwar durch das Mittelglied der Metaphysik selber."

[2] Wundt's criticism of philosophy as "*Guterlehre*," in his *Einleitung in die Philosophie* (1901), pp. 37 ff., is, although one of the earliest, still in many respects one of the best. Its chief weakness is a failure to grasp the real meaning of the onception of the "value character of the theoretical."

Common sense will, perhaps, always find this idea paradoxical, and will always strive against such an interpretation of the ontological instinct. But common sense, though essentially sound, is also confused. There are other objections, much more critical, which, however, amount, I think, to the same thing. Value, when taken by itself, is, as Creighton has said, "no more a complete thought than existence." But when he goes on to say that "things when *clothed upon* with the category of value become more significant and in a sense more real," there still survives—in a more subtle form, to be sure—the old notion of value as a predicate added to being. I cannot escape the feeling that all the objections to the value point of view in philosophy, even in their most critical form (and I have examined many of them), are all really but a survival of the old idea of value as an addendum, and ultimately as merely psychical in character.

The reason for this survival, for this deep-seated reluctance to accept the primacy of value, arises, in the last analysis, from the feeling that to do so is, to use an expressive phrase of Cyril Walker, "to overload the value category," or, in Croce's words, "to base philosophy on something so unsubstantial as value." The feeling is natural in a sense, but it can be decisive only for a thinker who is really still immeshed in the subjectivism of the psychological point of view, who has not yet grasped the fact that our conceptions of and distinctions within being have significance only within a world of discourse in which values are already acknowledged. One cannot overload the value category when it is thus understood.

The elimination of these prejudices is so important for all that follows that I must, even at the risk of unnecessarily labouring my point, consider one other possible criticism of our view. Critics of the value philosophers have, in general, not sufficiently grasped their main thesis—namely, that, while it is possible to "reduce" truth and existence to value, the converse reduction is not possible. It is on this that the whole conception rests. There is one American philosopher, however, who hsa completely grasped the point and has seen all its implications. His criticism of this point of view is, indeed, the most understanding of any yet written, and may well serve as a means of bringing the whole issue to a head.[1]

Professor Sheldon recognizes the entire possibility of the reduction of existence and truth to value, but this reduction does not, he holds, forestall the converse reduction. It is, therefore, a choice between the "ontological" and the "value" points of view. "The only justification for our preferring either reduction lies in its fertility." On these grounds he himself chooses the ontological point of view. It will be worth our while to examine this position with some care. It will serve to formulate, and perhaps to solve, the last problem with which our conception of philosophy is faced.

Granting that a complete reduction of the categories of existence and truth to value is possible, "should the value attitude then replace the scientific and theoretical one?" Do we get a better understanding of the world when we put it all into terms of willed end, frustrated or fulfilled purpose— yes, even an impersonal *Sollen*? "Do we get a better understanding of the world when we put it in terms of value? Does it help us to see more of the make-up of the universe to regard it in value terms rather than in the cold impersonal way of the rationalists?" Sheldon finds that it does not. "It gives a correct, though inadequate, formulation of the panorama; so does the existential rendering. As far as results go there is no ground for asserting the primacy of either value or fact."

The discussion from which these passages are taken is in every way an interesting one, and one deserving of fuller quotation and worthy of consideration in detail. I must confine myself, however, to two points—namely, his recognition of the equal possibility of the two reductions, and, secondly, his reasons for the inadequacy of the rendering of the world in terms of value. The latter is in a sense the crucial point, but it is closely bound up with the first.

After all that has preceded we must, of course, deny the equal possibility of both reductions. It was, indeed, precisely Sheldon's own attempt to reduce value to being which we found to be patently circular in form. On the other hand, reduction of existence to value is, on Sheldon's own showing,

---

[1] I refer to the discussion of Professor W. N. Sheldon in his recent book *The Strife of Systems and Productive Duality*, chapter vi.

perfectly possible. In any case, he would have to admit with Cyril Walker that "there is much more basis for the sublimation of fact into value than for the reverse process of reduction of value to fact." But suppose we were to admit the equal possibility of the two reductions, which is the more fertile of the two? Do we get a better understanding of the world when we put it in terms of value?

For my own part I am sure that we do, but all depends here on what it is to *understand* the world. If by the "make-up of the world" is understood the discovery of some hypothetical stuff out of which the world is made, or if to understand that make-up is to generate it out of abstract universals, then clearly to view it in terms of value does not help us. But if, on the other hand, by this make-up is understood its intelligible structure—the relative significance of its various qualities and levels—then I am quite sure that we understand it better if we conceive it as a system of values and validities. In fact, as we shall hope to show, system *is* a value concept and cannot be formed otherwise than in terms of values.

Obviously this is a belief that can be substantiated only by the developments of the following chapters. Only after we have examined much more fully the whole idea of what it is to *understand* the world—what an "intelligible world" is—can we finally pass judgment on the value point of view. Only after we have seen this point of view at work in its interpretation of the world, can we determine its fertility or lack of fertility. We might, to be sure, make the point here that fertility is itself ultimately a value concept, and that in making fertility the ultimate and only test as between the two reductions or interpretations, Sheldon has already admitted the primacy of the value point of view. But this is after all, perhaps, merely another instance of the despised "dialectic," and it would not do to make too much of it. One serious misunderstanding of the value point of view must, however, be exposed and answered before we leave this subject: "Should, then," we are asked, "the value attitude replace the scientific and theoretical one?" The very form of the question exposes the misunderstanding that underlies many criticisms of this position. There can be no question of substituting one attitude for another. The value attitude is rather but the complete development of the scientific and theoretical. It is the very "value character of the theoretical" itself that makes philosophy ultimately value theory.

The conception of metaphysics as value theory here developed is, I have contended all along, the true inwardness of traditional philosophy put in a modern form. The deeper initiatives of speculative thought have always had their roots in that orientation of intellect towards value which, as we have seen, constitutes the primal and natural metaphysic of the human mind. A certain tendency to fall away from this view, to make value secondary and adjectival, has, indeed, always been present even in the great philosophers. But it was not the true inwardness of their thinking. Everything in their thought depends upon the fact that an *ought* is there, an ought that sets the play of thoughts, of ground, cause, purpose, etc., in movement. As we see this movement of thought, this natural metaphysic, unroll itself in the succeeding chapters, we shall become aware, not only how constantly they thought more truly than they spoke, but also how repeatedly in their better moments they become conscious of this orientation. For them the world is intelligible, and an intelligible world is always a world of values. For them our whole scheme of thought is *value-charged*, and this value-charged scheme is the *form* of an intelligible world. To the development of this general theme the following chapters are devoted.

PART II

THE RETURN TO PERENNIAL PHILOSOPHY

CHAPTER V

THE RETURN TO PERENNIAL PHILOSOPHY: THE CONDITIONS OF PHILOSOPHIC INTELLIGIBILITY

"Plus veritatis inest virorum egregiorum dictis quam vulgo putatur, etsi quid insit pervideri nequeat, nisi ea aliunde jam fuerint perspecta."

CHRISTIAN WOLFF

"Jede Philosophie ist notwendig gewesen, und noch ist keine untergegangen, sondern alle sind als Momente eines Ganzen affirmativ in der Philosophie erhalten."

HEGEL

I

WHO is there that does not envy the ages of Reason in philosophy? Who of us would not at times gladly exchange his hard-won intellectuality for the greater intelligence of the masters? All his complacent subtlety and sophistication for their larger simplicities?

One thinks of Plato. Of the irrecoverable joy with which he follows the natural light of a reason oriented towards the Good, of the almost equal confidence with which he follows the light of reason in myth and figure when the dialectic stumbles. One thinks of Aristotle—that great form that rose to speak the final word for Greek civilization—the essential inward truth of his "realm of ends"—the simplicity of genius that knew how to find right words for the relations of mind to matter, of life to thought, of God to the world—that genius which makes him still the master of all those who really know. One thinks of St. Anselm and of St. Thomas—of the "ontological argument," that masterpiece of magnanimous thought upon which the criticism of the minute philosophers has for centuries broken itself in vain—of the *doctor subtilis*, in whose catholic conception of reason subtlety was always subordinated to common sense—that sublimated *sensus communis* which is but the natural metaphysic of the human mind. One thinks of Leibniz, of Hegel, of all those who have thought the really great thoughts over and over again. One thinks of these men and a profound nostalgia assails the soul. We would go back,

back to the great masters of thought—much as we would go back to the great masters of music—back to certain irrefutable ways of thinking, back to certain intelligible and inevitable movements of reason which, like certain *motifs* of the great symphonies, permit themselves to be thought over and over again. For there is an "intelligible world"—there is an essential intelligibility, in art and philosophy alike, innate systems and relationships that are eternally right because in some way they embody that objectivity and universality which belong to the typical spirituality of the soul.

Once in so often, it appears, the world is brought by the multiplicity of man's thoughts and desires to such an intolerable state of confusion that he loses the power of coherent thought and even of intelligible expression. A sense of loss of essential intelligibility, it is surely not too much to say, underlies the unrest of our modernity. There are "tired radicals" in philosophy as well as in politics, and this weariness is but another word for futility. Exuberance of intellectual activity but covers fundamental poverty of thought, subtlety and brilliancy essential incoherence. I think it was Mrs. Fiske who said of a certain actress: "She has great intelligence, by which I do not at all mean intellectuality." The possibility of the divorce of intellect from essential intelligence and intelligibility is, alas! ever present in art and knowledge, as it is in life. A continual redefinition of reason and reasonableness is the price of real intelligence. It is this redefinition of reason, the rediscovery, as it were, of its true and original course, that constitutes, if I mistake not, the one great desideratum of the modern world.

Perhaps at no other time have men been so knowing and yet so unaware, so burdened with purposes and so purposeless, so disillusioned and so completely the victims of illusion. This strange contradiction pervades our entire modern culture, our science and our philosophy, our literature and our art. The same tendencies that have driven literature and the arts to the *nuance* and into the blind alleys of impressionism and psychologism, have driven thought and knowledge to relativism and pan-fictionism to a scepticism which has become decadent through its morbid association with an animal conception of the mind. It was Ibsen, I believe, who said of his compatriots:

"All these men had to fight their way to scepticism, and then to fight their scepticism." The fight against scepticism has been a losing battle. The modern sense of futility is a sign that we know that we have not been able to break through.

Modern thought has come to an *impasse*, and when one comes to an *impasse* there is nothing to do but to go back. In a sense, of course, we cannot go back. Thought is endlessly mediated. It is, in fact, precisely this idea of a return to the primitive that constitutes one of the illusions of modernism in many of its forms. Nietzsche said that he took a step backward only that he might make a leap forward. But the leap was not successful. He sought to destroy old values, but the new values never came. Speaking of the return to the primitive in art, a critic of the new art cries: "We cannot go back. To do so we must be either children or frauds." Nor can we really return to the primitive in thought—to any naïve realism, to any world of "pure experience," or to a pre-critical dogmatism. To one who has once tasted criticism, uncritical thinking is nauseous. The entire movement back to the naïve in thinking is as futile as it is tasteless. "Scepticism and Faith" is an honourable philosophical title, but when one changes it to "Scepticism and Animal Faith" we have one of those bizarre combinations in which, indeed, decadence delights, but one which, like so many of the intellectual dissonances that delight our modern ears, seems significant only because we have lost the sense for the deeper harmonies of thought.

In a very real sense, in the sense of such naïve reaction, we cannot go back. The only cure for sophistication is to be "twice subtle." Not one of the ancient forms of thought in which the masters achieved intelligibility, a *Weltanschauung*, but can be refuted and surpassed. The ontological argument of Plato and Anselm, the "principle of development" of Aristotle and St. Thomas, the whole conception of causality, of the identity of efficient and final causes, upon which the Great Tradition rests—every one of these forms of thought has been refuted over and over again. More than this, and this is of even greater significance, we no longer seek to refute them; we explain them and understand them.

Ah, but that is just the question. Do we really understand them? These ancient forms of thought, I repeat, are among the best-refuted things in human thought. And yet there is in them something that escapes all refutation, something eternal as the great works of art. It is for us to think these old forms over again, in a new way perhaps. Part of the natural metaphysic of the human mind, as they are, it is for us to find out wherein their essential and eternal intelligibility lies. In a sense we cannot go back; but in a sense we can and must. We must recover again the great initiatives of reason which we have lost. For with their recovery will inevitably come those forms of thinking which are perennial, for the reason that they are the only forms in which these deeper initiatives can find expression.

II

In these introductory paragraphs has been suggested briefly the task which shall occupy us in the ensuing chapters. We shall attempt to restate some very old things in a new way—to put that which is irrefutable in the Great Tradition in terms that are intelligible to modern thought. All that has preceded is, in a sense, but preparatory to this task. Whatever intrinsic value these studies may be found to have, their primary object is to furnish the background for philosophical reconstruction, or better, perhaps, to provide the philosophical idiom in which these ancient truths can now alone be adequately expressed. We shall achieve our end all the more surely if we restate briefly, in a manner more suited to our present purpose, the chief conclusions of these studies.

The setting free of philosophy's energies is, we have seen, one of the chief demands of all those attempts at reconstruction which we have described as "modernistic." This demand implies, however, that philosophy is somehow bound, suffering, perhaps from certain external restraints or internal inhibitions, and that because of these philosophy has been shut off from its true and natural bent, and compelled to revolve about phantom problems. This implication is, indeed, present in all forms of modernism, and our psycho-analysts of philosophy are more or less in agreement as to the sources of these repressions.

One of the most popular theories is that of the metaphysical "ghosts" which from the days of Plato and Aristotle have haunted the souls of the philosophers. "We have," writes a popular exponent of this ghost theory, "an uncomfortable and perturbing suspicion that much if not most of our philosophy and social science will be brushed aside by future generations as so much rationalizing."[1] What single sentence could conceivably express more completely the repressions from which the modern mind is suffering? This turning of the activities of reason into "rationalizing" in the dyslogistic sense of the word, the turning of all the necessary postulates and presuppositions of intelligible thought and its communication into prejudices—the fear of "animism" that has become almost an obsession, the "suppression of anthropomorphic tendencies" which has become little more than a euphemism for the suppression of all spiritual initiative: what but these are the sources of that *malaise* from which we are suffering?

A more responsible exponent of this same theory, John Dewey, also finds that "the hands of philosophy are tied." Philosophy will recover itself, he thinks, "only when it ceases to be a device for dealing with the problems of philosophers" (problems of ultimate reality) "and becomes a method cultivated by the philosophers for dealing with the problems of men."[2] In calling philosophy back to the genuine human problems the pragmatists have done a real service, only they have been singularly insensitive to the fact that it is precisely these problems of the philosophers that alone permanently hold the interest of men. The real interest, the divine *libido* of philosophy, has, to continue our figure, indeed been drained off from its natural movement and forced to consume itself in fruitless circular movements about phantom problems. *But the inhibitions have been of our own making.* Any philosophy that narrows the human reason to a mere pittance of its former self must by that very fact suppress its fundamental spiritual initiatives, and compel it to consume itself on insoluble problems. Any philosophy that contracts and degrades the

---

[1] A popular presentation of this ghost theory is found in J. Harvey Robinson's *The Mind in the Making*.

[2] John Dewey, *Reconstruction in Philosophy*, in which one of the chief contentions is that we must abandon the ghosts of Greek metaphysics.

intellect to a biological rôle must, instead of freeing it, end in enslaving it all the more completely. Enough that it does not understand the very spiritual initiatives that it would set free.

Pragmatism is the last philosophy to hope to speak the freeing word. Yet the pragmatist's diagnosis, though faulty, is not without its truth, and his cure, though worse than the disease, is suggestive. The abandonment of the exclusively ontological point of view for the point of view of value, which he proposes, is in the direction of the freedom from those inhibitions which an over-sophisticated intellectualism has fastened on philosophy. When we are freed from the obsession that the ultimate object of knowledge is pure being, abstracted from value, we are, indeed, freed from many of the repressions that this divorce has engendered and from many insoluble problems. With this position, properly understood, we have already expressed agreement. But the shifting of the philosophical centre of gravity from being to value must be still more radical than that conceived by pragmatism, if it is really to set philosophy free. It must involve the recognition of the deeper truth that the intellect itself is oriented towards value, and that the problems of the intellect are value problems. It must abandon once for all the idea that intellect thus oriented is "rationalization." It must learn that, in the words of Münsterberg, "the connected system of valuations is reason."

It is this, and nothing else, that was in the last analysis the burden of the preceding chapters. It was with this in view that we examined the so-called "prejudices of the philosophers," and developed a method of distinguishing between prejudices and necessary presuppositions. It was with the same end in view that we examined the concepts of genuine knowledge and *bonâ-fide* logic, seeking to determine the values presupposed in logic itself. Our definition of logic as a value science was a specific expression of this view. In a like spirit we examined the relation of value to existence or being, and sought to justify, as well as to interpret, the concept of metaphysics as value theory. It is not, as we insisted in the preceding chapter, a question of the value attitude replacing the scientific and theoretical. It is rather the recognition of the value character of the theoretical itself, with all that this implies.

Such a view, it is clear, does set free the deeper initiatives of reason. It preserves the vitality of the ontological instinct by showing that, though this instinct may often have misunderstood itself, its fundamental character is, nevertheless, grounded in the inseparability of reality and value. In seeking the true values of things it finds reality, for value is of the very essence or substance of that reality. On the other hand, it frees us from all those inhibitions which arise from narrow and *ex-parte* definitions of reality and truth, and thus sets free the deeper initiatives of the soul.

But this is only the beginning of a genuine freedom of speculative thought. There remains the re-entrance into the "intelligible world" of which the great masters of philosophy have always been the free citizens, the reinterpretation of those great forms of thought in which intelligible expression and communication have been achieved. Thus far we have attempted merely to show that the "prejudices of the philosophers," the spiritual initiatives out of which philosophy arises, are not prejudices but necessary presuppositions. That the world is a totality in some sense, that it has meaning, that value and reality are ultimately inseparable—these are not only assumed in all the great philosophies, but are presuppositions without which all thought becomes incoherent and unintelligible. But the great forms of philosophical thought have gone much farther than this. They have developed *rationalizations* of the universe which have become the characteristic forms of the great systems of philosophy. They have developed the great interpretative ideas of substance, cause, purpose, etc.—these ideas which modern criticism has banished from speculative thought. It is the idea of "value" which, as Lotze says, sets these ideas in motion, and it is this idea of value which, as we shall hope to show, gives the key to the intelligible world.

III

Philosophia perennis, the Great Tradition, as we have called it, contains the *form* of an intelligible world. It is this form, this essential structure—of which the fundamental lines remain

M

even when certain parts have fallen—that constitutes the ultimate goal of our interest and endeavour. But we must first realize that back of this form, this structure, lies a conception or ideal of intelligibility which gives this form its meaning and its truth. It is, we have seen, the loss of this sense of essential intelligibility that underlies the unrest of our modernity. It is of the first importance that we should understand that sense for philosophic intelligibility that the modern has lost.

The intelligible world has been variously conceived—as a world of "ideas," a realm of ends, a world of freedom, a kingdom of spirits. Only in a world of this general character, it is felt, can a life that is intelligible be lived. Whether thought of as a world of universals or of individuals, as a unity or a plurality, as a system or a hierarchy, however varied in detail, it is always, in the first place, set in contrast with a world of sense. But there is another constant character of the intelligible world. From Plato to Kant and Hegel it is always as a world of values that it is ultimately thought. For this very reason there are those who have not hesitated to see in it a world of the imagination. Thus F. Lange: "Plato would not see, as Kant would not see, that the intelligible world is a world of poetry, and that it is precisely in that fact that its value and worthiness consists." Plato would not see it and Kant would not see it, of course, for the simple reason that such a proposition is itself unintelligible. The inseparability of value and reality is the one constant character of the intelligible world, and a world in which they were divorced would no longer be intelligible. None of the great philosophers, it has been said, has ever doubted the spiritual character of reality; the difficulty has been to express that belief adequately. To be convinced that only a world of ideas, of ends, of freedom can be ultimately intelligible is one thing; to express that belief intelligibly is quite another. Philosophy deals ultimately with concepts, not with images and feelings; with propositions, not with intuitions. An intelligible world must accordingly be a coherent world.

The ideal of intelligibility, as it has functioned in historic philosophy, includes, accordingly, two distinct but closely related elements. On the one hand, there is the ideal of an intelligible world, an intelligible order, in which a life of meaning and significance can be lived. On the other hand, there is the ideal of intelligible concepts, of a form of philosophic intelligibility, in which this world, this order, can be adequately apprehended and expressed.

"The object of ancient science," says Lévy-Bruhl, "was to understand. Modern science limits its ambition to knowing." Nowhere is the sophistication of modern thought so completely shown as in this paradox of science: that it wishes to know, but not to understand; it seeks knowledge but not intelligibility. Whether such expressions are themselves ultimately intelligible, whether the human mind in its integrity can actually abandon the ideal of understanding, may well be questioned. In any case, the fact remains that understanding is the goal of philosophy. "The need to represent nature as intelligible," may, as Levy-Bruhl continues, have "been abandoned by science," although even in science, as we shall see, the need continually reasserts itself; but, so far as philosophy is concerned, the situation is clear. Faced with this self-limitation of science, integral human thought has but two alternatives. It can, on the one hand, keep the name of science and with science renounce all understanding, all real intelligibility, or, allowing science to go her own way, it can follow the deeper initiatives of reason, and demand of philosophy that deeper integration of experience which issues in the understanding and interpretation of its meaning. A long period of doubt and indecision has but served to make final the choice in which all modern self-critical philosophy has issued. If science renounces intelligibility, philosophy will make precisely this intelligibility its goal. If science proclaims itself *wert-freies Denken*, philosophy will in turn become the interpretation of meanings and values.[1]

[1] The distinctions between description, explanation, and interpretation are, accordingly, distinctions that philosophy has been compelled to make. It is the very artificiality of science itself that has forced these distinctions upon her. They are but part of the modern subtlety and sophistication which we cannot escape, but which we must surmount if a return to the larger simplicities of traditional thought is to be possible. For a simpler way of thinking, description and explanation themselves were inconceivable without understanding. For a mode of thought that finds it possible to divorce explanation and understanding, things must, in the words of Windelband, be conceptually described, genetically explained, and axiologically interpreted. "Knowledge," in the sense of conceptual description and genetic explanation, may well be possible and yet reality remain

The ideal of philosophical intelligibility differs alike from that of common sense and that of science. Science in the main says that it does not care to understand. Common sense, however, says that it already understands, that the world as given is intelligible. "What," asks Tolstoy, "can be more intelligible than the words, the dog has pain, the calf is gentle, it loves me, the bird is glad, the horse is afraid, a good man, a bad animal?"[1] To this question common sense has but one answer; there is nothing more intelligible. And, in a sense, the answer is true. The entire world of human social communication, of objects and persons—including the predicates we apply to them—has a certain intelligibility. Recurring impressions, familiarity, habit, do, indeed, breed meaning of a sort, a kind of primary intelligibility of common sense. To deny completely this intelligibility, to describe and explain, as science sometimes does, in such a way as completely to contradict the deliverances of common sense, is doubtless to court ultimate unintelligibility. Yet for science and philosophy alike this primary intelligibility, as we may, perhaps, call it, leaves much to be desired. It is just the difference in what they desire that is important—the difference between "knowing" and "understanding."

This primary intelligibility here described is for many the whole of intelligibility. A proposition is intelligible when the terms or words which make it up can be referred to an observability, something observable by the "outer" or "inner" sense. The propositions, "the dog has pain," "the calf is gentle," are intelligible because the terms denote objects that are recognizable in experience. The condition of intelligible communication is the mutual acknowledgment of this identity of reference. But the craving to understand is only partially satisfied by these identities of common sense. Beneath this world of common sense and its intelligibility are sought a

fundamentally and essentially unintelligible. Absolute physics, says Nietzsche, is intolerable. Yes, but it is more than that, it is unintelligible. If genuine intelligibility is sought, the essential function of philosophy must become axiological interpretation, and it is at this point that the distinctive ideal of philosophical intelligibility is to be found.

[1] Tolstoy's philosophical work, *On Life*, from which this and other quotations are taken, should be read, marked, and inwardly digested by anyone who wishes to know the difference between intelligible and unintelligible thought.

deeper unity, a real simplicity, a genuine continuity, which only conceptual analysis can attain. This is the ideal of scientific intelligibility.

Unity, simplicity, continuity, do constitute, as Boutroux says, a certain kind of intelligibility, the scientific; and for this reason many may argue philosophically, as he does, that "it is, therefore, no chance life of mentality that is manifested in scientific invention; it is the special life of an intelligence, of a reason that has a certain standard of intelligibility." For science, then, the gross and visible frame of things is not intelligible. In place of it is gradually substituted a finer and more invisible frame of an intelligible world. Yet this finer and more invisible frame is itself unintelligible. "The facts that serve the purpose of scientific orientation cannot," in the words of Mach, "themselves be understood. Our intelligence always consists in the reduction of unusual to usual unintelligibility." "As is usual in the case of great scientific advances," writes Professor Russell, the astronomer, of Einstein's theory of relativity, "it leaves us with a view of nature more complex and harder to understand than our preceding conceptions, but which at the same time introduces greater unity and continuity."[1]

Perhaps the limits of understanding are reached when we reduce unusual to usual unintelligibility. But the very fact that this unintelligibility is realized indicates, at least, that another ideal or order of intelligibility is acknowledged. Be that as it may, the recognition of a higher order than those of common sense and of science is a constant character of philosophy. The need to represent nature as intelligible may be renounced by science, but the need of making life, and the

---

[1] The nature of scientific intelligibility (?) here described is well brought out in a paper by A. S. Eddington entitled "The Meaning of Matter and the Laws of Nature according to the Theory of Relativity," in *Mind* for April 1920. "Whilst," he writes, "it is a reasonable procedure to explain the complex in terms of the simple, this necessarily involves the paradox of explaining the familiar in terms of the unfamiliar. Thus the ultimate concepts of physics are of a nature that must be left undefined. . . . The word æther brings before the mind the idea of a limitless ocean pervading space; but during the last century all the properties that would make the æther akin to any known fluid have been abandoned one by one." "There is," he continues, "no particular awkwardness in developing a mathematical theory in which the elements are undefined, but it is desirable that at some stage of the discussion we should get to know what we are talking about."

world in which our life is lived, intelligible to ourselves is the essence of philosophy.

Philosophy has always acknowledged this ideal; it has always been able to state more or less clearly wherein other notions of intelligibility are lacking; but it has not always been equally successful in formulating positively the conditions of intelligibility as it understands them. Nevertheless, there are three fairly constant "notes," if we may so describe them, which can be more or less definitely characterized. The first of these is *penetrability*.

"The world is not intelligible," says Renouvier, "until it is penetrable." Conceptual unity, simplicity, and continuity do constitute intelligibility of a certain sort, but the world remains as impenetrable as before. Indeed, the finer and more invisible frame of things which science builds up often seems to rob the world of that initial and primary intelligibility which it appears to have. All those "important and intelligible words," the bird is glad, the animal loves me, become ultimately meaningless. They cannot, as Tolstoy says, be defined in space and time. On the contrary, the less intelligible a thing is in the primary sense, the more exactly can it be defined in space and time. Who can say that he "understands" the law of gravitation according to which the motions of the earth and the sun take place? Yet the eclipse of the sun is most exactly defined in space and time. "Nothing," says Ravaisson, "is distinctly intelligible to us save as we can picture it in imagination." No relation of cause and effect, for instance, is *penetrable*, according to Renouvier, "unless it can be understood as something analogous to our own volitional activity. The concept of will alone renders that of force really intelligible. But will itself cannot be defined by anything more primitive."

It is doubtful whether any ideal of philosophical intelligibility can be formulated which does not include this notion of penetrability. Penetration into the inner essence of things, by ways other than that of abstract conception, seems to be the *sine qua non* of such understanding. But the ideal of intelligibility is not exhausted in this notion. According to an almost universal feeling, an intelligible world is a comprehensible world—comprehensible in the sense that "the ends of the world are brought together" in some unifying conception or insight. "Nothing is intelligible to us," Croce says, "unless it is contemporaneous." Intelligibility implies a reality fully presented to consciousness, an organized whole of experience, and this involves the ideal of an eternal present. On this view, anything is still unintelligible to us so long as the parts are external to each other. We have philosophically intelligible concepts only when they express concrete individuality. This *synoptic* character of genuine knowledge is recognized as a condition of intelligibility of objects *within* the world, and if there is any intelligible *world* at all our knowledge of it must also be of this character.

The world, to be intelligible, must be penetrable. It must also be comprehensible. But it must be something else to be really intelligible; it must be *livable*. This aspect of the philosophical ideal of intelligibility is difficult to characterize, but that is largely because it is so deep-lying; it underlies, in fact, all the others. An intelligible world is, as we have seen, in the last analysis one in which a life of meaning and significance can be lived. In a world ultimately impenetrable, ultimately incomprehensible, such a life is, indeed, impossible. But what makes a penetrable, a comprehensible world? Is it not finally and solely the fact that it provides the context for an intelligible life? Any life, to be intelligible, requires to be understood through the ideals or values by which that life is lived. But a world, in order to be an intelligible context for such a life, must also be one in which the values, by which the individual life is lived, have their counterpart in an order of values that is cosmic. This involves also the notion, first clearly presented by Kant, that intrinsic values constitute the key to an intelligible world, and that the separation of value from existence means ultimate unintelligibility.

In these three concepts is expressed the whole ideal of an intelligible world. What, we may ask, is common to these notions? They are at one, in the first place, in their dissatisfaction with the kinds of intelligibility that suffice for both common sense and science. Things must be practically manipulatable and conceptually describable, but they must also be axiologically interpretable. In the second place, they are almost equally at one in their idea of what this interpretation is. Interpretation, understanding, implies the attainment of *intrinsic intelligibility.* Whatever the method of its attainment—whether by an act of penetrating imagination, of integrating thought, or of moral postulation—it is always some ultimate essence, some internal meaning, in short, some intrinsic intelligibility, that is sought. It is of the utmost importance to understand and evaluate this ideal of an intelligible world. On the one hand, it is an ideal that has been inseparable from the Great Tradition in philosophy. On the other hand, it is the ideal which, in one way or another, most of modernistic philosophy denies. For the latter this ideal appears to be but a refined and sublimated animism—a reversed psychology, a reversed logic, or a reversed ethics—and with such question-begging epithets, it is supposed, the last word has been said.

The intelligibility which all these characterizations have in mind I have described as *intrinsic.*[1] I have chosen this term in order to contrast it with the intelligibility of common sense and science, which to a large extent remains external and *instrumental.* Intelligibility in this sense is quite different from that of mere familiarity, as also from that of conceptual description and explanation. Now, this notion of intrinsic intelligibility, so constantly present in traditional philosophy, is gradually being re-established in present-day thought. The idea of intuition and of an intuitive method in knowledge, whatever we may think of the use of so difficult and ambiguous a term, is a sign of this reinstatement. That there is no genuine knowledge of that which is living—still less of that which is conscious and personal—which proceeds wholly by the way of conceptual analysis, and which does not involve some intuitive grasp of totalities, of inner meaning and value, is almost a commonplace of the newer movements in the study of life and mind. The real question at issue is the extension of this ideal of intrinsic intelligibility to knowledge as a whole.

It is a commonplace, then, that in our knowledge of persons real intelligibility involves more than the mere familiarity of common sense or conceptual description and explanation. I say that I do not understand a man's acting like that. This does not mean that the act is one which I have not learned

---

[1] In developing this idea of intrinsic intelligibility I have found an article by Archbishop Temple, entitled "Symbolism as a Metaphysical Principle," and published in *Mind* for October 1922, extremely suggestive.

practically to identify with men; nor that it is not familiar to me with that familiarity on which I can base my actions. Nor does it mean that I am unable to give a psychological analysis nor explanation of the act. It means that I cannot put myself in the man's place, that I cannot imagine myself doing it. In other words, I cannot identify myself with the act; I do not acknowledge the purposes, meanings, and values which the act presupposes.

Such understanding, it is said, involves sympathy, sympathetic intuition, and this is true enough so far as it goes. The statement is not so much untrue as inadequate. That knowledge of other selves is primarily immediate and not a matter of inference, seems to me to be one of the most certain things in human knowledge, and the arguments for this immediate knowledge, like so much of philosophy, merely an elaboration of the obvious. It is the interpretation of that knowledge that is important. Elsewhere[1] I have sought to show that knowledge of other minds is simply the implication of acknowledgment of mutual values. We know that our fellows are real, and have an inner life of their own because they furnish us with meanings, our full meaning, our hidden reality. When we say that we know our own minds, if we know what we mean when we say it, we mean not that we know our own psychic states, but what we mean or intend. The only form of intrinsic intelligibility in connection with persons is "a will acting for the sake of the good," or, more generally, a will oriented towards values.

The necessity of such intrinsic intelligibility, is, I repeat, generally recognized in connection with the persons in relation to whom our lives are lived. Moreover, only through such understanding of others does our own life become intelligible to ourselves. Only that which is the centre of meanings and values has such intrinsic intelligibility. But it is also intelligibility of the same sort, I think, that alone satisfies us in connection with the "world" itself. The only linkage of facts

[1] "The Knowledge of Other Selves and the Problem of Meaning and Value," *Philosophical Review*, May 1917. Since the writing of this article this general position has been developed on a large scale, notably by Eduard Spranger in his famous book, *Lebensformen*, and made the distinctive method of *Geisteswissenschaftliche Psychologie*, a point of view characteristic of so much of German psychology at the present time.

that is really ultimately intelligible is one which is interpretable in terms of value. Any explanation, to be really intelligible, must somewhere in the chain of explanation involve the idea of purpose. Purposive activity, within our own experience, with its "links of intelligible connection," we in a very real measure understand, for we actually live through it many times a day. It is accordingly only in so far as the descriptions and explanations of common sense and science alike (which are essentially instrumental) retain a vital connection with intrinsic intelligibility that they themselves are intelligible. The only thing that is self-explanatory is a will oriented towards value. Any explanation to be intelligible—yes, even to be communicable at all—involves the acknowledgment of this orientation.

It is often said that intelligibility of this sort is not really demanded by the mind, and indeed, as we have seen, much of modern thought is apparently ready to renounce "understanding" in this sense. That such a limitation of knowledge is possible I have already ventured to doubt, and the reasons for this doubt will become clearer when we come to study the conditions of intelligible communication. Here it will be sufficient to repeat that even those who renounce such understanding have, by their very act of renunciation, already acknowledged what real intelligibility would be. The very fact that, as we have seen, the intelligibility of science consists only in reducing "unusual to usual unintelligibility" shows clearly enough that for science also genuine understanding of the world really implies something else. Such understanding may be impossible, but surely the mind demands it.

IV

The ideal of philosophical intelligibility here sketched is, of course, the driving force of all the great classical systems. Every such system is a universe of discourse in which it is sought to give adequate expression in terms of "philosophical concepts" to the meaning of a world common to all. It is for this reason that, as has often been suggested, we find a more familiar illustration of that insight which constitutes philosophy in the understanding of some part of the world with which we are more familiar, such as the circle of the home, or the life of a small community whose members have known each other long and intimately. In such situations, it is pointed out, the spirit of the whole is comprehended as the common life of which all the individuals partake. Of such is, indeed, philosophic intelligibility but the ideal limit. The participation in a common life which is the condition of understanding in these situations is the acknowledgment of identical values, and it is this, as we have seen, which constitutes the very essence, as it is the first condition, of intelligible communication. We are thus brought to the second of our main contentions—namely, that *intelligibility is bound up with intelligible communication*. In other words, the conditions of philosophical intelligibility involve the more ultimate question of the conditions of intelligible communication. We are led to ask the question whether there are not certain *criteria* of intelligible philosophical concepts, and ultimately whether there may not be some *form* of philosophical intelligibility in which alone the world can be intelligibly expressed.

Philosophers have the words "intelligible" and "intelligibility" constantly on their lips, but there are few words more ambiguous in their meaning. Except in the case of those thinkers who deny philosophy itself, intelligibility is the goal of thought. The philosopher seeks a world that is intelligible even when, as in the case of Schopenhauer, to be intelligible it must be irrational. He seeks to make his thought intelligible to the intellect even when he depreciates the intellect itself. The worst that one philosopher can say of another is that he is unintelligible.

Intelligibility, accordingly, whatever else it means, means intelligible communication. Interpretation is once for all, as Royce insists, the main business of philosophy. Even the question about the real world itself, the very distinction between appearance and reality, is "simply the question as to what this antithesis is and means." Such interpretation, however, and this is of the utmost importance, implies community of meanings, acknowledgment of identical meanings and values. Intercourse, communication, and the meanings and values they presuppose, are beyond all distinctions in philosophy, even the distinction of realism and idealism itself. They themselves cannot be "described" and "explained," for they are pre-supposed in all description and explanation.

The recognition of this principle is the beginning and the end of philosophical wisdom, because it is the condition of the understanding of philosophical intelligibility. Every philosopher —even the mystic—assumes this minimum of intelligibility and intelligible communication. It is not uncommon, however, for scientists to find the propositions of philosophers unintelligible, and philosophers readily reciprocate the compliment. Among philosophers the lack of a common idiom is notorious. Natural-istically minded philosophers find Hegel unintelligible; and it is no less frequently the case that propositions, which to positivism and naturalism seem to have meaning, are for critical philosophers little less than nonsense.

The primary meaning of the term "intelligibility" is, of course, simple enough; it has to do largely with verbal meaning. In the sense of using words that are understandable, intelli-gibility is incumbent upon all, as is the requirement that a man shall think logically, in the narrow sense, even when his philosophy is based on a disdain of logic.

Let us consider the idea of verbal intelligibility first. It may, I think, be identified almost completely with familiarity. A word is intelligible when we can equate it with experience, more particularly with perceptual experience. The simplest form of making a term intelligible is pointing to the object to which it refers. Thus the propositions, "the calf loves me," "the dog has pain," are completely intelligible. I understand the word "calf" because I have a familiarity through my senses with the objects for which it stands. I understand the word "love" because of a like familiarity with the state to which it refers. Yet the slightest reflection serves to show us that this is only the beginning of intelligibility. This practical intelli-gibility is only one of its various forms. The real problem comes when we put concepts or terms together in judgments. I say the dog has pain, the calf loves me. In these propositions I can convey meaning even to a Behaviourist in psychology. He understands the words, of course, and does not hesitate to use them. They have practical intelligibility for him also. Yet in the next breath he will make other propositions which, if they have any meaning at all, rob the first of all intelligibility. He will describe the dog, the calf, or even a man, as a machine. He will make propositions that implicitly deny that the calf loves me and that the dog has pain, for he will deny the existence of consciousness. The propositions which he thus employs likewise have verbal intelligibility. We know what they mean. To one who finds the whole of intelligibility in unity, continuity, and simplicity, to one who acknowledges these as the sole values, it would be quite intelligible to describe the calf, the dog, or even man, as a machine and to deny the reality of consciousness itself. Yet even the arguments designed to make consciousness superfluous admit, at any rate, that we know what consciousness is; and, as Laird says, "Anyone who denies this is beyond the pale of argument." Should he not, rather, have said, "outside the world of intelligible discourse"?

There are many propositions that thus have verbal meaning but lack all real intelligibility. If I say that love is lust, mind is matter, to be is merely to be perceived, it is always open to you to say, But that is not what I mean by love, by mind, and by being. Unless there is mutual agreement, acknowledgment of mutual meanings and values, intelligible discourse is impossible. Somewhere vital contact must be made with intrinsic intelligibility, or our judgments, our descriptions, and our explanations are really unintelligible. What, then, is this difference between verbal and real intelligibility? The difference is, I think, sufficiently clear. In all these cases the words themselves are, in a sense, understood, but they lack wholly the intrinsic intelligibility of which we have previously spoken. In a sense these judgments retain the meanings of the terms used, but in a very important sense—in the sense, namely, that they retain the values which these meanings presuppose —they do not. The first condition of intelligible communication is, then, the retention of the accumulated connotation of the terms used—and this connotation *always implies the acknowledgment of values*. To make a really intelligible proposition about a living being implies, for instance, that we shall, in the words of J. A. Thompson, "keep the category of the living intact." So also, if we would make intelligible propositions about love or mind, the community or God, we must keep these categories intact. There are, as we shall hope to show, certain categories which have this intrinsic intelligibility, and out of these alone a "form of philosophical intelligibility" can be developed.

This, then, is the first part of our thesis—namely, that there is a genuine, a significant distinction between verbal and real intelligibility, just as in an earlier connection we found a valid distinction between verbal and real definition.[1] There are "proper" meanings to terms, and this proper or intrinsic meaning depends upon purpose and acknowledgment of values.

This thesis is, indeed, challenged by that realistic line of thought which conceives of value as a mere addendum to existence. In order to carry out a logical atomism resort is made to a pan-objectivism which makes meanings themselves entities or qualities inherent in things. Meaning, it is said, for instance, is an ambiguous concept. On one interpretation it presupposes value, on another it does not. Meaning is sometimes synonymous with intention. My meaning is what I intend to convey, to communicate, to some other person. Now, intentions are, of course, intentions of minds, and these intentions presuppose values. But, it is held, the "facts" I intend to indicate have no necessary relation to the values implied and acknowledged in my intention. There is, then, a second meaning of meaning. When I say that such a perceived thing means so and so, this merely expresses a certain perceived state of the perceived facts, i.e. the way in which such fact or aspect of fact indicates something else in the facts. It is this second meaning of meaning that contains no implication of value.[2] Now, I must confess that such statements are to me wholly unintelligible. It is extremely difficult for me to understand how the perceived facts can indicate anything to me unless they have reference to some purpose or value, practical or scientific, that gives them their indicative character. It is even more difficult to see how I can convey this indication to anyone who does not appreciate and acknowledge the same purposes and values. Meanings and values are inseparable. To make meaning, in any fashion whatever, part of the perceived object, part of the reality of any object, involves making value part of the reality of this object. This is, indeed,

[1] Chapter III, p. 123.   [2] John Laird, *A Study in Realism*, p. 33.

the thesis I have throughout maintained, that value and reality are inseparable, and that to divorce them is the source of all philosophical unintelligibility. But this is also to say that intelligible communication and interpretation is the *sine qua non* of an intelligible world.

Let it be understood that we are here talking about intelligibility and unintelligibility, not truth and untruth. There is, indeed, a close relation between truth and intelligibility. An unintelligible proposition cannot ultimately be true. Probably such propositions as we are now considering are also untrue, but here we are concerned with their intelligibility.

The distinction between untruth and unintelligibility has sometimes been expressed in the following way. False propositions are those that do not correspond to existence, but have coherent meanings that might so correspond. Unmeaning propositions are those that not only do not correspond, but are positively incompatible with existence and reality. Thus, for example, it is false to say that human beings can live without eating; it is meaningless to say that ropes can be made out of sand or capital out of debts. Such propositions, as we have seen, have the grammatical form of propositions, and as such can be uttered verbally and understood, but they are unintelligible.

Now, that there is a genuine distinction here I am not disposed to deny, but I do doubt whether it is adequately expressed. Apart from the fact that it is made on the assumption of the correspondence theory of truth, itself an assumption of the nature of truth which need not be acknowledged, I find a certain difficulty in the definition of intelligibility as incompatibility with existence and reality. In a sense it is true, but it is inadequate for our purpose. In the propositions quoted, the terms "ropes and sand," "capital and debts," are incompatible with each other and with "reality." But what does this mean? All these terms have what I have called instrumental intelligibility. Ropes and capital, sand and debts, all get their meaning through their relations, positive and negative, to certain purposes and values which we appreciate and acknowledge. It is the acknowledgment of these that determines the conditions of intelligibility of the propositions. Real intelligibility, as distinguished from merely verbal, may be defined as compatibility with reality, but only if reality is conceived as inseparable from value.

This can be generalized, I think, to include all cases of real intelligibility and unintelligibility, both intrinsic and instrumental. To say, for instance, that "to be is to be perceived" is intrinsically unintelligible, has meaning only if, in making the distinction between being and non-being, appearance and reality, certain evaluations are assumed that are nullified by calling being and perception the same thing. The definition of unintelligible propositions as those which are positively incompatible with reality has meaning only if value be considered part of the reality of any object, so that separation of reality and value means unintelligibility.

The distinction between verbal and real intelligibility is a genuine one. So also is the distinction between real intelligibility and truth, although this latter distinction is only relative. But let us develop a little more fully the nature of this real intelligibility and unintelligibility. With this we shall be able to determine more precisely the relation of logic to philosophy which was stated in general terms in an earlier chapter.[1]

There is, we found, a certain incompatibility or contradiction between the terms of all unintelligible propositions. The nature of that contradiction begins, I think, to become clear. It is evidently something more than merely "logical" contradiction, if logic be taken, as it should be, in the narrow formal sense. Logical contradiction does, indeed, make propositions unintelligible, but there may be absence of such contradiction and the propositions still be unintelligible. Logicians have an expression, *contradictio in adjecto*. The contradiction they have in mind here is one in which incompatibility between subject and predicate destroys the meaning by an implicit denial. A round square is said to be such a contradiction, and also, it has often been held, is a "partial identity" (an identity is total or it is no identity at all). Such contradiction makes the proposition unintelligible. But the absence of this unintelligibility does not necessarily make a proposition intelligible. There is another type of unintelligibility involving a *contradictio in adjecto* of a different kind. This also is an incompatibility between subject and predicate which involves an

[1] Chapter IV.

implicit denial, but it is a contradiction which arises from the separation of the existence of an object from its meaning and value.

It is of the utmost importance that this point be made clear. To say that lust is love contains.no contradiction in the first sense, unless lust be made equivalent with not-love. "To be is to be perceived" is not contradictory unless to be perceived is made equivalent to non-being. Contradiction or incompatibility arises only because in our descriptions and explanations we have made use of predicates that implicitly deny the value, and therefore the reality, of the thing described or explained.

We have been trying to distinguish between real and merely verbal intelligibility, between the intelligibility that is conditioned merely by expressibility in logical form and a form of intelligibility not exhausted in fulfilment of logical demands. The question of real intelligibility, we now see, lies not merely in the terms, but arises only in the bringing of the terms together in a judgment. Deeper than any judgment, in the sense of merely bringing terms together in relations, is a reflexive act in which the judgment itself is claimed to be meaningful, and ultimately true or false. This claim, however, since its very existence as a claim depends upon the recognition of its meaning, involves the acknowledgment of the values which the meaning presupposes. Merely verbal intelligibility has to do with terms—with their familiarity, their reference to particulars. Real intelligibility has to do with the expression of meaning in the judgment.

All this constitutes but a fuller development of our general position as to the relation of logic to language developed in an earlier chapter. The two functions of language there discussed, that of naming (vocabulary) and that of judgment (involving syntax), are both subordinate to a still more ultimate function, that of communication or *expression*.[1] To call an object something which implicitly negates the meaning which it has when we pass a judgment upon it is to make intelligible communication impossible. To pass a judgment

[1] These three functions of language are studied by A. Marty in *Untersuchungen zur Grundlegung der allgemeinen Grammatik und Sprachphilosophie*, in which valuable beginnings of a philosophy of language are to be found.

on a thing that similarly implicitly denies the reality of the object upon which the judgment is passed, leads to a similar result. For both naming and judging are but parts of a more fundamental function of expression of meaning. The technique of intelligibility as embodied in logic (the condition, for instance, of absence of contradiction in the narrow sense) is, therefore, only one of the conditions of intelligible communication. There are other compulsions which arise out of the fundamental nature of communication, and it is these that we have been attempting to describe. Logic is *die Moral des Denkens*, but this morality of logic is but part of a much larger morality of communication. An intelligible world is a world of intelligible discourse or it is nothing.

We shall, perhaps, be allowed to call this the "higher" intelligibility, to distinguish it from the merely verbal and formal, or logical. In any case, such an ideal of intelligibility has been assumed, either implicitly or explicitly, by all the major philosophers, and insistence upon it has been a constant mark of the Great Tradition. It underlies the continuous use of the dialectic in one form or another, the essential principle of which is that an intelligible world is inseparable from a world of intelligible discourse.

Thus the fundamental character of the principle of self-refutation, by means of which philosophers have always sought to establish some constant meanings and values, is the acknowledgment of the existence of meanings and values which may form a common basis for intelligible communication. As used by them, this principle has never meant that a proposition refutes itself. The self-refutation applies to the enunciator of the proposition if by that proposition he intends to convey an intelligible meaning. It has been argued—and rightly—that the determinist, in denying all choice, makes it impossible to choose what is called truth instead of what is called error, and that the meaning of the distinction between truth and error itself vanishes. The utilitarian, when he so distends the meaning of the word "selfishness" as to say that a man is self-indulgent when he wants to be burned at the stake, is really talking nonsense. He may, indeed, give us an illogical kick, as Chesterton says, by using a bad word for what is better expressed in better words, but if we took him seriously, as fortunately we do not, all intelligible communication of moral meanings would cease.

In this connection I cannot forbear to refer to what seems to me one of the most flagrant violations of this principle of the higher intelligibility—namely, that which is to be found in some of the modernistic conceptions of God. The idea of "God in the making," more particularly of the "emergence of Deity," seems to me to be a perfect illustration of the "futuristic" types of construction to which I referred in the first chapter, and which seem to follow inevitably from the premises of modernism. Here I wish merely to point out that such a notion is really not an intelligible conception. *Verbally* understandable it doubtless is when we are told that Deity is the next higher level after mind. But it is *really* not intelligible; for if Deity is not yet here we have the contradiction of trying to express in that ancient term the meanings and values (religious) which it connotes, and at the same time denying the assumption of existence or reality on which those values depend. If, on the other hand, Deity is the next higher level after mind, the next higher level after Deity will not be Deity, and we have again applied the concept to something which denies the very meanings and values which the term connotes. This use of "weasel words," so characteristic of much of modernist thought, is but one significant phase of that general violation of the higher morality of thinking which is its constant feature.

V

It is necessary to cast but a glance over the history of philosophy to assure ourselves that the great philosophers have always insisted upon this "higher intelligibility." A second glance suffices to indicate that, for this very reason, disputes in philosophy have revolved mainly about the nature of philosophical concepts or categories. The ideal of philosophical intelligibility includes, as we have seen, two aspects. The first of these is penetration into, or comprehension of, the meaning of the world. The second is the adequate interpretation and communication of that meaning. Of these two aspects the latter is, if not the primary, at least the ultimately determinative. "The first and last condition of truly philosophical concepts is," as Croce says, "expressiveness. Lacking this, they in a sense lack all."

Philosophies are known by the categories they keep. All of us find ourselves compelled to talk—yes, to express our inmost meanings—in terms that cannot be made clear and distinct in the sense of analytical logic. Abstract definitions, spatial diagrams, etc., may be made thus clear and distinct, but who would say that such concepts as life, spirit, self, society, God, etc., can be reduced to transparent simples? Yet who would deny that the retention of these very terms, with all their accumulated intension, is precisely the first condition of intelligible communication between man and man? These are *expressive* concepts, and, in so far as intelligible communication and interpretation are considered part of the task of philosophy, philosophy must retain these concepts. An important dividing line between traditional philosophy and much of modernist thought is, accordingly, the retention or exclusion from philosophical discourse of such expressive concepts.

Philosophical intelligibility, we shall maintain, requires the retention of these concepts, and the grounds for this contention constitute the substance of this part of our study. We shall, however, understand better the development of our theme if we make a preliminary distinction between two types of philosophical concepts, the retention of both of which, however, is necessary for intelligibility. The first class is that from which the examples of the preceding paragraph are taken, and which may be described in the terms of one philosophy as "concrete universals." Life, the organism, personality, self— such terms as these are, indeed, universals. Interpretation, no less than description and explanation, is possible only through universals. That which distinguishes these universals is their expressiveness, their retention of the accumulated connotation of concrete experience. Another class of philosophical concepts is, however, equally important for intelligible communication. Substance, cause, purpose—these, too, are universals. Without them we cannot describe, explain, or interpret the world. Yet, in so far as by use of these deeper-lying categories we appear to achieve an intelligible world, it is only in so far as they too retain the accumulated intension of experience and resist analysis into logical simples. Both of these classes of concepts have intrinsic intelligibility. They are concepts in terms of which alone all others are to be understood. The second class of concepts must also be retained in all their original and living significance if intelligible communication and interpretation are to be possible. In the following chapter we shall, indeed, attempt to show that they are integral parts of a necessary "form of philosophical intelligibility" as such. For the present we shall confine our study to philosophical concepts of the first type.

The extrusion of these "concrete universals," these expressive concepts from *science*, is, as we should expect, a natural consequence of the limited ideal of intelligibility that science has constructed for itself. It is also, we are not surprised to find, the professed programme of all that part of modernist philosophy that accepts this ideal, and models itself more or less on the pattern of what it calls science. In the case of philosophies of this type, however, reasons are given for their extrusion which involve considerations of a more fundamental kind. The very use of these expressive concepts involves for this way of thinking a fundamental fallacy which has been called, not inaptly, the fallacy of *pseudo-simplicity*. In general, it is, of course, argued that this very ideal of intrinsic intelligibility is but the survival of primitive animism, cleverly and elaborately disguised in an epistemological form. On this general position further words are, perhaps, unnecessary. Let us examine it in the more technical form in which this position has found its clearest expression.[1]

The term "pseudo-simples" is applied to all those terms, concepts, universals, by means of which philosophy seeks to retain, communicate, and interpret the meaning of our more "integral" experience. On the assumption that the essence of knowledge is analysis, that, in Herbart's words, "the leading principle of all metaphysics and logic is that reality is simple," it is proposed to rule out as pseudo-simples all those concepts

---

[1] This fallacy, and others connected with it, are conceived by the modernist to be the source of the prejudices of traditional philosophy. We have already considered it in connection with the relation of logic to language. We shall later consider it in its relation to allied fallacies (in Chapter VIII).

and categories that lack the clearness and distinctness of logical simples. The problem raised by such a proposal is, to be sure, in principle the same as that which appeared in connection with our discussion of the relation of logic to language, and must in principle be solved in the same way. Of the two functions of language there considered—of naming, or vocabulary, and of syntax—that of vocabulary here involved is the more primary. The expressive concepts here under consideration are, indeed, *names* which we give to integral experiences. Just as when we use the particular name "Socrates" we suppose that there is a more or less persistent being to which the name applies, so here, when we use the universals described as concrete, we assume that they express a more or less persistent meaning which we must retain if the real nature of the reality to which they are applied is to be expressed. Thus the charge that the "fallacy of pseudo-simplicity consists in confusing the simplicity before analysis with the simplicity after analysis" is wholly untrue. There is no confusion here; the difference is well enough understood. It is rather a deliberate and conscious retention of these unanalysed simples, because those who retain them insist that for intelligible communication they *are* simple whatever they may be for the more specialized, and in a very real sense arbitrary, purposes of science. They insist that if we do not retain them in their integrity, the propositions in which these terms are used, although verbally understandable, will lack real intelligibility. In terms with which we are now familiar they will contain that inner incompatibility, that form of *contradictio in adjecto*, which consists in separating the reality of an object from its meaning and value.

None of these concepts—such as life, personality, etc.—is simple in the sense of the radical analyst. None of them but is capable of being analysed into elements of which no vestige of their original meaning is retained. In what sense, then, are they simple? In the sense, I think, that they are *value concepts*, or, at least, have a value connotation that cannot be eliminated without the loss of their essential meaning, and, ultimately, of the intelligibility of all discourse in which the terms are used. By calling them value concepts I mean two things—in a sense different but ultimately closely related. They are value concepts, in the first place, because, to express any meaning, they presuppose certain values which must be appreciated and acknowledged. Whoever uses them assumes, in their very use, a world of discourse in which identical meanings and values are acknowledged as the condition of the very subsistence of that world. They are value concepts in the second place, because, as we shall see, the objects which they represent or express have meaning and value as part of their very nature or reality.

Let us examine briefly the concept of life—that concept upon the significance of which so much depends in any attempt to conceive an intelligible world. Even in the limited biological sense of the term it is really simple, and the condition of its retaining meaning is the acknowledgment of certain values. "The word life," says Tolstoy, "is intelligible to all, not because it is very accurately defined by other words and concepts, but because, on the contrary, this word signifies a fundamental concept (category) which alone makes many other concepts and ideas understandable. And so, if we wish to do this, we must above all accept it in its central indubitable meaning." This is particularly true of "life" in its human sense. But even in its limited biological meaning life includes, at least, the concepts of growth, generation, survival, development. These terms have significance, however, only with reference to a totality, an organism, which the survival or growth *concerns*. Except as conceived as a centre of values, values realized in the process of growth and survival, the living organism has no meaning, and "life," as applied to it, is unintelligible. Try to apply the concept of life to something not conceived as a centre of values. We do, indeed, speak figuratively of the "life" of a machine, but even here it is only by thinking of it as an instrument for the realization of human values that the term has any meaning.

What is true of life in the narrow biological sense is *a fortiori* true when the concept is extended to cover psychical and "spiritual" activities. Indeed, as Tolstoy continues in the paragraph quoted, "I cannot present life to myself otherwise than as a striving from bad to good." This is its "central and indubitable meaning," the application and acknowledgment of which alone make other concepts and ideas associated with it intelligible. But this is, of course, as he says, precisely what has been overlooked in many of the descriptions and explanations of life. The "centre of life is completely transposed"; it is reduced to non-value terms, with the result that we have an ultimate "nonsense." What has been said of the concept of life itself applies equally to such concepts as those of personality and State, which are terms representing forms of life in this sense. All are centres of values, and when otherwise conceived are unintelligible.

Life, and such other integral concepts as personality and State, are simple because they are "value concepts." They are value concepts, in the first place because the use of them in intelligible discourse involves the acknowledgment, on the part of those who use them, of certain values, without which they are meaningless. But there is a second sense in which these so-called pseudo-simples are genuine simples. The objects which they "represent" have meaning and value as part of their very reality.

To show this in the sphere of the human and historical sciences has now become a work of supererogation. That an element of selection or "value reference" is the very material of these sciences itself is now a commonplace. We may, indeed, compare two styles of art or two forms of the State wholly impersonally and quite in the spirit of the most rigorous science —as impersonally as we may compare two minerals or two types of vertebrates. But who is any longer naïve enough to think that he can form the concept of *style* itself without reference to æsthetic values, or concepts of *the State* without reference to moral and social values? These values are woven into the very texture of the material itself.

But is this truth any less certain in the non-human and non-historical sciences? We may compare the growth and development of two organisms or two species in a wholly impersonal way, but who again is naïve enough to think that we can form these concepts of growth, survival, etc., without reference to a centre of values? Value is already an element in the "material" with which the science deals. We can no more have the concept of organism without this value reference than we can have a body without the category of substance or a happening without the category of causality. For my own part I think the same holds also of the inanimate world, in so far at least as anything like real time and "direction" is included in our picture. The concept of "degradation of energy," I agree with Oswald Spengler, makes of physics a science in which the material can no longer be called *wert-frei*. The concept may, indeed, be figurative, but it cannot be constructed, much less retain any intelligible meaning, without reference to distinctions which imply values. Be that as it may (and this last point is scarcely necessary for our general position), the fact remains that the concepts with which we are dealing are value concepts, and for that reason are simple.

All of which must serve to make it clear, I think, that the term "pseudo-simples" as applied to these concepts is a question-begging epithet of the most unpardonable kind, and rests upon an assumption as to the nature of genuine knowledge which is wholly gratuitous. The advocates of radical analysis, it should be said, do not all carry their empirical atomism to its logically complete conclusion. Dr. G. E. Moore modifies it in a way especially interesting in the context of this present discussion. He asserts that, although wholes are not to be regarded as organic unities from the point of view of existence, they may well be so regarded from the point of view of value. In other words, he says that the whole is not organic in the sense that the part implies the whole and reflects its nature, yet it is organic in the sense that the value of the whole is greater than the value of the sum of the parts. Only from the point of view of existence, not from that of value, can the whole be accounted for by an analysis of the parts. Here, then, is the crux of the whole problem. If reality, existence, can be divorced from value without contradiction, then that form of analysis which neglects this element can give us genuine knowledge of reality. If, on the other hand, the divorce of the reality of a thing from its value leads ultimately to unintelligible propositions about the thing, then genuine knowledge is possible only in terms of those concepts which retain the meaning and value of wholes. "To attempt to understand the simpler entities in terms of their complex aggregates," says one representative of radical analysis, "is the vice of latter-day philosophy, by which I mean idealism." But to assume that these wholes are merely aggregates is to assume the whole point at issue. It is an assumption, moreover, which, as we have seen, ultimately makes intelligible communication and interpretation impossible. Whatever else logic is, it must be, at least, the etiquette of intelligible thought, *die Moral des Denkens*. This, many of the representatives of the New Logic seem wholly to have forgotten.[1]

VI

This discussion of philosophical concepts leads us to the question of a philosophical language as such, of the *Language of Metaphysics* as it is employed in the Great Tradition in philosophy. Into this question we shall go more fully in the next chapter. We shall attempt to show that there is such a language, a metaphysical idiom as it were, which alone makes intelligible communication possible—an idiom, moreover, which embodies or corresponds to a necessary "form of philosophical intelligibility." Our general thesis throughout this and the following chapter is, indeed, that this tradition alone speaks an intelligible metaphysical language, and alone communicates philosophic truth. Up to this point, however, we have been chiefly interested in discovering the sources of the unintelligibility of so much of the language of modernism, and of the deep-seated incoherence of which that unintelligibility is the expression. In other words, we have been interested in the nature and conditions of philosophical intelligibility as such.

In developing this theme we have connected the standpoint of modernism with a certain conception of science which more or less definitely renounces the ideal of an intelligible world— and with it the notion of intelligibility—as they have been understood by historic philosophy. I have no intention, of course, of suggesting that all scientists take this point of view. Even in science there are those who still wish to understand, and in so far as they do, they recognize, consciously or unconsciously, the conditions of intelligibility upon which we have been insisting. Of these an enlightening instance is that of J. A. Thomson, who, in his *System of Animate Nature*, takes as the cardinal principle of an intelligible interpretation of

[1] See Chapter III, pp. 116 ff.

living nature the acknowledgment of the living organism as a centre of meanings and values, and the retention of the category of the "living" intact. From this point of view he criticizes equally, for instance, mechanism and vitalism as attempts "to explain everything in terms of something else, which in essence amounts to the denial of the organic beings which we actually see and deal with." This is obviously in principle but a recognition of the thesis that the organic unity which wholes have from the point of view of value must be retained in any intelligible interpretation of existences. It is, however, also an acknowledgment in principle of the point of view from which "idealistic" philosophy in its various forms exercises its critique upon science.

Even more in the sciences of the spirit—the *Geisteswissenschaften*—is the number of those who wish to understand increasing. Of the sciences of psychology, sociology, and history, it is scarcely too much to say that they are all more or less face to face with a methodological crisis. Sooner or later all will have to face the question whether they shall keep intact the special categories that belong to these fields of reality, or abandon them for the categories that belong exclusively to the physical sciences. The fundamental motive of that entire recent development of psychology in Germany—of which Eduard Spranger's *Lebensformen* is so brilliant an illustration—is precisely the demand that we *shall* understand, shall make intelligible and interpret, the fundamental forms of the human spirit. Nor is it surprising that such understanding should include precisely the penetrative and synoptic *notes* of intelligibility that we have described, and that understanding of these life forms should be conceived as possible only through the "values" which constitute the determinants of these integral forms. In any case, the number is increasing of those who realize that to abandon these value categories means to accept the principle of the rénunciation of all real understanding.

But such a desire for intelligibility can, of course, seem only a weakness to those whose chief claim to distinction is that they have the strength to renounce it. Yet to anyone not blinded by the prejudices of the moment it must be clear that there are certain elements of comedy in the present situation. Surely it must be clear to most of us that there are limits to the amusing game of calling things other than they are. These limits have certainly been reached—and, indeed, long since passed—in some of the more extreme interpretations of the theory of Behaviourism in psychology. One cannot go on long denying the existence of the very things he is talking about without risking the laughter of men and gods alike. Still less can one reduce all language, even all science itself, to mere biological forms of behaviour (at the same time claiming the truth of one's own theory), and still expect to be taken seriously.

This latest chapter in the story of the human mind is a chapter in logic, but also, if logic is *die Moral des Denkens*, one in the higher morality. The desire to understand—to interpret things in terms of that which is intrinsically intelligible—has, indeed, begotten many and gross anthropomorphisms at times. But the most comical lapses—even the crudest of pan-psychisms —are philosophically harmless in comparison with the errors of reduction and over-simplification. The latter cease to be merely comic; they form rather a dismal chapter in the tragi-comedy of the human mind. "These monomaniacs," says Chesterton in his brutal fashion, "are logical as the insane man is logical." We need not allow ourselves pleasantries of this sort, so ill-befitting the philosopher. It is quite sufficient for the philosopher that he finds them outside the field of intelligible discourse.

It is the violation of these conditions of intelligibility that, as we suggested at the beginning of this chapter, underlies the intolerable state of confusion and incoherence to which the modern mind has come. Are we ever to work our way out of it? Who shall say? Forces surely are at work, and gathering with significant power, that are demanding an entire reconsideration of the premises of our most recent thinking. There are those who, like Professor Whitehead, believe that these forces are rising in science itself, and that science will again demand intelligibility. Perhaps they are right. Of one thing, however, we may be certain. Even now we are fully aware that we are ever so much larger and better than the philosophies that seek to express us. Even now, as we read the great masters of philosophic thought, we feel not only that we are much more at home; we feel also that we know our-selves better, and our world more truly, than as they appear to us through the eyes of the moderns. We know ourselves better for the "living reason" with which they envelop us than by merely looking into the polished logical mirrors that do but reveal the meaningless detail of existence. We know the world more truly for that it is, at least, an intelligible world —not merely a chaos of lucidities or a meaningless passage "out of nothing into nowhere."

This growing realization, this more profound conviction, cannot much longer be stifled. Nor can a return to the genuine spirit of philosophy be much longer delayed.

CHAPTER VI

THE FORM OF PHILOSOPHICAL INTELLIGIBILITY[1]

How unfailingly the most diverse philosophers always fill in again a definite fundamental scheme. . . . Something within them leads them, something impels them in a definite order, the one after the other—to wit, the innate methodology and relationship of their ideas.

NIETZSCHE

An irresistible attraction continually brings the intellect back to its natural movement, and brings the metaphysics of the moderns continually to the conclusions of the Greeks.

BERGSON

AN intelligible world, a *mundus intelligibilis*, we have said, is the world in which the masters of human thought have lived and moved and had their being. Their "grandiose and primitive schemes" may not, indeed, meet the more complicated problems of modern times, but there remains something in them that is irrefutable, something to which the mind returns again and again, as it returns to the simplicity and lucidity of the greatest works of art.

We may now see, I think, wherein the essential intelligibility of traditional philosophy is to be found. The insights of the great thinkers remain perennially significant for us because in general they fulfil the conditions of philosophical intelligibility. Consciously or unconsciously, they acknowledge those postulates and presuppositions, that *Moral des Denkens*, without which intelligible communication and interpretation are impossible. More particularly, in all their descriptions, explanations, and interpretations they retain the meaning and value of things. The one thing that they all understand is the difference between explaining things and explaining them away.

This much is obvious to anyone who has lived himself into those ways of thought that we call classical. The further question naturally arises whether this philosophical intelligibility does not involve something more, whether retention of the meaning and values of terms, the keeping of the fundamental

I am indebted for this expression, as indeed for much of the impulse to write on this subject, to the valuable paper by Professor J. E. Creighton, under the same title, and published in the *Philosophical Review* for May 1923.

categories of interpretation, does not imply also some specific, *structural form*—whether, in short, there is not some natural metaphysic of the human mind which generates a form of thought innate in intelligibility as such? Whether, finally, violation of this form does not result in essential unintelligibility?

To this question our answer must be, I think, in the affirmative. All world views that are intelligible have a specific form which is *a priori* in the sense that it develops necessarily out of the attempt to interpret and express adequately in the form of reflection the meaning and experiences of life. The form of an intelligible world is determined directly by the conditions of intelligible communication and interpretation. The mere fact of the existence of such a form, of a *philosophia perennis*, which, despite the controversies of the sects, remains relatively constant, is, I think, one of the most certain facts of human thought. It is our task now to develop that form and to show its validity.

I

There is, as Bergson has made clear to us, "a natural metaphysic of the human mind," a form of reflection in which alone the world seems to us to be made intelligible. To him, at least, it seems clear that it is a form to which everyone will come if he follows the intellect to its natural conclusion. His greatest service to philosophy, perhaps, as I have indicated elsewhere,[1] is the cogency with which he has made the alternative clear—between following out that natural metaphysic of the intellect, or turning our backs upon it and renouncing intelligibility for intuition. Let us look, first, at this natural form.

The starting-point of this natural metaphysic is the riddle of life, the burden of this unintelligible world, the problem alike of the highest poetry and the deepest philosophy. The similarities between philosophy and meditative poetry, so interestingly worked out by Dilthey, arise from their common starting-point and the form which it necessarily generates.

[1] "Origin and Value," *Philosophical Review*, September 1923.

In both, the apprehension of objects in the life process, of the gross and visible frame of things, forms the basis for reactions upon these objects, for distinctions between appearance and reality, the changing and the permanent, and ultimately between the true and false, the worthy and the worthless in the world in which our life is lived. In place of the gross and visible frame each seeks a finer and more invisible. Both seek an intelligible world, although in different ways. But when, as in the case of the philosopher, a complete solution of the riddle is sought, reflection predominates over emotion, expression is taken up into system, and the natural metaphysic assumes a logical structure and form.

This natural metaphysic is, I repeat, present alike in the highest poetry and the deepest philosophy. Their common problem dictates a common form. It finds significant expression, for example, in Matthew Arnold's lyric, *The Buried Life*:

> But often in the world's most crowded streets,
> But often in the din of strife,
> There rises an unspeakable desire
> After the knowledge of our buried life.

Thus the "metaphysical instinct"; then sometimes, "but this is rare,"

> A man becomes aware of his life's flow. . . .
> An air of coolness plays upon his face
> And an unwonted calm pervades his breast
> And then he thinks he knows
> The hills whence his life rose
> And the sea where it goes.

Perhaps he only thinks he knows, but unless he knows, his life and the world in which that life appears remain wholly unintelligible.

The essential form of metaphysical knowledge appears in these last lines; origin and destiny have always been necessary parts of the form of philosophic intelligibility. All questions of life revolve around the problems of generation, development, and death, of beginning and end. Life is unintelligible unless expressed in these concepts and the form of reflection they generate. Without them, without this *life form*, the meaning of life is unrealizable and incommunicable. We cannot think of life except as a centre of values, except as a movement towards the good. No intelligibility without finality. But it is equally true that we cannot think finality without origin. Origin and destiny are the same thing seen from two different points of view. The essence and meaning of a thing involve both. To penetrate to, or comprehend the meaning of, life is impossible without these concepts. Intrinsic intelligibility involves this form.

But this is only the beginning of the natural metaphysic of the human mind. To bring the ends of the life process together is the condition of its intelligibility. But the life process is part of a larger context, and to make life itself intelligible the form of reflection must be extended to the cosmos as a whole. No intelligible theory of our own existence is possible that divorces it from this larger context; that divorces our duration from the context of eternity, our place in the cosmos from its infinity, man from his context in the totality of things. But can we make this larger context intelligible? Can we bring the ends of the world together?

This is the problem that life itself sets. It is also the problem that generates all the significant and difficult questions of philosophy—the technical problems of space and time, of causality and finality, of philosophical system itself. It may be that the world is not penetrable, not comprehensible. It may be that the ends of the world cannot be brought together, that all attempts to bring them together, as in the speculative insights of the great systems, are but "rationalizations." None the less must they be brought together if there is to be any intelligibility in the philosophical sense.

In any case, we have here, as Bergson says, the "natural metaphysic of the human mind," that to which everyone will come if he follows the intellect to its natural conclusion. Thus it is, as he continues, that the identification of efficient and final cause is not only the last word of Greek philosophy, but together with the concept of being it implies, the essence of the traditional form of intelligibility. We perceive God or Idea or Spirit as efficient or final cause according to the point of view, and it is this insight that alone makes the world intelligible for reflection. It is for this reason that an irresistible attraction continually brings the intellect back to its natural movement and brings the metaphysics of the moderns continually to the conclusions of the Greeks.[1]

II

The nature and conditions of philosophical intelligibility constituted the theme of the preceding chapter. The results of that discussion may be summarized briefly as follows: The ideal of intelligibility and of an intelligible world includes two distinct but closely related elements. On the one hand, there is the ideal of an intelligible world or order in which a life of meaning and significance can be lived. On the other hand, there is the ideal of intelligible concepts, of forms of reflection, in terms of which this world can be adequately apprehended and expressed. It was the second problem that chiefly engaged our attention, for the reason that the first is ultimately reducible to the second.

The detail of that argument need not be repeated here. It must suffice to recall the main points. All intelligibility ultimately goes back to intrinsic intelligibles. The only thing that is intrinsically intelligible, however, is a will oriented towards values. Intelligibility in its lowest and simplest form already presupposes communication, and communication presupposes acknowledgment of identical meanings and the values which these meanings presuppose. There is no type of meaning separable from value. The conditions of intelligibility are the conditions of intelligible communication, and the conditions of intelligible communication are the acknowledgment and retention of the meanings and values of things. To separate reality and value means unintelligibility.[2]

---

[1] H. Bergson, *Creative Evolution*, English translation, p. 329.

[2] The basal character of communication in philosophy is also emphasized by C. Delisle Burns in his recent book, *The Contact Between Minds*. "Communication, then, which somehow rests upon meaning, is a kind of reality which is ultimate within the world of minds: and, as a relation between minds, cannot be reduced to or entirely explained by the terms of that relation, for the relation is not its terms and the terms are not their relation" (p. 73). Mr. Burns recognizes that awareness of values is bound up with communication and contact of minds, and that it is in the mutual enjoyment of values that we apprehend the reality of other minds. He recognizes that values "are not distinguished from other realities

Philosophies, we accordingly said, are known by the categories they keep. The first and last condition of truly philosophical concepts is their expressiveness; lacking this, they in a sense lack all. The condition of intelligible communication and interpretation is the retention of the meaning, the value, and the *reality* of the things to be explained and interpreted. It is unnecessary to recall here the ways in which these conditions of intelligibility are violated—how the mania for reduction, for calling things other than they are, has led to the abandonment of categories of description and interpretation without which intelligible communication is impossible. It is equally unnecessary to recall the significance of the "concrete universal" as a logical formula for these expressive concepts, or our arguments to the effect that such concepts are genuine simples, as against the charge of logical atomism which thinks to find in these concepts the fallacy of pseudo-simplicity. Let us recall, rather, here the kinds of concepts or categories that a philosophy must keep if it is to be intelligible.

In our discussion of philosophical intelligibility and philosophical concepts we distinguished two classes of such concepts. On the one hand there are those which correspond to organic wholes, such as life, personality, the State; and on the other hand those deeper-lying categories, such as substance, cause, purpose, without which the interpretation of these organic wholes is impossible. So far as the wholes themselves are concerned, our contention was that the meaning and value of the whole are greater than the meaning and value of the sum of the parts, and, since these values and meanings are inseparable from the reality of the whole, they must be retained in any concepts which shall adequately describe and interpret it. This is the first condition of expressive concepts and the beginning of philosophical intelligibility. But it is only the beginning.

Description is but the first step to explanation and interpretation. Things must be conceptually described, genetically

by the actual contact of minds in the perception of them: for this contact is universal and necessary in all mental activity" (p. 97). Even perception has no meaning without communication. Yet for some reason he fails to see that the distinctions between existence and non-existence, reality and unreality, themselves also arise in and presuppose this communication. He insists upon a pure contemplation of existence apart from communication, and thus preserves a brute realism at the cost of an unintelligible dualism.

explained, and axiologically interpreted. Description passes insensibly into explanation and explanation into interpretation. No description is intelligible which does not retain the meaning and value of the thing described—as part of its reality. No explanation really explains which in essence amounts to explaining away the meaning and value of the thing explained. All explanation, if it is to be ultimately intelligible, must eventuate in axiological interpretation, for it is only in this "higher intelligibility" that any genuine understanding, intrinsic intelligibility, is found.

One has merely to realize the implications of these statements to see that a further step in our thinking is involved. To keep intact the categories of intelligible description, these expressive concepts, *involves keeping intact also the categories of explanation and interpretation, the categories of cause and purpose, of substance and essence.* They are interpretative, as well as descriptive and explanatory in the narrower sense. Retention of their intrinsic intelligibility, their value connotation, is part also of the conditions of intelligible communication.

With such a conclusion, if it is justified, we should be led back, it is immediately apparent, to the natural metaphysic of the human mind, to that form of philosophical intelligibility which emerged in all the freshness and lucidity of Greek thought, and to which the mind, unless it renounces intelligibility completely, must in one way or another constantly return.

It is not necessary to hold that the language of this metaphysic, as worked out by the Greek genius, is in all points final. Many statements of this "form of intelligibility" have been, if not actually refuted, at least surpassed in various ways. What we do insist upon is rather this: that it represents the natural and inherent movement of thought as such; and in so far it contains an element that is irrefutable. Reconstruction, reinterpretation of this form, may be necessary, but to turn our backs upon it entirely means that our thought, and the language in which that thought is expressed, must ultimately become unintelligible. This reconstruction or reinterpretation is the task of the following chapters. The present chapter is concerned rather with the examination of this form in its more general aspects.

III

The vigour and intelligibility of traditional thought are due in large measure to its following the natural metaphysic of the human mind, and therefore to the retention, in all their full-blooded meaning, of the fundamental categories of substance, cause, purpose, which belong to that metaphysic. Yet these categories have also been classed by the modern radical analyst as pseudo-simples, and banished from the polite conversation of the "minute philosophers"—with the result that philosophy has been shorn of the very concepts that have hitherto made communication possible.

There is little doubt, I think, that these fundamental forms of human thought have become largely lifeless and meaningless. The ordinary consciousness understands by them, as Lossky says, "something living and real, something that has in it no merely intellectual significance." By substance, for instance, is understood the ultimate core of being, the independent individuality; by causation we understand activity, expenditure of energy. When critical analysis gets through with these concepts no trace of their original living significance remains.

It is entirely natural that modern logical atomism should be eager to give to these dead and dying concepts their *coup de grâce*. On this view, they are but survivals of that primitive animism that infects all our natural thinking, of that mythology which sticks in all our language. They represent earlier stages in the natural evolution of thought; why not abandon these earlier stages entirely for the survivals they are? We have already seen the fallacy that underlies this very popular line of thought.[1] The assumption that the "improvement of thought" for certain purposes involves necessarily the abandonment of earlier forms is no more valid than the assumption, for instance, that the development of language itself demands the complete displacement of gesture or any other non-verbal means of communication. "Does anyone really believe," asks Maeterlinck, "that by means of mere words any real communication can pass from man to man?" Similarly we may ask, Does anyone really believe that by means of words from which all intrinsic meaning has been banished the actual meaning of

[1] Chapter III, pp. 118 ff.

things can be communicated? Does anyone believe that concepts which are devised merely to control phenomena necessarily give their nature also?

The actual situation is quite the contrary. The development of "scientific" concepts, far from displacing the more primitive, only shows the latter to be the more indispensable. The universals of science, it is now generally admitted, are nothing more than possibilities of describing things, the utility of which depends largely, if not solely, upon the ease with which they allow the phenomena in question to be manipulated. In the case of the great scientific universals, such as inertia, mass, element, atom, energy, etc., the one and only question is the degree to which they enable us to achieve the specific scientific ideal of simplicity, unity, and continuity. But a world so conceived is not necessarily intelligible in any other sense, as we have already seen. It may even become progressively more impenetrable, more incomprehensible and unlivable. The very perfection of scientific language (which is, after all, only language well made—for a certain purpose) may serve but to make it all the more incapable of communicating the original and living significance of things. The extrusion of the deeper-lying categories embedded in natural language means not only the loss of philosophical intelligibility, but also of the *primary* intelligibility of the every-day consciousness. The primary intelligibility of these deeply-lying categories has also been ascribed to their humanly practical character. This also is true. But while they are more human and practical than their scientific substitutes, they are also more metaphysical. To these categories all philosophical reflection and interpretation must ultimately return. Only in terms of substance or essence as the ultimate core of being, of causality as efficient and final activity, of restless becoming and self-contained being —only in such terms can the mind apprehend and communicate the meaning of its own life, and with it the meaning of the world in which that life is lived. In fine, the language of metaphysics must contain these expressive concepts if it is to be intelligible, and it must retain them in their vigorous and full-blooded meaning. Much of modern philosophy has been talking "weasel words," from which all genuine meaning has been sucked.

It is of the utmost importance that we should make our position on this question entirely clear. It is but a further development of our general position on the relation of logic to language. As we have maintained that it is impossible to divorce logic from natural language, so here we maintain that no logic can banish the fundamental metaphysical categories of this language without ultimate unintelligibility. As the traditional formal logic, conceived as dealing with the universal relation of predication, is neither excluded nor superseded by any specific calculus dealing with more specific relations, just as little are the traditional metaphysical categories either excluded or superseded by any more specialized language devised for certain specialized purposes of science. In maintaining this position it is, of course, not necessary to deny that a constant criticism of language is necessary. Still less is it necessary to maintain that these fundamental categories are immune from criticism. Speculative and logical difficulties enough cluster about these notions which, we may admit, are not necessary for "science" in the narrow and sophisticated sense of that word. The fact that they are part of the necessary form of an intelligible world does not, of course, dispense the philosopher from the obligation to make these concepts themselves intelligible. What we do maintain is this: that while criticism is necessary, no criticism is valid that suppresses the original initiatives out of which reflective thought arises. Logic is reflected thought. But all that is reflected presupposes the spontaneous. The reflected cannot negate that on which it rests; it may only clarify it and determine its true direction.

In later chapters we shall consider the speculative difficulties in these notions which have been exploited by the various modern logics, realistic and idealistic alike. It is sufficient here to make clear the general position. Of one of the elements of the form of intelligibility, namely finality, Bergson has well said that "it will never be definitely refuted," that "if one form is put aside it will take another; it is very flexible." This is true of all these concepts; they are all very flexible. The real question is as to the limits of this flexibility. The limits of the reconstruction of these notions by logic, whether realistic or idealistic, are determined by the fundamental fact that logic, whatever else it is, is *die Moral des Denkens*—and that this morality has as its first law the mutual acknowledgment of meanings and values, and the retention of the categories in which these meanings and values are expressed. The destructive criticism of a too intellectualized logical monism may, so far as these categories are concerned, have much the same result as an equally over-intellectualized logical atomism. Both may reduce them to appearance and illusion, with the result that the form of philosophical intelligibility falls apart.

IV

The retention of the original and living significance of these categories is, accordingly, the condition of philosophical intelligibility. The reason for this is the same reason that bids us retain the living significance of the things to be explained. To separate the value of an object from its nature is contradictory. Not otherwise is it with these deeper-lying categories. They too, in the last analysis, are categories of interpretation, not merely of description and explanation. To use them intelligently we must realize that everything depends upon the fact that an "ought" is there, that sets the play of thoughts, of ground, cause, purpose, etc., in movement—that interpretation is throughout a *value-charged scheme of thought*.

That this is so, the whole body of philosophical tradition witnesses. The "natural light of reason," to use Descartes' words, tells us that the ultimate cause must contain *eminently* all the reality, meaning, and value of the effect. The less can be derived from the more, never the more from the less, *e minimo maximum non fit*. These axioms, as Nietzsche with his usual insight tells us, are the typical prejudices by which the metaphysicians of all time can be recognized. This is part of the natural metaphysic of the human mind. The intellect is ultimately oriented towards value, and this orientation requires that the "sufficient reason" of any reality shall retain the reality of the thing to be explained.

Now, the meaning and value of anything (and therefore its nature) can be expressed only in terms of purpose or finality. Consequently its ultimate origination, its *sufficient* reason, requires that this element of finality shall in some way be included in the notion of cause or ground. Causality and finality must in some way be brought together in a more ultimate concept. Thus it is that if we seek to bring the ends of the world together, if we seek to make our life and the world in which it is lived at all intelligible, there is necessarily generated this form of intelligibility. It is the only form that has *intrinsic* intelligibility.

To this natural metaphysic of the human mind, I have said, the whole body of traditional philosophy bears witness. To this "form of intelligibility" modern thought, I believe also, shows signs of returning. It is interesting to observe that even science, when it seeks to understand, is forced back to this form of thought. J. A. Thomson has expressed himself in a significant way on this question. Speaking of the question of *epigenesis*, he says: "In so far as this view (the traditional) means that there is nothing evolved which was not in kind originally involved, that there is nothing of lasting value in the end which was not present in kind in the beginning, it is acceptable."[1] Elsewhere he says it is the only intelligible view. Whatever science when it becomes philosophical may say, for philosophical interpretation itself it is the only intelligible form. Lloyd Morgan voices the same general conviction in his *Emergent Evolution* when he distinguishes between causation and causality. With an "intelligible causality" science may have nothing to do. But "philosophy throughout the ages has had very much to do with it."[2] Without such metaphysical causality the *nisus* implied in all evolution cannot be understood.

V

Thus far we have maintained two things: first, that the fundamental metaphysical categories, substance, cause, purpose, are all necessary parts of one value-charged scheme of thought; and, secondly, that this form is the essential principle of all traditional philosophy. Our general position may be made clearer by examining a recent and typically modern attempt to interpret these metaphysical categories in terms

[1] *The System of Animate Nature*, p. 169.   [2] *Op. cit.*, p. 289.

of value. I refer to the original and enlightening effort of William James to develop the pragmatic method into an instrument of philosophical interpretation. For him also these categories are value concepts, but in contrast to traditional thought he attempts to separate the notions of origin and destiny, and ultimately to divorce all problems of value from problems of being. In distinguishing what seems to me to be the element of truth from the element of error in this modern interpretation, we shall be enabled to make the traditional position stand out all the more clearly.

James explicitly recognizes a world of interpretation and a type of philosophical intelligibility different from that of common sense and science. Under the heading "Some Metaphysical Problems Pragmatically Considered"[1] he takes up successively the alternatives, materialism and spiritualism, mechanism and teleology, determinism and free will. On his pragmatic principles, it will be remembered, he argues that these alternatives are irrelevant from the retrospective, scientific point of view. Any decision, preference, for spirit, free will, monism, purpose, "have as their *sole* meaning a better promise for the world's outcome. Be they false or be they true, the meaning of them is their meliorism."

James's own decision on these great alternatives is itself interesting. In the main he chooses those characters which the great philosophers have always found inseparable from an intelligible world. It is not this aspect, however, that chiefly interests us. It is rather *why* he chooses them. And here the answer is clear enough. It is only in such a world that a life of significance and meaning can be lived; only such a world is intelligible. But wherein does this intelligibility consist? The meaning of these categories lies in their meliorism. In other words, the question of the truth of these metaphysical concepts cannot be separated from the question of their value. Nay, more, their truth lies wholly in their value—their practical value.

This reinterpretation of the traditional problems of philosophy is as original as it is fascinating, and has naturally elicited a great deal of interest and comment. An attempt such as this, to dissociate questions of meaning and value from

[1] *Pragmatism* chapter iii.

questions of being, has naturally disclosed itself to most thinkers as the interesting *tour de force* it really is. But the recognition of this fact should not be allowed to obscure the important half truth in James's conception. The complete meaning of these metaphysical concepts does not, it is true, lie in their meliorism, their practical value, but an important part does. A still more important part of their meaning lies in their value, if value be freed from its purely practical associations. For description and explanation, in the narrow and sophisticated sense of the word, these metaphysical questions are, indeed, as James says, irrelevant. In a world in which certain values were not already acknowledged it would be immaterial whether the world had its origin in matter or spirit, whether there were freedom or pure determinism. In a word, these conceptions are really significant only for interpretation, and interpretation presupposes communication with its acknowledgment of values.

This partial recognition on the part of James of the conditions of philosophical intelligibility is something for which modern thought owes him much. If in the enthusiasm of his genial insight he was led to the extravagances of thought we now realize, we may, perhaps, recognize them as necessary incidents of new ways of thinking. But the *tour de force* is patent. In attempting to separate destiny from origin, thus renouncing the traditional form of intelligibility, he was simply attempting to combine incompatible ideas. What it really means, of course, is that an attempt has been made to combine philosophical intelligibility with ontological agnosticism, to make the world intelligible and livable despite its ultimate impenetrability and incomprehensibility. And *that* must for ever remain impossible. To separate the nature of things from their meaning and value means, as we have seen, unintelligibility, but it is no less true that to separate their meaning and value from their nature comes to the same thing in the end. The essential incoherence of James's thinking—from any standpoint but the most popular and limited—is now apparent in many connections. Perhaps it is at this particular point that this incoherence reaches its maximum—a point, moreover, at which, as in a flash, the essential unintelligibility of much of modernism can be seen.

VI

This examination of a famous but futile attempt to keep the spirit of traditional metaphysic, while breaking with the form in which that spirit has inevitably embodied itself, should serve, at least, to give force to our main thesis—namely, that there *is* such a necessary form of philosophical intelligibility. It should also serve to make clear why the simple mind always finds this form intelligible, and why the tired philosophical radical, when he becomes "twice subtle," tends to revert to this ancient form.

All this will become clearer, however, if in the light of what has preceded we now examine two aspects of philosophy which have been fairly constant elements in traditional thought, but which modernism has in the main considered it its duty to suppress. I refer to the so-called *a priori* and speculative features in traditional philosophy, features which the human mind could not conceivably seek to deny except as it misunderstood their real character and the true nature of its own activity. Certainly in the constant use of this form it is always assumed that there is something *necessary* in it, and that in following it we achieve speculative insight into the ultimate nature of reality.

Speculation in the bizarre and imaginative sense has, indeed, as it has been truly said, passed largely from philosophy to science. It is now generally recognized that it is not the business of philosophy either to prove that the world exists or to show how it is made. Its task is not to show us how to make a world, but to help us to understand the actual world in which we find ourselves. Nevertheless, all this modesty on the part of philosophy, becoming as it doubtless is, may be so interpreted as to give aid and comfort to its worst enemy— that form of criticism, namely, which seeks to suppress all its deepest initiatives. Those who insist that to understand the world we must be able to deduce it logically are doubtless asking impossible things of philosophy, but the fact remains, however we may interpret it, that the masters of philosophy have uniformly sought to communicate their insights into the nature and meaning of the world in the form of speculative deduction. It is, therefore, of the utmost importance to understand just what is the significance of this fact, what is true and what is false in the notion of speculative philosophy.

What is here understood by speculative deduction may be well illustrated in a statement of C. S. Peirce, to the effect that "the one intelligible theory of the universe is that of objective idealism, that matter is effete mind, inveterate habits become physical laws." However crude we may find this description of objective idealism, we may, perhaps, understand why Peirce should call it the only intelligible theory. But that is not what first interests us in the statement. It is rather a more ultimate assumption underlying the statement, that *any* intelligible theory of the universe must involve deduction, derivation of the world in some sense—in short, intelligible causation.

It is not difficult to see what *our* interpretation of speculative deduction must be. On our view of the value character of the ultimate metaphysical concepts such deduction can mean only one thing—namely, axiological interpretation, or, in other words, the placing of things in an order of meaning and value. The first condition of such interpretation is giving the privileged position to something. The whole idea of intelligible causation with its axiom of derivation—that the less can be derived from the more, never the more from the less—is but a development of this notion. The idea of a privileged position is inherent in the notion of value as such. If the interpretation of experience leads us to the dichotomy of matter and spirit, that same demand for interpretation requires us also to give to one or other of these notions the privileged position. Which of these *should* be given this position is a problem for later discussion when we have learned what the dichotomy means. The only point that interests us here is that such position must be given something, and that it is out of this necessity that speculative deduction arises. That such notions of speculative deduction, ultimate derivation, need not be conceived in temporal terms has always been clear to traditional thought. The genesis of which it speaks may be an "ideal genesis," but some genesis, some derivation in the sense described, are inevitable.

These statements are unquestionable, and are, indeed, borne out by every attempt of the most modern philosophy to make itself intelligible. Bergson may deny intellect in favour of intuition, but an "ideal genesis of matter" which shall in some way be apprehended by the intellect becomes necessary if the import of this intuition is to be matter of intelligible communication. So New Realism, if it is to be more than a mere polemic against traditional interpretation, if it is to be an intelligible world view, must itself become speculative and deductive, and such a book as *Space, Time, and Deity* is the result. If space and time have not their genesis in Deity, Deity, if it is to be kept in the circle of our ideas at all, must have its genesis in them. Some element of deduction is, I repeat, involved in any intelligible world. We may merely analyse and describe, and a certain limited intelligibility results. We may explain genetically, up to a point perhaps, without giving any aspect of reality a privileged position, and a certain further increment of intelligibility appears. But somewhere, if there is to be any real intelligibility, axiological interpretation must appear; a privileged position is given to something, and speculative deduction necessarily enters in. Or it would be truer to say, perhaps, that something *has* been given a privileged position from the beginning, axiological interpretation is present from the start, only the sincerity to acknowledge it is lacking. All evolutionary naturalisms, for instance, of whatever type, are in the last analysis speculative deductions in this sense, only the normal and traditional order of interpretation is reversed.

Every attempt of the most modern philosophy to make itself intelligible ends, I repeat, in speculative deduction of some form. The only question is whether the form it takes is itself intelligible. According to Peirce, objective idealism is the only form that is. Now our present problem is not whether this is actually so, but rather what is *meant* by calling it intelligible at all, or the only intelligible form. Surely, it will be said, the attempt to deduce matter from mind has been as complete a failure as the converse deduction. Surely the attempt to reduce the not-self to the self is as futile as any of the reverse reductions. It is entirely possible, for instance, to say that any such idealistic theory as suggested by Peirce is merely reversed psychology, reversed logic, or perhaps reversed ethics, and these, if one cares to use such expressions, may all be classed as forms of animism, "amiable" or otherwise. Objective idealism may be, from one point of view, but an hypostatization of values as first cause, as ultimate end, or as immanental essence or substance to which both cause and end are reduced. But what of it? To say these things is to stop just where the real problem begins. The real problem is rather this: *why do such reversed movements of thought appear to make the world intelligible, while the other movements do not?*

It is at this point, I think, that the significance of the form of speculative deduction, and the distinction between the true and the false in that form, first come to light. Why do the idealistic movements of thought appear to make the world intelligible, while the others do not? I should answer unhesitatingly, because by the character of that to which such movements of thought give the privileged position, they express, always more or less inadequately to be sure, the true meanings and values of things. I do not agree with Rickert that "ontology is *merely* a roundabout way of solving the value problem," but it is at least—and perhaps first of all—*just that*. And it is this for the reason that, as we have already seen, the only form of thought that has *intrinsic* intelligibility is a value movement of some kind. In the last analysis, perhaps, the only thing that we immediately understand is a will acting for the sake of the good. But for our present purpose it is not necessary to go so far as this. It is enough to insist that speculative deduction, evolution, or devolution, some form of movement along the value scale, is the form which any interpretation of reality will inevitably take. Only in such a form can the meanings and values of things be communicated. Such a movement can, however, really be *thought* only in case the *nisus* of the movement is expressed in terms of activity, in terms of an intelligible causation. In so far as this means that there is nothing evolved which was not originally involved, that there is nothing of lasting value in the end that was not present in kind in the beginning, it is not only acceptable, as Thomson says, but the only form of thought that is intelligible.

Speculative deduction is, then, the necessary form of the communication and interpretation of the meanings and values of things. For my own part I believe that the great philosophers have all instinctively recognized this, and that all have thought better than they spoke. As Plato and Plotinus both instinctively distinguished between that which was philosophy and that which was myth in their thinking, so Fichte and Hegel were wholly aware of the element of figure in their generation of concrete reality by the dialectic. All of them, if we take them at their best moments, express themselves with reasonable sense and intelligibility. One of these best moments was that in which Fichte, *à propos* criticism of his laborious attempts to deduce the Non-Ego, or object, from the Absolute Ego, or bare subject, with which he starts, tells us that "he never attempted what would be comparable to writing a man's biography before his birth." He tells us, in other words, that he has not been narrating what ever took place, but attempting to give an interpretation of reality in its distinguishable but inseparable aspects and moments. It was Hegel who said, in the *Encyklopädie*, that "Nature must be regarded as a system of stages or degrees in which one necessarily proceeds out of the other, *not, however, in such a way that one is necessarily produced out of the other*, but in the inner idea that constitutes their ground or nature."[1] Shall we ever get over the *naïveté* of thinking that the great systems are descriptions of what is supposed to have taken place? As though such description of the sequence of phenomena were the beginning and end of intelligibility! Shall we ever understand that the great philosophers are not quite the naïve people we in our own simple-mindedness have taken them to be? That they have the desire neither to make a world nor to re-make it, but rather to understand it? Shall we ever learn what the language of metaphysics really is?

VII

Speculative deduction, as we have now come to understand it, is, then, the necessary form of the communication and interpretation of meanings and values of things, and for the reason that the meaning and value of things cannot be separated from their nature, the necessary form of an intelligible world. To make the world intelligible we *must* bring the ends of the world together in some concept of ultimate reality, and this means philosophic system. The introduction of this word "must" leads to our second question—namely, that of the *a priori*

[1] § 249 (Kirchmann ed., p. 208).

element in this form of philosophical intelligibility. This is in a sense the most important part of this chapter—the contention that the traditional form of thought is the *necessary* condition of philosophical intelligibility.

The word "must" has, indeed, a most unmodern sound. "Must," it is said, "was made for human beings in the relation of superior to subject. It has no place in science, though the science of man takes account of the 'must'." How can any-one nowadays speak of an *a priori* form of an intelligible world? We point to the incalculable element in reality, and ask how any one can presume to say that the world must be so. We point to the story of the mind, of the "mind in the making," and ask how such a mind could presume to dictate an eternal form. We ask, finally: Why any necessity of a really intelligible world at all?

To answer the first question—yes, even to understand it—we must begin with the more ultimate question: Why any necessity of an intelligible world at all? And here we must admit, as has indeed been admitted in the preceding chapter, that such necessity may always be denied. One may be content with mere living, with mere immersion in life. One may be content with merely external description, with the limited concept of know-ing to which so much of modern science has accustomed itself. From such extra-philosophical standpoints it is undoubtedly a *petitio principii* to demand a form of philosophical intelligibility, or, indeed, an intelligible world at all. Yet even in mere living a *minimum* of meaning and value is assumed; still more, in merely external description a *minimum* of meaningful com-munication is presupposed. In these purely extra-philosophical standpoints a demand for an intelligible world is already presupposed. When once this demand is acknowledged other demands, other necessities, immediately make themselves felt.

A minimum of this "must," this "internal necessity," is at once evident. But we have still to ask how we can speak of an *a priori* here, how we can speak of an *a priori* form of an intelligible world, and how the human mind can presume to dictate such a form. But let us look at the notion of necessity a little more closely. "Must" was, to be sure, made for human beings, but not necessarily in the relation of superior and subject. It is a relation that arises *wherever there is any kind of relation or communication.* There is a minimum of compulsion which no one—not even a philosopher—can escape, unless he takes refuge in pure impressions and solipsism. But as we have seen in an earlier chapter, the nature of this compulsion may easily be misunderstood. *A priori* truth is necessary as opposed to contingent, but not as opposed to voluntary. Necessary truth is necessary, not because it *compels* the mind's acceptance, as does sensation, but precisely because it does not. It is that which is acknowledged, and involves all the freedom of acknowledgment. But this freedom is freedom only from external compulsion, not from such compulsions as arise out of the very conditions of intelligible communication.

It is most important that this notion of the *a priori* should be made entirely clear. It is part of the modern spirit that all philosophy, idealistic as well as realistic, should emphasize the claims of what is called "experience" upon us. To acknowledge this is merely to admit that no speculation in the bizarre and romantic sense is desirable, and that no individual system of philosophy can be final. But this does not exclude, as every competent thinker knows, the fact that there are *no* fundamental truths of experience itself, for which we can give any reasons, that are not, in part at least, *a priori*, reason being defined in terms of that internal necessity which makes itself felt in every act of thought and its communication. Now this internal necessity is almost universally recognized as being present in our thought and discourse about all those entities and relations that are described as essences or subsistents. It is generally acknowledged that we cannot think—much less talk—about these things intelligently without acknowledging aspects which are not dependent on experience and its contingencies. It is only propositions about reality to which this *a priori* character is denied. And yet it must be clear that there must be some propositions about reality that *must* have this character also. Where denial of existence of objects leads to self-refutation and makes intelligible communication impossible, we have a similar internal compulsion which may very properly be called "metaphysical necessity."

Something of what this internal compulsion necessitates we have already seen in earlier chapters. We distinguished between prejudices and necessary presuppositions, and to the latter we gave the name of the *a priori* in the sense here defined. A certain *minimum* of this "must" we discovered to be the necessary acknowledgment of the self and the others inhabiting a world. Certain statements regarding that world were also seen to be the necessary presuppositions of philosophical intelligibility. It now remains to see whether this internal necessity goes farther and includes the *form* of an intelligible world; whether the natural metaphysic of which we have spoken has this character; whether there is a natural bent of the reason which it is impossible to unbend.

I have already indicated in a general way that this is so. In later chapters I shall seek to show it in detail in connection with the special questions of intelligible causation, intelligible finality, intelligible evolution, and intelligible progress. Here I shall content myself with trying to show *why* this form is *a priori*. The *a priori* is an internal necessity that arises out of the very conditions of intelligible discourse themselves. Discourse involves description, explanation, and interpretation, but the first passes insensibly into the second, and the second into the third; they can be separated only by a sophistication which ends ultimately in sophistry. Another way of saying the same thing is that interpretation is already involved in explanation and even in description. Merely to *describe* a thing, for instance, as coming out of nothing and going into nothing is already to evaluate or interpret that thing as the nothing out of which it comes and the nothing into which it goes. To explain a thing by deriving it out of something it is not, and developing it into something it is not, is ultimately to explain it away, to deny it that identity in difference upon which all intelligibility depends. Thus it is that a natural metaphysic involves of necessity concepts of ultimate origination and ultimate destiny, and more than this, it involves the bringing of causality and finality together in an underlying unity.

All this, as we have learned, Bergson saw clearly enough when he admitted that precisely this is what every mind *must* do if it follows the *natural* bent of the intellect to its conclusion. The only alternative to the acknowledgment of this internal necessity is to turn our backs on intellect and to renounce intelligibility for intuition. But Bergson also saw something more—and this is the point to which we have been leading up—he saw *why* this is so. He saw that there is in the human mind or reason a still more ultimate notion or "postulate" (the latter is his own term) which constitutes the basis or driving force of the traditional form, and of its compulsion. He calls it "a kind of metaphysical necessity."

It is possible, he tells us, to bring the concepts of causality and finality together, as did the Greeks, "only if you postulate a kind of metaphysical necessity in virtue of which the confronting of the all (or perfect being) with the zero (non-being) is equivalent to the affirmation of all the degrees of reality between them." In other words, he holds that that which alone makes it possible to bring beginning and end, cause and purpose, together (and also that which, *if* we postulate it, also *forces* us to bring them together) is a sort of innate conception of a scale of value, levels of being, degrees of reality.[1]

Now it is quite clear, I think, that the question of the existence of such an "innate" metaphysical necessity turns upon two things. The first of these is whether there is an *a priori* and necessary relation between value and reality; the second is whether the notion of degrees, or of a scale of value, is an essential part of the notion of value as such. The answer to both these questions I believe to be in the affirmative. We have already argued sufficiently for the inseparability of value and reality and for the position that, because reality is essentially a value concept, the idea of degrees of reality is an essential part of the notion of reality. In a later context we shall attempt to show that the principle of scale is an *a priori* character of value as such, and that there is, accordingly, precisely this metaphysical necessity of which Bergson speaks.[2] Here I will content myself with pointing out that Bergson is entirely right, at least, in seeing in this "postulate" the driving force of all Greek thought, and of all the metaphysics that derives from it. It is this that, so to speak, generates the traditional form of philosophical intelligibility. We may also point out that to assert this necessity is simply another way of saying that becoming is itself unintelligible unless it is a passage from lower to higher, or from higher to lower, levels,

---

[1] *Op. cit.*, p. 327.
[2] See Chapter X, pp. 336 ff. Also Chapter XIII, pp. 453 f.

and that the very acknowledgment of these levels within becoming implies that the levels are not temporal. This necessity of traditional thought is, however, just what any philosophy that attempts to make the world intelligible must "postulate" or acknowledge. There is no type of thinking, surely, for which the world is not assumed to be intelligible in some sense and in some degree. But as soon as this assumption is made these non-temporal levels are implied. The presence of any meaning in the world, it requires little thinking to see, implies the existence or subsistence of differences in meaning and value. If every phenomenon has equal significance, if one is, so to speak, as good as another, there are really no significance and no value. Now, I take it that the first condition of any intelligible communication and interpretation of experience is the recognition of the differences of meaning and value within the temporal experience, and this presupposes the acknowledgment of non-temporal levels. But what, now, does this imply? With Bergson, we may say that to bring causality and finality together in an underlying principle implies this "postulate." But we may equally well say that to postulate these levels means no less certainly the bringing of causality and finality, origin and destiny, together in one system of interpretation. System in philosophy is, as we shall later see, equally an *a priori* condition of intelligible communication and interpretation.[1]

We have not hesitated to use the word "must" in our argument despite its most unmodern sound. But our real contention after all is, not so much that philosophers must, but that they actually do, acknowledge this *form of intelligibility* whenever they try to make the world intelligible. Nor should we be surprised that to this very compulsion, this "invisible spell," the moderns themselves are yielding—even against their will. They too, as has been indicated, are returning to the "one, definite, fundamental scheme" which, as Nietzsche saw, "the most diverse philosophers are always filling in again." There is "an innate methodology and relationship of ideas" that leads them or impels them in a definite order, the one after the other. It may be that such thinking is, in fact, as Nietzsche continues, "far less a discovery than a recognizing, a remembering, a return, and a homecoming," and in so far "a

[1] Chapter XIII, pp. 453 ff.

kind of atavism of the highest order." Perhaps it is, rather, the "Divinity that shapes our ends, rough-hew them as we may."

VIII

The *a priori* and speculative elements in traditional thought are, I ventured to say, features which the human mind could not conceivably seek to deny except as it misunderstood their real character and the nature of its own activity. Yet they are features which modernism constantly denies, and doubtless will continue so to do. Men will continue to point to the incalculable element in reality, and ask how we can presume to say that the world must be so—to the mind in the making, and how such a mind should presume to dictate an eternal form. They may indeed, as many are now doing, make change and history ultimate, and deny the possibility of all form whatsoever. If one cares to go to the limits of possible paradox, one may even express the most modern of sentiments and say that every attempt to give form to the world but increases its confusion and irrationality, for that very form itself is but a new element in the empirical content of the world, one more novelty to master. In short, the only final element in thought is that there is no finality.

Now, I know of no way of compelling people to cease saying such things as this. Indeed, I am not sure that we should want to stop them if we could. The gaiety of that joyful science known as philosophy would be greatly moderated if thinkers were disallowed their intellectual play. Yet when all is said and done, there are limits to the things we may reasonably say, and this seems to be one of them. For after all there is no reason why one should want to say anything about the world at all if the only result is to add to its confusion.

The contradiction between the timeless form and the ever-changing content of knowledge is, it is true, the philosophic "worm that dieth not," but its gnawing has become so intolerable that the modern mind has sought surcease from pain in the counter-irritant of the most appalling paradox. Life to be intelligible requires form, but form, we are told, kills life, so life must ever be the enemy of form. Forms of thought, like the commandments of morality, are made only to be broken. With the vain and heart-breaking attempt to put some meaning into words like these—to make absolute becoming in some way intelligible—all the distinctively "modern" minds have been engaged. Bergson, Croce, Simmel, Alexander—to take only typical examples—each in his own way wrestles with the problem, and none can wholly disguise a hidden sense of his own unintelligibility.

For the purpose of these closing remarks it is not necessary to make distinctions among these views. All demand that "we take time seriously," and no one will deny, I fancy, that they have a serious time in doing so. Of this denial of all finality to philosophy, Croce has said: "What was at the beginning of the nineteenth century merely a simple presentiment becomes changed into a firm consciousness at the beginning of the twentieth." The twentieth century will, above all things, take time seriously, and upon this seriousness it prides itself. One may at least be permitted to wonder whether time, with all its little ironies, will return the compliment. The classical, as Guyau has said, is reality purified by time. Will this firm conviction withstand the puriying process?

CHAPTER VII

SPACE, TIME, AND VALUE: THE AXIOLOGICAL INTERPRETATION OF SPACE AND TIME

The solution of the riddle of life in space and time lies outside space and time.

WITTGENSTEIN

Das alle Reele ist wohl von der Zeit verschieden, aber eben so wesentlich identisch mit ihr.

HEGEL

I

WE have seen that philosophic intelligibility is ultimately bound up with questions of origin and destiny and cannot be separated from them. When philosophy ceases to ask after the first and last things it ceases to be philosophy; when it drops from its vocabulary the terms "beginning" and "end" it ceases to talk intelligibly. Yet one of the most persistent characteristics of traditional philosophy is its despatialization of ultimate reality, its detemporalization of the concepts of beginning and end. What is the significance of this tendency? Clearly it is the feeling, the insight, what you will, that the significance of the problems of an *ens realissimum*, of origin and destiny, is in some way deeper than the spatial and temporal forms in which a natural prejudice of the intellect inevitably expresses them.

With this we come to the first of the great historic problems of philosophy, the problem of the nature of space and time. Are space and time ultimately real? Has the universe a beginning in time? Or is there an intelligible world that is spaceless and timeless? If so, why did the original simultaneity of content pass into those forms of self-externality which we call succession and co-existence? These are questions which the great philosophers have continually asked themselves. What is the real meaning of these questions? How did men come to ask them? What is the significance of the historic answers to them?

"The problems of space and time," Mr. E. D. Fawcett rightly says, "compel a philosophy to declare itself." When a philosopher says that space or time is real or unreal, he has hereby expressed himself, not only on the fundamental questions of philosophy, but, by implication at least, on the significance of philosophy itself. Scarcely any problem has been so thought over as this. Every other world problem, one might almost believe, hangs from this—the ultimate nature of space and time. The reasons are not far to seek. However we may ultimately think space and time technically, whether as entity or relation, as form of thought or form of being, they are in some sense, at least, all-pervasive aspects of experience, and our decision as to their reality or unreality is determinative of our interpretation of reality itself.

All the vital problems of philosophy depend upon this question, but not all the problems of space and time are equally relevant to the philosophical problem. Psychological analysis of the space-time consciousness may throw light on disputed points. Mathematical and logical analyses have their own interests, but may have much less significance for the general philosophical problem than is often supposed. Our "physical outlook may, indeed, be profoundly changed if we imaginatively realize the consequences of the theory of relativity, but it is by no means yet sure that our metaphysical outlook will be equally profoundly altered." Be that as it may, much that is ordinarily included in discussions of space and time has little interest for us here. The problem, on the solution of which so much depends for our philosophical outlook, is still the same problem as it has always been—namely, the relation of space and time to the intelligible world. In terms of the more general discussions of the two preceding chapters we may state the specific problems of the present chapter in the following way. To what extent are intelligibility and intelligible communication bound up with, or dependent upon, description in space and time? What is the relation of space and time to the *form of philosophical intelligibility*?

Traditional philosophy has uniformly conceived of the intelligible world as ultimately non-spatial and non-temporal. It has always felt that the solution of the riddle of life in space and time lies outside space and time; with equal conviction it has felt that the relations of space and time are not intelligible in themselves, but become so only on the assumption that they are "phenomenal" of something more ultimate than themselves. For many, on the other hand, the only world we have is the space-time world. If intelligibility is to be found at all it must be found within its confines. Moreover, they see no reason why the relations of space and time should not be intelligible in themselves, and they make every effort to show them to be such.

All this will constitute the material of our discussions. It is of prior importance, however, to see what this problem of intelligibility means here, and how it arose in human thinking.

II

"The ancient world," writes Spengler, "had no problem of space and time." If this is true—and in a certain sense and with certain limitations it probably is—it is because the sense for the reality of space and time was unimpaired. This sense of their reality was due to the ease with which they were connected with value. This it was that made them intelligible.

For the ordinary consciousness anything to be real must have a definite place in the world, i.e. must be localized. That which has no such place seems to have no reality at all. This prejudice in favour of the actual, of which we have spoken at length elsewhere,[1] is curiously illustrated by Plato's saying of the ideas that they are in τόπος ἀτόπων—a prejudice finally overcome only when the sophisticated modern logician finds himself capable of thinking of certain entities, that are still entities, but are homeless wanderers, nowhere and nowhen, neither in space, time, nor even in mind.

Now, localization of values is not difficult for the mythological consciousness. For the religion of the ancient world reality divided itself naturally into heaven and earth and a subterrannean hell. This graduated series of the regions of the world was palpable evidence of a graded series of values. It was not until these durable connections between an order of space and an order of meanings and values were severed that the problem of the reality or unreality of space arose. When, however, it dawned upon thought that there could be no

[1] Chapter II, pp. 67 f.

absolute determinations of space, since every place is determined by relations to other places, the old world-picture was, as Höffding says, doomed. With the passing of this old picture questions of reality and unreality necessarily appeared. Hitherto it had been possible to express "spiritual" distinctions, distinctions of meaning and value, by spatial distances and relations. Hence no sharp distinctions between the material and spiritual were drawn. Now, however, the natural prejudice in favour of localization contends with a tendency against localization and limitation. Two possibilities thus appear. Through dissociation from the "real" the spiritual or value order may become unreal. But with equal plausibility the question of the ultimate reality of space may be raised. Is space ultimate or is it a form of appearance in which a non-spatial reality manifests itself?

As with space, so with time. The sense of the reality of time remained unimpaired so long as it remained possible easily to locate values in time. As the religious consciousness located its gods in space, so it located the supreme values at the beginning and end of time. The question of the reality of time arose only when this connection was severed. When time came to mean, as for instance in the Hindu mind, movement leading to no end, movement without direction, no value could be attributed to time itself, and because of the inseparability of value and reality time became unreal. The traditional philosophical conception of the ultimate unreality of time has its origin in the idea of its meaninglessness; the depreciation of time, the idea of its essential imperfection as a corruption of eternity, is a necessary consequence. The philosophy, on the other hand, that seeks to find the ideal realized in the present, that finds the eternal in the temporal itself, is a direct attempt to overcome this ancient dissociation of time from value.

In such fashion, then, have space and time become the fundamental problems of an intelligible world. In such fashion, and in such fashion alone, could the problem of their reality or unreality ever have arisen. The "depreciation of space and time," so characteristic of traditional philosophy, is but the reverse side of a growing appreciation of other meanings of reality than that of localization in space and time—as necessary alike for intelligible communication and interpretation of experience—and which makes of the natural demand for localization a prejudice.[1]

The origin of the space-time problem is thus axiological. Its ultimate meaning and final solution must be equally so. But this axiological problem presents itself, as, indeed, we have seen all the historical problems of philosophy do, in ontological form. James Ward has classified the problems of time under three heads: (a) the formal; (b) the ontological; (c) the axiological. The same holds true of space.

"For traditional philosophy space and time have," as Bergson shrewdly observes, "necessarily the same origin and the same value. The same diminution of being is expressed both by extension in space and detension in time. Both are but the distance between what is and what ought to be."[2] This "depreciation" of space and time, characteristic of the main line of philosophical thought, issuing in many cases in a doctrine of their unreality, is the main element in traditional philosophy against which, in one form or another, modernism chiefly takes issue. The debate has mainly taken place in the broad and open spaces of abstract logic, but the real underlying issues have been axiological, as we shall seek to show.

These two problems are, of course, intimately related both historically and logically; but they must be carefully distinguished. The contradictions in space and time which are supposed to make them unintelligible and thus ultimately unreal, might conceivably be due to "certain obstinate prejudices now overcome by the labours of the mathematicians," but this would in no wise affect the second problem. The arguments of Leibniz and Lotze, for instance, for the relativity of space and time may be met by the absolutists. They may, for instance, have definitely refuted the claim that the existence of points or positions in absolute space involves contradiction. But this method does not enable them to prove that that which is free from logical contradiction has ultimate existence or reality. Still less does it enable them to answer those who maintain that the world is more intelligible on the assumption that space and time are not ultimately real. The reason for this is plain. The real problem of space and time is not whether they are internally contradictory or not, but rather whether they are intelligible in the sense that their absoluteness or relativity is consistent or inconsistent with the interpretation of experience as a whole.

It is, I repeat, of the utmost importance to make this distinction clear. I can do so in no better way than by referring to the form in which it is vaguely but no less genuinely expressed by Mr. Bertrand Russell. Thus, writing of time, he says: "The arguments for the contention that time is unreal and that the world of sense is illusory must, I think, be regarded as illusory. Nevertheless, there is some sense, easier to feel than to state, in which time is an unimportant and superficial characteristic of reality. Past and future must be acknowledged to be as real as the present, and a certain emancipation from slavery to time is essential to philosophic thought."[1] Thus Mr. Russell shares with traditional philosophy a certain depreciation of time; and he shares it for the reason that he knows, however inadequately he may be able to express that knowledge, that the real reason for the depreciation of time in traditional philosophy lay not so much in the arguments for the unreality of time as in the consciousness of the ultimate unintelligibility of a world in which temporal distinctions are taken as absolute, in the consciousness that meanings and their validity are in some sense non-temporal.

It is, then, the axiological problem of space and time with which we are primarily concerned in this chapter, the problem of space, time, and value. This is by no means to suggest that the other problems are negligible. In fact, from other points of view, as, for instance, that of the formation of a concept of nature or natural science, the other problems become the more important and our special problem may conceivably be ignored. Thus A. N. Whitehead takes the "homogeneity of thought about nature as excluding any reference to moral or æsthetic values." These *values* of nature are, however, he adds, "perhaps the key to the metaphysical synthesis of existence. But such a synthesis is exactly what I am not attempting."[2] Yet if the values of nature are the key to metaphysical synthesis or interpretation, as I for one certainly believe, then it is obviously the space-time problem as it is related to values that is central and determinative.

[1] *Logic and Mysticism*, p. 26.   [2] A. N. Whitehead, *The Concept of Nature*, p. 5.

III

Traditional philosophy has in the main felt compelled to deny the ultimate reality of space and time. We have now seen why it has felt compelled to do so. Yet common sense and science seem to agree that they can do nothing with the world except on the hypothesis of their concrete reality, and many forms of recent philosophy have followed their lead. The demand that time shall be taken seriously is one of the fundamental notes of modernism. In so far as, more and more, space and time are found inseparable in scientific description and explanation space must be taken seriously, too.

Now, I think it may be said without hesitation that, in so far as intelligibility is sought merely in description and explanation as understood by science, space and time must, indeed, be taken seriously and therefore as *real*. By this I mean that the mutual externality of parts in space and of moments in time is the condition of any such intelligible description and explanation. But the problem is, how far does this hold for *all* communication and interpretation? In other words, how far is philosophy compelled to retain this mutual externality in its more ultimate interpretation? May we not rather be compelled to reconstruct our space-time notions if there is to be genuine understanding and adequate communication of the meaning of reality? May it not be necessary to supplement this mutual externality with a type of category more intimate to the life of experience if there is to be any really intelligible communication of that experience?

It is clear, I think, that description, whether for science or practice, is in the last analysis localization, and necessarily involves taking the mutual externality of parts of space and moments of time *as though* they were ultimate and final. Nothing can be really described except as it is thus localized in space and time. This is true of the mental as well as the physical. Communication of meaning is possible without localization, at least definite localization, but description of any mental fact involves necessarily direct localization in time and, at least, indirect localization in space. Whatever we may think on the vexed question of physical space and mental space, in *some* space every describable fact or event must have its place. Moreover, the unit of scientific description, as modern science is coming more and more to see, is the "point-instant." In this sense the Einstein theory is, as Alexander holds, "a result of last importance." For description, at least, space-time is indissoluble. As the framework of all description anything that is describable at all in the sense of science can be so described by a system of space-time co-ordinates.

In this sense, but in this sense alone, are space and time "all-pervasive categories." In another sense, as we shall see more fully later, they certainly are not. For there are "objects" in the broadest sense of that term of which to say that they are localized in space and time is meaningless. There are many such objects—all those, in fact, for which the philosophers have been compelled to use such terms as "subsistence" and "validity." Description, properly speaking, is possible only of existents physical and mental. The *meanings* of these existents and the meanings of existence itself are not describable; they can only be acknowledged in communication. Communication itself, upon which description and explanation, no less than interpretation, ultimately rest, is not an object describable by science.[1]

All this is true, and as fundamental as it is true. But there is still a sense—and to this we must hold fast throughout our discussion—in which space and time *are* all-pervasive categories, in the sense, namely, that this mutual externality is the necessary condition of intelligible description. When the Indian mystic cries, "That art thou, that art thou," and points to the varied objects of the natural world, he is undoubtedly communicating a meaning that is both intelligible and valid. When the poet cries, "I am a part of all that I have seen," he is expressing something that surely is intelligible to the poet in all of us. But to neither of these experiences can science give any intelligible meaning, for both statements involve a negation of that very externality upon which all the clearness and distinctness which science seeks in its descriptions rest. This mutual externality, abstracted from concrete experience and

---

[1] Description of existents takes place, it is true, only in terms of universals that are nowhere and nowhen, and these, when taken apart from the existents they describe, are not actual. These alone do not, however, describe the actual. Such description is impossible without the localization which makes the individual actual.

represented as continuous homogeneous magnitudes, is precisely what we call space and time. To deny the reality of space and time is, accordingly, not only to impoverish the world, as Lossky says, but in a very genuine sense to rob it of part of its intelligibility. Even more does this appear to be the fact when we consider space and time in connection with explanation.

For some purposes of science, explanation and adequate description may, perhaps, be conceived to coincide. Ideal intelligibility (*Durchsichtigkeit*) is achieved when nature is reduced to a system of space-time co-ordinates. But there is a necessary element of intelligibility, even in science, which refuses to be exhausted in such description.

Most of what we have in the past considered necessary for intelligibility has been driven out as anthropomorphic fictions. We are even told that to say that the combination of H_2O gives rise to water is further than we can properly go. A functional relation is all that we can legitimately assert. Yet even in science such asceticism has not wholly won the day. The investigations of Professor Lawrence J. Henderson, for instance, compel him to the conclusion that there is revealed in nature something more than this—"a certain order or pattern in the properties of the chemist," an "element of direction," which must be taken into account. These things, it is true, are "hidden when one considers the properties of matter abstractly and statically, for it is recognizable and intelligible only through its effects. It becomes evident only when time is taken into consideration. It has a dynamical significance and relates only to evolution."[1]

Explanation, even in science, involves more than mere description. The historical categories will not be denied. They have, indeed, been bled white by the increasing abstractness of science. It is to pump blood back into these anæmic categories that Bergson and other modernists bid us take time seriously. Time, real time, is the necessary condition of the intelligibility of the vital and psychical processes, even of the chemical. It takes time for all "creative resultants." This much is fully understood. But what is not so easily seen, perhaps, is that *the same is true of space*. Nowhere is the inseparability of space and time so clearly seen as precisely in all those sciences in

[1] *The Order of Nature*, p. 184.

which to "description" is added "explanation," where, in other words, the historical categories enter. Let us consider space first.

We have seen that mutual externality, as represented in separate co-existing positions in space, is the necessary condition of all description. Without this externality all things fall together in a mutual interpenetration which, while it may have a meaning of its own, a meaning which can, indeed, be acknowledged and communicated, is incompatible with description. This mutual externality is, if possible, even more demanded where historical explanation supervenes upon static description. This principle of mutual externality we may, from this point of view, describe as the law of segregation or the principle of "necessary spaces." We shall find this principle all-pervasive in the organic and inorganic world in the realms of mental and social phenomena.

To this principle of segregation, for instance, the historical geologist ascribes fundamental importance and world-wide significance. "Segregation," writes J. W. Gregory, "converted the widely diffused nebulæ into planetary knots, and then divided each young planet into a metallic centre and stony crust. The beginning of the geological history of the earth was the segregation of the materials of the constituent meteorites into three zones. The making of the earth into a condition suitable for the abode of life and ultimately for the home of man was the continuation of this beneficent process of segregation. . . . All the materials required for the life and work of man existed in the rocks of the lithosphere and in the waters of the ocean or in the air: but they were practically useless until each had been connected in beds in which they could be obtained in the necessary quantity and purity."[1]

This tendency of similar materials to collect together in groups, Gregory continues, "has affected the world from the primeval knotting of the nebulæ to the crowding of people into towns. This all-pervasive impulse takes on, however, different forms as we pass from the inorganic to the organic. In biology, for instance, segregation or spatial separation is found necessary for the fixation of species. One of the most

[1] *The Making of the Earth*, pp. 75 ff.

important contributions made since Darwin to our understanding of the method of the origin of species is a series of suggestions coming from various sources, but all centring about the general idea of "isolation." "It is an absolute certainty," says H. W. Conn, "that single variations cannot perpetuate themselves if there is free possibility of breeding with unmodified members of the race," and he holds this idea of isolation to be of such importance as "to deserve to rank with natural selection and Lamarckism as a third great theory or factor in the origin of species."[1] Into the details of the methods of isolation, geographical and physiological, we need not enter. It suffices for our purpose that the principle of geographical isolation of necessary spaces is of the utmost importance for explanation. In the making of living organisms, no less than in the "making" of the earth, without the externality of space time cannot do its work.

In the mental and social life of man the evidence of this principle of necessary spaces is still clearer, as its influence is in a sense even more profound. Thus Eduard Meyer, the historian, begins with the "axiom" that the whole mental development of mankind has as its preliminary assumption the existence of separate social groups.[2] Imitation, assimilation, interpenetration, are in the minds of the social philosophers both the conditions and the ideals of historical development; but separation and opposition are found to be equally necessary for the emergence and fixation of those qualities of individuality in culture which we find most significant and valuable. Elsewhere I have developed in detail the central rôle which segregation and isolation play in the development of social values.[3] It is enough, perhaps, to say with Gregory that "human segregation, though often deplored, will not only continue despite all attempts to stop it, but is probably as necessary and beneficent as similar tendencies in the inorganic and organic world."

Even more fundamental than the law of necessary spaces—if, indeed, the two can be at all separated—is *the law of necessary times* or stages. To arrive at any "higher" or more complex

---

[1] H. W. Conn, *The Methods of Evolution*, chapter vii, p. 282.
[2] Quoted from Henry Adams, *The Degradation of Democratic Dogma*, p. 259.
[3] *Valuation: Its Nature and Laws*, pp. 339 ff.

stage of existence "takes time." Any explanation of the emergent characters and qualities of the universe requires us to take time seriously.

"It was the peculiar ability of Darwin," writes Professor E. G. Conklin, "to see nature in four dimensions—length, breadth, depth, and duration. He observed the activities of earthworms for a season, and then calculated the agricultural and geographical importance of earthworms acting through many years. He observed the minor variations of animals and plants, and then saw the evolutionary significance of such changes when extended through geological time." It is the sense for this fourth dimension that is the peculiar gift of the modern world, and which more than anything else sets modern thought in contrast with the ancient. The Greeks, it is probably true, had so little of this sense that things and events, so soon as they were past, tended to merge into a background of timeless myth. "Once upon a time" was all the temporal localization necessary to give an event reality. Be that as it may, the element of duration, of necessary times in explanation, in the making of the qualities of the universe, was almost wholly lacking in ancient science as in ancient life.

It would be superfluous to attempt to expand this thesis; to attempt to develop in detail that which has become a commonplace of modern knowledge. It would involve a *résumé* of all the dynamic sciences, and would be no more than a restatement, *mutatis mutandis*, of what we have said regarding necessary spaces. Enough here merely to state the conclusion that the principle of "necessary times" is absolutely indispensable for intelligible communication and interpretation. Both description and explanation imply it.

What, then, is the significance of this principle or "law" of necessary spaces and necessary times? It is, first of all, a general statement of their all-pervasive character. They are the necessary conditions of intelligible explanation as well as of intelligible description. In the second place, for the modern scientific consciousness as for traditional thought, space and time have "the same origin and the same value." Necessary spaces and necessary times both are, from the standpoint of their intelligibility, the distance between what is and what ought to be, the less meaningful and the more meaningful. As such they belong together and for an ultimate interpretation are inseparable. Finally, the intelligibility which space and time thus acquired in explanation is solely *instrumental*, to make use of a distinction of a former chapter, and as such presupposes *intrinsic* intelligibility.[1] The necessary and the "beneficent" character of space and time relations, of which the scientist somewhat naïvely speaks, presupposes a teleology, an acknowledgment of values, which alone make these relations significant. The problem of space, time, and value is thus before us.

IV

The origin of the space-time problem—as a philosophical problem, at least—we found to be axiological. Its ultimate meaning and final solution must, we insisted, be axiological also. The first condition of such a solution is naturally an examination of the relations of space and time to values. Otherwise expressed, our problem is somewhat as follows. The fundamental task of this chapter is to determine the rôle of space and time in the interpretation of reality, or in our conception of an intelligible world. We have repeatedly found, however, from various angles of approach, that the notions of reality and value are inseparable. It is clear, then, that no determination of the rôle of space and time in this interpretation is possible until we have considered the relation of space and time to value.

With this question we have come to one of the most difficult problems of this chapter, and one in the discussion of which the greatest confusion of thought is possible. If, as has been suggested, the values of nature are the key to metaphysical interpretation, then the question of the relation of values to space and time is fundamental. On the other hand, this very question is made extraordinarily difficult by ambiguities in the concept of value. The merely psycho-biological conception is of values as adaptations of organism to environment, and, from the genetic point of view, as certain adaptations which emerge as evolution runs its course. If this were the whole story of values, what we have said of space and time in the preceding

[1] Chapter V, pp. 183 ff.

section would apply without change to the sphere of values. But it is not the whole story, as we have seen.[1] The necessarily vicious circle inherent in this conception forces us to other conceptions of value, and demands that we shall consider the question of the relation of space and time to values on its own merits.

We may begin by asking, concerning "values," the same questions we asked about "things?" Are the principles of necessary spaces and necessary times involved in the description and explanation of values? Are relations of space and time part of the nature of values? These questions must, in a sense, be answered in the affirmative. It is in connection with space and time that values become *sichtbar*; in connection with them alone that the meaning and values of things are acquired. It is only as "evolution runs its course" that there emerge, at the reflective stage of mind, *tertiary* qualities, ideals of truth and beauty. and the ethically right, having relations of value.

Mutual externality of positions in space and of moments in time are, we have seen, necessary for description and explanation. In the descriptions and explanations of the geologist, biologist, and sociologist, moreover, an element of meaning and value has already entered. The "beneficent" character of these factors is emphasized. Necessary spaces and necessary times are postulated as the condition of all those qualities of the universe, all those adaptations to which we ascribe value—as necessary, in short, for the acquirement of meaning and value.

In this sense, and to this extent, space and time seem to be part of the nature of any value.

This seems to be true also when we come to the distinctively human values, although the problem then becomes more complex and more difficult. Here, as elsewhere, space and time seem to be part of the nature of any value; and we find that we can do nothing in the way of description and explanation of values without assuming the "reality" of space and time. It is unnecessary to comment on the significance of space and time factors in determining economic values. Change in space and availability in time may make all the difference between worthlessness and fabulous "value." But this is also true, in a

[1] See Chapter IV, pp. 136 ff.

sense, of those values which we call ethical and æsthetic. There is this much truth in all naturalistic explanations and interpretations of such phenomena, that it is only in their relativity to time and place—in other words, to the specific situation—that they become evident and are realized. For our purposes, however, it will serve to emphasize only one aspect of the situation, namely, the rôle of the principle of necessary times in determining the emergence and realization of such values.

The rôle of the prolongation of infancy in the development of the family has been frequently cited as an instance of the function of the spatial and temporal environment in "eliciting" values. Here time, both in the phylogenetic and the ontogenetic series, is "creative." In this case, and in all similar cases, the only natural and common-sense point of view is to say that, since time, or times, are necessary to elicit these values—since "it takes time," so to speak, to "make" them—time itself is creative and, as such, part of the nature of the value as such. It is at this point in our thought that there arises the idea of "emergence" of new qualities, and with it the whole idea of emergent or creative evolution, a notion which we shall consider more fully later.

All these facts may be summarized for our purposes in the following generalization. Space and time, and their relations, are not only a part of those aspects of reality we call *things*, but of those we call *values*. In a sense, this generalization is but the corollary of the conclusions of an earlier discussion in which we found that value is part of the nature of things, part of the very material with which science deals.[1] And, in fact, all our actual everyday experiences seem to justify this conclusion. Such experiences seem to derive all, or at least most, of their significance and value from the fact that one position in space is not with another, one moment in succession not with another. Mutual externality, with all that it implies of necessary spaces and necessary times, is a necessary condition of intelligibility in the sphere of values as well as of things. There seems to be no denying this generalization, no escape from this very law of life itself. The *not-yet* and the *no-more* consciousness seem to be an essential part of both the realization and communication of values. All our plans, of

[1] See Chapter V, pp. 198 ff.

course, depend upon them, and if for them be substituted a merely timeless order, our purposes and values seem to become unmeaning. The inmost meaning of time is the inalienable difference between that which is and that which ought to be, and, conversely, it seems, the inmost meaning of value is bound up with its expression in the time form.

Taken in a certain sense, this conclusion would scarcely be denied by anyone. Traditional philosophy, even in its most "mystical" form, always tells us that "the external world, as viewed spatially and temporally, has much to teach us about ultimate truth." Mutual externality stands for something in the "real" world, although there are "spiritual" realities to which it does not apply. This idea—that space and time are somehow "phenomenal" of value in its ultimate sense, that they are the necessary forms in which values are realized, and yet the values themselves transcend these forms—is an imperishable element in traditional philosophy. To make this view intelligible is the task of the following sections. Here I shall merely point out that it is but a special form of the problem of the relation of value to existence and reality as considered in an earlier chapter.[1]

The inalienable difference between what is and what ought to be is, in a sense, the ultimate mystery. It is this, our inability really to identify the actual with the ideal, that compels us to acknowledge the reality of space and time. It is, however, on the other hand, this that equally compels us to acknowledge values which transcend space and time.

V

The driving force of the traditional interpretation of space and time is to be found, then, in their essential limitations as the *a priori* of a significant, intelligible world. All-pervasive aspects of reality they may be; but this fact, while important for description and explanation, is not final for interpretation. If to maintain this is a depreciation of space and time, then traditional philosophy must be charged with consistent and continuous undervaluation.

[1] Chapter IV, pp. 158 ff.

With this depreciation, however, there is a corresponding appreciation of their significance and reality. Space and time may be "phenomenal," but they are phenomena *bene fundata*. By themselves they may be meaningless and unintelligible, but as expressions or "symbols" of non-spatial and non-temporal meanings and values they are highly significant. To this positive side of traditional thought we must presently turn, but it is first necessary to examine a characteristic view of modernism which, while denying absolute reality to space, emphasizes all the more strongly the absolute character of duration.

The extent of Bergson's break with the past is shown precisely by his putting asunder things which traditional thought had, apparently, effectually joined. According to his view, space is, indeed, but an instrument of description and explanation, unintelligible in itself and by its very limitations incapable of making the world intelligible. But with time, properly understood, the case is wholly different. Not only is time real, but the only reality. Not only has time in itself meaning and value, but duration *is* meaning and value. In other words, the key to all interpretation and intelligibility is the intrinsic and absolute nature of time, the identification of being with becoming.

Now, it must be admitted that, despite the close relations of space and time, the phenomenal character of time is much more difficult to sustain than that of space. It encounters immediately the objection that the interconnection of psychic states and activities has, though no space aspect, yet certainly a temporal character. There is also the difficulty that, while space is in a sense irrelevant to value, time is not. The idea of duration as absolute is much more difficult to meet than in the case of space.

But is absolute duration intelligible? Can the metaphysical identification of being and becoming be carried out? Bergson's doctrine of time has been examined from every conceivable angle. Here we shall concentrate our attention on one single aspect, the axiological—the particular aspect, however, which, if our interpretation of the historic space-time problem is valid, is fundamental. It is an aspect, moreover, which will be highly significant for the discussions to come.

The historic attempts to interpret the world have, according to Bergson, uniformly failed because they have all refused to take time seriously. This is true alike of historic idealisms and spiritualisms and of modern naturalistic evolutionism. All have attempted to derive the more from the less, when it is possible only to derive the less from the more. For these philosophies there has always been more (of meaning and value) in the static and permanent, when, in fact, there is really more in the changing. The assumption underlying Bergson's entire philosophy is, accordingly, that time, taken in itself, has intrinsic meaning and value and that, consequently, the world becomes intelligible only on the assumption of a "creative evolution" in which time is the matter and womb of creation itself.

With the consequences of this assumption we are not at present concerned.[1] Rather let us examine the primary assumption. Time is in itself meaningful and has, indeed, more of meaning and value than the things within or without time. This is, of course, the negation of all traditional insight. Like space, time also acquires meaning only when seen as the distance between that which is and that which ought to be. Detension in time, like extension in space, is, as Bergson says, for traditional thought merely the expression of degrees of reality, of increase or diminution of value. For Bergson, on the other hand, time not only has meaning without this "direction," but is itself the essence of meaning and value.

Such a complete transvaluation of all metaphysical values is hard to understand. One phase of this morbid evaluation of time is indeed intelligible. Mutual compenetration and mutual interpenetration have, indeed, always been felt to be the condition of appreciation and understanding of the "spiritual world." For traditional philosophy also, there has always been, to use Bergson's own words, "more" in interpenetration than in externality. But now appears that phase of his thought which is not understandable. This meaning and value of interpenetration he thinks to find in an immediate intuition of pure duration itself—in mere becoming, as though this interpenetration were in any intelligible sense in the becoming itself.

Now, it can be shown, I think, that the meaning he appears to find in becoming does not belong to the becoming itself.

[1] They will be considered in Chapters IX and X.

An analysis of our experience—taken at its highest points, such as, indeed, Bergson himself undertakes—disproves his position. Our consciousness does not perceive sequence, our acts and states do not really follow one upon the other *except as they are held together by value.* The very interpenetration, continuity itself, is felt only through direction introduced into the becoming from a source other than itself. The weakness of Bergson's view, as, indeed, of the whole group of philosophies that make evolution itself creative, is the false assumption that time, process, tendency, are themselves matters of intension, themselves carry meanings and values, when they represent merely the "means of approach to values." This "packing" of time or space-time with meanings and values is, as we shall see, the only thing that gives to modern doctrines of emergence the apparent intelligibility they seem to have.

I think that this can be actually shown from Bergson's own analysis of becoming.[1] At the risk of labouring the point let me indicate more exactly what I mean. Bergson speaks of "an infinite multiplicity of becomings." Becoming is infinitely varied. That which goes from yellow to green is not that which goes from green to blue; that which goes from flower to fruit is not that which goes from larva to nymph and from nymph to perfect insect. The action of eating and drinking is not the action of fighting. And these three kinds of movements themselves—qualitative, evolutionary, extensive—differ profoundly. "It is but a trick of our intelligence that abstracts from these profoundly different becomings the single representation of becoming in general." Whence, now, I ask, the different "colourings" of these different becomings? Whence other than from the different meanings which these movements embody, directions which could not be recognized except by the apprehension and acknowledgment of the values which the meanings presuppose and which determine the directions?

The more of meaning which one seems to find in becoming does not, I repeat, belong to mere becoming itself. To grasp meaning in a movement, one must grasp direction; and the directions of all these different types of movement, the very continuity and interpenetration which make of them indivisible

[1] *Creative Evolution*, pp. 304 ff.

wholes, are determined by that which can be grasped only by intelligence oriented towards value.

The intellect, it is said, cannot grasp movement. If we mean by movement particular local motion, it is true that the intellect does not seize it as the senses do. But it does not follow that the intelligence solidifies movement in grasping it. All depends on what we conceive intelligence to be, and what the natural orientation of the intelligence is. The intellect grasps *intelligible* movement only by means of concepts, the concepts namely of potentiality and realization, of potency and act. These concepts, as we shall see later, are neither merely practical, nor are they intellectual dogmas forced on a resisting reality. They spring from the fact that interpenetration and continuity are themselves intelligible only as successive states are held together by value. They are value concepts, and the only way in which meaningful becoming and movement can be grasped.

"Time," as Guyau has ironically said, "is too often made a sort of mysterious reality designed to replace the old idea of providence and made almost omnipotent." This subtle temptation is seen in a large part of modern thinking about time. We moderns are right in taking time seriously; but to do so, it is not necessary to read into it meanings which, by itself, it never has. We are right in saying that time and space are real. They are existents on much the same grade of reality as the objects for which, without them, there is no intelligible description and explanation. As such, and in so far, they are of the very tissue of the given. But they are limited in that they cannot lead beyond themselves in any other way than by repetition of themselves, thus giving, as the last word they can say about themselves, the endless in space and time. They have, in the words of Leibniz, no "sufficient reason" in themselves.

Taken by itself, each is dumb; neither is able to make itself intelligible. It is supposed by some that they do become intelligible when we make of them a sort of Siamese twins; the entity called space-time. But is the situation really changed? Does the adding together of two unintelligibles make an intelligible? For myself, I cannot see that it does; for either we interpret this space-time as something in which there is no "direction," or else we endow it with a *nisus*, with potentiality—whether we use the terms or not. But this immediately transforms it into something quite other than the becoming or space-time of either common sense or science, something so like that mysterious reality designed to replace the old idea of Providence that it becomes the begetter of the very Deity out of which providence itself comes.

VI

Appreciation of the reality of space and time, more particularly of time, is then the characteristic of modern thought. The conclusion that space and time are part of the nature of any value sets the seal upon the doctrine of the reality of space and time. Yet depreciation of space and time—especially of time—is equally, as Mr. Alexander says, a sentiment widely spread among thinking men. Quoting certain expressions of these sentiments from poet and philosopher, he remarks: "A person might well be content to be an idealist in philosophy in order to have the right of saying these noble things." Perhaps it is the need of saying these noble things, at least, of acknowledging certain human meanings and values, which requires poet and philosopher alike to reconstruct their conceptions of space and time.

These needs, these exigencies, are there, but they are not particularly easy to express. "Space," Mr. Merz admits, "obtrudes itself everywhere, not only on our outer, but also on our inner, view, and is directly or collaterally the all-embracing receptacle of the whole of our experience. And yet we feel that, although space and spatial features obtrude themselves everywhere, they do not give us that which is most interesting and important to us. . . . We feel instinctively that the refined and spiritual experiences do not belong to objects or persons in their purely spatial existence, but form a world for themselves in the same way as in the purely intellectual region—numbers, mathematical formulæ, and logical connections form realities by themselves."[1] The arguments for the unreality of time, Mr. Russell, we have seen, finds illusory. "Nevertheless, there is some sense, easier to feel than to state,

[1] *A Fragment of the Human Mind*, p. 184.

in which time is an unimportant and superficial characteristic of reality."

These things, easier to feel than to express, are precisely what traditional philosophy has uniformly felt and acknowledged. It is these things that the "idealistic" doctrine of space and time has sought to express, however inadequately. Traditional philosophy has never denied, at least, in spirit, I think, the reality of space and time, although in its confusion of existential and axiological categories it has often appeared so to do. It has merely insisted that ultimate reality, that is reality in its really intelligible form, cannot be adequately expressed in the relations of space and time. For this we must go beyond externality to a type of category more intimate to the life of experience. In a sense it can be said, perhaps, that traditional philosophy, at least in its more magnanimous forms, has attempted the impossible—impossible at least to common sense—in calling space and time both real and unreal at the same time. Impossible or not, it is the *sine qua non* of intelligible communication and interpretation.

Reinterpretation of the traditional doctrine of space and time is, accordingly, our first task. As a primary condition of its adequate interpretation, it is necessary to recognize, first of all, that it is beyond the distinction of epistemological realism and idealism. Although associated in later thought with epistemological idealism, historically it has been maintained by realist and idealist alike.

It is important to emphasize this point if we are to understand the real driving force of traditional thought. The phenomenal and dependent character of space and time has been recognized by thinkers whose theories of knowledge are realistic. Again, while for idealists much of the force of the phenomenalistic position has seemed to arise from the contradictions which appear in our notions of space and time when they are conceived as independent entities, it is, nevertheless, entirely possible to find these arguments illusory and yet accept, in its essence, the traditional position. In fact, the real driving force of the argument is axiological. As the origin of the space-time problem is axiological, so must its ultimate solution be also.

It is in Leibniz, perhaps, that the deeper motive of the

traditional doctrine appears at its best. We think of Leibniz, to be sure, as the one who did most to press that form of idealism which regards space and time as private to finite sentients and without ultimate cosmic standing. In space, for instance, he says, we have an *ens mentale* which derives from our confused perception of other kinds of relations of simple entities, themselves not spatial. As thus explained, space is an order of coexisting which obtains only for qualitative contents of this or that monad. It is not an order which includes the monads themselves. It has, therefore, no ultimate cosmic standing. Generalized, and freed from the particulars of Leibniz's system, the essentials of this doctrine are that space (and time also) constitute an order that does not include any of the monads, ideas, and values that are considered ultimate. Leibniz's disproof of the independent reality of space and time is indeed largely formal and logical in character. It emphasizes certain contradictions which conceivably rest upon misunderstandings which mathematical logic can remove. But beneath these surface arguments is a deeper one, *axiological* in character, arising from certain assumptions or presuppositions without which intelligibility is ultimately impossible.

Leibniz's disproof of the independent reality of space and time, when stripped of the particulars of his own system, is, I repeat, the essence of the traditional line of thought. We must accordingly examine it with some care. "I say then," Leibniz writes, "that if space was an absolute being, there would happen something for which it is impossible that there should be a sufficient reason, which is against my axiom, and I prove it thus. Space is something absolutely uniform; and without the things placed in it, one point in space does not absolutely differ in any respect whatsoever from any other point in space. Now from hence it follows (supposing space to be something in itself besides the order of bodies among themselves) that 'tis impossible that there should be any reason why God, preserving the same situations of bodies, among themselves, should have placed them in space after one certain particular manner and not otherwise, and why everything was not placed in the contrary way, for instance, by changing east into west. But if space is nothing else but the order of relation, and is nothing at all without bodies but the possibility of placing

them, then these two states, the one such as it now is, the other
supposed to be the contrary way, would not at all differ from
each other. Their difference, therefore, is only to be found in
our chimerical supposition of the reality of space in itself."[1]
The case, Leibniz holds, "is the same with respect to time."
In other words, space and time are unintelligible when conceived as independent entities and the world in space and
time is unintelligible when they are so conceived.

It is easy to miss the force of Leibniz's argument in our
dissatisfaction with the form in which he expresses his ideal
of intelligibility or *sufficient reason*. We may question the assumption that space and time are objects about which the question
"why?" can be intelligently and legitimately asked. We may
question his appeal to the ideal mind or will of God as a
criterion of intelligibility. Yet both these forms of expression
may be discounted and the essence of the argument remain
unimpaired. Both the why, as an external purpose, and a God
as a purposer, may be taken as symbols, or even as convenient
fictions, without affecting its meaning or force. For the point
of the argument is this, as he states it in his fourth letter to
Clarke: If space and time are uniform, and they are, and if
their mutual externality is conceived as existing or subsisting
wholly independently, then "there can be neither any external
nor *internal* reason by which to distinguish their parts and to
make any choice or distinction among them."[2] In other words,
so conceived, there is no element of direction in space and time,
and without direction they are ultimately meaningless and unintelligible.

In maintaining this position, however, Leibniz is but
insisting upon that which most thinkers, both ancient and
modern, have fully realized. Given the idea of spatial endlessness of the universe, it is impossible that any one direction in
the universe can be distinguished from another. But just as in
a spatially infinite universe there can be no over, nor under,
so just as truly is it impossible to have an earlier or later in one
that is temporally infinite. Rather must the total condition
of the universe at all moments of time be, as we instinctively

---

[1] Third Letter to Clarke, quoted from R. Latta, *Leibniz, The Monadology, etc.*,
p. 102.
[2] *Op. cit.*, p. 104, note.

feel, really the same. The ultimate meaninglessness of absolute space and absolute time, and the ultimate unintelligibility of a world without limits and without beginning and end, are among those insights of traditional thought which no amount of sophistication can really darken. If there is to be direction in space and time, if space and time themselves are to have meaning, they must get it from something other than themselves. For this reason it remains true, as Mr. Russell says, that "a truer image of the world is obtained" (if, indeed, we must have an image) "by picturing things as entering into the stream of time from an external world outside than from a view which regards time as the devouring tyrant of all that is." It is truer because more intelligible.

This refusal of traditional thought to identify being and becoming either with duration, or with space-time, is, I repeat, ultimately axiologically motived. This appears most clearly, I think, when we examine from this point of view the contradictions or antinomies which traditional thought has uniformly found in space and time when made absolute—the antithesis of the finite and the infinite in its various forms.

These problems have, it is true, been uniformly conceived as logical and ontological, but they are gradually being recognized as deeper both in origin and nature. On the one hand, one may well question whether the removal of the problem to the subjective world is more than an evasion. On the other hand, it may be doubted whether any mere "logical" proof that space and time when conceived as absolute are free from logical contradictions, really proves that they are ultimately intelligible. In any case, the unintelligibility of space and time, as argued from the antinomies, really implies the problem of the relation of space and time to value.

This is, perhaps, best seen in the difficulties of the antithesis of the finite and the infinite which any attempt to conceive the ultimate metaphysical reality of time brings out. The idea of time as finite implies the end of time, and therefore an end of happening, change, life, and volition. The idea of the infinite, on the contrary, opens out a vista of an infinite series of events in infinite time, and therefore implies that the will can never come to rest; the gates of the future are for ever open. These contrasting ideas are respectively congenial to different men according to their respective temperaments. But if we look closely at them, "it is," as Windelband says, "difficult to say which idea is the more *intolerable*, that of an absolute rest, or that of a never-ending restlessness of the will. Both elements have their emotional value in relation to the finite time-aspects of empirical reality and our varying experience of it. At one time rest is welcome after long unrest; though it is tolerable only if it does not last too long. By others the struggle, even if it does not attain its end, is gladly welcomed; yet if such a state of things is conceived absolutely, it threatens to make the will itself illusory. Thus we see that the things that are certainly real in the finite world of experience become *impossibilities* the moment they are converted into absolute realities by metaphysical thought."[1]

I have quoted this passage at length for two reasons: first, to bring out the essentially axiological origin of the antinomy problem and its relation to the phenomenological doctrine of time; secondly, in order to comment on this use of the concept of the *intolerable*. That the antinomy of the finite and the infinite is no puzzle of the mere intellect, but gets its real drive from its relation to volition and value, is obvious, as was indeed made clear by Hegel's distinction between the "good" and the "bad" infinite. The identification of metaphysical impossibility with the intolerable, moreover, indicates the close relation of intelligibility to value. This relation has already been indicated in our doctrine of intrinsic intelligibility,[2] but the further thesis, that the axiologically intolerable is also one aspect of the metaphysically unintelligible, constitutes one of the main theses of certain discussions to come.[3] I will not stop here to develop this idea of the intolerable as the unintelligible. In this connection it is merely another indication of our general thesis (which the present section has made clear), that as the origin of the space-time problem is axiological, so must its solution ultimately be.

I have dwelt rather long, perhaps, on these old things. If so, it is because only by so doing could the essence of traditional thought regarding space and time be made clear. It is because Leibniz's conclusions, as well as his line of argument, exhibit

---

[1] W. Windelband, *Introduction to Philosophy* (1921), pp. 98 ff.
[2] See Chapter V, pp. 183 ff.   [3] See Chapter X, pp. 334 ff.

the axiological motive so clearly that I have made use of them. It is because this argument, quite independent of any secondary questions of subjectivity or objectivity, of mental or non-mental character, embodies an insight which no amount of sophistication can darken, that I have used it to display the ultimate intentions of traditional thought.

VII

The phenomenal character of space and time is the essence of traditional interpretation. We are now familiar with the negative side of the argument, with the "depreciation" of space and time. Let us turn now to the more positive side of the conception.

Space and time are not intelligible in themselves because they have no "sufficient reason," neither external nor internal meaning. Whatever meaning they have—and they have a genuine meaning and reality according to traditional thought —comes from something other than themselves. For interpretation space and time are phenomenal of an intelligible world, of an order that is really "logical" or "teleological." Space and time are the very warp and woof of the canvas on which the meanings of the world are spread out. But they constitute only the canvas. This genuine meaning and reality —that which they have precisely because of their "phenomenal" character—we must now seek to understand.

Steinmetz, the distinguished scientist, has said that "poetry, revelation, philosophy, mathematics, and science, all agree that space and time are not entities, but are conceptions of the human mind." To this dictum there will be many to take exception. But if he had said that all agree in recognizing objects or entities whose "meanings" are non-spatial and non-temporal his statement could scarcely be challenged.

With regard to mathematics and science nothing is clearer than the gradual substitution of logical relations for the empirical intuitions of space and time, of a logical order for a space-time order. We speak of the depreciation of space and time in traditional philosophy. Minkowski, with whose mathematical and physical conceptions those of Einstein are closely related, draws a picture of the world as four-dimensional with space and time "degraded to mere shadows, leaving nothing of their substance save a sort of unitedness of the two." The absolute world-order which both Minkowski and Einstein postulate, is one in which objects, and the definite relations which are what we mean by space and time, have not yet been constructed. Much discussion has arisen as to the relation of this view of space and time to that of Kant. The view, expressed by Cassirer and others, that there is a significant divergence between the views of Kant and Einstein is probably true. For Kant, as for Newton, space and time were unchanging frameworks in which the objects of nature exist. For Einstein they are always empirical, and not pure transcendental forms. For Kant, space and time are relative to the intelligible world of meanings and values. For the modern doctrine of relativity they are relative to the empirical world also. But, significant as the divergence is between the most modern mathematics and science and the traditional philosophical conceptions, as they found expression in Kant, this divergence should not be allowed to obscure the fundamental agreement of the modern doctrine with the essence of the tradition. The substitution of logical relations for the sensuous intuitions of space and time means that the intelligible world is non-spatial and non-temporal.

When it comes to the intuitions of "poetry and revelation," the very essence of those intuitions and, as we shall see, the very condition of their communication, are the acknowledgment of objects whose meanings are non-spatial and non-temporal. "A poet," writes Shelley in his *Defence of Poetry*, "participates in the Eternal, the infinite, the one. As far as relates to his conceptions, time and place and number are not. The grammatical forms," he continues, "which express the moods of time, and the difference of persons and the distinctions of place, are convertible with respect to the highest poetry without injuring it as poetry; and the choruses of Æschylus, the Book of Job, and Dante's Paradise would afford, more than any other writings, examples of the fact, if the limits of this essay did not forbid." The agreement of the poets on this interpretation of the "reality" with which their imaginations deal is so unanimous that at this point, where we are concerned only with their own interpretations, we need only note the agreement with traditional philosophy.

Whatever may be said of poetry and revelation, of science and mathematics, the instinct of philosophy is sure and its idiom definite and distinctive. Space and time are "phenomenal" of more ultimate meanings and values. For traditional thought mutual externality in space and time is the condition of things in the world of sense, mutual inclusion or compenetration the distinctive character of the "spiritual" or intelligible world. Spatial relations are phenomenal of inner affinities, temporal process of inner meanings and values. Non-spatial and non-temporal intuition is the condition of the interpretation of the space-time world itself.

That space and time are phenomenal of an order of meaning and value is, as we have seen, assumed even in the "descriptions" and "explanations" of science. Necessary spaces and necessary times are necessary for the development of qualities and totalities, meanings and values, themselves not spatial and temporal. Even in the sub-human world, organic and inorganic, space and time relations are intelligible only with reference to a non-temporal and non-spatial order. It is, to be sure, only in space and time and through space-time processes that such qualities and meanings emerge. But space and time acquire meaning only with respect to directions which are themselves non-spatial and non-temporal. Mutual externality is a law of this world, but not its deepest law.

This is true even of the sub-human world, but it becomes still more evident when we enter the world of persons and their relations. The phenomenal character of space and time, in the sense described, is assumed in all interpretations of community and State, of whatever type. A correspondence between the space-time order and a non-spatial and non-temporal order of values is taken for granted in every interpretation of the human order. By this correspondence I understand something very definite and something the meaning of which is immediately evident. The idea of "community" is essentially a non-spatial conception—it is the mutual acknowledgment of common values. Yet, as we have seen, the very "axiom" of the historical understanding of such community is the existence of separate social groups. Actually, the local contiguity and the spatial isolation of a group from other groups are always taken as outward and visible signs of an inner or spiritual community of social aspiration. It is this immediate correspondence between the spatial and non-spatial orders, always assumed, that constitutes in this connection the phenomenal character of space.

This correspondence between the spatial and non-spatial orders is, of course, only approximate. Only in those sections of mankind which have not yet succeeded in actively controlling the physical order for their purposes is it true that spatial contiguity and inner similarity, spatial remoteness and inner dissimilarity, coincide. But these facts only serve to show the more completely how the spatial order is related to the non-spatial. In proportion as man's conquest over space becomes complete, he seeks to devise means to extend and retain this inner unity of aims and interests, in spite of spatial separation. The abolition of distance effected by science and civilization is, as it were, a practical vindication of this philosophical doctrine of space. Humanity's ideal seems to be to make communication in thought with our fellows free from the restrictions of space and time. Mutual com-penetration, community, is assumed to be the meaning of the human, social world. It is assumed throughout that there is more of meaning and value in com-penetration and community than in externality. The mere fact that men can communicate with each other more widely and more quickly does not, to be sure, of itself mean increase of value, as is so often assumed in superficial conceptions of progress. This very communication brings with it negative values that must be taken account of. But this wider and more rapid communication forms a necessary condition of progress. The elimination of space and the binding of time are the conditions of civilization. But these conditions have no significance unless civilization and culture themselves are apprehended as having non-spatial and non-temporal significance.

The interpretation of human life thus assumes that the spatial relations of human beings are phenomenal of non-spatial meanings and values. Similarly, any interpretation of human life presupposes that the temporal strivings of intelligent purposive beings are phenomenal of inner meanings and values, themselves not temporal.

All concepts of development, whether in the ancient sense

or in the more modern sense of progress, presuppose this phenomenal relation between temporal stages and non-temporal levels of value. This is not yet the place to take up specifically the problem of an intelligible conception of progress. Here we shall content ourselves with pointing out that, while the principle of necessary times is a law of all human striving and development, it also is not the deepest law. "It takes time" for new qualities to emerge in the inorganic and organic world. It takes time for human meanings and values to be realized. The principle of "necessary stages," through which all development, individual and social, must go, is fundamental. All short cuts in development mean movement in a circle. Time is phenomenal here, but it is also, in the special sense in which we are using the term, a *phenomenon bene fundatum*. But just as with the idea of a mutual compenetration that shall transcend space, so the idea of an order of values that transcends time is presupposed in all intelligible concepts of progress. The only intelligible concept of progress, as we shall see later, is a transcendental one.[1]

For traditional philosophy, space and time have necessarily the same origin and the same value. Both are but the distance between what is and what ought to be. The same diminution of being is expressed by extension in space and detension in time. The general truth of this characterization is now obvious. The truth of the traditional position itself now appears in the fact that distances, whether spatial or temporal, have meaning only as they are conceived of as instrumental to the realization of meaning and values. From the axiological point of view, phenomenal and noumenal can be translated into instrumental and intrinsic.

VIII

I have now developed what seems to me to be the real meaning of the traditional conception of the space-time order, as phenomenal or symbolic of non-spatial and non-temporal relations. Are the upholders of this view forced to regard the conditions of space and time, under which alone the meanings

[1] See Chapter XI, pp. 386 ff.

of this order emerge and through which alone we learn to realize them, as themselves unreal and mere appearance? Not at all. The conditions of space and time, though when taken by themselves without meaning and value, are yet essential to this realization; and our idea of them suffers loss if divorced from these conditions. If space and time are in this sense symbols they are symbols which are part of the truth.

This is one aspect of the traditional conception, but only one. It has as its correlative, as we have seen, the recognition and acknowledgment of objects whose meanings are non-spatial and non-temporal. The very condition of making space and time themselves intelligible is the assumption of the non-spatial and non-temporal order of meaning and value. With this traditional view there has, accordingly, always gone a doctrine of non-spatial and non-temporal intuition, and the philosophers who represent it have always maintained the genuineness of such super-sensible knowledge. In this all the precursors of Kant have believed, to this view all who have sought to escape phenomenalism have returned. What shall we say of this persistent element in philosophical thought? Is there such intuition? To this question our entire chapter has in a sense been leading up. On our answer to it much of our future discussion must inevitably turn.

Let us recall, then, first of all what this position really means. One might be glad, it was said, to be an idealist in order to say certain noble things. The noble things in question were precisely those idioms in which poet and philosopher express their insight into spaceless and timeless realities. There are, in fact, certain "idioms" of "spiritual" communication and interpretation—idioms which imply non-spatial and non-temporal experience—without which the higher ranges of human experience are incommunicable. Two that we shall specificially consider are the idioms of "omnipresence," and of the "timeless present." The first embodies the realization of that compenetration or confluence that negates the externality of space; the second that interpenetration that negates the mutual externality of successive moments in time. Without these forms of speech communication of that which man is at his highest pitch is impossible. The necessary interdependence of communication and intelligible interpretation, as we have worked it out, makes the acknowledgment of these meanings the presupposition of all interpretation. *But the point which we wish to insist upon here is the existence of this idiom.* If there were no such experience as is represented by this concept of intuition, there would be no understanding of this idiom.

To the poet and religionist these idioms are familiar and wholly intelligible. What could we do, asks Dean Inge, with the entire range of the higher poetry—with Shelley's Alastor or Wordsworth's interpretation of nature, for instance—if we did not understand these idioms? What could we do with the religion of a Plato or a Paul, or with St. John's life of Christ? Literally nothing. Without an experience corresponding to these idioms, they would all become nonsense, as indeed they are perhaps to some. Now it is, of course, possible to say of the language of poetry, as of the language of metaphysics, that it is meaningless words. This is the common retort of the "matter of fact" mind, for which the nature of reality is already pre-determined by the prejudice in favour of the actual in space and time. Here we shall simply insist, with Hegel, that the first condition of philosophical knowledge is the acknowledgment of all the forms of human experience. Philosophy must also understand and speak this non-spatial and non-temporal idiom; for without it philosophy would also remain stupid and dumb.

This philosophical idiom has its difficulties and, as we shall see, is not wholly easy to make intelligible. Thus the philosopher—to say nothing of the poet and the religionist—speaks of the "things" that are temporal and the "things" that are eternal, for he must use the only language that the natural prejudice in favour of the "actual" permits him. He must speak in existential terms when it is really with meanings and values that he is concerned. Yet despite all the difficulties inherent in metaphor, the essential intuition expressed in this idiom cannot be darkened. Let us examine these forms of expression more closely.

Take, for instance, the spiritual idioms of omnipresence and immanence. In them some of the deepest human meanings are, and indeed alone can be, expressed, for it is the form of thought in which non-spatial meaning is acknowledged. It is highly figurative, but for that reason none the less ultimately intelligible. Over the shifts to which the literal and purely analytic mind has been put adequately to express this insight, one knows not really whether to weep or to smile. The school-men, for instance, in attempting to express that *ubeity* which they called omnipresence, distinguished three kinds of "where-ness" : circumscriptive, definitive, and repletive, the first being attributed to bodies, the second to souls, the third to God. They illustrate perfectly the consequences of the confusion of the axiological and existential points of view. With his charac-teristic wisdom and intellectual magnanimity, Leibniz remarks, however, that "he does not know whether or not this doctrine deserves to be turned into ridicule, as some people endeavour to do." Here, it is possible, the philosophers, even the school-men, thought better than they spoke, for in the "repletive ubeity" they rather humorously attributed to God, they were translating, were they not, into technical terms, an idiom which in their more human moods they all thoroughly understood?

It is not different with the idiom of the "timeless present." "Timelessness," says Fawcett,[1] "is a favourite term of the philosophers. . . . There is a voice in the study, but no answering experience shows in the vasty deep." This dictum the most superficial survey of human experience must compel us to deny. Timelessness is indeed a "command concept," as Fawcett calls it, but not of the study; rather of all intelligible communication and interpretation. The poet sings: *"Dem Glücklichen schlägt keine Stunde."* We not only understand what he means, we also know that it is true. "So let him wait God's instant men call years," cries another poet. Bring to bear upon this expression of the eternal element in experience the analysis of the schoolmen and you will get results equally ludicrous, as, indeed, some of the serious discussions of the infinite prove.

The point I am trying to make here is a simple one, but, I think, one of great importance. It is the necessity of the non-spatial and non-temporal idiom for the communication and interpretation of experience. In other words, there is experience, intuition, which this idiom alone expresses. Can this idiom itself be made intelligible? It all depends upon what we consider philosophical intelligibility to be.

"The effort of philosophy to rationalize" (in our terms to make intelligible) "the non-temporal is," says Rogers, "a

---

[1] *The Divine Imagining*, p. 107.

total failure." Acceptance of the temporal character of reality is necessary, he holds, "not only to save human values, but speculatively necessary also" if we are to find for our words about the concrete world a definite and intelligible meaning. "The moment I try to reduce time to a logical category in an eternal and unchanging universe, that moment I am forced to abandon outright my everyday descriptions; and since I am not recompensed for the loss by an increase of intelligibility, I hesitate to make the exchange."[1]

If the acknowledgment of non-temporal meaning meant the abandonment of our "everyday descriptions" we might well sympathize with this reluctance. But it does not, as we have seen. Mutual externality of things in time, the principle of necessary times, is not only the condition of the emergence, of the realization of values, but this principle itself is unintelligible without the assumption of a non-temporal order of values. On the other hand, as we have also seen, there is an increase of intelligibility if we acknowledge non-temporal objects. In fact, "if we are to find for our words about the concrete world itself a definite and intelligible meaning," we must use this idiom. The rôle of space and time in civilization and culture is a practical vindication of this philosophical doctrine.

In the experience of this concrete world, permanence, lastingness, is a test of value and reality. We increase the value and meaning of things in ordinary life when we lift them above the temporal level and secure them from the ravages of time. May we not, then, think of eternity or the "timeless" as a mode in which we express value? When we speak of God as eternal, the core of our meaning is that we look upon God as the absolutely valuable. This conception of value, this mode of expressing value, does not necessarily imply something that has never been in time, but rather something which, having been in time, is then raised to a higher level, the process of time having made its contribution to value, or having been the condition of the emergence or realization of value.

The point we are insisting upon here is merely the necessity of this non-spatial and non-temporal idiom for the expression of the meaning of the spatio-temporal order itself. It is not necessary to deny that form of experience which is described

---

[1] A. K. Rogers, *What is Truth?* pp. 175 ff.

as super-sensible intuition. The fact that there are such experiences, realizations, remains, of course, the ultimate source, as it is the final ground, for that universal agreement of poetry, revelation, mathematics, and philosophy of which Steinmetz speaks and also for the Great Tradition which expresses that agreement. But it is not necessary for our argument to appeal to such insights here. It is enough for our purpose to insist that the acknowledgment of *the reality of such moments is actually presupposed in the entire idiom of spiritual communication—in every attempt to communicate the meaning of our spatio-temporal experiences themselves.*

Otherwise expressed, there is constant expression of these "things" that are outside space and time. Of the things in space and time we say, this thing is outside that, they cannot coincide and amalgamate: this thing comes after that, the former must disappear before the latter arrives. But our minds tell us that there is a large class of objects of which these statements are not true, and the meanings of which are wholly incommunicable in these terms. "These things do not interfere with each other. They are alive and active, but they are neither born nor do they die. They are constant without inertia, they are active but they do not move." Our knowledge of this order is as direct and certain as our knowledge of the spatio-temporal order, and we have an idiom to express that knowledge.

If there were expression, communication, of meaning only when there is description in space and time, we should have to choose between ineffability and despair. But every yes and no, every affirmation or negation, proves the possibility of expressing that which is not so describable. The truth remains—and it is perhaps the deepest truth, underlying all other truths—that communication transcends space and time and is itself not describable in space and time. The solution of the riddle of life in space and time, if there be a solution, lies outside space and time.[1]

[1] Here again one sees that the fundamental problems of metaphysics all go back ultimately to the problem of the *philosophy of language*. The "language of metaphysics" always implies a doctrine of realism as opposed to nominalism. It is true that, as Mauthner has said, there never has been, nor could there be, a consistent nominalist. He who talks at all is always a realist. But the metaphysician is he who believes that language can express objects, or refers to objects, which, while real, are not describable as existents in space and time.

IX

The traditional conception of space and time as we have now developed it and interpreted it contains two elements. Space and time are phenomenal of a non-spatial and non-temporal order of meanings and values. This presupposes a super-sensible intuition of a non-temporal and non-spatial order. Our interpretation of these two elements provides us, I think, with the means of understanding and solving what is, perhaps, one of the central and most difficult questions of traditional thought.

For traditional philosophy origin and destiny are essential parts of "the form of philosophic intelligibility." Yet the all-pervasive character of space and time seem to eliminate all intelligible meaning from the concepts of absolute beginning or end. Has the world a beginning in time or an end in time? Is it limited or unlimited in space? About these questions, as well as others, has raged the discussion of the intelligibility or unintelligibility of space and time.

Now, so far as mathematics and physical science are concerned it may probably be said that the question whether the world is endless or not in space and time is at present unsolved if not insoluble. In an article entitled, *Ist die Welt in Raum und Zeit unendlich?* the Vienna physicist, Erich Hass, expresses the belief that while it is "*widersinnig*" to seek in physical laws a proof for the infinity of the universe, at the same time he believes that the physical facts can never bring a cogent proof for the opposite position.[1] One thing that seems to militate against an unlimited universe is, however, the fact of direction in it, the fact, namely, that all events, including the physical, appear to possess a definite direction—at least, if we take the principle of entropy as "metaphysical," that is, as more than symbolic description. Be this as it may, and we shall consider this problem in a later connection, all that concerns us here is to comment on the questionable character of the dogma of the endlessness of the world in space and time.

More important than this, however, is the recognition of the fact that the problem of ultimate origin (and, as I think, the problem of ultimate destiny also) is not affected by the all-pervasive character of space and time as we have come to

[1] *Archiv für Systematische Philosophie*, 1912.

understand it. The reason for this is that in our terms the ultimate problems of space and time are not logical, but axiological.

The position of traditional thought on this point is as definite as it is constant. The argument for a first cause, for intelligible causation, is, as it has been understood from Aristotle on, entirely independent of the philosophical consideration of the eternity of the world. Eternity as such is only a chronological attribute and can never be made equal to the reason—the sufficient reason—of a thing. One might find many expressions of this position, but here again we may with advantage take a classical formulation as found in Leibniz's paper "On the Ultimate Origination of All Things," especially useful for our purpose here for the reason that it was Leibniz also who furnished us with the best insight into the driving force of the traditional view of space and time. "Even by supposing the eternity of the world," Leibniz holds, "we cannot escape the ultimate extra-mundane reason of things, that is to say, God. For in eternal things, even if there be no cause, there must be a reason, which for permanent things is necessity itself, or essence. But for the series of changing things, if it be supposed that they succeed one another from all eternity, this reason is the prevailing of inclinations which consist not in necessitating reasons, of an absolute and metaphysical necessity, the opposite of which involves a contradiction, but in inclining reasons. These inclining reasons are the superiority of the good over the bad in the things that come to pass. The balance or preponderance inclines the will of God without absolutely necessitating it, to create these contingent things."[1]

Leibniz's idiom, it may be admitted, is sufficiently remote from our present ways of expressing ourselves. But for the discerning thinker, this difference will not serve to obscure the perennial truth of these conceptions which belong to the natural use of the intelligence as such—namely, that cause and substance in their metaphysical use are axiological concepts and belong to philosophical intelligibility as distinct from scientific description and explanation. The traditional argument does not ask where the world came from. It asks something much more fundamental—how to account for its character

[1] *Op. cit.*, p. 338.

and the directions of its becoming. If the world is eternal, then it is eternally unmeaning unless it gets its meaning from something beyond space and time. The answer to the riddle of the world in space and time lies outside space and time.

To this question of ultimate origination and intelligible causation we shall turn in the following chapter. Here I wish merely to suggest that the "phenomenal" character of space and time, as we have sought to understand it, opens up a way to the understanding of this problem also.

X

The characteristic of the traditional solution of the space-time problem is that reality is *both in and out* of space, *both in and out* of time. The Great Tradition is the magnanimous tradition, and it is characteristic of the magnanimous philosophers of all time that to the *"either, or,"* of the downright mind they have wanted to say "both, and." Reality is both in and out of space and time; space and time are both real and unreal. However inadequate his formula, it was this that led Kant to say: "Empirically real, transcendentally ideal."

But this, Bergson, like many others, finds an "appalling contradiction." Rather than formulate such a contradiction philosophers were necessarily led, he holds, to sacrifice the weaker of the two terms and to regard the spatio-temporal aspect of things as mere illusion. For myself, I find no such contradiction. *"Das alle Reele ist wohl,"* says Hegel, *"von der Zeit verschieden aber eben so wesentlich identisch mit ihr."* With this I can fully agree, as also with a further statement of his, in the same connection. *"So geht auch die Zeit der Unterschied der Objectivität, und einer gegen dieselbe, subjectiven Bewusstseins, nichts an."* [1] These two sentences are almost the most significant things ever said on this question. For they summarize in a few words the traditional conception as I understand it.

The distinction of subjective and objective is irrelevant to the real problems of space and time. The significant problems lie beyond the distinction of epistemological realism and

[1] *Encyklopädie,* § 258 (Kirchmann ed., p. 216).

idealism. The motives which underlie the conception of space and time as phenomenal of a non-spatial and non-temporal order, while historically closely connected with the motives of epistemological idealism, are not necessarily bound up with them. That a Leibniz should call them "mental entities," a Kant "necessary forms of perception," is understandable, but the same conception was equally present in ancient philosophy in which the element of modern subjectivism had not yet appeared. Moreover, the absolute world order which both Minkowski and Einstein postulate is one in which objects with the definite relations which are what we mean by space and time have not yet been constructed. The dissociation of this traditional doctrine from subjectivism is the first condition of our understanding it.

It is equally true that the ultimately real is different from time, even as it is essentially identical with it. That space and time are all-pervasive in the sense of being the necessary conditions of the description and explanation of existence, does not exclude the equally important truth that reality has other aspects that are not expressible in these categories. Reality is both in and out of space, both in and out of time. This we all know, for we assume it in all our attempts at the communication of the meanings of reality. Communication itself transcends the spatial and the temporal. We all know this. But we can understand it only on the basis of the fundamental axiom of intelligible thought and its communication—the inseparability of value and reality.

The significance of this chapter in the development of our main theme is, then, twofold. We have, on the one hand, reinterpreted and, as I think, justified the traditional position which refuses to identify "reality" with existence in space and time, in other words with becoming. But we have also, by our reinterpretation of that position, also cleared the way for a restatement of the traditional "form of philosophical intelligibility." Such intelligibility is, as we have seen, ultimately bound up with questions of origin and destiny and cannot be separated from them. Yet one of the most persistent tendencies of this same tradition is to detemporalize and despatialize these conceptions. We have at least come to understand the significance of that tendency. The solution of the riddle of life in space and time—if there be a solution—does, indeed, lie outside space and time. But certainly there can be no solution of that problem which involves the abandonment of the one *form* in which thought alone can intelligibly express itself. To the development of the elements in this form we must now turn.

CHAPTER VIII

ORIGIN AND VALUE: POTENTIALITY—MATTER AND SPIRIT

Surely it is not likely that fire or earth or any such element should be the reason why things manifest goodness and beauty both in their being and their coming to be, or that those thinkers should have supposed it was; nor again could it be right to ascribe so great a matter to spontaneity and luck. When one man declared then that reason was present—as in animals so throughout nature—being the cause of the world and all its order, he seemed like a sober man in contrast with the random talk of his predecessors. . . . Those who thought thus stated that there is a principle of things which is at the same time the cause of beauty and that sort of cause from which things acquire movement.

ARISTOTLE, *Metaphysics*

The present depression of humanity has its origin, I believe, solely in man's degraded sense of his origin. The human race feels itself like a rat in a trap. We began in mud and shall end in mud. Life is reaching the end of its tether. Humanity rots for a new definition of life.

The Glass of Fashion, p. 170

I

THE problem of an intelligible world begins with the problems of space and time, implicates inevitably the alternative of matter and spirit, and finds its culmination in questions relative to the origin and end of all things. The what, the whence, the why and the whereto, are the questions with which philosophy started, and in some form they will be the questions of philosophy until the end of time. When the philosopher ceases to ask about "the first and last things," he ceases, *ipso facto*, to be a philosopher.

But while these continue to be the root questions of any cosmology, their form changes. From one point of view the entire history of speculative thought might be written in terms of changes in the form and meaning of these questions. It was, indeed, the realization of this truth, however imperfectly, that gave the touch of genius to the thinking of William James. In considering metaphysical questions pragmatically he reckoned, it is true, with imperfect and incoherent concepts of value and reality, but he at least recognized that these questions about "first and last things" are genuine

s

problems of philosophy because they are the problems of men.

Many, indeed, speak of the "absolutely false and superannuated conception of philosophy, according to which the object of the latter is the beginning and end of things." Thus Couturat, voicing this modern fashion in thought, says: "Such questions, in so far as they are at all soluble, evidently belong to the scientific and historical methods, and have nothing really philosophical about them unless by confusion of ideas, springing from the ambiguity of the word *principium*, according to which principle is identified with beginning." That they should be considered not to be soluble at all one can well understand. That is, indeed, a necessary consequence of the separation of questions of "fact" from questions of "value." But that there should be thought to be anything in the scientific or historical methods as such, even to take hold of these problems, to say nothing of solving them, is an illusion which critical science itself has abandoned. It may be a superannuated philosophy that asks these questions. But if philosophy ceases to ask them, something else in the human spirit will continue to do so. What we call that something— that fundamental initiative of the human spirit we call speculation—matters little. One does not get rid of metaphysics by calling it question-begging epithets. Nor are questions any less metaphysical for being pragmatically considered.

The speculative form characteristic of modern thought is that of evolutionism in some form or another. Evolutionary naturalism, creative evolution, emergent evolution, such are some of the formulas in which it is sought to make the world intelligible. The idea of evolution, it has been well said, is "the lord of all our present thinking." As Mallock has said, "it gives speculative meaning to the history of humanity and excites men by suggesting great social changes in the future." In so far, however, as it gives this speculative meaning, it does so ultimately only by some conception, either explicit or implicit, of ultimate origination. In so far as it excites or interests men by suggestions concerning the future, it does so ultimately only by conceptions, either explicit or implicit, of ultimate destiny. It is the metaphysics of the modern.

That any intelligible conception of evolution is essentially and necessarily a metaphysic is a position few, I think, would care to deny. It is, nevertheless, a question we shall consider in its proper place. Here we shall content ourselves with pointing out that the recognition of its metaphysical character brings with it necessarily the recognition of the problem of the ultimate nature of the reality which has evolved, and the question of the destiny or character of the direction in which the evolution takes place. It is on these questions that modernism in all its forms takes an exactly contrary course from that of the "natural metaphysic" of the human mind, from the form in which an intelligible world has been traditionally conceived. The concepts of both origin and destiny (direction) have been separated from value. Questions of value, we are told, have nothing to do with questions of origin. The concepts of "direction," even the concept of "perfection," as used in naturalistic evolution, has nothing to do with value. These far-reaching dissociations of hitherto durable connections of ideas involve consequences of such magnitude that a most searching examination is imperative. In a sense the whole question of intelligible discourse is at stake.

II

For traditional thought origin and value have always been held to be inseparable. On this question the greatest thinkers have never been in doubt, although they have had difficulty in expressing this belief adequately. The reason for the belief is clear enough. There is, it has always been felt, *more* in spirit than in matter, more of meaning and value, and therefore more of "reality."

Underlying this traditional way of thinking is, however, an assumption which modernistic philosophy in the main insists upon calling a prejudice. Nietzsche, in many respects the epitome of modernism, calls it "the typical prejudice by which the metaphysicians of all time can be recognized." "How could," so these metaphysicians ask themselves, "how could anything originate out of its opposite? Such a genesis is impossible; whoever dreams of it is a fool—nay, worse than a fool. Things of the highest value must have a different origin, an origin all their own. In this transitory, seductive, illusory, paltry world, in this turmoil of delusion and cupidity, they cannot have their source. But rather in the lap of Being, in the intransitory, the concealed God, in the thing-in-itself— there must be their source and nowhere else."[1]

Nietzsche is undoubtedly right in seeing in this the typical attitude of traditional philosophy. Whether prejudice or necessary presupposition, this feeling constitutes its life-blood, its driving force. Bound up with this "prejudice," back of this way of thinking, are, as Nietzsche sees, a certain "mode of valuation," a certain "antithesis of value," which he holds are open to serious question. He doubts, not only that the popular valuations and antitheses of value, upon which the metaphysicians have set their seal, are anything but superficial estimates; he also doubts that such antitheses exist at all. More than this, he doubts the very assumption which connects value at all with origin, and finds in it nothing more than a "moral prejudice."

Is, then, this prejudice of the metaphysicians really a prejudice, or is it, rather, one of those fundamental presuppositions without which intelligible thought and its communication are impossible? It is my belief that the latter is the truth, and that the arrest of the spiritual initiative which it embodies is the source, not only of much of our philosophical depression, but also of the sophistication and sophistry in which so much of modern philosophy has involved itself.

It is to Bergson we owe the setting of the constant "form of intelligibility" of traditional philosophy in so clear a light. It is to him also that we owe the clearest statement of the necessary relation of origin and value that goes with it. There is, according to him, immanent in perennial philosophy "a particular conception of causality which it is most important to bring to light. For it is that which each of us will reach when in order to ascend to the origin of things he follows to the end the natural movement of the intellect." Now, this conception, as he develops it, is precisely that "mode of valuation" which Nietzsche and so many other moderns relegate to the limbo of outworn prejudices. As Bergson states it, "Philosophy can derive the less from the more, never the more from the less."

[1] *Beyond Good and Evil*, chapter i.

It is interesting to note that Bergson himself does not challenge this principle of intelligible causation. It is the driving force of his own thought and he appeals to it explicitly as the ultimate basis of his own "philosophy of change." It is, he says, because "there is *more* in movement than in the successive positions attributed to the moving objects, more in becoming than in the forms passed through," that the latter can be derived from the former, never the former from the latter. "Philosophy," he continues, "can therefore derive terms of the second kind from the first, but not the first from the second."[1] It is not, therefore, the "traditional mode of valuation" that Bergson challenges, but rather the traditional antithesis of values. The irresistible movement of thought, from the less to the more, drives traditional thought from the changing to the permanent. This same movement of thought drives Bergson in the reverse direction.

Of Bergson's own transvaluation of metaphysical values we shall have more to say in a later chapter when we take up the question of intelligible evolution. Even now, however, we may see that this transvaluation has its roots in his misconception of the relation of time to value which we have already examined, namely, in his failure to recognize that the *more* of meaning one seems to find in becoming does not belong to mere becoming itself, but rather to the value that gives continuity and interpenetration to the becoming.[2] But this is not the point that I wish to emphasize here. The significant thing is that he recognizes in this "prejudice" of the metaphysicians, not only the essence of traditional philosophy, but the condition of all philosophical intelligibility as such.

In this Bergson is, I think, fundamentally sound, however inconsistent he may be in carrying out the principle. For in accepting this principle that the less can be derived from the more, never the more from the less, he accepts also the principle that reality and value are inseparable. Intellect, in the narrow and special sense of his definition, may be oriented towards externality and matter, but philosophic insight, whether a matter of intuition or reason, is oriented towards value. Now, it is precisely this orientation that modernism in the main challenges, and in so doing challenges the entire structure of traditional thought.

[1] *Creative Evolution*, English translation, p. 310. [2] See Chapter VI, pp. 249 ff.

III

English-speaking philosophers are indebted to Professor R. B. Perry for an excellent exposition of the position of philosophic modernism on this point. Traditional speculative philosophy is for him, as for modernism in general, a bundle of prejudices which he calls the characteristic philosophical errors. These are the fallacies of "speculative dogma," of "indefinite potentiality," and of "pseudo-simplicity." Of them Professor Perry says: "These three errors have perpetually played into one another and have begotten certain well-nigh inveterate habits of thought." They are characteristic of all idealistic philosophies and all forms of activism; in short, of all forms of philosophy that attempt to make the world intelligible at all.[1]

These so-called "errors" are, one may easily read between the lines, merely aspects of the original and typical prejudice of the metaphysicians which we have been examining. The key fallacy, so to speak, in this complex of philosophical errors is obviously that of pseudo-simplicity, to which, as we shall find, the others are plainly reducible. Of this "fallacy" we have had a good deal to say in another connection.[2] Here we shall consider it only in connection with the errors of indefinite potentiality and speculative dogma, said to be inherent in traditional philosophy.

The fallacy of pseudo-simplicity consists, it is said, "in confusing the simplicity before analysis with the simplicity after analysis." This, we pointed out, is not true; there is no confusion here. The difference is perfectly understood. The perpetrator of this supposed fallacy knows perfectly well that the concepts he keeps intact are not simple in the sense of the radical analyst, but he also knows that they are *expressive* concepts that must be kept intact if intelligible communication is to be possible. After our study of space and time the reason for this becomes clearer. This simplicity, we now see, means that intelligible communication requires non-spatial and non-temporal categories. There is more in the whole than in the sum of the parts, more in the process than in the sum of the successive stages of the process. Intelligible communication

---

[1] *Present Philosophical Tendencies*, pp. 65 ff.   [2] See Chapter V, p. 197.

requires the use of the categories of immanence and omnipresence, and, as we shall now see, of the category of potentiality also.

For it is this, is it not, that the natural metaphysic of the human mind has always said. It is this that it means when it says that the less can be derived from the more, never the more from the less. It is also this that it means when, following out this natural movement of thought, it constantly and necessarily makes use of the category of potentiality. The "error" of indefinite potentiality, if it is an error, "the fallacy of the implicit," if it is a fallacy, is but another phase of the same mode of thought. This concept of potentiality is, as we shall see, the crucial problem of an intelligible concept of evolution, but it is also the *crux* of traditional thought as such. It must, therefore, be examined with great care.

Potentiality is a many-sided category. It helps to interpret the past and to anticipate the future. It stands for the significance and richness of terms. It tells us that terms are not reducible to their relations without a remainder. But it is even more than this; and it is for this further reason that it is, so to speak, the cement of all traditional systems. It is part of the *a priori* conditions of intelligibility. We feel that the stream cannot rise higher than its source. But in cosmic development, we are told, it is apparently the rule for the stream to rise higher than its source. It is this contradiction—between the *a priori* conditions of intelligibility and *apparent* actual experience—that the concept of potentiality attempts to meet. It does so by inverting the process in idea after it has been realized in fact.

Such procedure is, however, for modernist philosophy wholly indefensible. The concept of potentiality, we are told, does not explain. Reality is wholly actual. Perhaps. In any case, the concept is necessary for intelligible interpretation. Its indispensability for practice is admitted. But it is much more than merely a name for a practical attitude; its meaning is not wholly prospective, as some have maintained. It is essentially a value category, but the value is theoretical as well as practical. The philosophical meaning of potentiality is simply the postulate, or insight, that in the interpretation of any process it is the process as a whole that is to be considered if we wish to know the nature of the reality revealed in it. In other words, the concept of potentiality merely maintains that any valid speculative derivation presupposes the retention of the meaning and value of the thing to be derived.

The whole question of potentiality, it is obvious, is bound up with the question of our conception of the nature of time. If the philosophical meaning of potentiality is the insight that it is the process as a whole that is to be considered, if we wish to know the nature of the reality therein revealed, then it is clear that the intelligibility of the concept of potentiality depends on our conception of the nature of time and of the relation of value to time. For the traditional concept of time as phenomenal of an order of values not temporal, the later is clearly thus potential in the earlier. But it is generally considered that the more "modern" conceptions of time are antagonistic to the concept of potentiality.

Whether this is true or not depends, to be sure, on what we find the "modern" concept of time to be. Certainly one important aspect of it is the abandonment of the idea of instantaneous "presents" and insistence on continuity of past and future with the present. In this concept, as, for instance, developed by Whitehead, the notion of potentiality seems to be implied. Otherwise I am at a loss, I confess, to understand what he means. "The theory which I am urging," he writes, "admits a greater ultimate mystery and a deeper ignorance (than the materialistic theory with its notion of the instantaneous present). The past and future meet and mingle in an ill-defined present. The passage of nature, which is only another name for the creative force of existence, has no narrow ledge of definite instantaneous present within to operate. Its operative presence which is now urging nature forward *must be sought for throughout the whole* (italics mine) in the remotest past as well as in the narrowest breadth of any present duration. Perhaps also in the unrealized future. Perhaps also in the future which might be as well as the actual future that will be."[1]

In such a concept of time, I repeat, the idea of potentiality seems to be involved. What else does the seeking for this operative presence throughout the whole mean? "It is

[1] *The Concept of Nature,* p. 73.

impossible to meditate on time and the mystery of the creative passage of nature" (I think we shall all agree with these words in which he closes the passage) "without an overwhelming emotion at the limitations of human intelligence." But I feel sure also that such meditation increases our respect for those concepts, however inadequate, in terms of which thought has sought to grasp the nature of this passage. Among these concepts is certainly that of potentiality. Is it not the idea of the "instantaneous present" in the "old time" of science that excluded potentiality?

IV

The traditional use of the category of potentiality must then, it would seem, be retained in any intelligible interpretation of reality. If the "operative presence" of the "creative force of existence" must be sought for throughout the whole, past and future are brought together in one conception, and this conception is what traditional thought has meant by intelligible causation and intelligible substance.

It is in the use of these concepts, however, that there arises that "fallacy" to which has been given the name of speculative dogma. The natural metaphysic to which this error is ascribed consists in "the assumption of an all-general, all-sufficient first principle." It also means "the assertion of a maximum or superlative ideal having metaphysical validity." This natural metaphysic, as is fully realized, is beyond the distinction of epistemological realism and idealism. The motive involved in it being "quite independent of the cardinal principle of idealism," it must be recognized as being part of the form of philosophical intelligibility irrespective of any particular theory of knowledge.

The form in which this assumption has expressed itself is naturally in connection with the two categories of substance and causation and the two questions of ultimate origination and ultimate essence. It is the sophisticated critique exercised on these two categories by the monistic and pluralistic logics, and their consequent relegation to the level of appearance, that has led to the abandonment of this principle also.

On this general question we have already said most that needs to be said in another connection.[1] That they are necessary moments in any form of philosophical intelligibility we saw reason to maintain. But this modern depreciation of causation and substance calls for some further consideration in the present context. We shall attempt to show that these modern attacks are misdirected, and to maintain against them the traditional notions of intelligible causation and intelligible substance.

Depreciation of the category of causality proceeds from two sources, atomistic and monistic logic, both of which, we have seen, identify logic with the ultimate science of the real. Ambiguities in the natural use of the category are seized upon by both, and for both the contradictions to which they give rise are resolved by dispensing with the concept altogether.

Logical atomism points out that causes and effects, regarded as entities or things, are in the first instance qualitative, and that it is only in the first stages of knowledge that we are concerned with such relations of qualities. Knowledge begins, indeed, with such propositions as "fire expands bodies," but the higher stages of science become to a large extent attempts to formulate processes in purely quantitative terms. What we seek is not causes but formulæ expressible in equations. "In the notion of mutually gravitating bodies," it is said, "there is nothing that can be called a cause and nothing that can be called an effect. There is merely a formula."

This depreciation of causality is matched by another line of thought, according to which the relation of cause and effect tends to pass over into that of ground and consequent. Here criticism takes hold of the temporal element in the ordinary causal conception. The cause as a mere event in time contains, it finds, something irrelevant to the characters of logical system. Causality is abandoned in favour of logical correlation, and we have, as the outcome, the reduction of causation to metaphysical appearance characteristic of certain modern forms of absolute idealism.

Of this modern depreciation of causation in both its forms many things could be said. To say them would involve threshing over all the old straw that has accumulated since

[1] Chapter VI, sec. iii.

Hume and Kant. But there is only one thing that really needs to be said, and that concerns the fundamental question of the nature and function of logic and its relation to thought and language.

No doubt from the reflective, abstract, logical point of view we can reduce causation to mathematical formulæ and to logical correlation. We are driven from one "cause" to another without being able to reach an intelligible cause, and the natural metaphysic of the human mind becomes a mythology or metaphysical appearance. But the analytical and reflective point of view cannot be the only one at our disposal. For whatever is reflected presupposes something that is natural and spontaneous. Our reflected language presupposes the non-reflected. Intelligent reflection on any object implies the reality in some sense of the object reflected upon. Reflection that negates the natural light of reason that gave birth to the reflected would be contrary to all principles of philosophic intelligibility. Everything depends upon the fact that an ought is there that sets the play of thoughts, of ground, substance, cause, and purpose, in motion.

But this will become clearer as we examine the concept of intelligible substance with which that of intelligible causality is so closely related.

It is possible to form a concept of causality without that of substance, but not a concept of intelligible causation. It is possible to form a concept of causality without the idiom of immanence and omnipresence, but not an intelligible one. Hegel has put this truth in the following fashion: "Substance is cause in so far as it is reflected in itself, as against its transition into accidents, and so is the original thing."[1]

The category of substance, it must first of all be understood, is a value category. In the words of Münsterberg, "substance is the development of the values of existence." Or, putting it in a way to bring out the full significance of our own position, it is impossible to develop, to communicate, the values of existence without the concept of substance. The retention of the meaning and value of the "individual" is the axiological basis of substance in its meaning of thing-hood, the retention of the meaning and value of the universal the basis of substance

[1] *Encyklopädie*, § 153 (Kirchmann ed., p. 150).

in its sense of essence, the retention of the meaning and value of concrete totalities the basis of its use of important or characteristic elements. When Hegel said of the State that it is "ethical substance," he was entirely conscious of the axiological character of the concept. It was for this very reason that he said of substance that it is "the original thing."

The modern criticisms of the substance concept are, *mutatis mutandis*, the same as those of causation, and are carried on from the same general standpoints. The natural use of the category of substance contains certain ambiguities which reflective analysis is not slow to disclose and of which modern destructive criticism has taken full account.

Substance has meant any individual real thing, any entity; it has meant the unknown reality that underlies the known properties of anything, whether mental or material; it has meant the generalized reality which is manifested in a variety of particular things; and it had finally meant essence, the important or characteristic elements in any subject of discourse.

Now, it is precisely this ambiguous character of the category of substance that leads partly to the widespread proposal for its abandonment. And indeed, when we regard these different, and often contradictory, attempts of our ordinary thinking to determine the essential underlying unity of things, it is obvious that the "essential" is distinguished from the non-essential from a definite point of view, and that what is essential from one point of view is not essential from another. This is undoubtedly true precisely for the reason that concepts of substance are the development of the values of existence. These different and often contradictory conceptions are the results of those ontological prejudices examined elsewhere.[1] But, as we have seen, the admission of these particular ontological prejudices does not mean that the presupposition of an *ens realissimum* is itself a prejudice. It is just this presupposition that the demand for an intelligible substance or essence expresses. This point of view may, perhaps, best be indicated by again relating it to that of Hegel. "Substance," says the latter, "though a necessary stage in the evolution of the Idea, is not the same as the Idea." It does not, in other words, exhaust the meaning of the Idea. "But," he continues,

[1] Chapter II, sec. vii.

"it gives the basis of all real further development."[1] That is the important point. Retention of the concept of ultimate substance, as of ultimate origination, with which it is closely connected, is the *sine qua non* of all further intelligible thought. It is a *necessary stage* in the development of the Idea, or the meaning of reality, and in the interpretation and communication of that meaning.

Like the other fundamental categories of intelligible thought, such as causality and finality, substance is very flexible. Like them it may be despatialized and detemporalized. It may be transformed but not eliminated. On this question of despatialization and detemporalization we have, perhaps, said all that needs to be said in the chapter on "Space, Time, and Value." Our contention there was that intelligible communication of the meanings of experience requires a non-spatial and non-temporal idiom. More particularly we emphasized the necessity of the idioms of omnipresence and immanence, of intelligible ground and cause, as *modes* of expressing meaning and value. Again, with regard to the question of the endlessness of the universe in space and time, we found that, while no cogent proofs could be brought from "science" for ei her position, yet the concept of endlessness is really unintelligible, for it is in contradiction with any meaning or direction in the universe. But even the idea of endlessness in the universe does not exclude, as we found Leibniz pointing out, questions of ultimate origination and ultimate substance. However foreign to our modern way of expressing ourselves his metaphysical language may be, it remains a "form of sound words," for it enshrines the principle of the inseparability of value and reality on which the whole conception of an intelligible substance, as well as of intelligible causation, ultimately depends.

But what is the upshot of this rather lengthy discussion of these two conceptions—these "philosophical errors," as the modernist would call them? It is that questions of ultimate origination, far from being meaningless, are the only questions that give other problems any meaning. It is the popular thing just now—one hears it in the most varied quarters—to insist upon the meaningless character of these questions. It

[1] *Op. cit.*, p. 153.

is admitted that with all our sophistication the "torturing question" still remains. What then, after all, is the substance of the world? Even if everything is turned into a flux of sense data, a deed of the will, into pure activity and endless becoming, yet even then the imagination may be unwilling to stand still before this boundary-line of knowledge. The world must, after all, it would seem, have some quality or essence which we must ultimately be able to describe or characterize. But here, we are told, all questioning becomes meaningless—not because we do not have enough knowledge, but because such a question "negates the presuppositions of modern thought."

If so, so much the worse for modern thought and its presuppositions. For this is the crux of the whole matter. If we are genuine philosophers we shall do well to avoid this form of the *argumentum ad populum*. We shall not be interested in the presuppositions of *modern* thought as such, but of *intelligible* thought.[1] We shall do well to avoid calling questions meaningless which are actually the only supremely meaningful questions man has ever asked himself, and recognize that they are meaningless only because of the peculiar logical dialectic in which we have chosen to express ourselves. We shall, indeed, recognize that there are certain questions of proximate origins —of the planetary system, for instance, and of life on this planet—that interest philosophy only indirectly. The real metaphysical question concealed in this language of origination is, as all see more or less clearly, rather the difference between the two orders of the living and the non-living, and of the bearing of this difference on our ultimate interpretation of things. All questions of temporal beginnings, of historical emergence of qualities and values, are in this sense secondary; but is this true of ultimate origination? "Do not origins qualify values?" asks Balfour, and he answers truly, "Notoriously they do." We may have learned in the dire distress of evolutionary thinking to separate, as a matter of mere method,

---

[1] This form of *argumentum ad hominem*, namely, an appeal to the *Zeitgeist*, is to be sharply distinguished from that more fundamental form which in an earlier connection we found to underlie all philosophical discourse. An appeal to "absolute" or "timeless" values involves, to be sure, by implication at least, an appeal to the minds that acknowledge them, but an *argumentum ad hominem* in this sense is the presupposition of all communication.

questions of genesis from questions of value and validity, but we have not yet learned, and, as I think, never shall learn, to form an intelligible concept of evolution by separating them. But this is the substance of the next chapter.

The language of metaphysics must include the concepts of intelligible substance and intelligible causality. Part of this language is of course, and of necessity, the term uncaused cause—*causa sui*—to which the natural metaphysic of the human mind always comes. Of this concept the modernist would doubtless say with Neitzsche that, "It is the best self-contradiction that has yet been conceived, a sort of logical violation and unnaturalness; but the extravagant pride of man has managed to entangle itself profoundly and frightfully in this very folly." To this the seasoned thinker, with a full sense of all this idiom has meant in human thought, can but reply: If this be folly, if this be treason to logic, make the most of it. If it be wisdom to deny the intelligibility of this idiom, then it is not wisdom to be only wise. For one can still insist with Hegel that cause in its full truth *is* "*causa sui*." Many, indeed, like Jacobi, whom he is criticizing in this connection, "bound fast in the one-sided idea of mediation," have "taken this absolute truth of causation as a pure formalism." The truth of necessity is, however, spontaneity, or, in Hegel's terms, "freedom."[1] The transition from necessity to freedom, or from actuality to the notion, is, indeed, the hardest to make, but it is one that must be made, and is, in fact, always made, by all those who pass from mere description to explanation and interpretation.

The upholder of traditional ways of thinking may, indeed, point out to the modernist that he himself has not been able to get along without the use of the idea of the uncaused cause. The very general concept of "a reality that creates itself gradually" is but the old idea of the *causa sui* in modern guise, but used, as we shall see later, in a most unintelligible way. The significant thing is that the transition from necessity to spontaneity must be made in any conception of an intelligible world. A recent illustration is the, for the moment, popular conception that by combining space and time in one concept we can find in it a creative principle which

[1] *Op. cit.*, p. 150.

neither has in itself. But it is entirely clear that on such a view we must do one of two things. We must either interpret reality strictly in terms of space-time substance, in which case the question of *nisus* or emergency does not arise, or we endow it with an attribute of anticipation, of what is not yet, but has the capacity or potentiality of becoming, which transforms it into something quite other than the space-time either of common usage or of science. If we take the latter course the beginning is interpreted by the end, the beginning and end are brought together in a more ultimate concept, and that is inevitably the notion of the uncaused cause, however it may be camouflaged in order to avoid drawing its inevitable implications.

V

So much, then, for the characteristic errors of traditional philosophy. We can well understand how they have perpetually played into one another. For they form a complex which constitutes the natural bent of the human intellect, an irreversible movement upon which it is well-nigh impossible for us to turn our backs. It is our contention that we should not try to turn our backs upon it. The intellect is ultimately oriented towards value, not towards space, matter, nor logical simples. The mode of valuation that lies back of these ways of thinking is not a prejudice, but the essential form of philosophical intelligibility itself. On the other hand, the language of metaphysics, with its idioms of intelligible causation and substance, is a language without which intelligible communication and interpretation of the meanings of reality are impossible. This has all along been the main thesis of this chapter, to which the examination of these so-called philosophical errors has been merely subsidiary. In developing this thesis we shall also find the root of this entire complex of errors, a root, moreover, which strikes deep down into the very heart of thinking, of both logic and reality—into the "heart of darkness" of an atavistic animism, or into the central light of intelligence, according to your point of view.

Here again Bergson may well be our guide—into a realm

of thought in which he, more than any other modern thinker perhaps, is at home. Back of this entire traditional way of thinking, he holds, there lies an idea, or rather an antithesis of ideas, which requires to be brought to full light if we are to understand its driving force. Philosophers, he tells us, have paid very little attention to the idea of the "naught," yet it is "often the hidden spring, the invisible mover, of philosophic thinking." *Ex minimo maximum non fit* is the postulate of all philosophical interpretation, including his own. Back of this lies the simpler and more ultimate formula, *ex nihilo nihil fit*. Now, according to him, curiously enough, it is precisely this idea of the *naught*, together with its antithesis, *the all*, that constitutes one of the two great theoretical illusions of traditional thought. It is this illusion more than anything else that has necessitated the idea of a reality outside duration, and the showing up of this illusion enables us to see that a self-sufficient reality is not necessarily foreign to duration, but may rather be identical with it.

Now, we may agree with Bergson that this antithesis of ideas does lie back of traditional thought, and that it requires to be brought to the full light of day. First of all, one may well ask how it is possible to accept the axiom *ex minimo maximum non fit* without thinking the more ultimate formula also. How we can think of the more and the less without the all and the naught which they imply is hard to understand. Be that as it may, the concept of the *naught* is for him a theoretical illusion, and his "demolition of unreality" is one of the feats for which he is famous.

His argument, in brief, is that the idea of the naught is wholly a product of the practical intellect. Entirely legitimate in the sphere of action, it becomes an illusion when transferred to the sphere of theoretical speculation. He has no difficulty, of course, in showing that between thinking an object and thinking it as existent (in the broadest sense of the word) there is no difference: that to represent an object as unreal cannot consist in depriving it of every kind of being, since, as he says, representing an object at all is necessarily representing it as *being* in some sense. Every thing that can be thought at all is an entity in some sense.

All this is, of course, true enough, but for the purposes of the present argument wholly irrelevant. It is, to be sure, as we have already seen, quite natural to say that whatever is exists, and whatever exists must be real. But we have also seen that little reflection is necessary to show that the situation cannot be as it first appears. The "predicate" real itself gets its meaning only by suggesting a contrast with something unreal which, however we may understand the term, must itself fall within the universe, which by hypothesis includes everything. The only way out of the paradox which this situation creates we found to lie in recognizing that when we judge anything to be real or unreal we are not opposing a general class of unreal things to real things, but are comparing one particular content with another, from which it ought to be, but in a certain judgment has not been, distinguished. In other words, we found that the question what is real or unreal is meaningless if being is abstracted from value.

In short, the antithesis of reality and unreality as it functions in philosophic thought is essentially a value concept.[1] Bergson recognizes this, indeed, by implication, but he is wrong in thinking it of wholly practical origin and significance. In any case, it is clear that the contrast of the unreal with the real, so understood, *must* be the hidden spring, the invisible mover, of philosophic thought. It is also clear that his demolition of unreality, so widely heralded, turns out to be, like the reports of many other demises, grossly exaggerated. Its demolition would, indeed, mean, as Bergson sees, the destruction of the traditional mode of thinking, but it would also mean the loss of philosophic intelligibility.

Be this as it may—and this is a position which we shall hope to justify more fully when, in the next chapter, we consider in more detail the intelligibility of certain modern evolutionary philosophies, including Bergson's itself—it is, at least, clear now, I think, that the concept of the naught is at the root of the so-called error of speculative dogma, and, indeed, of the whole complex of "errors" under discussion. It is precisely because the concept of the naught *has* meaning for thought that the axiom *ex minimo maximum non fit* has meaning, and because the less can be interpreted in terms of the more, never the more in terms of the less, that we are

[1] See Chapter II, pp. 74 ff.

compelled to think of a self-sufficing reality and to ascribe
to it such characters as retain the meaning and value of our
higher experiences.

"There can be no such thing as nothing. The garden is
full, not empty." Thus Eve, in Bernard Shaw's *Back to Methu-
selah*. To which the Serpent replies: "I had not thought of
that. That is a great thought. Yes; there is no such thing as
nothing, only things we cannot see. The chameleon eats the
air." This is, indeed, a great thought, but its greatness depends
entirely on how we think it.

From the impartial point of view, to which, as we have
seen, modern thought strives, there is, indeed, no such thing
as "nothing." If we identify reality with being in the widest
sense, everything that is the object of discourse has being—
even impossible objects, even the naught itself. If we identify
reality with being in the widest sense, then to the question,
What is the real? we can only answer, The real is everything.
But when we judge anything to be unreal, we are not opposing
a general class of unreal things to another class of real things.
We are rather comparing one form of being with another,
and such comparison involves degrees of meaning and value.
Nothing, or the null point, is but the limit of such a series of
which the other limit is perfection or the "all." It is from this
nothing that nothing comes.

There can be no such thing as nothing. Taken one way, it
is nonsense. Taken another way, it is a great thought. To say
that the garden is full, not empty, is simply another way of
saying that the less can be derived from the more, never the
more from the less. There is no such thing as nothing, only
things we cannot see. God is in the garden, even if he is a
concealed God.

"There is no more tragic spectacle in this age than the
philosophers who, like Herbert Spencer, having reduced the
whole universe to a nebula, try to bridge the gulf between
the nebula and nothingness. The great intellect of Spencer
grovels below the mental capacity of a child of ten as he makes
the absurd attempt, announcing that, perhaps, the primal
nebula might be conceived as thinning itself out until nothingness were reached." Thus the unsophisticated mind, as represented by old Peter Ramsay, the lighthouse-keeper, in his

diary.[1] But he was mistaken. There is something still more tragic because it is still more absurd. It is the spectacle of the philosophers who, having realized the absurdity of Spencer's attempt, seek to correct it with concepts still more unintelligible—namely, concepts which pack time itself with that "more of reality" which it can but reveal and never create.

VI

Two main problems constitute the task of this chapter, the two problems of "origination" set by modernism and so vividly formulated for us by Nietzsche. The first of these is whether the "mode of valuation" which lies back of the concept of ultimate origination in traditional thought is valid. The second is whether the particular mode of valuation, that antithesis of values which is typical of the philosophers of all time, is, as modernism holds, the result of merely "popular and superficial estimates," or whether it belongs to the natural bent of the intellect as such. The first question we have answered in the affirmative; it is to the second that we must now turn.

The discussion of the first question has been rather lengthy, for the reason that it involved an analysis and evaluation of the entire complex of habits of thought which make up the structure of traditional philosophy. The second problem can be treated much more briefly, for the major part of the work has already been done.

The popular estimations, the popular antitheses of value with which we are concerned, are those of materialism and idealism, of permanence and change. It is only in terms of these distinctions and contrasts, we have said, that it is possible to express the *meaning* of our life and of the world in which that life is lived. The development of matter from spirit is intelligible, the development of spirit from matter is not. Change can be understood through the permanent, the permanent cannot be understood through change. Thus speaks traditional philosophy, *uniformly*, and in so speaking it assumes an antithesis of values which it holds to be ultimate. It is,

[1] Alfred Noyes, in his story "The Light-House," published in a volume called *Walking Shadows*.

however, precisely the ultimate character of these antitheses which is challenged by typical modernistic conceptions, more particularly by the various forms of evolutionary naturalism in which modernism has found expression.

From the standpoint of traditional thought all these naturalisms must in the end mean nothing more nor less than a disguised materialism; not materialism of the older type, to be sure, but of the subtler modern kind to which so much of modern thought seems necessarily to gravitate. Whether we start with atoms or electrons, neutral stuff or space-time, the primary prerequisite of carrying through any naturalistic programme is to drive mind or self from its privileged position and to give that position to something else. All interpretation means giving the privileged position to something, and in the end this is what every philosophical interpretation does. The antithesis of values expressed in the terms "matter" and "spirit" may be superficial, but intelligible communication and interpretation are so constituted that one element of the antithesis must be subordinated to the other.

It will be worth our while to dwell on this point for a moment. The most deeply marked fissure between schools of thought is not, as one might think, between monism and pluralism, or realism and idealism, but the gulf between spirit and matter. All systems must in the end be called by one of these names, for all favour in a more or less degree the supremacy of something that may fairly be called spiritual, or something that may fairly be called material. Neutral monisms are ultimately unintelligible for the reason that so soon as the monist seeks to communicate his meaning definitely the monism becomes, as all history shows, materialistically or spiritualistically toned. So also all those philosophies of change, those philosophies that make life the fundamental character. All suffer from a fundamental ambiguity in the concept of life itself, the distinctively biological and the more spiritual conceptions. So soon as such a philosophy seeks to make itself intelligible it becomes materialistically or spiritualistically toned.

In general, it is true that the popular antithesis of materialism and spiritualism, fundamental as it is, is not the one that chiefly interests the present-day thinker. In comparison with what seems to him to be the more fundamental contrast of

294 THE INTELLIGIBLE WORLD

permanence and change, that of materialism and spiritualism
seems secondary. Indeed, on his view, the latter antithesis is
bound up with the substance concept, the concept of the
permanent; and a philosophy of absolute change, of pure
dynamism, as it would make fictions of the substance concept,
would at the same time reduce to a superficial significance the
antithesis or dualism bound up with this concept.

Now, there is a certain truth in this contention. It seems
beyond doubt that the transvaluation of metaphysical values
that finds more in becoming than in the thing that becomes
is one that has the greatest number of consequences for interpretation. It is in terms of this contrast—of restless becoming
and self-contained being, more than in any other—that the
mind apprehends and communicates the meanings of its own
life and of the world in which that life is lived. Pure dynamism
has always seemed paradoxical to the natural mind, and in
terms of pure dynamism no intelligible communication of the
meaning of life and reality is possible.

All this is true, and its significance for interpretation, as,
indeed, the whole question of the significance of the antithesis
of permanence and change, will be considered in the following
chapter. But this is not what I wish to insist upon here. It is
rather that, however we may interpret this antithesis, the
antithesis of matter and spirit is no less fundamental. Whether
we give the supremacy to permanence or change, in neither
case can we avoid the dichotomy of materialism and spiritualism. If we give the supremacy to permanence, any characterization of the permanent must be in terms of this antithesis,
for it is only in terms of this dichotomy that the value distinctions in things can be expressed. If, on the other hand, we
give the supremacy to change, we still need this dichotomy.
For either we interpret reality in terms of mere duration or
space-time, in which there is no "direction" and our thinking
inevitably gravitates to the "physical," or else we endow
duration or space-time with a direction or *nisus*, with potentiality (whether we use the word or not), and this immediately
transforms duration into something quite other than the
becoming or space-time of either common sense or science.
In the latter case we have the inevitable drift towards something that may fairly be called spiritualism.

Superficial, then, the antithesis of values implied in the alternative of materialism and spiritualism certainly is not; it is fundamental and unavoidable. It is, to be sure, the result partly of popular and practical estimations, but it is for that reason no less profound.

Secondary tendencies, superficial estimations, there undoubtedly are that emphasize the cleavage. "Matter, we say, is gross, coarse, crass, muddy; spirit is pure, elevated, noble; and since it is more consonant with the dignity of the universe to give the primacy in it to that which appears superior, spirit must be affirmed as the ruling principle." To this it has seemed sufficient to answer: "A matter so infinitely subtle and performing motions so inconceivably quick and fine as those which modern science postulates in her explanations has no trace of grossness left."[1] As a matter of fact the question has even been raised, by one professing to uphold materialism, whether that word is any longer a suitable name for a doctrine that dissolves all matter away into intangible energy. If, then, it is upon these popular and superficial estimates that, as Nietzsche says, "the metaphysicians have set their seal," then they have, perhaps, merely raised popular prejudices into absolute values. But it is not. If these popular estimations have largely disappeared, as, indeed, they have, their disappearance has not affected in the least that deeper antithesis of values of which they were, so to speak, but the secondary characters. Philosophically, and even according to the new physics, perhaps, scientifically speaking, matter may not be any longer really matter. But the fact remains that "something having all the properties we have attributed to matter is perpetually getting into our way, and that our minds do, in point of fact, fall under the dominion of certain bits of this matter, known as our bodies, changing as they change and keeping pace with their decay."[2] The changes in the scientific conception of matter have, perhaps, much less significance for philosophical interpretation than is often supposed.

This popular antithesis of values is, then, not superficial. This "persistent and treasured dichotomy of the universe" is persistent and treasured because life and the world are

---

[1] William James, *Pragmatism*, p. 94.
[2] Aldous Huxley, *Those Barren Leaves*, p. 368.

unintelligible without it. The plain man will not be argued out of the feeling that the ontological status of matter is the key question of philosophy, and when the real meaning of the antithesis, in its modern as well as its ancient forms, is understood, the philosopher will not be argued out of it either. "For the world must be cogitated," as Wundt says, "either as a material or spiritual unity, in so far as it is to be a unity at all. There is no third way."[1] It is just as well for us finally to come to that realization. From a purely logical point of view, it is, perhaps, true that we have no right to assume that reality is exhausted in these two alternatives. Even if we know only material and spiritual reality in our experience, we have no right to assume that they exhaust the complexities of reality. But the problem is not logical except in that broad and general way which arises from the fact that logic itself is *die Moral des Denkens*, the science of those values and value distinctions which must be acknowledged if intelligible communication is to be possible.

It is enlightening to observe the transformation through which materialism has gone as the result of changes in the concept of matter. Present-day materialism, as one of its most consistent upholders maintains, is "infinitely different" from the old. It may even make vast concessions to agnosticism, and it concedes the whole foundation of knowledge to idealism. Materialism, as he defines it, amounts to three things: the uniformity of law, the denial of teleology, and the denial of any fundamental form of existence other than that envisaged by physics and chemistry. Materialism thus defined amounts to little more than a *method* dogmatized.

The conception of a methodological materialism is, however, not unfamiliar. When F. A. Lange constantly insisted upon the methodological validity of materialism, but equally strongly on its metaphysical invalidity, there appeared the first clear recognition of a point of view which has become increasingly influential. The picture of a philosopher fighting with the one hand for materialism and with the other against it might, indeed, seem like a philosophical curiosity or even perversity, but it really indicated a long step in the direction of understanding the true inwardness of this antithesis. The recognition

[1] *System der Philosophie*, p. 411.

of the fact that this opposition is primarily methodological, that it may be even above the distinction of epistemological realism and idealism, brings with it also the recognition that it stands for two fundamental and irreconcilable ways of interpreting life and the world.

The inevitableness of this opposition of methodological materialism and methodological idealism lies, then, in the *a priori* character of the axiological principle that we can proceed intelligibly from the more to the less, but not from the less to the more. The development of matter from spirit is intelligible, the development of spirit from matter is not. If by development is here understood analysis of the one into the other, neither procedure is, of course, intelligible. The reduction of spirit to matter has always been felt to be unintelligible, and never more so than to-day, when, as we shall see in a later connection, it is the distinctive claim of the most modern naturalisms that they are not reductive. On the other hand, the reduction of matter to spirit in this sense is no less unintelligible. "The idea of dissolving matter into spirit," says Mr. Hugh Elliot, "has never entered into the wildest dreams of the scientist."[1] And in this he is, of course, right. If interpreting matter in terms of spirit meant this, the philosophy that attempted it would always find itself unintelligible.

Qualitative dualism is the "most certain of all facts," for the reason that the antithesis, or dichotomy, it represents, far from being superficial, represents the necessary condition of intelligible communication of our meanings and values. The category of substance or essence, we have seen, is the development of the values of existence. These values cannot be developed without this antithesis, and the insistence upon two irreducible substances is but the acknowledgment of these values. But this fact does not for one moment exclude the other fact: that one or the other of them must be given the privileged position. It is precisely because they represent values

---

[1] See Hugh Elliot, *Modern Science and Materialism* (1919). Materialism, as he defines it, reduces wholly to a matter of method. Present-day materialism, he recognizes, is "infinitely different" from the old one. While professing to uphold materialism, he doubts whether that term is any longer suitable for a doctrine that dissolves all matter away into intangible energy. It "may even make vast concessions to agnosticism and it concedes the whole foundation of knowledge to idealism." See especially Chapter VI.

that one of them must be dominant. The world must be cogitated either as a material or a spiritual unity, if it is to be a unity at all. There is no third way. Two things may be equally real, equally necessary, but not equally significant.

It is this, I am sure, that the great idealisms have always attempted to express. The difficulties which they have found in expressing it arise from those ambiguities inherent in the idea of unity, or the whole, to which we were forced to give attention in an earlier connection. There is, however, one meaning of the whole which seems to me to express more adequately than any other the true intent of traditional thought. It is the conception of "dominant unity" as developed by Leibniz, or, as expressed in our terminology, that of axiological unity.

The key to the understanding of all spiritualistic metaphysic is to be found at this point—the value character of the theoretical, and the conception of axiological totality which is part of it. The relation of value to being, of validity to existence, is, we have repeatedly seen, the ultimate point to which an analysis of knowledge leads. It is also the point beyond which analysis cannot go. From this point of view value is more ultimate than existence, for any judgment of existence involves the acknowledgment of meanings and values which themselves do not exist, but are merely valid. But value and validity are "no strangers to being." It is at this point, I think, that the inevitableness of metalogical speculation appears, and the type of speculation that alone has intelligible meaning—namely, the *spiritualistic*. For is it not clear that if we thus seek to turn the forms of validity and the ideals of value into realities, there is but one course open to us, namely, to give them "spiritual actuality," to connect them with a spiritual first-principle, such as Plato's Good, Aristotle's *Nous*, Berkeley and Leibniz's God, Kant's Intellectual *Architypus*, Fichte's *Ego*, Hegel's Idea, or the Voluntarists' over-individual wills?

Such metaphysical speculation is inevitable for, while we must learn to speak the language of validity, it is an idiom that is not sufficient for communication. But can this language of a spiritualistic metaphysic itself be made intelligible? "The great metaphysicians," it is often said, "announce to us in a rapturous *Eureka* that they know the unknowable, have discovered the undiscoverable; the only pity is that every one of them has discovered something different." But do these varying terms in which the spiritual first principle is expressed really invalidate, as is supposed, the truth of the insight which they pretend to communicate?

The question here raised involves the whole problem of the nature of metaphysical language and of its intelligibility and its truth. One thing certainly the critics of this language overlook: the fact that, in the history of philosophical interpretation different and sometimes conflicting concepts of the spiritual first principle have followed each other, does not affect the fundamental insight that the methodology of philosophical interpretation demands the axiological dominance of this principle. In science also, different and often conflicting concepts of matter and energy have followed each other (the history of the principle of conservation, with its varying formulations, is instructive in this connection), but this fact does not affect the methodological continuity of physics.

If this suggestion is important, there is another which is even more so. It is that this entire metaphysical language, this language of spiritualistic metaphysic, is the only one in which an intelligible rendering of the meanings and values of reality is possible. Modernism has attempted to develop another idiom, to develop a language from which the concepts of substance and causation, of immanence and potentiality, are eliminated, in which the contrasting values of permanence and change, of matter and spirit, these treasured dichotomies of the human spirit, have been abandoned. I have tried to show in a general way why this new language cannot be made intelligible. In the following chapter on Evolution we shall see at certain more specific points why this is necessarily so. An intelligible concept of evolution, we have suggested, is the desideratum of the modern world. That any such intelligible conception is necessarily a metaphysic we have also maintained. Is it not possible that such a conception can be formed only within the traditional "form of philosophical intelligibility"; that it must speak the language of a spiritualistic metaphysic, and, finally, must recognize the axiom of intelligible thought: that the less can be derived from the more, never the more from the less? To this question we must now turn.

CHAPTER IX

INTELLIGIBLE EVOLUTION

I

THE idea of evolution, we have said, is the lord of all our present thinking. We do not consider that we understand anything rightly, neither plant nor animal nor man, nor even the fixed *strata* of the earth's crust, nor the planet itself, until we understand its place in a process. For modern thought, the whole order of nature is a movement. Evolution is now generally felt to be the *one* form of an intelligible world. It is easy to see why this should be so. The concept of evolution, it should be remembered, is but a more modern form of a much older concept, namely, that of development. Development and growth, however, are inseparable from life and living process, the "life-form" in which all meanings and values are realized. The extension of this form to the cosmos seems of necessity to make it intelligible.

This close relation between evolution and life should be emphasized. We may, indeed, if we wish, speak of a mechanical evolution in which nothing of life is to be found. It is clear, however, that in the case of merely mechanical processes and events nothing, strictly speaking, of development appears; we have here nothing but transfer of movement. In the concept of evolution, on the other hand, an element of new meaning is brought to logical expression. This necessary relation of evolution to life and its meaning is easy to establish. However the meanings and values of life arise, it is always and only in the form of development and evolution that they can be expressed. Only that which develops or evolves has the meaning and significance of life. On the other hand, only that which in some sense lives, or has the meaning of life, evolves. One can, therefore, speak of an identity between life and evolution.

It is this relation of evolution to the experience of life that gives to evolution the character of a form of an intelligible world. Life, *as it is merely lived*, is meaningless, unintelligible. It is only as it is brought to conceptual expression in evolution, development, that it becomes rational and intelligible. By means of such concepts the non-rational elements of life are brought into the sphere of rational knowledge. Only by means of concepts of cosmic evolution, of the evolution of a cosmos which contains and includes life, can the irrational elements of the cosmos be brought into the sphere of rational knowledge.

It cannot be too often repeated that evolution, development, are intellectual and rational concepts—the Western world's form of an intelligible world. We have but to show the place of a thing in this process to make it intelligible. An evolutional philosophy is thus essentially a systematic philosophy. But evolution is an idea, a concept, a category if you will. As such, it must itself be made understandable, intelligible. That prevailing concepts of evolution are not always found to be intelligible is clear enough from the revolt against evolution in high places as well as low. "The world, my dear friend, does not evolve," says D. H. Lawrence, in his *Philosophy of the Unconscious*. Many there are who think that the world itself does not evolve, and some who, like Tolstoy, do not think that evolution is even the fundamental character of things within the world. Many others hold that certain formulas or concepts of evolution are untrue and unintelligible. Darwinian evolution, with its "circumstantial selection," is frankly called nonsense, and cosmic evolution of the Spencerian type is without hesitation described as one of the most unintelligible philosophies ever invented. An intelligible concept of evolution is plainly the great desideratum of the modern world.

Within the purely biological sphere, the conditions of such intelligibility are in principle relatively simple. Transformism, or the mutation of species, and the different ways of interpreting it, are the problems here. In this restricted sense an intelligible concept is one in which the theory of variations, their selection and retention, is central. How is transformation of species *possible*? On the other hand, the extension of evolution to the cosmic process raises questions of an entirely different type—questions of a metaphysical character, and here the conditions of intelligibility are the conditions of philosophical intelligibility as we have developed them.

This is immediately apparent from the fact that evolution, like certain other general concepts, cannot be used intelligibly except as qualified by certain descriptive adjectives. Materialistic evolution, naturalistic evolution; emergent and creative evolution; even such terms as logical and theistic evolution—until such descriptive adjectives are applied we do not know *what* evolution we are talking about. *Evolution, roughly speaking, is the general form of an intelligible world. The kinds of evolution represent the attempts to make the evolutionary process itself intelligible.*

These different concepts of evolution, moreover, indicate the essentially metaphysical character of the concept. Methodologically, evolution permits only of descriptive procedure. Scientific research is satisfied as soon as it succeeds in showing the elements or moments from which a system historically evolves, and describes the steps or stages through which it passes. It makes the system, order, connections, intelligible or conceptually apprehensible, in that it derives them genetically. For the completion of this procedure evolution is not only a valid category, but the final category. In this sense evolution is, as Lloyd Morgan says, but "the name we give to the comprehensive plan of sequence of natural events."[1] With such a plan of sequence, science as such stops, and, indeed, must stop. Not so evolution in the interpretative sense in which we have been considering it. It is not sufficient merely to form a comprehensive plan or sequence of natural events, a system of animate nature, or of nature both animate and inanimate. The system, like the constitutions of which Carlyle speaks, must also "be made to march." An evolution that does not evolve is no evolution at all.

The natural science of the day is permeated with the idea of development and evolution, and, while it recognizes different concepts or theories of evolution, does not hesitate to speak of evolution itself as a fact. But here again, we must insist, it is a "fact" only in the sense that it is a name for a comprehensive plan of sequence of natural events. "We know," it is said, "how world bodies developed new and ever new from rotating nebular masses, how the earth developed from the sun, how the surface of the earth cooled off, how the first little living lump developed from inorganic substances, and how from this little lump came first the lowest protists, the other invertebrates, fish, reptiles, and mammals, and finally men; we

[1] *Emergent Evolution*, p. 1.

know all these things for 'facts,' we say, and yet the critical thinker, the thinker who knows his business, must insist that while the sequences are undoubtedly facts, anything else read into the situation belongs to the sphere of the idea. More than this, anything read into the concept of evolution beyond the comprehensive plan of sequence involves an evaluation of the facts. Development, evolution, cannot even be asserted of any sequence of events without evaluation."[1]

It is in the attempt to form an intelligible philosophical concept of evolution that the divergent interpretations appear. It is at this point, also, that the break between the typically modernistic philosophies and traditional thought is chiefly found. The descriptive terms applied to the word evolution indicate, as I have said, the nature of that attempt, and it is in the prosecution of that attempt chiefly that the novelties of modern thought have come into being.

Evolutionary naturalism, in its various forms, has been prolific of a number of philosophical novelties, all of which go back, in the last analysis, to the divorce of reality and value, more particularly the dissociation of origin and value which, as we have seen, is the most fundamental difference between modernism and the past. The separation of destiny from origin, as in pragmatism, the doctrine of epigenesis and emergents in evolutionary realism, the idea of creative evolution, of a reality that creates itself gradually—all these are typically modern, and all, for reasons that we shall see, equally unintelligible to traditional thought. It is my belief that they are intrinsically unintelligible if the real nature of philosophical intelligibility is understood. It is to the development of this thesis that we must now turn.

II

One form of evolutionary naturalism, it is now pretty generally recognized, is wholly unintelligible. For Bergson it

[1] The confusion of thought on this point is widespread. Quite recently, as reported by the daily press, the President of the Science League of America appeared before the California State Board of Education to protest against action of the Board declaring evolution could be taught in the public schools only as a theory, not a fact.

is, perhaps, the most unintelligent philosophy ever constructed. For others it is, perhaps, not so much absolutely false as inadequate.

Without going into differences of detail, it may, perhaps, be said that the majority of modernists in philosophy agree that the older *Evolutionary Naturalism* had decided limitations, due to a certain philosophical immaturity. In its passion for the logical values of unity, simplicity, and continuity, it followed the method of reduction to such lengths as to become unintelligible. "An up-to-date evolutionary naturalism is not a reductive naturalism." The old naturalism ignored novelty and evolutionary synthesis. An adequate naturalism must not make this mistake. Though founding itself on science and evolution, the older naturalism did not take some of the sciences seriously. "Past naturalism did not take evolution seriously, nor did it take mind seriously." Perhaps the one outstanding characteristic of this more modern naturalism is the recognition or acknowledgment of different levels of being, matter, life, and mind, and that the higher levels cannot be led back to the lower without a remainder.

Naturalistic evolution, it is admitted, "has been so completely identified with the reduction of the higher to the lower that it will be hard to rescue the term from opprobrium, but the attempt must be made." It is, perhaps, not so much opprobrium as unintelligibility from which it needs to be rescued, and the task is not a light one. The method of rescue has been to point out that the older forms of evolutionism grew up under the influence of a certain dogmatic monism, under the influence of the "speculative dogma" that intelligibility and rational explanation meant reduction to one ultimate substance, the matter and energy with which the physical sciences deal. Modern thought has but to show the fallaciousness of the dogma of substance in any of its forms, to free evolutionary naturalism from the particular materialistic form of the dogma. The removal of this fallacy, together with a better understanding and evaluation of the particular concepts of the other sciences, such as biology and psychology, makes possible a new concept of evolution which does full justice to the varieties of existence as they reveal themselves in experience. This conception of evolution may be called Emergent Evolution.

The concepts of emergents, creative resultants, and epigenesis represent, then, the high-water mark of modernistic thinking. Emergent Evolution is the name which best characterizes the speculative conception that includes these concepts. If evolution, in the broad unqualified sense, is but the name we give to the comprehensive plan of sequence in all natural events, emergent evolution lays stress on the incoming of the new, salient examples of which are afforded in the advent of life and the advent of mind. If nothing new emerge, if there be only regrouping of pre-existing events, then there is no emergent evolution, strictly speaking, no evolution at all.

The "fact" of the emergence of novelties that cannot be reduced to pre-existing events is, then, the foundation of the structure of emergent evolution which we are to examine. Evolutionary naturalism is built on science, and the failure of the older concepts of evolution lay in the fact that while it professed to build upon science, it did not take some of the facts of science itself seriously. Our first problem, therefore, is to see in what sense *emergents* and *emergence* may be said to be scientific facts. For most of those of this way of thinking, emergents are assumed to be a "fact" and emergence a "law of nature."

Now, the insistence upon fundamental differences between the inorganic, the organic, and the mental, upon different levels of meaning and value in reality, is in itself most welcome. It is, in fact, the very essence of our doctrine of "expressive" philosophical concepts, or of the necessity of the retention of those concepts which radical analysis calls "pseudo-simples." As such, it is not only the first principle of all traditional thought, but also the very condition of all intelligible communication and interpretation.[1] But in what sense is the recognition and acknowledgment of these differences based upon the facts of science? In what sense, and to what degree, does the recognition of these differences afford a basis for the "law" of emergence based upon them? The negative aspect of the theory, its anti-reductionism, is welcome. What shall be said of the positive aspect?

Reductive naturalism, it was said, erred by not taking science seriously. Biologists, supposedly, tell us to keep the

[1] Chapter V, pp. 195 ff.; Chapter VI, pp. 210 ff.

category of the *living* intact. But which biologists? Some undoubtedly do, but others do not. Psychologists, it is assumed, tell us to keep the category of the *mental* intact. But which psychologists? Again, some of them undoubtedly do, but which? The Behaviourists? Psychology, a certain wit has said, first lost its soul, then its mind, and finally it lost consciousness. No, it is not to "science" that one must look for this fundamental wisdom.

We may say without hesitation, I think, that these emergent "qualities," these novel meanings, are "facts" only in the sense that they are *objects of acknowledgment*. Ultimate entities, in the sense either of sense data or of universals, they are not. I know of no strictly scientific grounds on which one can say to a radical analyst that life and mind cannot be analysed into simpler elements, none except those which arise out of the demands of intelligible communication and interpretation. How shall we say that life or mind represents unique and integral forms of reality? It is always open to a reductive naturalism to say of life that it is but

> Water and saltness held together
> To tread the dust and stand the weather.

Without doubt that seems a non-sense to many of us. But it is only because we acknowledge certain meanings and values bound up with the experience and concept of life and to apply the term life to a group of pre-existing events that does not include these meanings and values involves an inner contradiction that can end only in unintelligible discourse.

Certain representatives of evolutionary naturalism are not without some inkling of this situation. Lloyd Morgan even goes so far as to admit that we can but acknowledge these emergent qualities or meanings with "natural piety." I will not stop to expatiate upon the novelty of the use of such terms in "science." Acknowledgment is assuredly a new term to apply to any relation of the mind to "brute" fact. Piety, even if it be qualified by the word "natural," is hardly an attitude with which science as such will be able to do much. It is, rather, the implications of this admission of Lloyd Morgan's, when they are thought out, that interest me. These implications are clear enough. These "emergent qualities" are not "facts" as distinguished from the meanings and values of the facts. It is only meanings and values that are "acknowledged." There is no piety, natural or other, in the perception of a fact, but there is in the acknowledgment of certain meanings and values which must be retained if intelligible communication is to be possible. In fine, to our earlier statement that development cannot be asserted without valuation, we may add a second, namely, that *the very "facts" on which development is predicated are themsslves inseparable from values that must be, and can only be, acknowledged.*

It is, accordingly, only in the very loosest sense of that term that we can apply the term "fact" to these "emergent qualities." It is in an even looser sense that men speak of the fact of emergence, or, indeed, in some cases, of a "law of emergence."

Here, again, distinctions are very much in order if there is to be any clearness of thought. If we acknowledge as a fact the unique character of these qualities—and this acknowledgment is necessary only if we acknowledge certain meanings and values—then it is, of course, also true, a "fact," that such qualities appear or emerge in the world. But to say this is really to say nothing. It is, to be sure, a fact that things appear which are not reducible to pre-existing arrangements or events. We may, perhaps, say that it is a law, in the sense of an empirical generalization, that novelties do thus appear. But that is not what is meant by the law of emergents. If the concept is to have any meaning at all, it must be that things emerge from that which they were not. It is one thing, however, to say that things appear which cannot be reduced to preceding events; it is quite another to say that they emerge out of what they are not. The first represents merely a limit of scientific analysis and description. The second is essentially a metaphysical conception. It is one of the blind spots of evolutionary naturalism that it does not see this distinction.

III

The attempt to rescue evolutionary naturalism from opprobrium by the doctrine of "emergents" is a welcome gesture. But it is only a gesture. It lacks sincerity and reality, for it is really unintelligible. For one thing the method of rescue, the denial of the dogma of "substance," is questionable. Someone is bound to ask in the end, *What is it* that evolves?" And the answer can be only in terms of matter or spirit, one of the so-called emergent qualities. If evolution is made "cosmic," this is inevitable. For, as we have seen, if the world is to be cogitated as a unity at all, it must be cogitated in one or another of these terms.[1]

But this difficulty is merely one of many that arise out of the complete break with the traditional form of intelligibility which the doctrine of emergence implies. There is one point at which this break occurs which is diagnostic for the whole position, the whole complex of novelties called modernism, namely, the abandonment of the category of potentiality. Any doctrine of emergents that is consistent and coherent must do this. It must break with the category of potentiality, not only in its Aristotelean form, but in any form in which it has functioned in traditional thought. And in doing this it must accept consequences of far-reaching importance. For, not only is potentiality the great interpretative category; it is also, so to speak, the cement of all traditional systems.

The reason for this break, so we have seen, is fundamental. The break was inevitable so soon as the *a priori* character of the form of philosophical intelligibility was denied, so soon as reality is divorced from value, and therefore origin dissociated from finality. Yet we find a curiously vacillating position on the part of many representatives of emergent evolution. The need to retain it in some form seems to arise out of the need of making themselves intelligible. For precisely the acknowledgment of integral qualities, such as life and mind, the insistence upon the retention of these categories in the face of radical analysis, is what distinguishes them from the old-fashioned reductive naturalism. But this is just what the category of potentiality has always stood for—for the retention of the significance and richness of expressive terms, and the truth that these terms are not reducible to their relations without a remainder; in short, that there is more in these things than in the entities out of which they appear to emerge.

[1] Chapter VIII, p. 296.

Can this aspect of the category of potentiality be retained without retaining its classical implications and meaning?

To me, at least (I cannot refrain from saying it), a large part of present-day thinking is thoroughly incoherent on this point. Illustrations of this situation are everywhere present in recent literature. I take one from Lloyd Morgan's *Emergent Evolution* as perhaps best fitted to bring out my point.

"It will be urged," he writes, "by many critics of our thesis, that mind *does not* emerge" (italics his). "That is true," he goes on to say, "of mind in one sense, but not of mind in another. If we say that mind emerges at a certain stage and others say that mind does not emerge and cannot be treated as an emergent, this may be because the word 'mind' is used in these two different senses." "Mind as a correlate," he continues, "does not emerge, but there are emergent levels of such mind, as correlate, and it is at an assignable level that mind in the second sense does emerge. It is an emergent quality of the correlated psychical order at an approximately definable stage of evolutionary advance."[1]

Nothing would be easier than to amuse one's self over this very human desire to eat one's cake and have it too, over this antinomy into which Lloyd Morgan's thinking seems to drive him. But it is well to remember that it is just such antinomies as this that constitute a challenge for all large-minded philosophies—problems the solution of which has brought greater light in the past. If we did not draw back from the seeming paradox that reality is both in and out of space and time, surely we ought not to be disturbed by this apparent paradox.

The truth of the matter seems to be that we are somehow compelled to use mind in these two senses—that is, if we are to talk intelligibly. This is the crucial point. Mind, as a correlate, does not, then, emerge. But is it possible to think of mind as a correlate of all existence without thinking of it also as immanent? And can we think of its immanence or "operative presence" without the traditional concept of potentiality? I do not think so. We must insist that emergent levels of a non-emergent mind cannot be thought without this concept of potentiality. We must, further, insist that we cannot make use of the negative side of potentiality, its opposition to

[1] *Op. cit.*, p. 37.

reductionism, without its positive implications. The very
essence of potentiality is that it stands for the significance and
richness of terms. It tells us that they are not to be reduced
to their relations without a remainder. But this also implies
the positive conception that the *nisus* of these emergent levels
is immanent or potential in the *total* process.

But there is a still more fundamental consideration. Evolution is intelligible movement, or it is nothing at all. Unless it
be merely a *name* for the comprehensive sequence of natural
events, it is intelligible movement. But it is only the intellect
that grasps such movement, and it can grasp it only by means
of concepts—the concepts, namely, of potentiality and realization, of potency and act. These concepts are not intellectual
dogmas forced on a resisting reality. They are the conditions of
the apprehension of intelligible movement, because the interpenetration and continuity of such movement are themselves
intelligible only as successive states or events are held together
by value.[1]

The only possible alternative to this conception is that of
Creative Evolution—of *a reality that creates itself gradually.* Now
this idea is, to my mind, one of the most unintelligible concepts
that it has ever entered into the mind of man to invent. One
sometimes wonders how such ideas could ever have got
possession of modern thought. That a certain plausibility
seems to attach to this idea need not be denied. Why say—so
we find the modernist asking—why say that the more cannot
be derived from the less, the higher and more complex levels
from the simpler, when precisely this is actually taking place
before our eyes? We are even told that there is nothing
materialistic in this when the rule of all development is for
the stream to rise higher than its source. Of course, it is *not*
taking place before our eyes. No eye can see any such thing
taking place. Eyes do not even see the differences between life
and the non-living, between mind and the non-mental. If we
did not appreciate immediately the meaning of life and mind,
if we did not acknowledge the values which those meanings
presuppose, there would be no differences between life and
"wetness and saltness held together," no difference between
cells held together and mind. Certainly no emergence of the

[1] Chapter VII, pp. 279 f.

higher from the lower takes place before our eyes.[1] If it did, we should have to deny the witness of our eyes. It is only for thought that it takes place, if at all, and anything that takes place for thought must be intelligible. The whole doctrine of emergence of higher levels of meaning and value from forces or entities originally devoid of value has seemed thus plausible, I think, only because those who think the idea are themselves placed at the end of a process of development, as so far continued, and are themselves part of the conclusion. But could such emergence have been foreseen, or even understood, by a mind of like endowment placed at the beginning of the process? Surely not. The process could be understood only by a mind itself independent of the process and capable of intuiting or apprehending the higher grades of reality at the outset. It is intelligible only to a mind that in some sense transcends the process.

Yet *Creative Evolution*, with its conception of a reality that creates itself gradually, is the only conception compatible with the doctrine of "emergents." It is also, as we shall see, the only one that goes with the idea of cosmic evolution—with evolution as a universal category. Those who "take evolution seriously"—and to take it seriously means for them to make time absolute and to identify becoming completely with being—are forced to this conception. "The evolutionary naturalist," says Sellars, "is not a finalist. He is a believer in novelty, time, and creative evolution." But whether an intelligible concept of evolution can be formed without finality is the real question at issue. Our contention is that it cannot. Evolution, if it is anything, is a form of the intelligible world, and part of that form is the concept of finality. But of this more later.

At the end of a summary of the different levels of being, in which it is said of these successive levels that they are the "emergent stuff of which the natural togetherness at the lower levels is the substance," Mr. Lloyd Morgan asks: "What more

[1] All this may seem a little strained. May we not speak of the "eyes of the mind," and is it not this that is here meant? It is, however, precisely my point that this emergence is not an "observability" in any sense of the word which conceives this observability as something abstracted from the acknowledgment of value. See in this connection my discussion of the same point in Chapter IV, p. 146.

need one ask for? Is not such a scheme of interpretation complete?" What more need one ask for? Nothing—but intelligibility.[1]

IV

An intelligible concept of evolution is, we have said, the great desideratum of the modern world. Evolution seems to be the form of an intelligible world; but the need of making that form itself intelligible is imperative. The unintelligibility of current evolutionary naturalisms, as it has gradually disclosed itself in the last quarter-century, has given rise to the question whether an intelligible concept of cosmic evolution is at all possible. An intelligible concept of evolution within the sphere of biology itself involves chiefly a credible view of the origin and transformation of species. But when the concept of evolution or development is extended beyond that sphere to the cosmos, quite different conditions of intelligibility arise. Naturalistic evolution has become systematic—that is, has included the inorganic processes and the human and cultural

[1] In bringing this part of my discussion to a close I may, perhaps, profitably comment on a criticism by Professor G. K. Patrick of these views as I have presented them in an article, "Origin and Value."

In the preface to his *Introduction to Philosophy*, Professor Patrick does me the honour of maintaining the concept of Emergent Evolution against the strictures I felt compelled to make upon it. He thinks that Lloyd Morgan and Alexander "have done philosophy a great service in introducing the word emergent to designate the relation in which spiritual values stand to the organization of material elements." That service, in its negative aspect at least, I unhesitatingly recognize. Professor Patrick does not, however, feel the difficulties in the divorce of origin from value implied in this doctrine. He agrees with me that the dissociation of value and reality would indicate the decadence of philosophy, but he cannot agree that the special form of it, dissociation of origin and value, would be equally fatal. "Even if," he writes, "we speak of new values as novelties, there is no necessary divorce of value from reality. But even if there are laid up somewhere in the heavens, patterns by which we measure these values, even then there is no reason why they may not emerge in any given local process of evolution."

Is it necessary to point out that this really begs the whole question? If these "patterns," or, better, the scale of values, are non-temporal, they do not themselves evolve and evolution becomes a "local process." If, however, evolution is only local and not universal, these values do not emerge in any ultimate sense. They merely become *sichtbar*. Emergence in any local process becomes merely a local appearance. With such a doctrine of emergence no one can have the least quarrel.

elements in its whole—only by embracing under one concept the most varied processes—of change, growth, development, progress. In particular, no completely intelligible concept of evolution can be developed which does not imply or eventuate in some concept of progress. Any philosophy must give some interpretation to human history if there is to be no gap in our view of the universe. But it is doubtful whether any intelligible history can be written without the postulate of progress, and there can be no intelligible concept of progress without intelligible finality. These are, however, topics which are yet to be considered in our discussions. It is, accordingly, only within the most decided limitations that we can attempt to determine the conditions of an intelligible concept of evolution at this stage.

On the other hand, there are certain problems in connection with such a conception that we are in a position to consider now, and these, perhaps, the most fundamental and important. They are the metaphysical problems involved in the concept of eosmic evolution. The idea of evolution as itself creative is, as we have seen, the only one that seems to go with a doctrine of emergence. It is also, it seems to many, the only one that is consistent with the idea of universal evolution, with the extension of development to the totality of things, to the universe or cosmos as a whole. It is the problems connected with this idea of universal or cosmic evolution that concern us here. The idea of evolution, as not a mere name for, nor description of, the sequence of phenomena, as not merely the method of creation, but as the creative thing itself, cannot be made intelligible without involving the questions of intelligible substance and intelligible causation already considered.

An examination of the history of the concepts of development and evolution, the stages of growth in the idea itself, serves best, perhaps, to reveal the nature of these problems. First, there is the original meaning of the word "evolve"—a mere unfolding, as in the opening of an unrolled scroll or the expansion of a bud into a full-blown flower.[1] This conception

---

[1] In this limited sense we may, perhaps, speak of development even when we are dealing with purely mechanical atomism. The transformation of a nebulous globe into the solar system, the breaking up of the masses into separate bodies,

is, then, enlarged so as to take in at the same time the idea of growth, not only in volume but in differentiation. This meaning is also illustrated by the development of a flower bud. Not only do its parts unfold, but they also change in size and shape and their tissues become continually less and less homogeneous. A still further meaning is gained when all the particular stages of the process are explicitly referred to one developing individual and an antithesis is drawn between the beginning from which, and the end toward which, the subject develops. The end of the development is, then, conceived as revealing what the beginning contained, as the oak reveals the true nature of the acorn. Finally, when the concept of development is made to extend beyond particular individuals to the whole range of the organic world, or even to the cosmos itself, it has reached its deepest meaning. But in establishing this meaning we find certain difficulties which lie in our inability both to fix upon an unequivocal meaning for development or evolution itself, and to fix definitely upon the subject to which the universal development is to be applied. In other words, *it is precisely at that point where evolution becomes the form of an intelligible world that it becomes difficult, if not impossible, to make the form itself intelligible.*

It is, I repeat, at this last stage of the historic development that the deepest meanings of the concept of development appear. But it is also here that we find its deepest problems and its greatest difficulties. For in the passage from development, as the form of an individual process, to evolution as a cosmic principle, we try to conceive the latter process without an end (with which development has always been connected), and we also try to apply the concept, formed to deal with concrete individuals, to the whole of reality for which it was never intended.

These difficulties are undoubtedly partly linguistic. The concept of evolution is a metaphor, and involves a gradual transference of evolution as a mere unfolding to that which does not merely unfold, or the transference of development

---

the process on the particular planets by which their surfaces take shape, may all be described as development from an original total state, in so far as the states implied in the forces or the elements and in their spatial distributions become successively real ; but only in this limited sense.

and growth to that which, strictly speaking, does not grow. We say, for instance, that there is no evolution without involution, meaning by this that if we are to use the concept of evolution intelligibly we must also use the correlative concept of involution with which it was originally bound up. It is always possible to say that in such a case we are imposed upon by language. The element of metaphor in the terms develop and evolve creates, it may be said, merely sophistical difficulties which give way before the demands of fact. But these difficulties are not merely a matter of language, or, better expressed perhaps, they are also matters of intelligible communication. The "language of evolution" must be intelligible. When we say that a thing evolves, or that the universe evolves, we are saying things that are significant only in case we can give a definite meaning both to the subject and predicate of our proposition. There is no point in saying that things develop or evolve rather than merely change, unless we mean to convey something by the word evolve that is not expressed in the word change. Similarly, there is no point in saying the world or cosmos evolves unless we mean to convey something more by the word cosmos than is expressed in the word all, when we say that everything changes. To say that all things change or flow is, indeed, a judgment of totality that has consequences, but it means very little in comparison with the judgment that the world evolves.

V

It is at this point, as is well understood, that the first and fundamental difficulty in the language of evolution appears. That which distinguishes evolution from mere change is always, and necessarily, the element of direction or *nisus* in the change, and no such elements are intelligible without some concept of permanence within the change. So long as the concepts of evolution or development were confined to those individual things for which they were first made, the ideas were clear enough. The scroll that unrolled had a permanent way of unrolling, the organism that grows or develops, a permanent path of development. In both cases an antithesis is drawn between the beginning and end of the process; and the end is conceived as revealing what was contained in the beginning and as the permanent and intelligible cause of the process or development. When, however, the concept is extended to embrace the whole of organic life—or, indeed, the cosmos itself—one of two possible consequences seems necessarily to follow. Either we make of the whole of life or of the cosmos an *individual*, and unconsciously use the old concept of development, or else inevitably, if insensibly, the element of direction is minimized and evolution tends to become synonymous with continuous change.

The antithesis of permanence and change is, we have seen, one of the two great dichotomies that have dominated the history of metaphysical thought. This antithesis is fundamental, for it is an *antithesis of values*, and it is only in terms of this contrast, of restless becoming and self-contained being, that the mind can apprehend and communicate the meaning of its own life and of the world in which that life is lived.[1] Modernism in general gives the privileged position to change: there is more in becoming than in that which becomes—a position which may be described as pure dynamism.

Pure dynamism has, however, always seemed paradoxical to the ordinary mind. To say that there is more in becoming than in the thing that becomes is unintelligible to the natural mind and essentially a transvaluation of all natural metaphysical values. A natural metaphysic demands things of which the forces shall be functions. Forces which are suspended in the air and supposed to produce things have no meaning for the ordinary mind, however much philosophers might like to see the contrary. The reason for this is deep-seated. There is, in the first place, that "prejudice" in favour of the permanent. "Deep down somewhere, the ultimate test of reality appears to be the law of conservation." An element of prejudice there may, indeed, be in this form of the ontological postulate, but it cannot be wholly prejudice, for permanence is a mode in which we express significance and value. In the second place, and this is more important still, it leads to the paradox that it is the becoming that is significant and valuable, not that which becomes. The final end of a development is not

---

[1] Chapter VIII, pp. 214 f.

more valuable than the starting-point. It is the transition from one to the other that is valuable. It is possible, to be sure, to say that this paradox is present only for the practical consciousness and not for the theoretical. But this is no answer if we recognize the "value character of the theoretical" itself.

The paradox of pure dynamism remains a paradox because it sounds the very depths of the unintelligible, as we have come to understand that concept. It is just as well for us to try to plumb these depths. For it is an intelligible concept of evolution that we want, and it is of considerable moment to see just how far short of such a concept the prevailing notions of evolution fall.

One of these depths is reached in the modern transformation of finality and teleology into the conception of "heterogeneity of ends," with the associated idea of an "ever fuller volume of free activity." Of this conception we shall have more to say in a later connection.[1] Here we are concerned merely with its relation to the conception of evolution as continuous change. The law of heterogeneity of ends is at bottom an attempt to combine the idea of direction or *nisus* (without which evolution or development cannot be thought) with continuous change. This is done by applying the notion of continuous change to the idea of the end itself. In this way it is thought possible to escape the dilemma of mere change without direction or end, or change towards a specific end— by means of the middle ground of continuous change of the direction itself. This is what the principle of heterogeneity of ends really amounts to.

Of this idea it has been said that it describes the actual experiences of every individual life. It is the miracle of every first-rate artistic creation, the whole story of human invention. When carried over to life as a whole, or to the cosmos, it has the additional advantage of being a conception of direction or finality "that is apparently more applicable to the earlier stages of evolution, where the objective realization of adaptations that were never subjectively intended must have played a still more conspicuous part than in human history." Now, as a merely descriptive formula, as a protection against a superficial anthropomorphism when applied to nature, or a

[1] Chapter X, pp. 360 f.

superficial intellectualism as applied to human invention in all its forms, it has its value. But taken in any absolute metaphysical sense, it is simply unintelligible. It is doubtful whether those who use these phrases so confidently quite realize how meaningless they are. In the life of the human spirit, from which alone the idea of "end" is taken, endless change of the end is a way of life which involves not endless self-renewal, but endless self-alienation. It is not different with the way of the "world," the cosmos. Here, also, endless change of the end could by no possibility be made intelligible as either development or progress. Endless change may, in a sense, be a law of the cosmos, but if so, there must be a deeper law of permanence in change. Otherwise reality is subject to perpetual estrangement from itself and admits of neither knowledge nor understanding.

The point I am trying to make here may be more simply and more concretely put. To suppose that all the variety in the world should have been directly created for variety's sake—"almost like toys in a shop," to use Darwin's phrase—is, indeed, as he himself urges, "an incredible view," in our phrase untrinsically unintelligible. Yet that is precisely what "creative accumulation" as a substitute for teleology means. But what is more important is that "creative accumulation" is, as the modernist well knows, the only concept consistent with pure dynamism.

But why incredible? Why unintelligible? The situation as here envisaged is not abstractedly impossible—certainly not unimaginable. We can very well imagine it. There are, indeed, those who envisage the world process, "creative evolution," as they call it, as a gigantic play of fancy. The "world as imagination" is not an unknown metaphysic. Indeed, there are possibly whole peoples who envisage the world in this fashion. What we mean to say is that *it is unintelligible to apply either the term evolution or development to such a process.* For these concepts are essentially concepts of the intellect, and processes that cannot be grasped by the intellect cannot be described as evolution or development. Both concepts imply intelligible causation. Creation for variety's sake may conceivably imply causality, but certainly no element of intelligible causation. When Bergson maintains that life and evolution cannot be grasped by thought, it is equivalent to saying that life is not apprehensible as evolution at all, but merely as change.

But we have by no means reached the depths. The paradox that it is the becoming that is significant and not that which becomes, or that there is more in becoming than in that which becomes, strikes deep. For it means that in transferring the concept of development or evolution from the individual thing for which it was made to the cosmos, we have been compelled in the process to abandon all that made the concept intelligible.

But pure dynamism involves a still deeper difficulty. In arguing against the Darwinian hypothesis, Agassiz is said to have urged: "If species do not exist, how can they vary?" and this rather naïve argument has found its way into the school logics as an illustration of the fallacy of *petitio principii*. Now that the objection, as stated, does beg the question is doubtless true. In the very form of the question it is assumed that existence and variation are incompatible, when it might be that to be or to exist is to change. And yet there is really more to this argument than meets the eye. It is really but a naïve way of saying that the language of evolution must be intelligible, that if you are going to say that species vary, the subject of your proposition must be an entity in some sense or else we shall not know what you are talking about. If you apply "existence" only to the variations, you must find another ontological predicate for that which gives meaning or significance to the variations. If a tendency to vary in all directions is regarded as a condition of attaining the most favourable form of life, then this tendency must be interpreted as a "seeking after" the most favourable form. The only way of finding fixed forms which have any counterpart in reality is from the point of view of the end, and those forms stand out among the chaos of differences which are the most perfect when the end is taken as a standard by which to measure them. The only intelligible language here is a teleological language; in other words, a language which gives subsistence to the species as a value.

It is for this reason that an intelligible concept of evolution must of necessity be teleological. If the idea of fixed species is given up, we must of necessity find a substitute for it. If the old basis of classification is destroyed by the theory of transmutation, a new basis is introduced, none other than the teleological, a principle that proves to be not only compatible with evolution but actually necessitated by it. The forms around which the members of a species group themselves become intelligible only in terms of adaptation, utility, and survival. Any intelligible system of animate nature, once the idea of fixed species is given up, is a realm of ends.[1]

It is here that the natural metaphysic of the human intellect is under a definite constraint. If it wishes to talk intelligibly it must talk a teleological language. It must say that that which becomes is more significant and more real than the becoming. The concept of substance, as we have seen,[2] is the development of the values of existence, and the only intelligible evolutionary language is that which gives substantiality to the species as a value. Nay, more, if our natural metaphysic wishes to extend the concept of evolution to the cosmos, it must say the same of the cosmos. Here, too, that which becomes is more significant than the becoming, the permanent more real than the changing.

The very significance of the concept of evolution—that which seems to make it the form of an intelligible world—is its close relation to life. If this relation does not persist, we have in evolution a mere name for a change in parts or a sequence of events. But the idea of mere change is incompatible with the idea of life. The fundamental characteristic of life is that while, in one aspect, it is unlimited, in another aspect it is always something individualized and limited. This characteristic of something limited that constantly transcends its limits is the inmost constitution of all that lives. A merely Heraclitean passage or flowing, without a definite permanent something, would not contain the limit beyond which this "going out," this transcendence, would be possible. Nor would it contain the subject which reaches out, which grows or develops. In sum, pure dynamism cannot be thought through; the complete identification of being with becoming excludes all intelligible concepts of evolution or development.

[1] For a keen argument for this position see Sigwart, *Logic*, vol. ii, pp. 524 ff.
[2] Chapter VIII, p. 283.

VI

The concepts of development, evolution, are thus themselves not without difficulties. Even when applied to individuals or to species within the whole, it is difficult to make these concepts intelligible. But the deepest problems of all arise when we speak of universal evolution. What is it that evolves? What is the subject to which universal evolution is to be ascribed?

The expression everything evolves, when taken collectively, when applied to the "world" as a totality, involves the greatest difficulties. In fact, the moment one begins to talk about the world or universe as we do about one finite being, one organism, or one society among others, one is "already on the brink of the unmeaning." From the fact that individuals grow or develop we can infer only that some things grow or develop. From the fact that everything that "exists" changes we may, perhaps, infer that all these things change, but never that the whole changes. In other words, we can find subjects for the predicates "grow" and "develop" and for the predicate "change," but none for the predicate "evolve," as it is used to include all these. I venture the statement that when we use the term evolution in a universal sense we never know quite what we are talking about. And this is what evolutionary agnosticism always really says.

To give an intelligible answer to the question, What is it that evolves?—if such an answer can, indeed, be given—we must divide the question into two parts, namely, whether evolution *is* of the whole, and, if so, what is the nature of the whole that evolves?

The answer to the first question obviously involves a consideration of the results of our discussion of the category of totality. The "prejudice in favour of totality" is, we saw, no prejudice, but a necessary presupposition of intelligible philosophical discourse. Something must be said about the whole, the universe. The universe must be the subject of discourse, not only in the logical sense but in a metaphysical sense also.[1] But while this is true, it is also true that there are some things that we must learn not to say about this whole. It may be that evolution is one of these things. I think that most certainly it is.

[1] Chapter II, pp. 53 ff.

x

The reasons for this are plain enough. In the first place, the "real world" in the sense in which the predicate "evolve" can in any meaningful sense be applied to it, is less than the universe. The real world, we have seen, always contains less than the universe, for the predicate "real" has inevitably the meaning of suggesting a contrast with something unreal which, however we may understand the term, must fall within the universe, which by hypothesis includes everything. Of the universe in this sense it is meaningless to say that it evolves. It is even meaningless to say that it changes. The universe cannot change, because any change introduces something that is, and this by hypothesis falls within the whole. The whole, if it changes is not the whole, but something less. All that is includes all that can be. There can be nothing more than it. This may be called dialectic, but what is dialectic but the determination of the conditions of intelligible communication?

If the "universe" cannot change, it certainly cannot evolve. But even of the real world of existents, in the limited sense in which it is intelligible to apply to it the concept of evolution at all, it is scarcely more intelligible to say that it evolves. For the real world in the sense of the existent, of which the law is the law of change, contains not only changing things, but the direction of change. To say that this direction changes (in any ultimate sense) is to negate direction and to give us nothing but change again.

Thus it is that, as we have seen, there obviously cannot be evolution of new levels. For then we should have, not only the whole problem of something coming from nothing, but we should also have the problem already pressed upon us by our consideration of the principle of "heterogeneity of ends," namely, of determining any direction of evolution at all. Development, evolution, cannot be asserted of any sequence of events at all without evaluation. But there cannot be any evaluation where absolute change is the law of value. Either we apply evolution to the whole, and evolution loses its meaning by becoming identical with mere change, or we apply it to "individuals" within the whole and it retains its element of direction.

"The world, my dear friend," says Lawrence, "does not evolve," and surely we must say the same. There is development, evolution, *in* the world, but not *of* the world. Logically, we have here precisely the same sort of an ambiguity with which we find Lloyd Morgan struggling when he speaks of the sense in which mind emerges and the sense in which it does not emerge, an ambiguity which inheres in all universals and totalities. Only to concrete individuals, totalities within the world, can the concepts of development or evolution be intelligibly applied.

Evolution, devolution, progress, decay—all such terms apply only to the part and never to the whole. In so far as they are temporal and not logical conceptions, they are necessarily local in significance. It is becoming fashionable in some quarters, in the revolt against the irresponsible extension of the evolution concept to everything, to go to the opposite extreme and to say that "the evolutionary concept has no more significance for philosophy than any other scientific hypothesis." This can scarcely be the case. For while it is a metaphor, as, indeed, any scientific hypothesis is a metaphor or symbol when extended beyond the realm of facts for which it was explicitly made, this happens to be a metaphor which has a maximum of consequences for metaphysical interpretation, which has significance in a larger context than, perhaps, any other. Yet it remains true that evolution can be applied —with any really intelligible meaning—only to the part, and never to the whole. When we speak of the world evolving, it can never be the world in the sense of identity with the universe, but only in the sense of some individualized totality necessary for intelligible discourse. Philosophy has always had a name for that totality. It has called it the phenomenal world.

The religious consciousness, no less than the metaphysical, has always struggled with this problem. If God is perfect in the beginning, then development, progress, can consist simply in the manifestation of His being, and progress simply in the betterment and enlightenment of human beings and of races in the universe. Even if we deny the divine perfection and think of a finite god, himself conceived as growing in insight and moral wisdom as individuals and races grow, even then, he himself being finite, progress applies only to the part and not to the whole. The idea of god in the making does not get over the idea that progress is only of the parts. It seems impossible to override the testimony of the religious consciousness on this point. But even if we do, nothing is gained from a philosophical point of view. From an ultimate metaphysical standpoint, progress is unintelligible as applied to the universe, and the temporal view of things with which progress is bound up is not ultimate.

VII

This leads us to the second part of our question, namely: What is the nature of that which evolves—what is the nature of any whole to which the predicate "evolve" can be intelligibly applied?

The outcome of the preceding reflections may be put in this way. It is only to that which is individual, to that which is at the same time limited and has the capacity of transcending its limits—in short, to organic wholes, that development and evolution can, strictly speaking, be intelligibly applied. When we regard development as an actual process in time, it requires a concrete individual subject existing in time. But the only subjects that thus actually "exist" are the particular organisms that succeed and produce each other. If we apply it in any other way and to any other subject, development or evolution tends to become simply another name for change, with a corresponding confusion of the issue. Nevertheless, there persists the attempt to think, if not the world or universe, at least "our world" as an evolving whole, as a subject of universal development. If, now, we wish to find such a subject, such a totality, this subject must itself be conceived as one that can be conceived in universal terms.

It is at this point that the treasured dichotomy of matter and spirit comes into play. Any philosophy, when it becomes articulate, must inevitably become dominantly materialistic or spiritualistic. For reasons that we need not repeat here, one of these must be given the privileged position. The world must be cogitated as either a material or a spiritual unity if it is to be cogitated as a unity at all. There is no third way. But—and this is the point of importance here—*to apply evolution to the world necessitates that it be cogitated as a unity.*

The older evolutionary naturalism of the reductive type of necessity gave the privileged position to "matter." In seeking for a subject of universal evolution it necessarily found it in matter or force, for, from its point of view, evolution and reduction are the same road viewed from its two ends. But evolution so conceived can be nothing but evolution in the sense of unrolling, or of successive unfolding of states implied in the forces of the elements and in their spatial distribution, and evolution in this sense, as creative and emergent evolution rightly insist, is no real evolution at all, if in that term we are to include the meanings of growth and progress.

The search for a subject of universal evolution in the latter sense naturally led to the concept of life as the ultimate category. For the modern *Lebensphilosophien* the essence of reality is life. To extend life to the cosmos must involve making biological categories world categories, as Bergson and all thinkers of his type have seen. That this is more intelligible than materialistic evolution in any of its forms few would deny. In so far as only that which in some sense lives, or has the meaning of life, evolves, then, if evolution is to be a universal category, life must be a world category also. Thought is in the position of either abandoning the category of evolution as in any sense a world category, or else changing our conception of the nature and "substance" of the world. But to make biological categories world categories is as unjustifiable as to make the categories of any single science ultimate. That which alone has made it seem plausible or intelligible is the fact that in thus expanding these categories of life and growth of organisms to the dimensions of world categories, from purely biological to metaphysical conceptions, the concepts of life and organism have themselves changed.

It is this equivocal use of the concept of life in modern philosophies that alone makes them plausible. It is, accordingly, upon this ambiguity that we must first fix our eyes. It consists, in brief, in taking a category from the organic world and then, in order to enable us to extend this category to the inorganic and to the hyper-organic, so changing or widening the concept that it may become a universal predicate. Such transformation of the concept, however, raises it, so to speak, to another metaphysical level. As Tolstoy says:

"I cannot present life to myself (in this sense) otherwise than as a striving from bad to good. This is, then, its central and indubitable meaning." In this case, however, *the category of life necessarily merges into that of spirit.* In other words, we have really taken the second half of the treasured dichotomy of human thought.

The essential unintelligibility of all mere life philosophies was exposed long ago by Hegel in his criticism of Schelling's formulation of the same hypothesis. In addition to pointing out the ambiguities involved in this use of the concept, he shows the impossibility of applying it to the totality of reality in any intelligible way. For either this totality is one organism among other individuals, or else it is the totality, past, present, and future, of all such organisms. The first hypothesis would, of course, make of life and its evolution a limited and local phenomenon. The second hypothesis conceives of life, not as the life of an individual, but of organic nature conceived as an organic whole. But such a totality of successive organisms is simply an indefinitely prolonged procession of living beings. It is a process of exfoliation, not of development. Out of such a succession of processes no *true* individual can be conceived as the subject of development.

The outcome of such reflections is as obvious as it was in Hegel's day. The only form of unity or totality that can provide the conditions for an intelligible concept of cosmic development or evolution is that unity which comes through the concept of the development of the "Idea." The concept of life, by reason of its ambiguous character, affords no intelligible middle ground between the dichotomy of matter and spirit. If the world is to be cogitated as a unity at all, it must be cogitated as either a material or a spiritual unity. If it is to be cogitated as an evolution, it must be as either a materialistic or an idealistic evolution.

In other words, any concept of total evolution, as distinguished from partial evolutions within a universe, can be conceived only as a development of the *Idea,* to use Hegel's terms. It is quite clear, I think, that any other concepts, such as those we have been considering, cannot be made intelligible. Perhaps this notion of the development of the Idea cannot be made intelligible either. We can at least present the process of thought which leads to the conception, and thereby make clearer this notion of the Idea and of its development.

It is clear that we cannot have an intelligible notion of universal development without a subject of such development. It is clear, also, that if we wish to find such a subject it must be characterized in universal or general terms. And to such general concepts as matter, life, mind we can attribute development only in an ideal, logical sense. When we regard development as an actual process in time, it can be development only of particular, concrete subjects, existing in time. If the concept of development is to be not merely a general formula for the sequence of events, if it is to be in any sense an interpretative concept, it requires *a subject of such a nature that by its successive changes new conditions of further changes in a fixed series are continually introduced, and that this series leads ultimately to an end in which the original disposition or potentialities are completely realized.* It is not by itself, but by virtue of the permanent nature of the developing subject, that each particular stage is the cause of the next. This alone is intelligible causation, and intelligible causation can never be thought as anything but realization or development of the Idea.[1]

By the term "Idea," as here used, I mean, then, a subject of just such a nature as is here described. Any philosophical conception of evolution requires such a subject, an immanent or underlying activity—a substantial activity—expressing itself in individual embodiments. It is, moreover, just because of this basal requirement that any intelligible philosophy of evolution must in the end conform to that traditional form of intelli-

---

[1] The point I am trying to make here may be brought out in greater relief by reference to Whitehead's discussion of Evolution in the chapter on the "Nineteenth Century" in his *Science and the Modern World*.

"The doctrine" (of Evolution) "thus cries aloud," he says, "for a conception of organism as fundamental to nature." "A thoroughgoing evolutionary philosophy," he points out, "is inconsistent with materialism." But the later developments of this theme indicate that in using the organic conception of nature he has widened the concept of organism precisely as I have indicated. He makes it quite clear that, after all, value, and with it the concept of spirit, are central in his thought. Speaking of the requirements of a philosophic conception of evolution, he says: "It also requires an underlying activity—a substantial activity—expressing itself in individual embodiments and evolving in achievement of organisms. The organism is a unit of emergent value, a real fusion of the characters of eternal objects, emerging for its own sake" (p. 152).

gibility (of intelligible substance and intelligible causation) that brings the cause and the end together in a more ultimate concept or idea. The only form of unity or totality that can afford the conditions of an intelligible concept of cosmic evolution is the unity of the idea. To the question, What is it that evolves? naturalistic evolution in its more reflective moments always gives an agnostic answer, and must necessarily do so. There is no single subject for cosmic evolution in the sense that the whole that evolves may be described as matter or life or mind. These can be but moments in a more ultimate concept.

Here, again, the point I am trying to make may be put in a more concrete and, in a sense, I think, more intelligible form. The language of metaphysics—and the language of evolution must be a metaphysical language—when it is most intelligible, when it approaches intrinsic intelligibility, also approaches the language of poetry, as when the poet cries:

> . . . the One Spirit's plastic stress
> Sweeps through . . .
> Torturing the unwilling dross that checks its flight
> To its own likeness as each mass may bear.

In such words, with all their accumulated intension, the poet has found expression for the natural metaphysic of the human mind. The likeness to the Spirit, as each mass may bear, is the only criterion that distinguishes evolution from mere differentiation or change. The One Spirit's plastic stress is the only element of unity or universality that can be found in the world process. Evolution seems to make the world intelligible to us. But it does so only when we conceive it, either consciously or unconsciously, as evolution of a divine idea, as a gradual revelation in time of that which was present from the "foundation of the world."

As a matter of fact, this is what we mostly do in our hearts, whatever we may say with our lips. The brute fact is that the panorama of evolution—that comprehensive plan of the sequence of natural events as it unrolls itself before us—may *seem* to be intelligible, but fundamentally we *know* that it is not. This is how it appears to a poet who has apparently long brooded over the passage of nature. In a poem called *The*

Passing Strange, John Masefield expresses in unforgettable words how passing strange the whole thing is :

> Out of the earth to rest and range
> Perpetual in perpetual change
> The Unknown passing through the Strange.

Strange, eternally and radically strange, are all the varied phenomena of change, unless they possess that intrinsic meaning which attaches itself solely to a will directed towards purpose and value. That which passes through these unintelligible things remains for ever in the deepest sense unknown unless it be throughout of the nature and essence of that which appears on the highest levels of the Spirit. The increasing recognition of this fact, not only in philosophy, but in the widest ranges of the human spirit, is, perhaps, the outstanding feature of the general culture of our time.

CHAPTER X

INTELLIGIBLE FINALITY AND THE PROBLEM OF DESTINY

> The doctrine of final causes will never be refuted. If one form of it is put aside it will take another.
>
> BERGSON
>
> It takes genius to make an ending.
>
> NIETZSCHE

I

NOTHING is more characteristic of us moderns than novel attitudes towards the future. A certain hilarious acceptance of the essential meaninglessness of a universe in which, as it is said, the gates of the future are for ever open, alternates with an almost equally hilarious acceptance of a universe in which the gates of the future are already shut. Modernists seem quite able to contemplate the world "unrolling as an endless serial novel"; but they seem almost equally ready to contemplate it as a crude tragedy in which all the players are killed off in the end.

I do not mean, of course, that men have not held these views in the past, that men have not constructed futile and intolerable worlds and called them philosophies. What I do mean to emphasize is, rather, this miracle of modern sensibility and sophistication which enables us, not only to conceive such worlds, but also to call them good.[1] Modernism is nothing if

---

[1] The following popular expression of this mood is worth quoting: "They tell me that our race may be an accident in a meaningless universe, living its brief life uncared-for on this dark cooling star; but even so, and all the more, what marvellous creatures we are! What fairy story, what tale from the *Arabian Nights* of the jinns, is a hundredth part as wonderful as this true fairy story of the simians?

"And it is so much more heartening, too, than the tales we invent. A universe capable of giving birth to such accidents is, blind or not, a good world to live in, even if not the best. We have won our way up against odds. We have made this our planet. It stirs me to feel myself part of our racial adventure.

"It is an adventure that may never be noticed by gods. It may lead to no eternal reward in itself. God or no God, we belong to a race that has made a long march, and in the future may travel on greater roads still" (Clarence Day, "This Simian World," *Harper's Magazine*, March 1920).

not spirited. The vulgar and unsophisticated might think to detect a note of hysteria here, a kind of whistling to keep up one's courage. But that would be to fail entirely to appreciate the miracle of the modern mood, to realize how completely we have learned to renounce all intelligibility, to renounce that "mythical philosophy" which connects the meaning and value of things with their origin and end. The philosophers of the Great Tradition knew, or thought they knew, whither they were going. Now, in the words of that artificially inspired individual of a popular song, "We don't know where we're going, but we're on our way."

Thus the evolutionary naturalist is not a finalist. He is a believer in novelty, time, and creative accumulation. In other words, he believes that he can make a way intelligible without any idea as to where it is going. It is doubtful whether we quite grasp all that is involved in such a conception, in this substitution of "creative accumulation" for teleology. It is the natural culmination of the unintelligible position of the preceding chapter. As it involves the idea of a reality that creates itself gradually, so it involves the idea of the evolution of the scale of values itself. We make our hopes of the goal, our very conception of it and so the goal itself, as we go. This necessarily involves either the denial, or an entire reconstruction, of the concept of progress. Instead of knowing what progress is by means of our values we try to know our values by means of progress. It is doubtful, I repeat, whether we quite grasp all that is involved in such conceptions. The whole question of intelligible finality and intelligible progress is at issue. In the present chapter we shall devote our attention to the first of these questions, leaving the fuller consideration of the problem of progress for the next.

For traditional philosophy there has been, in the main, one and only one way of finding the world intelligible. Obeying a natural metaphysic innate in the human mind, it has found itself unable to construe the world except in terms of origin and destiny. Intelligibility, it finds, cannot renounce the idea of ultimate origin. This idea may be modified, detemporalized, but it cannot be exorcized. As little, apparently, can it renounce the idea of ultimate end. This idea, we shall see, may be greatly modified, perhaps detemporalized also, but it cannot be exercized. The two *ideas* are, in fact, correlative, and the abandonment of either or both, as certain conceptions of science and philosophy propose, means, as Levy-Brühl rightly admits, the abandonment of the ideal of intelligibility.

Even Bergson, a modern of the modernists, recognizes that finality in some form is an essential part of the form of philosophical intelligibility. "The doctrine of final causes," he writes, "will never be definitely refuted. If one form of it is put aside it will take another It is very flexible."[1] Teleology needs no proof. It is a necessity of thought. It is the time-form of value, and without value there can be no thought. We do not, and cannot, move a step in our thinking without acknowledging that which for internal reasons of value and validity we recognize as the rationally intelligible way of interpreting our experiences. There are no fundamental truths of experience which are not, in part at least, *a priori* reasons defined in terms of an inner necessity, or rather obligation, which can be merely acknowledged. Part, at least, of finality is, we shall see, *a priori* and as such ultimately irrefutable. But while it is irrefutable it is extraordinarily flexible, and modern philosophy has exploited this flexibility "to the limit." I propose, therefore, to submit some of these recent modifications to an examination from the point of view of their ultimate intelligibility. To accomplish this we must first analyse finality, in order to try to determine the "essential characteristics of value," as Bosanquet calls them—to which finality, if it is to have meaning and validity, must ultimately be carried back. In other words, we must seek to determine the *a priori* element in finality, without which there can be no intelligibility.

II

Origin and destiny are obviously the same road viewed from its two ends. But there is an important difference in the way the road looks from the two ends, due to the privileged character which the practical reason gives to the future. William James insisted that the origin of things makes no difference except for its bearing on their future. This, we have

[1] *Op. cit.*, p. 40.

seen, is by no means true. But *a large part* of the meaning and value of anything—of its very nature, indeed—is bound up with its future, and it is the peculiar character of this meaning that first concerns us in the study of finality.

The relation of the meaning of anything to its future appears at two points. In the first place, the future of anything that has meaning and value cannot be thought of, much less expressed, except in terms of purpose and finality. In so far as the element of futurity, of what a thing is going on to be, is taken into account, that aspect of its being can be envisaged only in terms of end, or means to ends. If an object has value at all, that value, in so far as it is projected into the future, must be thought of either as an end or as a means to an end.

The second point at which this relation of the meaning and value of a thing to its future appears, concerns the *fate* of the object and of its value in time. Once an object "has been detached from its immediate objectivity and has entered into that subjectivity, that free existence, which makes it a purpose," or a means to an end, its meaning and value cannot be detached from its future or its fate in the future. To say that a man or an institution has no future is the same thing as saying that they have no meaning. In the mere process of temporal becoming means may take the place of ends, new and unforeseen ends arise out of old, but unless that part of the nature of an object we call its purpose is *in some way retained and conserved in its temporal end,* the identity of the thing with itself is lost and no intelligible communication of its nature and meaning is possible.

Finality, in these its two aspects of purpose and consummation of purpose, is then part of the time-form of value. Reference to its future is a necessary part of the expression and communication of the meaning and value of anything. So soon, however, as this future reference enters into our description, the only form of description possible is in terms of purpose, involving the relation of means to ends and realization of ends through the means. It is for this reason that, as has been said, the doctrine of finality will never be refuted: if one form of it is put aside it will take another. Another term for purposelessness is futility, and that which is futile is ultimately unintelligible.

All this has, of course, been said again and again in varying ways from the time of Aristotle to the present. It has, however, been expressed in an unusually telling way by Wundt in an eloquent passage in his *Ethics*, which stresses especially the second point in the relation of the meaning of a thing to its future, its destiny. "If," Wundt writes, "we could be absolutely assured of the misery of a descendant living two centuries hence, we should probably not be much disturbed. It would trouble us more to believe that the State and nation to which we belong were to perish in a few generations. The prospect would have to be postponed for several centuries, at least, before our knowledge that all the works of time must be destroyed would make it tolerable. But there is one idea that would be for ever intolerable though its realization were thought of as thousands of years distant; it is the thought that humanity with all its intellectual and moral toil may vanish without leaving a trace, and that not even a memory of it may endure in any mind." From the intolerability of this conception Wundt proceeds to infer the opposite. "The confidence of this reality, it is true, is born, not of knowledge, but of a faith based on a dialectical analysis of the concept of moral end, which shows that every given end is only proximate, not ultimate— is thus finally a means to the attainment of an imperishable goal."[1]

For Wundt, accordingly, there is an element in finality that is irrefutable. The point which especially interests us in his presentation of this element is, however, the form in which this irrefutable element is felt by us. For him it is the thing that is *forever intolerable* that is also the unintelligible and unthinkable. Its irrefutable character is, indeed, based upon a dialectical analysis of the concept of moral end. The relation of the meaning and value of any thing to its future is expressible only in terms of ends and means to ends. Every given end is only proximate, and implies, to be intelligible, an imperishable goal. But it is the *intolerability* of the opposite of this implication that is really the determining element, and it is at this point that the irrefutable element in finality is to be found.

It will be worth our while to pursue this suggested relation of the intolerable to the unthinkable and unintelligible

[1] *The Principles of Morality*, English translation, p. 82.

somewhat further. First of all, I may point out that, as a matter of fact, appeal is constantly made in the history of philosophical thought to the intolerable, much in the fashion that we find it in Wundt's passage. Indeed, often when a "thing" is said to be unthinkable, what is really meant is that it is intolerable. It is said, for instance, that it is unthinkable that God should condemn innocent infants to eternal punishment. Now, there is doubtless ultimately some "logical" contradiction in the conception, but the contradiction is, as we say, primarily moral, or more fundamental still, axiological, in the sense that we have defined it in an earlier chapter. The unthinkable here is the axiologically intolerable.[1]

The intolerable then, it is our contention, is *a special form of the unintelligible, the unthinkable.* It is that form which always appears in connection with the future reference of values, or in contemplation of their fate in the cosmos. It is because part of the very nature of a thing is bound up with its future reference that futility or absence of purpose, and the passage of meaning and value into nothing, are unintelligible. It is because of the relation of feeling to value that the unintelligible expresses itself in the form of the intolerable. Let us show this connection in detail; and first of all by examining the concept of the unthinkable.

The unthinkable is the inconceivable, and the "inconceivability of the opposite" has been connected with the idea of necessary or *a priori* truth. Similarly, the intolerability of the opposite has been connected with the idea of the *a priori* in the field of valuation.

In the case of the so-called inconceivable or unthinkable, many things have turned out to be so only because of obstinate human prejudices and because men have persisted in confusing the unimaginable with the inconceivable. None the less, while we have become exceedingly wary of the unthinkable, and have pretty well concluded that there is no proposition about existent things the opposite of which is not abstractly conceivable, there still remain certain propositions, even about

---

[1] Elsewhere, in an article entitled "On Intolerables," *The Philosophical Review* (vol. xxiv, No. 5), I have attempted to make a more complete study of the rôle of the "intolerable" in philosophic thought. Here I shall content myself with such aspects of this study as are necessary to develop our conception of finality.

existent things, which for all "practical" purposes of intelligible human communication we have agreed to find unthinkable.

The situation is not notably dissimilar in that region of the unthinkable to which we have given the name of the intolerable. In the case of those things found unthinkable because ultimately intolerable, many, indeed, owe their apparent intolerability to certain prejudices of feeling and sensibility we attribute to the tender-minded, prejudices which the tough-minded do not share. Here, also, it may be said, perhaps *a fortiori*, that there is no value, no proposition about value, the opposite of which cannot conceivably be affirmed. But here again, as I hope to show, for all practical purposes—purposes of intelligible human communication—there are propositions that are *axiologically* intolerable.

In general, such propositions are concerned with the fate of values, and of the bearers of value, in time-propositions involving finality and destiny. Such intolerability is quite different from any merely psychological sensibility. It strikes deep into the very metaphysical structure of things—expressing itself ultimately, as we have seen, in the antinomy of the finite and the infinite—of which both alternatives, if taken absolutely, are equally intolerable in the axiological sense.[1]

III

Our argument thus far is as follows. We hold, and are attempting to show, that there is that in the notion of finality which is irrefutable. The irrefutable in the sphere of ultimate metaphysical conceptions is that which is unthinkable. But the unthinkable in the sphere of values—and in the relation of value to existence and reality—cannot be separated from the element of feeling. The unthinkable here shows itself necessarily, therefore, in the form of the intolerable, the axiologically intolerable. The intolerable in this sense is whatever is in contradiction with *the essentials of value as such*. Our present task is, therefore, to seek to determine what these essentials are, to find out what *a priori* characters belong to value and valuation as such, quite irrespective of the empirical

[1] See Chaper VII, pp. 256-7.

content in our valuations. Only after this is done can we hope to distinguish the irrefutable element in finality from the changing forms which its very flexible character makes possible. The irrefutable in finality would then be that which cannot be denied without unintelligibility, in the sense in which we have been using the term.

With this we enter upon one of the most difficult, as it is one of the most unworked, regions of philosophic thought. We may take our start by first recalling briefly what we understand by the *a priori* in the sphere of "pure thought."

Now, the *a priori* in this sphere is that of which we cannot conceive the opposite. It is possible, for instance, to contemplate a world in which men never die, but not one in which two and two do not make four. "We feel that such a world, if there were one, would upset the whole fabric of our knowledge and reduce us to utter doubt." How is it now in the world of values? Are there any propositions the contemplation of the opposite of which is impossible—that would destroy the very fabric of our knowledge? Certainly not any propositions about the future; certainly not even the situation which Wundt finds intolerable. It may be intolerable, but surely not abstractly inconceivable. Absolute physics with its dying world may, as Nietzsche says, be intolerable, but it is not inconceivable. Indeed, there is none of our actual empirical valuations— upon which any thought of the fate of values must be based, the opposite of which it is impossible abstractly to contemplate. A world, for instance, in which lying should be put above truth, ugliness preferred to beauty, a world in which it were said "Evil, be thou my good," is not abstractly inconceivable. We can contemplate a world in which men never die, and perhaps equally one in which happiness is not better than unhappiness, or life better than death. There is no value the opposite of which cannot conceivably be affirmed, Transvaluation of values is conceivable indefinitely; and with this it follows that there is no fate of our empirical values which is not abstractly conceivable.

This is the element of truth in all merely relativistic theories of value, and to this relativism the critic of teleology always may, and always does, appeal. Yet, recognizing this element of truth in relativism, there is still something *a priori* in all

Y

valuation which the relativist overlooks, something here, also, the opposite of which cannot be contemplated.

Value itself (there are few who may claim competence in this sphere who do not now see) is a logically primitive concept. If I argue that good or value is the desired, I need a premise to the effect that satisfaction of desire is a good. If I argue that good is that which ought to be desired, I need a premise to the effect that everything that is better than some other thing ought, therefore, to be desired before it, and conversely. If, however, I say that one thing is better than another because it is more highly developed, I must first assume that development is necessarily improvement—that is, that there is always greater value in a thing in proportion to the degree of its development, and to do this I must already know what good or value is. In other words, all deduction of value from something else is an argument in a circle, as I have shown.[1]

This, I repeat, is now generally understood, but what is not so clearly seen is that this logically primitive concept *implies certain things the opposite of which cannot be conceived.* For one thing, although we may, perhaps, conceive a world in which there are no values, yet, given any values at all, it lies in the nature of values as such that they must be related as higher and lower. Values may conceivably be transvalued, "perverted," indefinitely, but any such transvaluation, however complete, leaves the value relation as such untouched. You find it possible to contemplate a world in which there are no values or in which values cease to be? But certainly not a world in which, if there are any values at all, they are not thus related.

True, there seem to be immitigable scales of value which we violate at our peril. Granted the acknowledgment of such values we may certainly speak of a perversion of values, as when Lord Alfred Douglas said of Oscar Wilde that "he perverted values, calling the physical spiritual and the spiritual physical." But there is nothing abstractly inconceivable about such a "perverted scale." He who says that the physical is the spiritual and the spiritual is the physical is not enunciating a proposition that refutes itself. But the enunciator of the proposition refutes himself if he thereby intends to convey an intelligible meaning. For his communication must take place

[1] Chapter IV, pp. 137 ff.

within a world in which the scale of values is already acknowledged. So long as a man remains a solipsist he can be refuted
in the sphere of values as little as in any other sphere. Such
immitigable scales of value there are, but they are not *a priori*
in the sense we are using the term here.[1]

This conception of *a priori* elements in value and valuation
is so important for all that follows that we may with advantage
develop the point somewhat further, especially in the way of
making clearer our notion of the *a priori* as defined in an earlier
section.

The *a priori* we defined as "that which is true no matter
what." Whatever is *a priori* is necessary, but this necessity,
while opposed to the contingent, is not opposed to the voluntary.
It is that which is acknowledged and involves all the freedom
of acknowledgment, but this freedom is only from external
compulsion, not from those compulsions that arise out of the
conditions of intelligible communication.

That there are such *a priori* elements in all value and valuation seems beyond question. One may admit the relative and
contingent character of all values, and yet there are essentials
or principles of value that are true, no matter what. Any
transvaluation of values, however complete, still leaves the
principle of an order of value untouched. The Chinese order
in the rescuing of the shipwrecked is, it is said, the exact
opposite of ours. Whereas custom demands of us the rescue,

[1] An interesting and suggestive parallel between the physical and the moral
world is drawn by Aldous Huxley in *Those Barren Leaves*, p. 377. "In the physical
world," he writes, "you call the Unknowable the Four-dimensional Continuum.
The continuum is the same for all observers; but when they want to draw a
picture of it for themselves they select different axes for their graphs, according
to their different motions—and according to their different minds and physical
limitations. Human beings have selected three-dimensional space and time as
their axes. Their minds, their bodies, and the earth on which they live being
what they are, human beings could not have done otherwise. And when we
want to draw a picture of that other reality in which we live—is it different,
or is it somehow incomprehensibly the same?—we choose, unescapably we
cannot fail to choose, those axes of reference we call good and evil; the laws
of our being make it necessary to see things under the aspects of good and evil.
The reality remains the same; but the axes vary with the mental position, so to
speak. . . . But the axes chosen by the best observers have always been startlingly
like one another; Gotama, Jesus, and Lao-tsze, for example. They lived sufficiently
far from one another in space, time, and social position. But their pictures of reality
resemble one another very closely. The nearer a man approaches these in
penetration, the more nearly will his axes of reference approach to theirs."

first of the children, then of the women, and finally of the men, another conception of "importance" calls for the reversed order in the case of the Chinese. But the conception of a necessary order of value is equally present in both cases. In other words, this necessary element in value and valuation remains true, "no matter what" the variations in empirical valuation.

We have said: Given any values at all, it lies in the nature of values as such that they must be related as higher and lower. But is it not possible to think the world without value at all? As a matter of fact, we can contemplate the complete absence of value as little as we can contemplate the absence of being, that is, if we assume a world at all. This is, to be sure, a statement that will be questioned by many, but only, I think, because the statement is really not understood. Things do not, indeed, have to be good and beautiful in order to exist in the narrow and abstract sense of the word "exist" employed by science, but things do have to be in relations of value, as well as in other types of relations, in order to be things in the full sense of our experiencing them as things.[1] But the inseparability of value and reality has been repeatedly argued throughout this book and need not be gone into here. For my own part, I believe that any object *qua* object must fall somewhere in the scale of positive and negative value with the same kind of necessity that an object must be existent or nonexistent. For our present purpose it is not necessary to insist upon this. It is enough to affirm that, *given* any value at all, it must, in order to be a value, be related to other values in the relations of more or less. If you affirm any value at all you must affirm a scale or system of values. An isolated value is a contradiction in terms. In other words, if one does not affirm merely dogmatically a value, this value is alone possible in that it goes back to a scale of values. A value is never a brute fact, and a brute fact is never a value.

IV

In all this we may seem to have strayed from our main topic, namely, the analysis of finality, the determination of the

<hr>

[1] Chapter IV, pp. 157-8.

irrefutable element in it, and the notion of the *axiologically intolerable* with which it is connected. As a matter of fact, it is only by doing precisely what we have done, only by seeking to understand the essential characteristics of value as such— to which finality, if it is to be valid, must be carried back— that we can hope to understand what is irrefutable in the notion.

Thus far in our argument we have merely developed two essential characteristics of value as such, namely, first, that value is a logically primitive concept like being and is applicable to all objects with the same necessity that an object is said to be existent or non-existent; and secondly, that given any values at all, they must fall into the relations of more and less, in a scale of positive and negative values. These essentials are, moreover, *a priori* in the sense that we really cannot contemplate the opposite, and in the still more important sense that if we do affirm the opposite, no intelligible communication of our values is possible. In all this, it is true, no element of purpose has as yet entered into our dialectical analysis, no connection between relations of value and the relations of means to ends has yet been made clear. But it is already evident at what point the notion of finality must enter in. Value is inseparable from reality, and it seems probable, therefore, that if there are propositions about value that are true no matter what, there are also similar propositions about the relations of value to reality. Our problem, now, is to determine whether there are such propositions and what their character is. Are there any such propositions about values when they become ends or purposes and about the realization of these values in time? Are there any elements in finality that are irrefutable?

This is evidently the turning-point in our argument. It is also clear that the key to the problem lies in the fact that, as we have already seen, purpose is the time-form of value, and that as soon as a value becomes thus a purpose, it thereby enters into relations to existence. In the first place, so soon as objects are valued and become the objects of volition, by that very fact they necessarily enter into the relations of means to ends. Time becomes part of the nature of any value and the mutual externality of the moments of time—which is of its very essence so far as volition is concerned—creates necessarily the relations of means to ends. Otherwise expressed, when once objects are detached from their immediate objectivity by valuation and volition, and enter into that "free existence" which makes them purposes, not only do they necessarily become related as means to ends, but this relation of means to ends is the necessary time-form of the relation of higher and lower, inherent in the nature of value as such.

In the second place, when an object enters into that form of existence which we call a purpose, immediately a certain relation of value to existence is established. The innermost essence of time is the inalienable difference between what is and what ought to be. If there were not this duality between value and existence there would be no volition. On the other hand, if there were not some necessary relations between the value and its realization in time—between value and existence —there would also be no volition, at least, no intelligible valuation and volition. In the light of this analysis we may state our present problem in this way: Is there anything that we may say *a priori* about valuation and the element of finality it implies? Are there any propositions about the relation of values to volition, and about the fate of these willed values in time, that may be said to be irrefutable? I believe that there are such propositions and I shall describe them as *the necessary conditions of intelligible valuation and volition.*

It is rather generally recognized that there is an *a priori* aspect to valuation. That the better ought to be chosen rather than the.worse, the greater value rather than the less, seems to be self-evident. This principle of "the maximization of value" is said to be the one absolutely evident moral law and, therefore, in the terms of Brentano, the natural and ultimate sanction of morality. It is something the opposite of which it is impossible to contemplate. The recognition or acknowledgment of value is already the beginning of willing it, the acknowledgment of degree of value is already the beginning of the choosing of the greater rather than the lesser good. It is impossible to conceive our will as willing otherwise. In other words, the *form*, or the essential characteristics of value as such, is so related to will that if we will at all we must will according to it.

This principle of the maximization of value is intrinsically intelligible. We may also say, as we have in another connection, that the only thing that *is* intrinsically intelligible is a will oriented towards the good. But with the entrance of will and the element of time, values immediately become ends, degrees of value relate themselves both as proximate and as more remote ends and as means to ends. Thus the principle of maximization of value becomes necessarily the principle of the *summum bonum*. The human and finite analogy of means to ends becomes the necessary temporal form of the essentials of value, and is *a priori* in the sense that without it there is no intelligible valuation and volition.

This is one side of the argument. If we will at all we must, as we have seen, will according to the essentials of value. Only volition of this sort is intelligible volition. This is, so to speak, the "demand that reality makes on us." But is there no *corresponding demand that we may make on reality*? Undoubtedly there is—*if* reality, including our own valuation and volition (which is a part of it), is to be intelligible. I mean by this to say that, if the principles of degree and of maximization of value, with its idea of a *summum bonum* and of an imperishable goal, lie in the nature of value as such; and if, further, it is true that if we will at all, we must of necessity will according to these principles, then a world in which the opposite of these principles were true, in which there were no finality in the sense of an increasing purpose, no finality in the sense of an imperishable goal, would be an *intolerable* world, and to this extent wholly unintelligible.

This is, I repeat, the irrefutable element in finality. If we acknowledge values at all, we must acknowledge, also, these implications of value and valuation. Finality in this sense is the necessary condition of intelligible valuation. But, what is even more important than this, the truth of these propositions is the necessary condition of the communication of the meaning and value of things, and is, therefore, part of the form of *any* intelligible world. But I would not be misunderstood here. I do not for one moment say that a world in which there were no finality, no increasing purpose, and no imperishable goal, is abstractly inconceivable. It can be *conceived* readily enough. All that I have said is that it is *intolerable* and that with this intolerability is connected an unintelligibility of a peculiarly impressive kind. There are, to be sure, as we pointed out, propositions about value as such, the opposite of which cannot be conceived without destroying the very fabric of value and valuation, but these apply, so to speak, only to the *form* and not to the content of valuation. No propositions about value and existence can have this character, but they may be irrefutable in the sense that their denial makes all valuation meaningless—and all volition ultimately futile.

It is now necessary to see just what this argument is worth. This entire line of thinking, it may be said, is nothing more than a presentation in different terms of Kant's doctrine of the Practical Reason. In a broad sense this is, perhaps, true. But there is a difference of such importance that to ignore it would be to miss the entire point of the argument. It is found in the contrast of knowledge with faith. The confidence expressed by Wundt, for instance, in the implications of intelligible purpose, "is born," he says, "not of knowledge, but of faith based on the dialectical analysis of the concept of the moral end." We should say that this confidence is based on knowledge. The task of the philosopher at this point is that of making transparent, as it were, the structure, the *a priori* structure if you will, of value and being in their necessary relations. We have carried the dialectical analysis of which Wundt speaks further back—back to the essentials of value and valuation as such. Surely this is knowledge in any but the narrowest sense of that term, and the significance of this analysis is not adequately expressed in terms of mere faith or of the merely practical reason.

The purely practical character of the category of purpose and finality is the contention of all those philosophies that would either exclude it, or, if it cannot be altogether exorcized, so transform it as to make it innocuous; and for this they seem to be able to appeal to Kant's authority. Now, the practical and human character of the category need not be denied. But it is our contention that it is much more than this. It is axiological and, to that extent, metaphysical. As the axiologically intolerable is the unintelligible and ultimately the metaphysically impossible, so the axiologically *a priori* is the metaphysically necessary.

It was one of Kant's most serious limitations that while he recognized that the knowledge of nature, in our terms its intelligibility, is conditioned, by certain forms immanent in

mind, to the equally necessary forms of the interpretation of
life and the world, he allowed merely the character of practical
postulates and regulative ideas. It escaped him entirely that
reality, as we live it and know it, is likewise our reality only
as the stuff of experience is formed by the categories of value.
We orient ourselves in the world by relations of over and under,
right and left, more and less, etc., but not less necessarily by the
relations of higher and lower, better and worse. Non-temporal
and non-empirical forms of value are also the *a priori* of an
intelligible world.

It is impossible to insist upon this point too strongly. Kant's
fatal distinction between the practical and theoretical reason—
and his no less fatal vacillation between knowledge and faith
in his characterization of the status of the "postulates" of value—
is the source of much of the sophistication and sophistry of
modern thought. As a necessary stage in thought it was inevitable. After the extrusion of all values from the objective
world—which seemed to Kant to be the necessary consequence
of the assumptions of science—it was possible to restore their
objectivity only by a line of reasoning such as that with which
he has made us familiar. But that was only the beginning, and
the position in which Kant left the whole problem of value—
including that of teleology—was one from which thought is
only with difficulty finally emerging.

V

The preceding discussion has been concerned wholly with
the element in finality that is irrefutable, with the attempt to
discover those essentials of value to which all teleology, if it
is to be valid, must be carried back. These essentials include,
on the one hand, certain *a priori* elements which belong to the
notion of value as such, and on the other hand, certain necessities which arise out of the fact that to separate value from
reality is contradictory. Now, it does not follow, of course, that
because there is that in the notion that is irrefutable, any
given formulation of it is equally irrefutable. It is one thing
to show that some notion of finality is necessary to intelligible
communication and interpretation; it is quite another thing

to show that any specific form is itself intelligible. Otherwise expressed, the notion of teleology, or final causes, cannot be extruded, but many doctrines of teleology have been found untenable. Modern thought has been continually engaged in the attempt to find substitutes for traditional notions of finality, and in the most modern thinking a point has been reached at which the new concepts bear little resemblance to the old. The heights of paradox to which the modern mind has been driven in its attempts to find such substitutes have already been indicated and will be developed more fully in the sequel. Our task is now to determine the conditions of an intelligible concept of finality.

The natural metaphysic of the human mind is always some form of teleology. So is also, for that matter, any natural science. The necessary retention of the concept of purpose and utility in biology, even if in a merely heuristic capacity, means that an intelligible description is impossible without it, and if it is necessary for description, we may be well assured that it is necessary, in some form, for an intelligible concept of nature. But we need not stress that point here: enough that finality is part of the natural metaphysic of the human mind.

The classical form of this natural metaphysic first developed in the lucidity of Greek thought and is chiefly associated with the name of Aristotle. It is at bottom nothing but an embodiment, to a degree unconsciously of course, of the essentials of value that we have been analysing. An intelligible nature was for Aristotle a *Wertzusammenhang*, and in developing that system the *a priori* elements of value were determinative.

In developing his conception of an intelligible nature, Aristotle worked with two different concepts of purpose, apparently without feeling any contradiction in them. On the one hand, he regarded individual things as self-realizing; and, on the other hand, he looked upon them as realized in other things. He did not expressly formulate these two different concepts, but he continually applied them in practice. The first conception of purpose he got from the development of organisms, the second from the world of human practice, more particularly from that kind of development which takes place when an artist purposely moulds plastic material. This seemingly unimportant difference was really fundamental.

For, if it is not wholly true that it is "the difference between Aristotle as he meant to be, Aristotle as the critic of Plato's dualism, and Aristotle who reverts to Plato's teachings," it is, at least, the difference between *internal* and *external* finality which was to become so important in later thought.

Aristotle's conception of external finality preponderates over his "original" conception of development and purpose. His view contains, indeed, as Hegel says, the inner finality and, therefore, "stands infinitely high above the later concepts of teleology" which only contemplated the *"endliche aüssere Zweckmässigkeit"*; but still the external predominates over the internal. And as in Aristotle, so in the long history of human thought as dominated by Aristotle's concepts. Aristotle does regard the individual things as self-contained and self-realizing, as "developing the perfection natural to each," but he also regards them as not self-contained. And when so regarded, as relative to each other, he has a different conception of the world. The world is still a developing world, but the essence that unfolds itself is not wholly in the phenomena. It is a goal for which the phenomena strive, the fulfilment of an ultimate purpose. Individual things are in a scale of values relative to some transcendent standard or end.

It is not difficult to see why both of these conceptions appeared in the first formulations of teleology. Aristotle was, in fact, but giving expression to the two fundamental principles of value we have been examining. The first, the principle of universality of value, when translated into the terms of development or purpose, generates the idea of an intrinsic end of each individual. The principle of degree of value, on the other hand, when translated into these terms, generates the relation of means to ends, the "practical" expression of the principle of subordination or scale. But it is also not difficult to see why the external or transcendental concept should have triumphed over the internal in Aristotle's thinking. The dialectical analysis of the moral end and of the practical concept of the good shows that every given end is proximate, not ultimate, and thus the means to the *summum bonum*, to the imperishable goal.

Both of these motives have been present from the beginning of philosophical thought and have given rise to a continuous conflict, not only in the concept of teleology itself but, as we shall see later, in the entire concept of philosophical system. In this long conflict the principle of immanent finality ultimately triumphed, only to be driven out, in many quarters at least, by the still more modern concepts of creative accumulation in which scarcely any vestige of finality remains. Thus our ultimate task is the achievement of an intelligible concept of finality. Such a concept is impossible, I believe, without the external or transcendental element. Our first task, however, is an examination of this debate between external and internal finality and of the processes of thought by which the modernistic transformations of finality have come about.

It is ordinarily supposed that the modern depreciation of the category of purpose has been due largely, if not wholly, to the long *critique* exercised by science and logic upon our natural anthropomorphism which reads the practical concepts of means and ends into non-human nature—a *critique* that has ended in the complete extrusion of external finality from nature. This is, however, but one of the causes of this depreciation. It is, indeed, argued that the category of means and ends is a practical category, made primarily to serve the purposes of life, but that when made theoretical and applied outside the human context, it develops contradictions and paradoxes, which show that it must be abandoned or transmuted into something else. To these logical aspects of the question we shall presently turn, but for the moment we must consider a still more fundamental and subtle source of this depreciation which has become most influential in modern thought, namely, *a depreciation of purpose and finality in life itself.* The category of means and ends is a practical category, made primarily for the context of human life. But even here, it is said, its service is of doubtful character. It represents, rather, an *external logic that falsifies life.*

It is of the utmost importance that this phase of the question should be understood first. All the modern *Lebensphilosophien* depreciate the category of means to ends. Even here, in life itself, an *intelligible* finality of human activity is, we are told, not external, but transcends the relation of means to ends. *A fortiori*, an intelligible concept of finality in nature must transcend these conceptions. The real driving force of the modern revolt against finality is this *a fortiori* argument. It is necessary, therefore, to examine its premises with some care.

Finality, in the sense of external purpose, arises in human life and activity; but even here, it is said, it is full of paradoxes and contradictions. It tends to go over into something it is not. Life tends to negate and to transcend this very form in which life alone can "carry on."

Teleology, as the time-form of value, involves the relation of less remote and more remote ends, culminating in an ultimate end which has supreme value. But innumerable times we are compelled to act as though the immediate end, however momentary "means" it may be, were the ultimate, as though our entire salvation hung upon it. If we did not concentrate our entire valuation upon the next step of the teleological ladder, we should have neither the courage nor the power to act. If we were to give it only so much interest as belonged to it in view of its relation to more remote ends, all our energy would be dissipated. Closely allied to this is the transference of valuation from ends to means. Omnipresent in human action, like the concentration of valuation on immediate ends, it seems to be the condition of effective activity. Knowledge, art, morals, industry for their own sake—in such valuations purposive activity often finds its highest form. The soul has, indeed, its scruples against these "abstractions from life," as in the protest against art for art's sake, but the will overcomes these scruples and gives absolute value to that which is but relative. And who will say that these very things which seem to destroy teleology do not often become its sublimest forms?

Still another paradox is exploited by those who would depreciate the category of external finality. We set ourselves ends or goals—man is *das Zwecksetzende Wesen*—but the ends we reach are not the ends we set ourselves. The pursuit of ends begets new ends not included in them, so that the idea of the consummation of the end, seemingly implied in the external finality, is an illusion. This contradiction in our purposive activity, first recognized definitely by Hegel, was later formulated as the principle of "the heterogeneity of ends." If there is this contradiction in our purposive activity must we not, so it is argued, transform the conception itself into something other than itself, into "creative accumulation" or into "totality"?

From all these facts the inference is drawn that life transcends the category of purpose, of means and ends. Mankind itself has reached a stage of existence which is above purposes and ends. "Man is man only when he plays," said Schiller, and the modern mood generalizes this to the effect that man is man only when he turns his back on that character of end-making which has hitherto been held to be his peculiarly human quality. It has even been said that "it is his peculiar value as a man that he acts purposelessly."

To the unsophisticated mind all this sounds paradoxical in the extreme and in the last analysis unintelligible—as, in truth, it really is. But it is necessary to get to the bottom of this modern mood; for not only is it the source of all the modern reaction against finality in life and art, but it is also, as we have said, the real driving force of all those modern reconstructions of teleology to which we shall presently turn. "There is no goal," cries D. H. Lawrence. "I loathe goals more than any other impertinence. Gaols they are. Bah—jails and jailers. Goals and Gaolers."[1] Childish and frivolous as this may sound, it is but an extreme expression of a more or less general position, not without its element of truth. It is necessary to separate the truth from the falsity.

It is the *dualism* of means and ends that is chiefly attacked in this aspect of modernism. Single moments in life ought not, it is said, to be merely means to other moments, past and present merely means to the future. The child is not simply the man in the making; childhood is an independent age with its special tasks and its appropriate value. Every period of life, every part of the course of time, should be thus understood. This dualism, "the most mischievous of all dualisms," in Höffding's words, distorts and mutilates life. This mutilation of life follows from the distortion of reality involved. Any external purpose, any in any wise distant goal, so we are told, appears as a fixed point, discontinuous and different from the present. On the other hand, the distinguishing character of life, of immediate living, is continuity—feeling, and thinking into the future. A purpose, a goal, allows the constant life-movement

[1] *Aaron's Rod*, p. 338.

to coagulate, so to speak, about a fixed point—a necessity in a sense to be sure, but a necessity only of intellect and practice. It tears a piece of the unbroken temporal life and draws it to itself, thus creating a chasm on the two banks of which are the two points of the present and of the future in substantial fixity. Expression of the truth of life requires, therefore, the transcendence of the category of purpose.

Such an argument is, to be sure, not without a certain plausibility. The concept of external purpose does introduce a certain fixity, a certain substance, into life, but without this substantiality which purpose gives it, would life have any communicable meaning? The "dogmatism" of ultimate ends may become mischievous, but can there be without it any intelligible expression of life? The unbroken temporal life, of which we speak so eloquently, is really an unlivable life and an inexpressible life. It is true that we may live from day to day, "from hand to mouth," so to speak, but that is not living in any but the most narrow biological sense. In order to live significantly we must make ourselves goals, we must break up the life movement with our concepts, for only so can we give any substance to our life. It is true that the ends we achieve are not the ends we set ourselves, but the substance of all achievement consists in establishing continuity between them. It is not true that the expression of the truth of life requires the transcendence of the category of external purpose. In *human* life, at least, finality is in some sense external or it is nothing.[1]

---

[1] As I have been rewriting this chapter, I have come upon a typical statement of this modernist position which illustrates rather perfectly the distinction I have been making throughout between linguistic and real intelligibility. In a paper entitled "Emerging American Philosophy," Mr. E. C. Lendeman writes thus: "Emphasis will be placed upon means, not ends" (in this new American philosophy). "End-gaining" will come to be seen as an inhibition to the discovery and invention of appropriate means. "The dogmatism of ultimate ends and static principles will be replaced by a fluid and evolutionary concept of means—means that create their ends. Only through this process can the modern world rid itself of stifling and fictitious allegiance to collectivities. Institutions such as Church and State will be viewed not as ultimate objects of loyalty, but as evolving means for individual fulfilment. . . ." "And if we should become courageous enough to live by the new philosophy, we would no longer be baffled into pessimism by unattainable ends: we could take possession of the only optimism true to our legitimate aspirations—namely, the optimism of a richly potential life in a world of unlimited means. Conflict itself, the necessary corollary

VI

The task of this chapter is to show that teleology, finality, purpose, are part of an intelligible world and, properly understood, an *a priori* part. We are attempting to show, also, that the traditional concept of external finality is the only intelligible concept. Thus far we have shown it to be so only for life—for the human context. We must now attempt to show that the same conditions hold in the application of finality to nature.

As there is no intelligible human life without purpose, so there is no intelligible world without it. As we have seen in an earlier connection, the principle of necessary spaces and necessary times is involved in all descriptions and explanations of nature. But the element of necessity of these spaces and times arises from, and is intelligible only in the light of, ends and values to be realized in the process. The "beneficent" processes of segregation and isolation of which the geologist and biologist speak must be assumed if the meaning of space and time is to be understood.[1] This can be seen in the principle of classification in biology. If the idea of fixed species is abandoned, the only principle of classification possible is a teleological one. Teleology is thus the condition of an intelligible nature, but there seem to be also certain conditions necessary to the intelligible use of the concept of teleology.

These conditions are, to be sure, but a special application of the conditions of philosophical intelligibility in general.

of adjustment, might come to be seen as a cumulative and creative opportunity" (*The New Republic*, November 19, 1924).

What, we may well ask, is, and *can* be, meant by these words? In a sense we know what the writer means by them, although even as writing they have that impressionistic quality so annoying in much of present-day popular philosophy. But when we seek to give them real intelligibility—the whole thing falls apart in our hands. There is, to be sure, one interpretation of them which is intelligible. If it is meant that no finite end is final, that every end is proximate, not ultimate, and thus the means to the attainment of an imperishable goal, then it is understandable and true, but there is nothing new about it. It is essentially what traditional philosophy has said from Aristotle to Hegel. If, on the other hand, it means, as it seems to mean, that there is no goal to give meaning to the means, we have simple nonsense. I know nothing of the optimism which the courage to live by such a philosophy gives, for I have not experienced the pessimism of a disillusioned pragmatism of which it is the outcome. But I do know that this *life* so conceived is unintelligible, and I have never been able to associate optimism with unintelligibility.

[1] Chapter VII, pp. 241 ff.

As we have seen in earlier chapters, intelligible communication—including description, explanation, and interpretation—involves necessarily the retention of the meaning of the things to be described, explained, or interpreted. It involves also the retention of the meaning of the categories in terms of which the things are described, explained, or interpreted. Otherwise we are using empty words, and really intelligible communication becomes ultimately impossible. We have seen how these principles apply to other elements in the form of philosophical intelligibility; let us now see how they apply to teleology.

In the first place, the end or *telos* must be an ethical end or value—ethical, at least, in the sense that it can be understood by the human intelligence and will. For it is perfectly clear that there is no use in using the concept of *telos* unless that *telos* or end can be appreciated. This is simply another way of saying that instrumental intelligibility must touch intrinsic intelligibility at some point; but there is nothing intrinsically intelligible except movement towards the good.

The second condition of an intelligible concept of teleology seems to be that the value that is thus appreciated and acknowledged must be conceived as the *cause* of the existence of something—that is, that the values are effective in reality. The cause must, moreover, be effective by reason of its value. Finally, any such cause must be the cause of effects that resemble it in some sense and some degree—that is, a "heterogeneity of ends" in which the result bore no such relation to the purpose would not be teleology in any intelligible sense.

This is the natural, and also the classical, conception of finality. If it be anthropomorphism, as it surely is in a sense, the critic may be invited to make the most of it. It is clever to say, when, for instance, the amœba is spoken of as a stage in the development of "higher" species, that the amœba's opinion has never been ascertained, but it is clever nonsense. Acknowledgment on the part of the amœba of any ends or values in terms of which his life is interpreted, or his place in the scale of being is determined, is not asked for. For he does not live in a universe of discourse in which such ends or values have any meaning.

This is, I repeat, the natural and classical concept of teleology.

z

The inevitable element of external or transcendental finality is obvious; it is, in fact, implied by each of the three conditions of an intelligible teleology. Finality is, as Bergson has said, *either external or it is nothing at all.* The idea of a finality that is always internal is a self-destructive notion. Yet this element of externality has, as we have said, gradually given place, first to a purely internal finality, and ultimately to substitutes for finality that retain no vestige of its original meaning.

In this transformation various motives have, as I said, played their part. Criticism of untenable forms of the design argument, the triumph of the mechanical analogy in human thought, logical criticism of the concept itself from the standpoint of atomistic and monistic logic, have all contributed, but the deepest source of the change is precisely that depreciation of the category of means to ends in human activity itself to which we have already given our thought. Finality in human life and action, that is wholly internal, we have already found to be a self-destructive notion. It is no less so, we shall find, in the sphere of nature and history. But let us examine the stages by which this transformation has taken place.

The transformation from external to a purely internal finality has involved an important change in every one of the elements of the classical conception. Since Kant the word "teleology" has constantly been connected with a theory in which the word "end" seems to be used in a much looser sense. In the classical conception the end was always a value that could be apprehended and appreciated by human intelligence. Internal finality in its pure form is but the polite denial of any such apprehension and appreciation.

In the classical conception end and means were distinguished, in that means denoted anything that was efficient cause of the existence of something resembling or approximating to the end, and which was supposed to be produced by the final causation of the end. In the modern theory there is little attempt to distinguish in what sense, if any, the end is the cause of the means. At the same time it is maintained that the end has to the means a closer relation than the mere fact that it is an effect of the latter. This closer relation finds its typical expression in living bodies where, it is said, all the parts are but means and ends to each other, and also all means to the whole.

And any whole in which the parts are said to bear this relation to each other is called a teleological unity. This, again, is but a polite way of denying the second element of the traditional conception. For the relation of means to ends, it is apparent, has been transformed into one of mutual dependence, and the element of end or value, without which we can scarcely speak intelligibly of teleology, seems to be taken by the whole, which is formed by the two things having this relation; this whole being assumed to be better than, to have more meaning and value than, either separately.

In the classical conception, finally, any final cause must be the cause of effects that resemble it in some sense and in some degree, and in an intelligible teleology such continuity must be capable of being appreciated and acknowledged. In the more modern conception this necessity is denied. The doctrine of the *heterogeneity of ends*, taken in its full significance, is again but a polite way of denying the third element in the traditional conception. Nowhere, perhaps, in modern thought is the use of "weasel words" so shameless as in this conception of finality which includes the idea of a realization which is wholly other than the end.

Such is, then, the transformation of finality from external to internal finality, and the corresponding metamorphosis of the idea of end into that of adaptation, or of the relation of the part to the whole. It will be readily seen that in this transformation various motives have been at work, motives logical and axiological. Of the latter we have spoken in another connection. It is rather with the logical aspect that we are here concerned. The essential contention underlying this entire transformation is that the human analogy of means and ends has only practical significance—that, taken in a theoretical sense, it develops logical difficulties and contradictions; and finally, and most important of all, the relation of means to ends has in it something irrelevant to logical system, and must be abandoned in favour of more ultimate logical relations. It is this latter contention that I wish chiefly to contest.

Now, this shrinkage from external to internal finality does, indeed, "save it," as Bergson says, "from many logical blows." But in its effort to avoid these blows it has lost a good deal of its self-respect and almost all its force. It seems to form a tenable theory of finality; but, as the theory is developed and its implications seen, it turns out to be a finality that is no finality at all.

Some of these implications are immediately apparent. If every individual is a teleological unity, is its own end—if teleology consists wholly in the development of the perfection natural to a thing—then every thing becomes an end, while nothing is means. The amœba, even the louse and the pebble, become ends in themselves; and when everything is equally a value, the very distinctions of value on which teleology is based tend to disappear. Finality that is confined to a single organism is no finality. If there is finality in the world it includes the whole of the world in an indivisible embrace. Again, on such a purely immanental view of finality the meaning and value of the process of development must lie wholly in the process and not in the end, in the becoming and not in that which becomes. This notion, which we found to be one of the paradoxes of pure dynamism,[1] is, however, equally involved in purely immanental finality.

The doctrine of immanental finality we are here criticizing has been developed by those philosophies which we have characterized as modernistic, but there are other doctrines of immanence which likewise counsel the complete abandonment of the finite analogy of means to ends, although for different reasons. I refer to certain modern forms of idealism, of which that of Bosanquet is for our purpose the best expression. Bosanquet's argument is of special importance because his transformation is based explicitly on the "essentials of value"; the assumption being that the principle of totality and the principle of value are identical, and that therefore teleology must be equated with the relation of part to whole.[2]

This attempt at a transformation of traditional finality demands a more careful examination than it has as yet received. Like the others, it also abandons the whole finite analogy of means to ends, the coincidence of *terminus* and end, all the "prejudices" connected with the practical character of the concept of purpose. But, unlike the other forms, it proposes

---

[1] See Chapter IX, pp. 316 ff.

[2] B. Bosanquet, "A Symposium on Purpose and Mechanism," *Proceedings of the Aristotelean Society*, 1911–1912.

specifically "to fall back on the characteristics of value, which, apart from sequence in time and selected purposes, attach to the nature of reality, which is perfection."

Of the difficulties of this substitution of the whole for the end Bosanquet is, of course, not unaware. To abandon all the psychological, ethical, and temporal elements in the concept of purpose and keep any intelligible meaning is, it is admitted, "no light task." To separate perfection from value, and value from satisfaction, and satisfaction from conation, Bosanquet admits, is not easy. And anyone who has realized the difficulty of expressing value without its time-form, the future, will understand why it is not easy. The answer to the difficulty lies, he thinks, in the fact that the essential nature of value "lies deeper" than this: that "it is not conferred by *de facto* satisfying conation, but is satisfactoriness rather than satisfaction. It lies in the character of completeness and positive non-contradiction, which gives the power of satisfying conation because it belongs to what unites all reality in itself."

The idea of finality is, as we have said, very flexible. Here again its flexibility has been exploited to the utmost. How far, we may well ask, is this transformation of finality successful? Much of the line of thought we may admit without hesitation. The subordination of the concept of purpose to that of value and the objective character of value may be welcomed as a *sine qua non* of a valid interpretation of finality. But it is precisely at this point that the real problem arises. It is the assumption that the essentials of value can be reduced to logical relations that we must question. That they cannot, has been the contention of this whole book. The relations of logic to language, and to the natural metaphysic which expresses itself in language, are such as to negate this assumption. Logic is reflected thought, but it cannot negate the spontaneous. As the critique of the ontological logics of the concepts of intelligible substance and intelligible causation lead to unintelligibility, so a like critique of traditional finality leads to similar results. As applied to this latter problem the situation is entirely clear. The essential nature of value, as we have come to understand it, includes the *a priori* forms of value which are constitutive of reality as well as forms of thought. The finite analogy of means to ends is bound up with these forms. In abandoning this analogy with its implication of external finality we abandon also the essentials of value, to which any teleology, if it is to be found intelligible, must be carried back.

A wholly internal doctrine of finality cannot be carried out. Finality is external or it is nothing. The doctrine of immanental ends is in truth a very dangerous principle. We may, indeed, use the expression in a negative way to protect our thought against an easy and limitless transcendence, both in human life and in nature. But we may not use it to undermine all teleology, which it really does. The concept of purpose implies a value scale or system. The individual is always one among many and always subordinated to a higher. Ends are immanent so long as we remain wholly within experience, but *any attempt to make these ends intelligible implies transcendence.* Otherwise expressed, there is a certain indispensable *minimum* to any intelligible concept of finality. In this minimum must be included the four conditions or elements of traditional conception which we have been examining. The end, or *telos*, must be humanly appreciable as a value, it must be conceived as a *vera causa*, and a cause, moreover, precisely by reason of its value; and, lastly, it must be the cause of effects that resemble it in some sense and in some degree. Not the least of these conditions is the final one—which implies that there must be consummation of the end if there is to be any intelligible finality. With this we are brought to the question of Destiny.

VII

For traditional philosophy, as I have said, there has been in the main one and only one way of making the world intelligible. An essential part of the *Form of Intelligibility* has been the idea of destiny. Without the ideas of the "one increasing purpose" and of an imperishable goal—yes, even the ideas of a climax of being and of a last judgment—it has been impossible to make any teleology intelligible. Now, modernism does not abandon the concept of destiny altogether; since it is an intrinsic part of the notion of finality or teleology, the idea of destiny can no more be exorcized from our thinking than

finality itself can be refuted. But with the modern transformations of our notion of finality have come necessarily
significant changes in the idea of destiny. With the abandonment of the traditional notion of a "climax of being," of the
"illusion of finality " in the sense of any coincidence of terminal
point and value, there have inevitably resulted substitutes for
the idea of consummation which have affected profoundly
both our life and thought. Let us examine some of these changes
and their consequences.

But first let us recall briefly why it is that the destiny of anything is an essential part of its nature, and why, therefore, if the
world is something to be understood at all, the notion of destiny
must enter into that understanding. We saw, earlier, that the
future of anything is a necessary part of its nature and meaning.
This connection appears at two points. In the first place, the
future of anything that has meaning and value cannot be
thought of, much less expressed, except in terms of purpose
and finality. In the second place, the meaning and nature of
an object is bound up with its fate in the future. Unless that
part of the nature of a thing we call its purpose is in some way
retained and conserved in its temporal end, the identity of the
thing with itself is lost, and no intelligible communication of
its nature and meaning is possible. This being true of the nature
and meaning of anything, it becomes wholly clear why even
modernist thought, in thinking about life and the world, does
not abandon wholly the notions of the "one increasing purpose"
and of the imperishable goal; it merely transforms them.

These transformations are in two main directions. For those
who take time unduly seriously the gates of the future are
open, and we have that contemplation of the infinite regress
in the future direction which modernism in one of its moods
finds so exhilarating. For those who, perhaps, do not take time
seriously enough there is also the denial of consummation of the
end. In the first case, we have as a substitute for destiny the
idea of "creative accumulation"; in the second, the idea of a
"timeless totality." An examination of these substitutes will
serve to bring out the full implications of these modern transformations of teleology. Let us begin by considering the first
of these substitutes—that connected with the modern mood
which we described at the beginning of this chapter.

The exhilaration of this modern mood cannot be denied. Yet it is not surprising that many have found this enthusiasm out of all proportion to its theoretical basis. With the best of will, they fail to find in this evolution *"ins blaue hinein"* any intelligible meaning. Life, the vital impulse, the primal urge, Mr. Balfour mildly remarks, seems to have no goal more definite than that of acquiring an even fuller volume of free activity. Bosanquet finds that such an opening of the gates of the future simply closes them to perfection, while Bradley finds it "as untenable in our philosophy as it is abhorrent to our hearts."

This "futurism," if I may so call it, quite general in modernism, whether artistic, political, or philosophical, is, it must be remembered, not so much a denial of finality as a substitute for it, and it is as such that we must view it. The typical modernist is not a finalist in the generally accepted sense; he is "a believer in time, novelty, and creative accumulation." As emergence is his substitute for origin, so creative accumulation is his substitute for destiny. For the concepts of "increasing purpose" and imperishable goal, for increase and conservation of value, we have creative accumulation, whatever that may mean.

It is nothing less than astounding what power such empty words have acquired over the modern mind. As the concept of emergence is without meaning, so that of creative accumulation is without a vestige of intelligible finality. To the criticism that, on this view, reality has no goal more definite than that of acquiring an ever fuller volume of free activity, the reply may be made, as in the words of Sir Oliver Lodge, "Is this not a good enough goal? Is it not the goal of every great artist?" Perhaps. And the whole argument seems plausible. We are already familiar with this argument from the analogy of artistic creation. As against the anthropomorphism of external finality, of radical finalism as reversed mechanism, it is argued that a higher level of meaning and value is found in those forms of artistic activity in which specific purpose or definite goal is either lacking or at a minimum. It is the second-rate works that are intellectualistic. If, we are then asked, *if* the highest form of finality in the hyperorganic world is of this nature, *a fortiori*, must it not be so on the lower levels? Why apply the lower form to the cosmos in general? Only, it is forgotten that this is not all there is to the great artist. His greatness does not lie in his mere "expressionism." Pure expressionists are likely enough to be unintelligible. The greatness of true art, after all, lies in its communicability. Novelties and inventions have value only when they survive some test of a pre-existent or subsistent scale of value, or a systematic whole of experience. The intelligibility of this analogy from artistic activity can be retained only by carrying over this second aspect of the situation also. When this is done the analogy from artistic creation must lead, as in the case of Aristotle's analysis, to the idea of a transcendent goal.

This futuristic substitute for the traditional concept of destiny is, then, not a good enough goal. The essential unintelligibility of such reconstructions is, of course, the burden of much of modern absolute idealism. Such conceptions are impossible, it holds, without a morbid evaluation of time and becoming, which involves the transvaluation of all metaphysical values. But is the complete detemporalizing of the notion of destiny, proposed as an alternative, really any more intelligible?

The great enemy of all sane philosophy is, in Bosanquet's words, the notion that the ideal belongs to the future. In a true teleology all presumption of coincidence of termination and end must be abandoned. If teleology is to retain a meaning "we must give up the whole finite analogy of means to ends and fall back on the characteristics of value which, apart from sequence in time and selected purposes, attach to the nature of reality which is perfection."[1] In other words, just as we must form a concept of finality that eliminates selected purposes, so we must form a concept of destiny which does not include the consummation of any selected purpose. Can such a concept of destiny be made completely intelligible?

We have but to put this view into simpler words to see the difficulty. The plain man and traditional philosophy ask after our destiny. For what can we hope? They do so for the reason that for any natural metaphysic the meaning and value of a thing can be no more separated from its destiny than from its origin. To this question the philosophy we are considering answers: "Where your question speaks of the future we speak

[1] *Op. cit.*, p. 126.

of the whole. What really interests you, if you but knew it, is not something yet to come, but inherently the comprehension and evaluation of the whole of which we are members." In other words, when finality is carried back to the essentials of value, the idea of a consummation of the end, of a climax of being, has no meaning.

The question here raised is definite and unavoidable. Can we substitute the whole for the future and still talk an intelligible teleological language? We have already seen that we cannot. The inseparability of the meaning of an object from its future, its not-yet, which we emphasized at the beginning of this chapter, seems to be, not merely practical, but theoretical. For any natural metaphysic the meaning and value of a thing can be no more separated from its destiny, its future, than from its origin. No detemporalizing of finality can go to the length of eliminating completely the coincidence of termination and end without risking unintelligibility. Not only must "the purpose of our earthly life be realized, but there must be," as Fichte says, "a time in which it shall be accomplished, as surely as there is a sensible world and a world of reasonable beings existent in time with respect to which nothing earnest and rational is conceivable besides this purpose, and whose existence becomes intelligible only through this purpose." To separate terminus and end completely is possible only if we separate value from conation and perfection from value, and this, by the very nature of the case, cannot be done.

VIII

As we examined the modern substitutes for teleology, so now we have examined the corresponding modern substitutes for destiny. We may say, without hesitation, that they cannot be made intelligible. We must now ask whether the traditional notion can be given an intelligible meaning. Can we make an ending of the time process that does not involve an internal contradiction? Can we form a notion of one increasing purpose, one far-off divine event, which constitutes sense and not nonsense? Can we form a notion of a climax of being that does not negate the very notion of being? Can we, in short, make any ending to life and the world process which has not, from the very beginning, the seeds of irrationality in it?

Now, I shall say quite frankly at the outset that the solution of this problem is only partly possible. I believe that practically it is being constantly solved in human experience, but that it always involves some "trenching on the mystical," and that this experience is never satisfactorily stated in conceptual terms. I must also point out that any indication of the direction in which the solution lies must be only tentative. A really satisfactory answer to the questions of the foregoing paragraph would be possible only after we have examined the problem of *intelligible progress*, to which the following chapter will be devoted. For it is in connection with the idea of progress—the idea of "the one increasing purpose," of "the one far-off divine event towards which the whole creation moves"—that the modern notions of human destiny have developed. An intelligible notion of progress would have to combine these two notions in an all-embracing concept. Our task in the present context is merely to examine the logical or axiological question of an intelligible notion of consummation of the end.

Just what this problem involves may perhaps best be seen by recalling certain conclusions from our study of time and value. There are two things which are certainly "real" enough in the world of finite experience, but which become impossibilities the moment that they are converted into absolute realities by metaphysical thought. These are the idea of time as finite—implying the end of time and therefore an end of happening, life, volition—and, secondly, the idea of the infinite, opening out a vista of an infinite series of events in infinite time, and therefore implying that the will can never come to rest. Both of these ideas have their emotional value in relation to our varying experience of reality, but it is difficult to say which is the more intolerable if either is taken absolutely. Both are axiologically intolerable—as untenable in our philosophy as they are abhorrent to our hearts. Now, it has been one of the constant objects of speculative philosophy to avoid either of these alternatives, and to find some concept that will include the truth of both. Traditional philosophy has found a language of a certain kind in which to express this notion. Let us consider this idiom for what it is worth.

It is to Hegel after all, I think, that we owe the best expression of traditional thought on this question. It is ordinarily thought that it was Hegel, more than any other modern thinker, perhaps, who turned the notion of the "consummation of the end," of the climax of being, into an illusion. As a matter of fact, the whole weight of his thinking is actually in the opposite direction. Speaking of the idea of the consummation of the end, he employs very much the same words as we found him using in connection with the notion of substance. "Substance," we found him saying, "although a necessary stage in the evolution of the Idea, is not the same as the Idea." "But," he continues, "it gives the basis for all real further development." So with the idea of the finite end and its consummation. Such a notion does not, indeed, exhaust the meaning of the idea. But *its retention is the necessary condition of the communication of the meaning which constitutes the idea.* In a famous passage of the *Encyklopädie*, we read: "As a matter of fact, the object is potentially *an sich* the notion; and so when the notion as end is realized in the object, this is only the manifestation of the nature of the object itself. Objectivity is thus, as it were, only a covering, under which the notion lies concealed. . . . The consummation of the infinite end consists, therefore, merely in the setting aside (*Aufhebung*) of the illusion which makes it seem as if the end was not yet accomplished. It is under this illusion that we live, and at the same time it is this illusion alone that stirs us to activity and in which our interest in the world depends. The idea in its process makes for itself that illusion—posits another over against itself—and its activity consists in setting that illusion aside." This passage and others like it have been made the basis for the charge that Hegel turns the entire life of valuation and volition into an illusion. But the drift of Hegel's thinking—of his handling of the fundamental philosophical concepts—is against that interpretation, as we have seen in his discussion of the concepts of cause and substance. Without these concepts there is no intelligible communication and interpretation.

The truth is that we *must* make endings to our lives—both our individual and social histories. Otherwise we can neither realize nor communicate the present meaning of these histories. Such endings can be expressed only in terms of the particular and the individual, and yet the very meaning we seek to express is universal. This is, indeed, the final metaphysical problem of life—that life is, in its very essence, at once limited individuality and limitless continuity. It is meaningful only if there is consummation of the end, and meaningful also only if every finite end is transcended. The innermost meaning of time is just this inalienable difference between what is and what ought to be—between the imperishable goal and its consummation. No thought can bridge this difference—no purely conceptual terms can rationalize this paradox, and yet it is constantly being solved in experience. In every perfect realization of life, however fleeting, the contradiction is resolved.

To this fundamental deliverance of consciousness the metaphysician must hold fast; but he must also realize that if he attempts to express that experience he must, so to speak, "speak in parables." As Nietzsche said, "it takes genius to make an ending," and for this reason all making of concrete endings to life—all writing of eschatologies—must be left to poets and seers. The prophetic insight which applies the eternal "form of perfection" to the changing empirical content of life can show itself only in those who have a singular combination of the sense for the richness of present experience and of the sense of the eternal. The task of the philosopher, even of the metaphysical genius, is much more modest—that of making the symbols, the imaginative constructions of the prophetic genius, intelligible to reason. The conceptual analysis of the philosopher is significant, but it cannot have as its objective the communication of the same kind of meaning and reality as the symbols of the more concrete thinking of mankind. The ideas of providence and of immortality, although the same ideas as those of the philosopher, are on a different level of meaning and expressed in a different context. The metaphysical statement of the problem has rather a heuristic significance—namely, that of making transparent, as it were, the structure—the *a priori* structure if you will—of value and being in their necessary relations. As for the more concrete ideas, the symbols in which this structure is embodied, they share in the validity of the relations which they express. He who has once come to see their relation to this structure can doubt neither their significance nor their validity.

IX

"It takes genius to make an ending," and it is doubtless for that reason partly that the modern thinker, no less than the modern novelist and play-writer, has decided that this is a trifle that can be conveniently dispensed with. The geniuses of the past may not have satisfied us with their endings, but our own loss of capacity, either to appreciate or to create, does not dispense us from recognizing that which is the *sine qua non* of all intelligible interpretation.

In his *Das Ende Allen Dingen*, Kant discusses the idea of a "last judgment," of a consummation of all things. He finds the idea significant (*zweckmässig*), together with that of an all-seeing eye, of a world judge, and indeed, as he says, "wonderfully interwoven with the universal human reason, because this thought" (like that of teleology which implies it) "is to be met with at all times and among all thinking pople, clothed in one way or another." There can be in Kant's mind no thought of its being a mere prejudice. Bound up with the universal reason as it is, it is in some sense a necessary presupposition of intelligibility. But it is not, he holds, to be taken literally. In doing so, "in making the end of things a matter of time," we may be guilty of a prejudice. We cannot, indeed, make it solely a matter of time—but partly a matter of time it must be if it is to be significant at all.

The making of endings will never cease. Yet, as G. H. Lewes says, "mankind alternately seeks and shuns finality." Characteristically, modernism shuns finality. That which appeals in it, we have seen, is its adventurous and dramatic quality. It stirs us to feel ourselves part of a racial or even cosmic adventure. With the gates of the future forever open, with progress only a possibility, a dramatic quality is given to thought. But if modernism is a dramatic philosophy, is it not rather poor drama? Life, we say, has no ending; why should a work of art? Life has no ending; why should a philosophy of life? We know what dramas emerge from this theory. Should we not expect philosophies of the same sort?

Mr. Charles Frohman, speaking of the demand of the public for the "happy ending," and of its incurable dislike for plays that have no finality, shrewdly remarks that this dislike is really due in most cases to the fact that the plays are bad plays. The playwright has created certain interests and expectations concerning his characters which the last act does not realize. This is simply bad writing. The same thing is, I am sure, true of philosophies. That which is so unsatisfactory in so much of modernist philosophy is not that it fails to satisfy an incurable prejudice for happy endings, or, at least, for some sort of ending; it is rather that it persists in the futility of expecting us to be permanently interested in values that come from nothing and come to nothing. This miracle of modern sophistication may, indeed, impose upon those for whom everything traditional is mythological, but for those who have penetrated beneath the mask of sophistication it is but an idle gesture.

Indeed, even the public's demand for a *cheerful* curtain is not so naïve as it may seem. It may be "inartistic" and unrealistic, as many think. I am not sure that it is unphilosophic. Certainly there is a much deeper reason than the mere sentimentality with which the critics charge it. The philosopher who finds a moral order, a meaning, in the universe is compelled by his logic to envisage a universe in which there is a last judgment of some sort, the triumph of good, the conservation of value. It is partly a matter of faith; but still more a matter of reason if the true nature of reason be understood. The public that eats candy in the gallery has the same fundamental reason as the philosopher; but not having so much time to spare, the good has to win, not in some thousands of millions of years, but in time to catch the suburban train. It is not surprising that the cosmic process gets somewhat rushed in the process and the *dénouement* is not always convincing.

Doubtless the cosmic process does not like to be rushed, and it has its little ironies with which it takes revenge on those who try to rush it. "The Absolute is not in a hurry." Neither the cosmos nor history takes very kindly to our dogmas, and both constantly rebuke the impertinence of our goals. But the rebuke is not wholly unkind; it is the chastening of one who loves. For they know, or seem to know, that in substance we are right. For have they not put in us, whom they have begot, a sense that they are not wholly "sound and fury signifying nothing"? Doubtless we make ourselves comic with our human ends, but we do not make ourselves absurd. Absurdity is left for those who try to think value without any destiny at all.

CHAPTER XI

INTELLIGIBLE PROGRESS: THE FORM
OF HISTORY

I

IF we consider the whole course of human thought in the last two centuries we shall realize that the idea of progress, in many different and even contrasting forms, is the one around which all our life, theoretical and practical, has centred. So completely has modern thought identified itself with this idea that it has now become the fashion in some quarters even to say that progress is a wholly modern concept.

The histories and discussions of the concept of progress, characteristic of the last decade, trace its lineage to wholly modern sources, and seek to show that it is an idea foreign to traditional thought in both its Greek and Christian forms. But this, to say the least, is an exaggeration, as Croce has taken pains to point out. Distinctively modern notions of progress there undoubtedly are, and it was some of these that the papal pronouncement had in mind when it denied that the Roman Pontiff "can and must be reconciled and compromise with progress, liberalism, and modern civilization." But progress in the broader and deeper sense of the word, as development towards a terminus or end, has in one form or another always been part of all philosophies of the traditional type. With their conceptions of finality they could scarcely express themselves intelligibly without it.

Yet this very fashion in recent thought is highly symptomatic of a change that has come over us. The tendency to see in the belief in progress largely an expression of eighteenth-century optimism and Victorian fatuity, has its source in a more or less conscious desire to dissociate it from the idea of intrinsic rationality and intelligibility with which it has been too closely fused. Our disillusionment with "modern" progress, our growing disbelief in the dogma that "a law of necessary progress is the most certain of all facts," has made it highly desirable for us to believe that there have been many—and among them the greatest—who have not found such progress a necessary part of an intelligible world. It is therefore not strictly true to see in belief in progress a necessary characteristic of modernity. In this, as in many things, the ultra-moderns are highly ambiguous and changing before our very eyes. To the large collection of prejudices that our highly sophisticated generation is assembling, the "illusions of progress" have recently been added. Like Nietzsche, they all take a certain pleasure in lacerating themselves, and precisely because the faith in progress has seemed part of the natural bent of reason, they feel obliged to turn their backs upon it.

Some concept of progress, I ventured to say, has always been a constituent part of the Great Tradition in philosophy. If, as has frequently been said, progress has taken the place of providence in modern thought (as it did, for instance, for a time in Tolstoy's thinking), it could do so only because something in it was in part at least the same as the content and meaning of providence. He who desires something new desires something old, only he desires it in a new way. If, as Guyau said, we make of time a sort of mysterious providence, designed to replace the old concept, it is because there is something in that old concept for which there is no substitute. It is this something, expressed in the concepts of "increasing purpose" and "imperishable goal," in the entire dialectic of valuation worked out in the preceding chapter, that is common to all concepts, old and new. It may be that these postulates of increase and conservation of value are not bound up inseparably with modern concepts of progress; it may be, indeed, that they are not, as Dean Inge and other critics of modern notions hold, even incompatible with the idea of cycles. In any case, in so far and in whatever sense this dialectic of valuation implies progress, progress always has and always will be part of the form of an intelligible world.

Broadly speaking, there are three elements in the notion of progress: (1) an absolute standard, apprehended, however dimly, by man; (2) intelligible causation, that is, a causal connection between being and value, existence and perfection, a connection without which, as we have seen, teleology is unintelligible; (3) a consistent or continuous advance through time. The first two elements all forms of traditional thought have had; while many, including the greatest of the Greek minds, have doubted if not actually denied the third. The reasons for this absence from Greek thought lie doubtless in their lack of our perspective—material and historical. But back of this is that lack of the time sense of which we have spoken in another connection. A modern who takes time seriously will hardly be able to think progress without the element of continuous advance through time. But it does not follow that no concept of progress is possible without it.

It is easy to see why the first two elements in the notion have always been a part of traditional thought. I cannot present life to myself otherwise than as a striving from bad to good. Only in such terms can its meaning be communicated. As growth, evolution, is the form in which alone the meaning of life can be expressed, so development is the only form in which the meaning of personality, progress the only form in which the over-individual meaning of humanity, can be expressed. A philosophy must give some view of human history if there is to be no gap in our view of the universe. But when a thinker looks at history his thoughts must inevitably centre around the idea of progress. He may believe in it or disbelieve in it, but his view of history will be determined by it just the same. By this I mean that a conception of history, such as Schopenhauer's, as mere succession without direction, is no history at all. It is conceivable, at least, that the concepts of devolution, degeneration, and regression might make an intelligible history, but there is no history without movement of some sort towards an end.

It is to evolutionism that the distinctively modern concept of progress largely owes its origin. But, paradoxical as it may seem, it is largely through this same naturalistic evolutionism that the belief in progress has lost its vitality. The significance of evolution, we have seen, lies mainly in the fact that it gives speculative meaning to the history of humanity and incites men by suggesting great changes in the future. This element of incitement has found its expression in the modern notion of progress. In so far, however, as evolution gives speculative meaning, it does so (as we have seen) only by some conception, explicit or implicit, of ultimate origination. In so far as it incites men or interests them by suggestions concerning the future, it does so in the last analysis only by conceptions, explicit or implicit, of finality and ultimate destiny. That the concept of evolution has lost much of its speculative value is obvious, that it has lost still more of its exciting quality is even more apparent. But it has not been as clear as it should have been, that it has really lost only something which, by itself, it has never had. It has merely lost its illusions.

Tolstoy was among the first to point the finger of scorn at the illusions of the nineteenth century. Now there is no one so stupid as not to see the pitiful ambiguity on which the whole artificial structure of Spencer's doctrine of necessary progress rested. The whole concept of evolution is, in fact, as we have seen, highly ambiguous. Apart from the mathematical idea of evolution, we understand chiefly by this term two closely related types of events which must, however, be clearly distinguished the one from the other. In the first place, we call evolution the process by which all the possibilities of a given complex are realized in their several forms, a process the purely causal nature of which is entirely independent of any ideas of value. In this sense the originally gaseous sphere evolves into a manifold planetary system; and in this we have no distinction except that between the simple and the complex. But in our ordinary way of looking at these things we have the tendency to regard the more complex state as the higher— that is to say, of higher value—and thus to conceive the process of evolution as an advance from simpler and lower to the more complex and higher. Now it is the assumption of the identity of complexity or elaboration with value which has given evolution the intelligible character it appears to have.

What shall we say of this ordinary way of looking at things? First of all we may say, I think, that if evolution is to be more than a mere description, progress must be included in it. This is what Spencer means by calling the law of progress the most certain of all facts. Without the value concept of progress evolution is a mere name for an orderly sequence of events. Science can, indeed, abstract this orderly sequence, this process of elaboration, from value. Integral human thought cannot. The attempt to abstract it is one of the characteristic notes of modernism, as illustrated, for instance, in Alexander's attempt to separate perfection from value. The consequences of this attempt are far-reaching, and will be fully examined in our chapter on System.[1] Here I wish merely to consider its bearing on the concept of progress.

II

The concept of progress is then, in some sense, part of the form of an intelligible world—in the sense, namely, that without that concept, no intelligible communication of the meanings of humanity is possible. The real problem of modern thought is not so much belief or disbelief in progress as the formation of an intelligible concept of progress. Some may speak of the superstition of progress, others think of it as an anthropomorphic prejudice. Superstitions there undoubtedly are, prejudices of the Time-Spirit to be abandoned. But there still remains a resistant core which no amount of sophisticated criticism can affect. A tenable and intelligible concept of progress is perhaps the chief desideratum of the present age. Some contribution towards such a conception is at least the object of this chapter. But our first task must be to develop more fully our grounds for maintaining that the idea of progress is part of the *a priori* of an intelligible world.

We may perhaps get the main point most vividly before us in the following way. "Sincerity," says H. Cohen in his *Ethik des reinen Willens*, "demands the belief in progress. If one says that this belief is utopian, a superstition, he gives up *Wahrhaftigkeit*. To draw from history the conclusion that it must always remain as it has been, is insincere. For without any inner progress there is no history." That is the great insincerity —to use history to disprove or deny the reality of history.[2]

This contention is again one of those cases of "mere dialectic" that either amuses or enrages the pure empiricist. And yet in reality it is merely pointing out one of those instances of *contradictio in adjecto* which, as we sought to show in an earlier connection, mean philosophical unintelligibility. "History," says Renouvier, "is the experience humanity has of itself." How can this experience be expressed except in terms of progress or development? It is true, as we shall see, that in a sense this experience could be expressed in terms

---

[1] Chapter XIII, pp. 443 ff.　　　　[2] *Op. cit.*, p. 512.

of regress or degeneration, or perhaps in terms of alternate cycles. But even then these concepts, when examined, will be seen to be unintelligible except as they presuppose the reality of progress. In any case—and that is all that we need to insist on for the present—the experience humanity has of itself can be expressed only in some form of movement—value movement from lower to higher, or from higher to lower.

The relative separation of the concept of history from the concept of nature is one of the most significant products of modern critical thought. For the recognition of the fact that history is the record of the experience mankind has of itself has brought with it also the recognition of the significant difference between that experience and the experience of what is called nature.

This difference is expressed in various ways: (a) by the statement that "history deals with man's unique activity in society"; (b) by pointing out that the uniqueness of this activity consists in the fact that its products, unlike those of nature, are themselves unique and non-repeated events, and that these events or products are *value-unities*, which can be described, explained, and interpreted only in terms of reference to ends or values. The concept, then, of history as a science that deals with values, and whose method is teleological, is an idea widely accepted by historians themselves.

This conception of history turns largely on the meaning of an "historical fact or event," and the explanation or interpretation of such an event. Description, explanation, and interpretation are, as we have seen, never wholly separable, but it is in the methodology of history that this inseparability is particularly manifest. For an event becomes historical, first of all, only when, in virtue of its individual significance, it is directly or indirectly related to values. The French Revolution, for instance, is a historical event, or a historical totality with individual significance. A description of this event is always, in part, an interpretation, for it is always a synthesis involving selection from a great variety of happenings. The first thing that a historian has to do is to separate the important from the unimportant. What this means is of the first significance. "It is a question of values," as Professor Fling says, "the fundamental question of historical synthesis and the one con-

cerning which there is the greatest necessity of agreement."
But what is the meaning of the term value in historical
construction? Clearly not the expression of opinion as to
whether a certain fact or group of facts is good or bad, useful
or useless to-day. The condition of history being more than
a purely arbitrary personal or class interpretation is, of course,
the elimination of such particular prejudices. One who is
already convinced that the triumphant progress of democracy
is the significance of modern political history will select his
facts accordingly, and his history will be an arbitrary construction. What is meant by value in historical construction
is rather whether any fact or group of facts has any importance
for a given historical synthesis or interpretation, and hence
should form an integral part of it. History works with the
category of totality, but totality in the axiological sense in
which we have defined it.[1]

Elimination of prejudices, personal and class valuations, is,
of course, the condition of any "science" of history. But the
elimination of these does not mean the elimination of the value
element from historical concepts. We cannot even form the
concepts of democracy or autocracy without the element of
valuation and acknowledgment of values. We may, indeed, as
in any science, compare these two forms of the State with the
same scientific detachment as we compare two animals or two
geological formations, but who is naïve enough to think that
we can form the concept of State without reference to ends
and values? But if we would avoid frequent and gross misunderstandings it must be constantly emphasized that this
relation of all concepts used in history to value, is by no means
a *judgment* of value. The value is part of the material of history
itself. Another way of stating this is that the entities with which
history deals are value totalities or individualities.

In the last analysis, therefore, the whole question of historical
synthesis and interpretation is a teleological question. Not,
for the most part, the question of what should be the goal

---

[1] F. M. Fling, *The Writing of History*, chapter vii, especially p. 129.
This book is a valuable presentation of the results of the studies in the
methodology and philosophy of history as carried on under the influence of
the axiologists, especially Windelband and Rickert. A recent and very important
work on the methodology of history—in which the chief positions of this chapter
are maintained—is Ernst Troeltsch's *Der Historismus und Seine Probleme*, 1922.

of man's unique activity in society—although ultimately that question cannot be excluded—but rather what has been the goal, what in specific cases was apparently the goal aimed at and attained by man's unique social activity. It follows inevitably that the very events of history, as distinguished from the separate happenings into which they may be analysed, can be separated out only on the basis of a mutual acknowledgment of values. It follows equally that an intelligible history is always a philosophy of history, as intelligible evolution is always a metaphysical conception. If no philosophical judgments, no metaphysical elements, enter into the particular synthesis, into the interpretation of particular historical events with which the specialist and the scientific historian busy themselves, this is partly due to the limits of the field with which the synthesis deals, and partly to the refusal to acknowledge the presuppositions of his own activity.

That this last statement is true will become clear if we merely raise the question of the possibility of a world history as a complex whole, and not as simply viewed in the external framework of a single abstract conception such as that of economic or political history. The first problem would then be one of selection. What shall enter into a history of the world? Shall it deal with all sides of man's unique development, economic, educational, political, scientific, artistic, philosophical, and religious? Or with only one or two of these, the economic and political, for example? Which of these activities is the more important? Important for what? Here we are at the very heart of the metaphysical question. For in such selection a privileged position is plainly given to something and, what is even more significant, we obtain a judgment of totality in which some all-explanatory first principle is used for the interpretation of the whole. That an economic interpretation of history is a metaphysic, and a very dogmatic one at that, is well understood by all who understand what the terms mean.

It should be entirely clear that the construction of a world history, a world synthesis, presupposes a philosophy of life. Is society in all its outward manifestations a means to an end or an end in itself? In either case, what is that end? Is it the development of the spiritual content of life, as Eucken says? Is the chief end of man's unique social activity the development of human personality to the highest point? Or is it the realization in time of over-personal and over-individual values? No history has even been written without the presence of these questions, openly or tacitly, in the historian's mind. Is there any possible proof of any such "end"? Possibly not. But even if it is only a working hypothesis, has it any less reality, so far as the making of history is concerned, than if it could be demonstrated? Can man in his unique activities as a social being, and in his story of these activities which we call history, escape the formation of such a working hypothesis? Certainly not.

It takes genius to make an ending, but an ending must be made—i.e. in any intelligible history. "If history does not mean the actualization in time of something that has eternal reality beyond change and time, if it does not mean bringing more of value, meaning, of God, into the world, it is difficult to see what it does mean."

III

History is indeed, then, the record of mankind's experience with itself. That experience, it is now abundantly evident, cannot even be recorded except in terms of purpose and value. To try to draw from that record the conclusion that no purpose and value has been realized, is to deny history itself; for without inner development of some sort there is no history. This I believe to be undeniable; but it is not at all clear as yet that an intelligible history requires for this reason the postulate of progress, to say nothing of the concepts of progress that some historians have constructed. Thus far, all that can be said is that man can record his own experience of himself, and communicate its meaning, only in terms of a value-movement, of a teleology of some sort.

In one sense, it may be said, it is immaterial whether we envisage the world as progressing or regressing. Both would make an intelligible history of a sort. Now, it is not dysteleology that is primarily unintelligible, but the absence of all teleology. It is possible to understand the time in which we live if we project a golden age in the past. It is possible also if we project it into the future. But it is not possible if there is no golden age at all. The historic connections (it has been said by Windelband) remain the same, independently of whether the whole is understood as an ascent or descent, or as an indifferent remaining on the same level of value. The last part of the statement is, I think, distinctly untrue. Strictly speaking, there are no *historic* connections at all if there is no value movement. The connections would then be merely causal, economic, etc. But some historic connections there would be, although not by any means the same, whether the value movement were progressive or regressive.

Value movement of some sort is then the necessary form of intelligible history. The popular mind says we must either go forward or backward: we cannot stand still. It says *must*; and here, as in many other places, it is highly philosophical, often more philosophical, in fact, than the sophisticated professional. What then is the source and meaning of that "must?" It is to be found in the combination of the scale of value with time. We cannot stand still—that is the law of time. Forward or backward—that is the form time must take if the forms of value, which are as necessary (we have seen) to grasp the world as are the forms of space and time themselves,[1] are connected with time. As motion arises with *a priori* necessity from the union of space-time, so with equal necessity the union of time and value gives either progress or regress. When the popular mind says we must go either forward or backward, it is, it should be noted, but saying in another way that to separate reality and value is self-contradictory and therefore unintelligible.

An intelligible history can then be written, up to a point, in terms of devolution no less than evolution, of regress no less than progress. But only up to a point, I think. For that which gives meaning to a regressive process is the presence of the value scale; and the value scale gets its meaning, after all, from the positive idea of perfection rather than from the null point that lies at the other end of the scale. While we can understand the movement from the higher to the lower, it is really only because we already know and realize the other movement. I cannot present life to myself otherwise than as

[1] Chapter X, p. 344.

a striving or movement from the bad to the good, and if the reverse movement seems to make things intelligible to me, it is only because of a derived meaning which it gets from the intrinsic intelligibility of the first. Thus, in history itself, periods of regress and decadence can be understood and measured only in terms of periods of progress.

In any absolute sense, then, regress is as unintelligible as immobility. The human mind has found various ways of expressing this fact. There is the idea that if the world is good at all, it must be getting better and must go on becoming better. Being more is itself the condition of mere persistence in being, if value is part of the nature of anything. Endless surpassing, increasing purpose, is the law of all that lives. This is the positive *a priori* element in the notion of progress. We postulate it as the necessity or obligation of all that endures.[1]

In this connection reference may be made to some interesting reflections of Mr. L. P. Jacks: "Suppose you were able to show that up to date the amount of happiness in the world has shown a steady increase until it has reached the grand sum total now existing. Now suppose that you were transferred to another planet where the conditions were the exact opposite; where the inhabitants, ages ago, started with the happiness we now possess and gradually declined until at the present moment thay are no happier than the human race was at the first stage of its career. Now add together the totals of happiness for both your worlds—the ascending world which starts with the minimum and ends with the maximum, the declining world which starts with the maximum and ends with the minimum. The grand totals in both cases are exactly the same. So far as the total result is concerned, the declining world has just as much to show for itself as the ascending. Valued in terms of happiness, the one world would be worth as much as the other. And yet we know that the value of these two worlds is not the same. The ascending is worth a lot more than the descending. Why? I leave you with the conundrum. Answer it and you have the key to the meaning of moral progress."[2]

---

[1] This may be said to be a corollary of our study of the *a priori* element in teleology, as developed in Chapter X, pp. 340–45.

[2] Quoted from L. P. Jacks, "Moral Progress," in Marvin, *Progress and History*, p. 149.

The answer to the riddle lies, we may suggest, in the preceding considerations.

There remains, however, to consider the intelligibility of an historical process which is conceived of as a combination of progression and retrogression, the concept of historical cycles, of alternating periods of development and decay. This idea, long familiar to the human race and coming again into a certain popularity, seems to many to give not only a truer picture of the facts, but a more intelligible understanding of them. Dean Inge says it is the only view of the macrocosm which is even tenable.

Of all concepts in this sphere of thought this is perhaps the most difficult to grasp, and for the very good reason that it is really essentially ambiguous. For let us assume that history is a series of cycles. If so, these cycles are composed either of a series of elements that are identical in each, or of a series of elements that are in some way and to some degree diverse. In the first case, as in the concept of the "eternal recurrence," we really have only permanence, and the movements, whether of "progress" or "regress," are merely appearance. If, on the other hand, the cycles are composed of things diverse, we have only change. On neither of these conceptions of cycles do we have either forward movement or backward movement, for in neither case is there any real gain or loss of value. If, however, we conceive this circularity as involving diversity in identity, we have precisely those elements that go to make up any intelligible movement; we have also the elements that alone make possible any distinctions of value. Value is not value unless it changes, but it is also not value unless it endures or is conserved.

It is easy to see why Croce should see in this concept of "historical circles" a wholly unintelligible conception. It is also easy to see why the modern tendency is to substitute the concept of spirals for that of circles. It is characteristic of the historical nineteenth century to assert the concept of progress. As Kant against Mendelssohn, Schelling against Schlegel, uphold the position that history moves, not in periodical circles, but in a *once-for-all* evolution or progress, so Fichte, especially in his *Reden an die Deutsche Nation*, rails against that conception of history which believes in *Still-stand, Rückgang und*

Zirkeltanz—in entwickelungsloser Naturgesetzmässigkeit, instead of the infinite progress of our species.

It is characteristic of historically minded epochs and historically minded individuals to believe in progress. But it is not the fact, so much as the necessity, of this belief that interests us here. For the concept of history itself involves the element of the *a priori.* Even when one conceives the field of history as concerned with the individual, the unique, the concrete, with *Wert-individualitäten,* or *value-unities*—as we have done—even then it involves the idea of the *a priori.* Only we must avoid the idea that the *a priori* is found only in the abstract universal. It is that which is true, no matter what, that which must be acknowledged, if intelligible communication of our meanings and values is to be possible.

IV

Thus far we have been concerned wholly with the "belief" in, or "postulate" of, progress as a condition of philosophical intelligibility, or as part of the form of an intelligible world. The idea of a "law of progress" is then surely not so wholly a prejudice, not so hopelessly dogmatic, as many would have us believe. But our ideas of what progress consists of, the intelligibility of our concepts of progress, is a wholly different matter. Here, doubtless, there are prejudices and dogmas aplenty. Both the nature of the law and the basis of its validity have been grossly misconceived. Our disgust with the fatuous notions, as well as with the artificiality of the logical basis, of nineteenth-century optimism is, doubtless, partly justified. Yet the "progress in which we have perhaps believed somewhat too readily is," to quote the words of Ferrero, "not altogether a delusion."

Many, like Ferrero himself, are busily engaged in trying to reconstruct their ideas of what progress in the historical world is, hastening to get rid of those prejudices of the Victorian epoch which make those of the utopian eighteenth century singularly innocent. This disillusionment, and the critique it has begotten, concern both the question of the criteria of progress and the question of its universality and necessity. Whether increase of happiness, of freedom, of knowledge, of power over nature, or what not, constitute valid tests of progress are questions which serve but to raise the deeper problems of the possibility of any intelligible criterion of progress at all.

What is involved in our saying: "Yes, that was progress"? First of all it is a judgment on change, on the change, let us say, from the stage-coach to the steam-engine; from the perspectiveless painting of the Pre-Raphaelites to modern art; from the Magna Charta to the British or American constitution; from the Greek to the Christian moral order. And this judgment seems always to involve at least three things: elaboration or increase of something; some continuing identity throughout the change; and finally some apprehension, however dim, of ends and values realized in the process.

Now the first two of these elements may properly be said to be determinable within the special fields of mechanics, economics, art, political science, etc., in which the facts are found. That an elaboration with a persistent core of identity is discoverable in these movements, taken by themselves, seems evident. That they are value movements, however—progress in the full sense of the word—it seems possible to say only if there be acknowledgment of the value, not only of the *proximate*, but also of the ultimate, end to which these elaborations lead. Thus I may well acknowledge the fact of elaboration from the hand-loom to the monstrous machines of the present, but it is quite a different question whether I shall acknowledge this elaboration as progress in any ultimate, or even intelligible, sense.

All this is a platitude, to be sure, but it needs to be constantly repeated. For the attempt is constantly made to construct concepts of progress which do not involve judgments of totality, and neutral concepts that do not involve this acknowledgment of value.

The idea of progress (progression) is, indeed, used in particular sciences and particular spheres of fact, without either of these implications. In mathematics, the idea of numerical progression is used even without any idea of temporal meaning. In logic, "progressive" means proceeding through a linear series in the natural order, as opposed to regressive, or proceeding in the reverse order. In medicine, progressive, applied to a disease, indicates a gradual sequence of development, often with a predictable order of symptoms. In general, then, progress may be used loosely for any sort of continuous change towards a terminus or end. In all such cases progress and progressive may be used intelligibly as a wholly neutral concept, and as a law solely of the specific series to which it is applied. So also in biology, the law of the "progressive" transformation of species is both neutral and specific in this sense. But it is immediately evident that none of these concepts is historical in the slightest degree, and to attempt to construct such concepts in the sphere of history can, as, indeed, we have already seen, lead only to nonsense.

History is mankind's experience of itself, and when we consider the idea of progress as applied to humanity and human phenomena, the situation alters completely. Here also, at first sight, neutral and particularistic concepts of progress seem possible. In economics, for instance, it may be assumed, as it was indeed constantly in the nineteenth century, that increase of population is a criterion, or increased control over the forces of nature for purposes of production. But it is always possible to ask, as indeed the twentieth century is more and more insistently asking, whether these things in themselves necessarily mean progress, whether increase of population and increase of production are really ends in themselves, and whether increase of elaboration in these directions might not go hand in hand with retrogression in other spheres. It is hardly necessary to labour a point which every one, if he sees anything clearly at all in this field of thought, has long since fully realized. But what needs to be emphasized is that just this point raises the most fundamental problems of an intelligible concept and criterion of progress.

It is not necessary, I repeat, to labour this point; but this very difficulty of forming neutral and particularistic conceptions of progress has driven men to makeshifts of thought which are, if anything, even more unintelligible. "Progress," says a recent writer, "is the discovery and application of the law of cause and effect." "Real progress," says Sir William Ramsay, "is learning how better to employ energy and better to effect its transformation." Definitions of this type, of which there are many, are, indeed, most enlightening for the purpose of this discussion. In terms of distinctions made earlier in our discussion, we have an attempt here to substitute instrumental intelligibility entirely for intrinsic. It is as though men said: We recognize the fallacies involved in any particularistic conceptions of progress and of the ends which it necessarily implies. We will, therefore, abandon all dogmas of ultimate ends and think only in terms of means. This is precisely that aspect of modernism described in an earlier section.[1] We will assume that we have progress whenever we increase the use of the discovery of the law of cause and effect, whenever we learn better how to employ energy and better to effect its transformation. This is, of course, *nonsense.* For either it means that the accumulation of means is valuable, no matter what they are used for, than which there is nothing intrinsically more unintelligible; or it means the optimistic assumption that elaboration of means works necessarily to the realization of good ends.

We began our discussion of the criteria of progress by asking: What is involved in our saying—Yes, that was progress? How shall we distinguish mere change from progress? What, in other words, is an intelligible criterion of progress? and in the course of our discussion certain principles have gradually emerged which indicate the direction, at least, in which such a criterion must lie. Particularistic concepts taken from particular sciences are, it is now clear, not only wholly inadequate, but likely to be fallacious.

One way of indicating the difficulty in such concepts is to say that they necessarily involve a form of the fallacy of composition. Elaboration, or increase of something, is the only concept of progress that can be formed within a particular sphere of human activity or a particular science. Elaboration of the means of locomotion, increase of population, development of perspective or subtle tone relations in music—all may be "good for something." But how are we to know that the goods do not cancel each other? It does not follow that this "progress" added to this "progress," etc., makes progress of the whole. It has been argued, e.g., that protection is good for this labour union, for that labour union, and for the other. Therefore the protection of all industries would be good for all

---

[1] Chapter X, pp. 348 ff.

groups of labour. We know how fallacious such an argument is.

But so soon as we realize the full implications of this situation we are driven to the recognition of another principle or criterion of intelligible progress. For any adequate criterion of progress must be a system—more specifically a *system of values*.

That no social change, no movement in history, can properly be called progress on the basis of any particularistic or limited conception of progress is now abundantly evident. "Every such social change," says J. A. Thomson, "must run the gauntlet of successively higher criteria. Is it sound physically, biologically, psychologically, socially?"[1] The principle is here unhappily phrased, but, nevertheless, true and important. If progress in history cannot be determined by any single criterion, but only by a series of successively higher criteria, it is evident that in the very notion of progress itself is bound up the notion of a scale of values; and this scale of values must be a system that transcends the change which it measures.

Our contention, then, is briefly that no conception of progress is intelligible which is not philosophical; and no philosophical conception is possible without the concept of philosophic system. Otherwise expressed, the only possible intelligible concept of progress is a transcendental one.

Despite the almost self-evident character of this proposition, men continue, and will doubtless continue, to try to form positivistic and particularistic conceptions. Even Thomson himself, with his more than usual insight into these problems, does not escape the fallacy. To the question, What is progress? he admits that the merely biological point of view can answer only, "Fuller and freer life." If, then, we ask why this spells progress there is no answer, as Thomson admits again, except that there are ends which mankind at its best has always valued. So it comes to this—that progress is a sociological concept derived from history.[2] But this answer is no better than the biological. For one thing, progress is not derived from history but presupposed by history. More significant still, however, is the fact that fuller and freer life, whether life is

[1] J. A. Thomson, *What is Man?* p. 297.
[2] *Ibid.*, p. 29.

conceived merely biologically or sociologically, has no answer to the question. The concept of life itself, as all intelligible thought has long seen, is a self-transcendent notion.

V

All of which leads to the inevitable conclusion that the only intelligible concept of progress is a transcendental one. The only intelligible criteria of progress that have emerged in modern thought are those that imply a transcendental subject of progress and a transcendental goal, that envisage a meta-physical humanity and a metaphysical task—in Fichte's words, *Dem metaphysischen Volke die metaphysische Aufgabe.*

An intelligible history is, as we have seen, always a philosophy of history, as an intelligible concept of evolution is always a metaphysical conception. What is the goal of man's unique social activity which we call history? Is it the development of human personality to the highest point? May we say that the self-forming of humanity is the ultimate meaning of the historical process, and, since this self-forming means self-determination, the history of progress is, in Hegel's words, the consciousness of freedom? Is it the development of the spiritual content of life, or the attainment of a standpoint from which every individual wills in accordance with over-individual values? In these and many other ways men have sought to express that transcendent goal, movement towards which alone can in any proper sense be called progress.

Only in such transcendental concepts can the meaning of progress be expressed. But, on the other hand, the penalty such concepts must always pay for their validity is their vagueness.

This vague and abstract character of all attempts to define the goal of progress is, however, frequently misunderstood. It arises not from any uncertainty regarding the law of "necessary and universal progress," nor yet again from any vagueness or uncertainty regarding the values to be realized, or the scale or system of values in terms of which progress is determined. It arises, in part at least, mainly from the defects of imagination that inevitably make themselves felt when we attempt to envisage the conditions under which this realization is possible, when we attempt to apply the "form of perfection" to the empirical content of life. These imaginative defects are fundamental and inherent in all thinking regarding the future.

An interesting sidelight is cast on this problem by the low value utopias and pictures of human progress always have. This is but part of the general fact that the future always has a lower æsthetic value than the past. In the main the vagueness of the future never has the same æsthetic character as the vagueness of the past. Even in epochs in which the idea of progress is dominant, this idea, in associating itself with our representation of the future, seems to lack the element of poetry that belongs to the past. Why is this? Is it that we can discern progress only in the parts while the unity of the whole escapes us? This is in part true, but it is not the sole, nor, indeed, the chief, reason. Is it because activity, progress, does not seem to be able to take place without depreciation or loss of that which the past contains of the desirable, the durable, the viable? Yes, in part also. But there is another and still deeper reason. It is that no representation of the future is possible without the inclusion of the novel and the strange, and the introduction of this element throws the picture out of perspective and so introduces false values.

It is an interesting fact that the strange or "unheard-of" can rarely appear beautiful in a description, because that which is novel attracts too much attention, and is given undue prominence in a picture. We miss that which would have taken away the effect of strangeness—the perfect balance of the parts and the harmony of the whole. For instance, so we are told, the blue eyes of the northern, when described to the black-eyed inhabitants of warmer regions, seem unbeautiful and a monstrosity, because the latter vividly see with mental vision that unheard-of blueness, but not in the same vivid way the accompanying flesh and hair tints with their harmonies. It is for a similar reason that utopias, with their novel elements, are rarely æsthetically satisfying. Their very novelties are their undoing; for we cannot envisage the total context in which these novelties would be harmonious.

These inevitable limitations of the imagination necessarily

make the conception of the goal of progress vague and abstract. Thus it is that progressive peoples—peoples who, so to speak, have their future largely before them—often tend all the more, as in the case of the American people itself, to affirm the values of the past and, by an instinct sure but vague, to emphasize the conservation of these values. But the source of this vagueness of the future lies even deeper still. It is rather with vagueness in another sense—a vagueness in the very notion of progress itself. This vagueness appears at two points—vagueness as regarding the "subject" of progress and regarding the "end of progress." Let us examine these two aspects in order.

Historical progress implies world progress—universal progress. For while it is only in the parts that we seem to discern progress, yet partial progress is unintelligible. The subject of progress must be a universal, a totality, and yet the idea of an evolving totality seems to contain a contradiction. Again, the idea of progress implies an anticipation of the future, the idea of an as-yet-unknown end, of a *dénouement*, the meaning of which vacillates between the idea of an increasing purpose, such as truth, well-being, freedom, etc., and the idea of a limit towards which we tend, a limit imposed upon humanity from without, which would not be attainable except by becoming a point of arrest in the sense of a termination of the life and destiny of man. It is from these contradictions in the notion of progress itself that its necessary vagueness arises: it is from these dilemmas that the mind takes refuge in positivistic and particularistic notions.

These difficulties, it is obvious, are in general of the same type as those that emerged in our attempt to form an intelligible concept of evolution. Vagueness regarding the *subject* and *end* of progress is the same vagueness we found in the discussion of the subject and direction of evolution.[1] It was, indeed, because an intelligible concept of evolution involves an intelligible concept of finality and progress that our attempts to solve the difficulties of evolution were but tentative. The full significance of these problems appears only in these *dilemmas of progress*, as they may be called.

The subject of a genuine progress must always be a totality of some sort. The connection between the concept of history

[1] Chapter IX, pp. 312–15; also 321 ff.

and that of society, or humanity, has always been very close. The mere concept of a real historical becoming appears to make the idea of some co-existent interaction or unity between the members of the historical process necessary. Without the assumption of some such unifying bond, of a grouping that is at once given and which it itself is bringing to pass, all occasion to think of progress would be lacking. This connection between history and community appears in the entire course of Christian thinking in the form of the idea of a divine world-plan or destiny with which the unity of the human species is closely connected. This necessary connection continued in the thinking of eighteenth-century France and in Kant and his successors, and is the driving force of all historical interpretation to-day.

On the other hand, what intelligible meaning can be given to the idea of a unity which is at once given and which it itself is bringing to pass? Now, it is fairly obvious that nothing of the nature of a completed whole can be found in a series of events. History, as chronology, shows no such unique social activity as an interpretative history assumes. No whole, as a subject of progress, is observable any more than a whole as a subject of evolution. It is by no means clear, however, as Bosanquet remarks, that unification may not be an empirical character of such events. And, indeed, such a process of unification we seem, with greater or less degree of certainty, to find. In other words, unity seems to be both the ideal and the actuality of historical process.

In an earlier connection we found that mutual compenetration or community is assumed to be the meaning of the human, social world; and to make such community and communication free from the limitations of space and time seems to be humanity's ideal.[1] Otherwise expressed, the reality of non-spatial and non-temporal wholes is the presupposition of the communication of the meanings and values that emerge in space and time. It is for this reason that unity and totality as merely the goal of effort are unintelligible conceptions. It is for the same reason that to speak of a progress that was, or is to be, but is not now, is in the end nonsense.

That the merely temporal view of things cannot be ultimate

[1] Chapter VII, pp. 260 ff.

appears no less clearly in the second of these dilemmas. The idea of progress, as we have seen, implies an anticipation of the future, of a *dénouement*, the meaning of which vacillates between the idea of an ever-increasing purpose and the idea of a limit towards which we tend—a limit imposed from without, and one which would not be attainable except by becoming a point of arrest in the sense of termination of the life and destiny of man. This vacillation in our thought is not to be wondered at; for to set before oneself as an ideal of action what one certainly knows to be incapable of attainment or accomplishment, incapable of coming to an end—that is surely futile and vain. Without a best, better, or better and better, have no meaning. Yet when the best is reached progress is no more. The ideal of a state in which we shall simply rest from our labours proves no more satisfactory and meaningful.

This is in principle, of course, merely a restatement of the paradox of finality with which we became familiar in the preceding chapter. Any solution of this dilemma, if it be solvable at all, must, therefore, be along the lines already indicated. I may, however, allow myself an additional remark regarding the special form it takes in connection with our ideas of historical progress, more particularly the vagueness that necessarily inheres in this notion.

It is, of course, obvious that just as nothing of the nature of a completed whole can be found in a series of events, so nothing perfect may be realized in such a series. But again, as the speculative philosophers point out, it is not at all obvious that perfectibility may not be a character of such a series. It is suggested that "if we read perfectibility for perfection we may get a quasi-fulfilment which realizes all the requirements of progress"—of the consummation of the end and of the imperishable goal. Perfectibility is a character of forms of life, and there is nothing intrinsically unintelligible in the idea of such perfectibility. The extension of the notion of perfectibility to such universals as society or humanity involves, it is true, all the vagueness inherent in the limitations of our imagination, but there is nothing inherently incompatible in the two notions. To stake the intelligibility of history, and ultimately of the universe of which history is a part, on the realization of some specific far-off divine event, is, indeed, "to make it rest on a *de-facto* sequence in the future of a partial and arbitrary type— a type which is, in fact, contradictory." There is a sense in which "the superman makes any discussion in which he enters ridiculous." There is a sense, also, in which any attempt to combine humanity and perfectibility has the same effect. But it must, also, be remembered that we are often most ridiculous when we try to express that which is deepest in us. In any case, there is nothing contradictory nor absurd in the notion itself.

Only in such transcendental concepts, then, can the valid meanings of history be expressed. But, I repeat, the penalty such concepts must always pay for their validity is their vagueness. Here, too, the philosophers have constantly cried *Eureka* as they have discovered one way or another in which to give concrete form to the idea of perfection. Here, too, we may say that it is a pity that they are so vague, that they differ so among themselves. But these difficulties in making an ending to history should not trouble us unduly. These differences are, after all, in a very real sense secondary. All agree on the general concept of progress as the development of the spiritual content of life. In the interests of an intelligible teleology, and an intelligible concept of progress, we are no more called upon to specify in advance what will be the details of a life that will satisfy a spiritual being as such, than we are called upon to specify in advance what will be the details of a knowledge that will satisfy an intelligent being as such. But neither our inability to define completely the goal of goals as such, nor our not being called upon to do it in the interests of practice, dispenses us from goal-making. Still less does it warrant us in saying there is no goal.

In a certain sense, indeed, we make our goal as we go. But we could not make it unless, in a sense also, we already knew it; and nothing is more certain in experience than that we have this knowledge. Nothing is more certain that that, in any purposeful and significant life, he who lives such a life constantly finds some coincidence between termination and end, that the envisaged goal can be found in the consummation even though in that consummation the goal itself is partly changed. But what does this mean? It means that we can "make endings" to our lives without fear that we shall be put to shame by the consummation. It implies that we do not err completely if we identify our true being with our end. If we think out what is highest and best, we shall not err unduly if we make that our goal. But it means more than this. It means that we may form ideas of progress that are not wholly illusion. If we think out what is necessary to understand and express the highest, we shall not err if we think of that as the goal of the highest.

The indubitable fact is that the life of the spirit does just this thing, and does it continually. For the basis of our belief in progress, after all, is not merely, although, perhaps, it is mainly, those *a priori* elements of value which make some form of finality irrefutable. It is rather *experience*—the knowledge, for one thing, that the spirit of man is able to determine when progress has taken place ãnd when it is the reverse, that he is aware, however vaguely, of that totality, that system of values by which alone progress can be known. Knowing this, he is not only able "to heal the wounds of time," to modify the historical life of man in the direction of the ideal. He is also able to make ever more clear and concrete the meaning of progress itself—to fill in the scale of values in terms of which that meaning is expressed. Such an idea will always have in it an element of the other-worldly. But that is merely because the very essence of significant life is life-transcendence.

VI

The faith in progress which marked the nineteenth century has been followed by the complete abandonment of assured progress, whether found in the operations of a Divine providence, in the ultimate triumph of reason, or in a merely naturalistic evolution. Progress thus becomes only a possibility, and its realization depends solely on humanity's own efforts. But more important than this abandonment of the element of necessity is the modification of the idea of progress itself. This idea, we are told, may itself progress until it resolves itself into something different—such, for instance, as the attainment of a new equilibrium.

There are two ways of expressing the idea of necessary progress, both of which have been found repugnant to the modern mind. These are the "mechanical progress" of a Karl Marx or of a Herbert Spencer, and the idea of a "progressive copying of a goal already fixed." The element of unintelligibility found in both of these ideas is summed up in the one word, *futility*. Why exhortation to action when the results of any effort we may make are inevitable anyway? What point is there in the progressive "copying of a goal already fixed"? On such a view there can be no ultimate value in the goal, for by the very fact that it is fixed it is only there to be transcended. The only meaning or value must be in the process of goal-making itself.

Now, futility is, indeed, as we have seen[1] in this sphere, but another word for unintelligibility. In it inheres that element of the intolerable which corresponds in the sphere of the axiological to the unthinkable in the sphere of pure contemplation. If any formulation of the traditional concept of progress has the taint of futility, it is by that very fact unintelligible. But it is a grave error to think that either of the notions thus found futile really represents traditional thought.

On the other hand, it is precisely the more modern concept of progress (which must of necessity, if it is to be coherent, substitute for progress the attainment of a new equilibrium) that is saturated with futility. What does it matter if humanity, setting itself a goal, does realize that goal, if that realization is but the achievement of an equilibrium, an equilibrium to be followed by ever new forms of equilibrium? *Equilibrium is equilibrium.* In it, properly speaking, no value distinctions can be made. What does it matter even if, reading value where we have no right to do so, we say the best is yet to be? The best must perish as the good, to give place to a yet better best, which will not have the virtue of enduring any more than the others. "Do we offer any real consolation to Sisyphus," asks Renouvier, "by promising him an annihilation, which is coupled with the promise of successors capable of lifting his old rock higher and still higher up the fatal slope, by offering him the eternal falling of this rock, and successors who will be eternally annihilated and endlessly replaced by others?"

Let us at least talk intelligibly. One can understand and sympathize with thinkers such as Schopenhauer and Tolstoy who deny progress utterly. They are responsible thinkers and

[1] Chapter X, pp. 334 ff.

know what they are doing. It is asking too much, however, even of a philosopher, to have patience with these weasel words with which our present thinking is afflicted. This vagueness began when, following Auguste Comte, we moderns began to talk of progress as the *aim* of the historical life of man. Progress is meaningless without the idea of a goal or aim; but we are now called upon to understand our aims in terms of progress. We make our hopes of the goal, our very conception of it, and so the goal itself, as we go. An essential incoherence! For if we explain our values away in terms of anything else, even of progress, they cease to be our values. But this was only the beginning of a process by which gradually all the meat has been sucked out of the idea of progress, a process which has reached the acme of incoherence in the idea of progress as something which depends wholly on humanity's own efforts. This is obviously but the expression in another form of the idea of "a reality that creates itself gradually," and shares all its inherent unintelligibility.

The truth is that the notion of progress is transcendental or metaphysical, or it is nothing at all. We moderns have been trying to retain the concept without acknowledging the absolute value it implies, and the ultimate metaphysical problems it involves. The development of the human spirit has, it is true, no absolutely reliable means in this world. A thousand different and often mutually inimical evolutionary processes cross one another. But the real aim of the spirit does not lie wholly in this world. Only if metaphysical being and becoming are synchronized completely would this be the case.

Finally, then, it is because progress is a transcendental concept that no intelligible idea of it can be formed without reference to the whole system of philosophical concepts. Problems of progress pass over inevitably into problems of ultimate destiny and immortality, because an intelligible concept of progress cannot be formed without the idea of conservation. Problems of progress pass necessarily over into problems of system, because an intelligible concept of progress implies an over-temporal system of values and validities. The first of these more ultimate problems is treated in the next chapter on "The New *Götterdämmerung*"; the second, in the concluding chapter of this book, on the "System of Philosophy."

CHAPTER XII

THE NEW GÖTTERDÄMMERUNG: DEGRADATION AND VALUE

There is no Entropy of Being.

SIMMEL

For a philosophy that knows its business, the Law of Degradation makes
no difference.

BOSANQUET

I

THE problem of world destiny has again entered the foreground of human interest and reflection in the form of a
magnificent dysteleology, the Second Law of Thermodynamics,
the Law of Entropy.[1] The pre-eminent significance which
this principle has for speculative philosophy is understandable.
While not a doctrine of "last things" in the absolute sense, it
is certainly such a doctrine in a sense sufficient to affect
vitally our interpretation of reality and its significance. The
thinking which thinks this principle into the universe is not—
and cannot be—a *wert-freies Denken*. It reintroduces finality into
the world picture—even if it is, as I have said, a magnificent
dysteleology. Dysteleology is a form of teleology, just as
meaninglessness is always negative meaning and negative
value a form of value. In a very important sense, on this view,
the gates of the future are shut.

It is not surprising, therefore, that attitudes towards this
conception are in a sense diagnostic for philosophical interpretation. It is also not surprising that the entire range of
variation in philosophical attitude and interpretation is
reflected in the reactions to it. They vary all the way from
the mood of exaltation to that of unyielding despair: from
those who see in it a challenge requiring an entire reconstruction of the humanistic sciences, and, correspondingly, of
our philosophy of humanity and history, to those who hold
that for a philosopher who "knows his business" it makes no
difference.

[1] More accurately, of course, the law of increasing entropy.

Clearly such variation must be due in part—as it, indeed, is—to difference of opinion as to the range of the implication and the validity of the law itself. But it is also due to wide differences in general philosophical attitude. A philosophy, for instance, which, like James's Meliorism, makes enormous drafts upon the future, must take such a conception very seriously, as, indeed, his correspondence with Henry Adams shows. On the other hand, to one in whose philosophy the future is not given a privileged position, its implications are of but relative importance. In any case, we have in the philosophical evaluation of this cosmological principle a key to much that is most s'gnificant in modern thought. The relation of the historical process to the cosmic process is, as we have seen in the last chapter, from one point of view, at least, the key question of metaphysics. It is, at least, the point at which the question of the intelligibility or unintelligibility of a philosophy attains maximum significance.

II

This problem we may, perhaps, get before us most vividly in the words of Mr. Henry Adams, to whom this law of thermodynamics presents modern thought with an ultimate dilemma.[1] "The universe," Mr. Adams tells us, "has been terribly narrowed by thermodynamics." Already history and sociology "gasp for breath." Assuming that the humanistic sciences are gasping for breath (or if they are not they ought to be), it is easy to see why Mr. Adams finds it so. Both of them of necessity, whether they recognize it explicitly or not, ply their trades on the implicit assumption that history and social life are the expression or realization of some meaning. Otherwise history is "but sound and fury, signifying nothing."

The life-blood of history (and of sociology—as a humanistic science, at least) has been the postulation of a law of progress. This postulate has included two elements—the one the element of direction towards an end, the other the identification of this end with increase of value. For Adams degradation of energy means an end true enough, a direction, but it also

[1] *The Degradation of Democratic Dogma* (1919), p. 261.

means inevitably decrease of value. Accordingly, modern thought is faced with this dilemma. Either this law must be abandoned in respect to vital and human phenomena altogether, for the entire realm in which meanings and values appear, or "vital energy" must "abandon reason entirely in one of its forms" and go over frankly to anti-intellectualism and mysticism. In either case we must frankly face dualism in the sciences and, *a fortiori*, in philosophy.[1]

All this, to be sure, presupposes the conception of history developed in the preceding chapter. There might be, indeed, a sociology, and in a sense a history, of a race "going to the dogs." If there is *any* value movement *at all* the process can be made intelligible in a sense. This is, of course, the sort of history that Henry Adams writes. But if history is what we have found it to be, we appear to be faced with the above dilemma. Whether this dilemma is ultimate or not, we at least see where the problem of the present chapter lies. It is to be found in a fundamental contradiction, apparent or real, between a "law of value" and a "law of exi;tence"—one of those contradictions that constitute the genuinely axiological intolerable, the unintelligible in the ultimate sense. Our task is, accordingly, twofold. In the first place, to examine the law of Entropy itself—its validity and its implications; and, secondly, to examine the relation of the ultimate laws of value, on which finality and progress rest, with this cosmic law.

III

The reason for this supposed dilemma, it must be pointed out at once, is that this so-called law of thermodynamics is itself a historical principle, and, like any history, essentially metaphysical in its implications. With it a historical element has been introduced into physics, and, in so far as this law is made a basis for any interpretation of life and destiny, brings it into relation to principles of life and of history.

It is important to emphasize the historical character of this law for several reasons. In the first place, it is in no sense a completion of the physical picture of the world as

[1] *Op. cit.*, p. 262.

developed by physical science, no perfection of the ideal of description which mechanics and physics have followed. It is rather essentially a disturbance of that picture—perhaps, as it has been suggested, its ultimate destruction. The historical element thus introduced into physics, for one thing, belongs to an entirely different order of ideas from the essentially non-historic concept of the conservation of energy, a leap into another order which threatens the internal coherence of the science. The sense of this precarious situation on the part of some physicists is indicated by attempts made to escape the logic of the theory by these very physicists themselves.

It is for this very reason, the historical character of this law, that the principle is generally recognized as, in the words of Bergson, "the most metaphysical of all the principles of nature." But it is, perhaps, not generally recognized how far this significance extends.

It is metaphysical, in the first place, because, as Henry Adams indicates, it is a law that stretches the tentacles of its implications far beyond the physical realm into that of life, mind, and history, squeezing the breath out of them. Ostensibly it expresses merely the fact that all forms of energy have the tendency to be degraded into heat, and that heat tends to be distributed among bodies in a uniform manner. Actually it also tells us that changes that are visible and heterogeneous will be more and more diluted into changes that are invisible and homogeneous, and that the instability to which we owe the richness and variety of the changes taking place in our solar system will gradually give way to the relative stability of elementary vibration continually and perpetually repeated.[1]

The law of degradation is metaphysical because it thus involves a judgment of totality—it applies not only to energy, but to the "world" process. It is metaphysical also because it includes the element of irreversible direction and thus makes of the world process a "unique event." But even more than this it purports to tell us *specifically* the direction in which the world is going, and so, by implication at least, something about a beginning and end. That this law involves a doctrine of first and last things is a point that should be made more clear.

[1] This is true, of course, of only *closed* and *purely physical* systems. But more of this later.

Already, in our discussion of space and time, we found that there is an inherent difficulty in the idea of a becoming without beginning and end. Those thinkers who have assumed the spatial endlessness of the universe have always realized that it is impossible to reconcile with this idea the notion that one direction in the universe could be distinguished from another. This general difficulty becomes specific and inescapable when, as according to the law of entropy, anything like a definite direction in the universe becomes an established fact. For among the numerous quantitative aspects of physical phenomena in which the totality of the universe can be numerically expressed—as, for instance, the average temperature, the average density, etc.—there is one, so this law informs us, that can change only in one direction, and in this case, with the continuance of time, become greater and greater. The physical quantity called entropy can only increase, never decrease, and the amount of available energy must correspondingly decrease.

This idea of a definite direction is, I repeat, an essentially metaphysical conception, for it implies the idea of beginning in time. The idea of the "ageing of the world" expresses itself in the fact that with the occurrence of physical events the relation of the energy still usable to the total available energy becomes smaller and smaller. When, for example, at any particular time of the world process, 40 per cent. of the total constant is available, it follows that at another moment of time, separated from the first by enormous yet still finite time, the available energy would be only 35 per cent. The decrease of this relation takes place constantly, and indeed, as physics teaches, the more rapidly, the greater the supply of available energy is. Accordingly, the farther back into the past we look, the greater this relation must have been. If it is now, for example, 40 per cent., it must have been at an earlier time 41 per cent. Consequently, the relation at some finite time must have been 100 per cent.—at a time, in fact, at the most sixty times as great as the time in which the relation sank to 1 per cent. But now comes the important point. Beyond this time we cannot follow the world process into the past. For the relation expressed in the law of increase of entropy could never have been more than 100 per cent.—

the part can never be greater than the whole. Consequently, the available energy of the universe could never be greater than the constant total. Since, however, available energy is still present in the universe, we must conclude that the world process could not have subsisted eternally, but that it has had a beginning, a beginning perhaps immeasurably remote, but none the less in finite time.

From considerations such as these it is clear that it is the historical character of the law of the degradation of energy that makes it metaphysical. It is this character, threatening as it does to disturb the unhistorical world picture of the mechanical sciences, that raises significant problems for science itself.

It is easily understandable that this disturbance of the scientific world picture is not wholly welcome to scientists, as its apparent implications are unwelcome to the philosopher. More particularly, there is more or less of a tendency to avoid the almost instinctive logic that seems necessarily to connect the idea of end with that of beginning, to avoid the metaphysical or even supernatural explanation of the world process which seems involved. Many have, therefore, sought ways out of the difficulty. In principle, they consist chiefly in disavowing the metaphysical character of the law; or, in other words, in maintaining that what is merely a description must not be turned into a dogma; and, above all, that the concept of degradation of energy must not be changed into that of degradation of the universe.

The easiest way of avoiding these difficulties consists in the simple denial of the universal validity of the principle of entropy. It is admitted that it is valid for that part of the universe which is open to our observation, but the possibility is left open, it is held, that, in addition to the systems in space in which the entropy increases, there may also be such in which the entropy decreases. It would then be possible that the total sum of entropy, like that of energy, would remain constant. On the other hand, it is also possible to contest the universal validity of the principle of entropy in time. On this view the assumption is made that we live in a time in which the world, in consequence of the increase of entropy or degradation of energy, approaches the dissipation of warmth and death; but it is held to be possible that, after the entropy maximum is attained, there will follow the period of entropy increase a period of entropy decrease, and that this oscillation occurs throughout eternity. We have, then, the doctrine of world cycles in a new form.

While this is an easy way to escape the difficulties suggested it is not a wholly satisfactory way. The doors of the future are still open on this assumption. But for the alternative hypothesis which the denial of the universal validity of the law makes possible there is, of course, no secure basis in experience.[1] As hypotheses they are scientifically uncontrollable, and it becomes really a matter of simple choice whether we choose this position or that of a supernatural or metaphysical cause.

IV

The challenge which the principle of the degradation of energy presents to the humanistic thinker is really a challenge only in case it involves the idea of the degradation of the universe. The second law of thermodynamics is significant for philosophical interpretation only in case it is metaphysical. Either the law is metaphysical, involving the whole of reality, vital and mental—the realm in which meaning and value appear—and we must, then, draw the consequences that Adams draws; or we must abandon it in the sphere of "vital energy," with the consequent dualism of existence and value. There is, according to him, but one limitation to be put upon this dilemma, and that is a very serious restriction which concerns the limitations of science itself.

It is to the "limits of science," accordingly, that most philosophers have appealed in the attempt to turn the edge of this dilemma. It would be difficult to count the number of those who have quoted the warning of Lotze against crediting as a prophetic announcement with regard to the

---

[1] It is, perhaps, unnecessary to mention specifically such alternative hypotheses as, for instance, (a) Clerk Maxwell's "demon," which is virtually the activity of intelligence; or (b) the possible capacity of vital and psychical processes to resist the processes of degradation (Bergson).

future, those ingenious calculations which draw conclusions as to the final state of the world from our experimental knowledge of the economy of heat. In strict logic, it is true that such pessimistic conclusions follow only if we assume that the given conditions are the only ones to be taken into account, while such an assumption is arbitrary. We may even go so far as to say that, "although we may use the symbolism of the degradation of energy, we must not take it too seriously and degrade the world system as well. This system does not begin with mere motions of mass particles, and it does not end in heat—that is, movements distributed in a uniform way among such particles. Situations of this class belong to the 'Neverland' of abstractions and representative fictions."

Such answers to the challenge of the new *Götterdämmerung*, as Spengler calls it, are always possible. To one who takes this critical attitude towards science it would also be possible to say, with a show of reason, that to the philosopher who knows his business this law makes no difference. And to such a limitation science itself is scarcely in a position to take serious exception. On this, as on all ultimate and significant questions, "science" is thoroughly ambiguous. On this very question of energetics itself there are two entirely different positions. The doctrine of energy, in its most modern phases, has developed in two directions: it has run into a metaphysics in the hands of Ostwald and thinkers of his type, and into a wholly mathematical formalism in the hands of Duhem and those of his way of thinking. For the latter science is mere description, and the language of science is symbolical. It disclaims wholly all ontological language.

To this critical attitude of the philosopher science as such is, accordingly, in no position to take serious exception. It is, indeed, possible—and I myself believe, as do many—that this extension of the law of the economy of heat to the universe as a whole is based upon assumptions far from unquestionable, and is likely to pass, if it has not already passed, in the form so common in the last decades.[1] Until science is agreed in its

[1] Thus, according to some, the Einstein theory enables us to avoid such cosmological consequences. Harald K. Schjelderup, for instance, writes as follows: "As" (in the theory of relativity) "the sphere surface, so is the universe a finite quantity, but unlimited. Through this conception," he continues, "a big

assumptions regarding space and time—until, in general, it knows what it is and what it really wants—philosophical interpretation is always in a position to insist upon the essential irrelevance of this law.

But this doctrine of irrelevance turns out in actual thinking to be far from satisfactory. And the reason for this is the fact that there persists in our thinking something that lies very much deeper than this particular law of physics—something which, moreover, whether we wish it or not, turns it into a metaphysical conception. This is nothing less than the element of history and direction that must inevitably be read into the universe in so far as the universe is viewed as a temporal process.

Let us put this more concretely. Just as some notion of development, evolution, progress will always be part of the form of an intelligible world, so such a world will always have to take account of the processes of devolution, dissipation, and decay, no matter whether they be formulated in terms of this generalization of physics or not. There will always be this *motif* in the symphony of philosophy, whether it be in terms of this new *Götterdämmerung* or of one as old as the oldest mythology. Whatever formulation of this *motif* may come with changes in our scientific concepts, some formulation there will always be, and philosophy will have the problem of its interpretation. It is for this reason that the second law of thermodynamics cannot be wholly irrelevant to philosophy. Some attitude towards, some interpretation of, this principle must find its place in any form of modern philosophy.

difficulty attached to our world image is solved. As long as the Euclidian geometry was regarded as holding true for the world space, it seemed that the physicist had to regard this as infinite. This infinite universe, however, he could not—if he presupposed the validity of Newton's gravitation law—regard as being filled with an infinite number of heavenly bodies. While, then, the universe was thought infinite, the material world had to be thought of as finite. The star world had to be imagined as a finite island in the infinite ocean of space. This conception was not, however, very satisfactory. The energy of the universe had to be regarded as spread out little by little and lost in the infinite space, without ever returning to the material world. The universe would, by and by, have to die out completely.

"Through Einstein's theory we evade such a conclusion. Also, applied to the world as a whole, then, the relativity theory seems to lead to more satisfactory conclusions than the earlier conception."

See his article, "The Theory of Relativity and its Bearing on Epistemology," *The Scandinavian Review*, September 1922, p. 40.

V

Let us examine, now, the philosophical attitudes toward this law which assume its metaphysical character—which recognize in it a direction in which the world is actually going. The problem for philosophical interpretation is, then, rather this: Assuming it to be "true" in the ordinary sense of the word, what difference does it make?

The popular philosophy of the nineteenth century has made enormous drafts on the future, and the form which these drafts have taken is the belief in universal, necessary progress. How far those drafts can be honoured in a universe that is growing old is one way in which the problem may be put. Another way of stating it is this. A law of progress is a necessary presupposition of an intelligible history and sociology. But in a world so conceived progress can be only an illusion, or at best of a very limited significance.

There are those, to be sure, who tell us that there is no incompatibility between the law of progress and the law of degradation, because the possibility of progress is guaranteed by the high probability, based upon astrophysics, of a virtually infinite time to progress in. While science assures us of the ageing and death of our universe, it also assures us that the stability of the present condition of the solar system is certified for many myriads of years to come. Whatever gradual modifications of climate there may be, the plants will not cease to support life within a period of time which transcends the efforts of the imagination. "As time is the very condition of the possibility of progress," writes Bury, "it is obvious that it would be valueless if there were any cogent reasons for supposing that the time at the disposal of humanity is likely to reach a limit in the near future. . . . It would be a delicate matter to decide what is the *minimum* period of time which must be assured to man for his future development in order that progress should possess value and appeal to the emotions. . . . But this psychological question need not be decided, for the reasons stated above."[1]

It is difficult to take an argument of this sort seriously. According to this line of reasoning the question we are

[1] *The Idea of Progress*, p. 5.

considering is a "psychological" one. As a matter of fact, it is a question of quite a different order—in the terms with which we have become familiar, an axiological one. There is, to be sure, an element of truth here. For the imaginations of beings of our time-span the extinction of life contemplated can have little or no emotional meaning. In comparison with the short life in which our ends are to be phenomenally realized, in comparison also, perhaps, with the times in which movements of civilization and culture work themselves out, the terminus as set by the speculations of physics is irrelevant. But if our distinction between the psychologically and the axiologically intolerable has any validity, all this is beside the mark. For a concept of progress to be intelligible it is not sufficient that it shall involve merely an indefinite evolution *ins blaue hinein*. Intelligible evolution involves perpetual surpassing, but it also involves a perpetual conservation—not only a goal, but an imperishable goal. A more significant statement of the position we are examining will, however, bring out the point of our criticism more fully.

"From our point of view," writes Bernhard Brunhes, "the principle of the degradation of energy would prove nothing against the fact of evolution. The progressive transformation of species, the realization of more perfect organisms, contains nothing contrary to the idea of the constant loss of useful energy. . . . On one side, therefore, the world wears out; on the other side, the appearance on the earth of living beings more and more elevated, and, in a slightly different order of ideas, the development of civilization in human society, undoubtedly give the impression of a progress and a gain. Only the vast and grandiose conceptions of the imaginative philosophers who erect into an absolute principle the law of universal progress could no longer hold against the most fundamental ideas that physics reveal to us."[1]

With this "impression of progress" we ought, perhaps, to be satisfied—*psychologically*, at least. But we are not satisfied, and the reason we are not becomes clear when we realize that, as the writer of the preceding candidly admits, the impression of gain is really an illusion, for the gain is really derived from an order due to the levelling of energies, from

[1] Bernhard Brunhes, *Degradation* (Paris, 1908), p. 193.

an order consequent upon the dissolution of a higher order which had supplied, by lowering its inequalities, all the useful energies that caused progress. The reality behind the illusion is, therefore, absence of power to do useful work—or what man knows in his finite sensibilities as death.[1]

The preceding remarks give the key to the apparent opposition between the doctrine of evolution and the principle of degradation of energy. Physical science presents to us the picture of a "world" that is unceasingly wearing itself out. A philosophy which claims to derive support from biology, on the contrary, complacently paints a world steadily improving—in which life goes on, always growing perfect to the point of reaching full consciousness of itself in man, and where no limit seems imposed to eternal progress. Surely such compromises as those suggested in the preceding paragraphs are impossible—impossible because they are essentially unintelligible. The irresponsible conceptions of popular thought and the vast and grandiose conceptions of the imaginative philosophers may, indeed, require considerable revision, but that revision can scarcely go so far as to transform the idea of progress beyond all possibility of recognition. A reconciliation of progress with dissipation which first turns progress into an illusion is one that has little to offer us in the way of an intelligible philosophical conception.

It is entirely understandable, therefore, that such compromises as these should not prove wholly satisfactory—neither to those who, taking time seriously, are compelled to make enormous drafts on the future, nor to those who, not taking time so seriously perhaps, make their drafts on that which is timeless. Even if the possibility of world progress is guaranteed by the "world bank" for many myriad of years to come (whatever that guarantee may be worth), the certainty of failure to come would dwarf those years into insignificance. There is one thing that would remain for ever intolerable, though its realization were thought of as thousands or myriads of years distant: it is the thought that humanity with all its intellectual and moral toil will vanish without leaving a trace, and that not even a memory of it will endure in any mind. The drafts which we make in our moral postulates cannot

[1] *Op. cit.*, p. 53.

be estimated in years, no matter how loosely we play with them. The world bank is the one bank of which it may be said that, if it is ultimately insolvent, it has always been so.

VI

With regard to the dilemma presented by the principle of degradation, there are, we have seen, according to Mr. Adams, only two possibilities: either to accept it for the world of life and mind, of history and values, and to draw his pessimistic conclusions; or else to reject it in the realm of history and values, and thus to hand life and mind over to the irrational. Now, as it happens, there have been recently two thinkers who have respectively accepted each one of these two horns of the dilemma, but in neither case have the pessimistic nor irrationalistic conclusions been drawn. On the one hand, Wilhelm Ostwald accepts the application of the law to the realm of life, mind, and values, but maintains that, far from its being inimical to the realm of values, it is only on the basis of this second law of thermodynamics that the world of values becomes intelligible. William James, on the other hand, attempts to meet the situation by accepting the principle, but showing that, save as it sets a terminus, it is wholly irrelevant to history. It will be worth our while to consider briefly both of these attempted solutions. They illustrate perfectly the only logical or axiological possibilities open to a philosophy that identifies becoming with being.

In a paper entitled "The Energetic Imperative" Ostwald insists that the principles of energetics, including the first and second laws of thermodynamics, must be applied universally to life and mind.[1] He exults in the thought that "natural science has at last been able to seize from its conservative guardians the world of values, hitherto conceived as the exclusive possession of the *Geisteswissenschaften*." For him there can be no compromise between physics and history; energetics must be extended to life and mind. But such extension is not inimical. "Far from this," he continues, "we infer the

[1] Wilhelm Ostwald, *Der Energetische Imperative*, 1912. Also article, "Wilhelm Ostwald," in *Philosophe der Gegenwart in Selbstdarstellungen*, 1923, vol. iv.

all-important opposite conclusion that the entire world of ends and values rises from the law of dissipation as its deepest source."

The title of the paper gives the clue to his meaning. He recognizes that an imperative is the essence of the life of values—that, further, all imperatives, however formulated, embody the idea of a maximization of good or value, whether that maximization is conceived as universalization, increase of pleasure, of cosmic energy, or what not.[1] He recognizes also that no imperative has any significance except as there is possibility of fulfilment. In other words—and this is the important point for our present purpose—Ostwald accepts "the dialectic of valuation," the irrefutable element in finality as we have developed it in a preceding chapter.[2] Is, now, such an imperative, such finality, possible in a world where the law of dissipation rules? It is, he holds, not only possible, but it is only in such a world that it has any meaning.

It is ordinarily assumed that between these principles and the law of degradation there can only be contradiction. Far from this being the case, it is, according to Ostwald, on the truth of the law of dissipation that these principles depend. It is at once obvious, as, indeed, we have already seen, that the principle of maximization of value is up to a point consistent with the law of dissipation. Evolution, progress, in a limited sense, contains nothing contrary to the idea of a

[1] The moral imperative itself, Ostwald believes, may be adequately formulated in terms of energetics. Act so that thou mayest transform the raw energies of life into higher with the greatest economy (*Güter-verhältnisse*). So the formula runs. That it will be received with scorn and even disgust, he is well aware, for "it smells of the technical." But it really embodies, he thinks, that which is essential in all significant moral acts. Whatever doubts we may have as to the adequacy of the formula to express fully the meaning of the moral imperative we may afford to pass over, for it does involve in its own way the two fundamental principles of valuation from which all imperatives spring. Transformation of lower into higher forms involves an order of rank, a scale of values. From what does this order depend? Obviously, he answers, from the extent to which the energy is humanized, that is adapted to human ends, as, for instance, when bread represents a higher form of energy than wood, although both are chemically very similar. Transformation of lower into higher with a maximization of value does involve the principle of increase or maximization which, as Brentano rightly said, is the one self-evident moral law. Now, it is precisely the fate of these two principles in a world where the law of dissipation rules that is the question at issue.

[2] Chapter X, p. 342.

constant loss of useful energy. Similarly, transformation of the
raw energies of life into higher forms with the maximum
economy is entirely possible in a world where the sum-total
of the energies thus available is constantly decreasing. We can
make the best of a world going to the dogs. But Ostwald's
point is a more fundamental one than this—namely, the essential
compatibility between the fundamental postulate of value and
this fundamental law of existence is much more deep-seated.

The point which attracts Ostwald's attention is one which
has been emphasized by others, notably Royce—the fact,
namely, that the law of dissipation, or of the irreversible
series, is the one aspect of reality in which matter and mind,
nature and humanity, pre-eminently meet. The irreversibility
of the time process is the deepest fact. From this essentially
metaphysical character of reality an idealism such as Royce's
may draw the moral that the distinction which common sense
and science draw between nature and mind is but appearance.
The moral for Ostwald is that irreversible process is the law
or postulate of values, and therefore, since it is also the deepest
law of nature, nature cannot be inimical to values.[1]

First of all, irreversibility of value series is the fundamental
law of valuation and values. Values are related to each other
in various ways. A may be a value because B is (relation of
means to ends, or a relation of part to whole); A may be a
value because it can be exchanged for B or transformed into B.
Now these relations are by their very nature irreversible.
That is, if A is a value because B is, B cannot in the same
respect be a value because A is. If A is of more value than B,
so that preference or exchange may take place, B cannot in
the same respect be of more value than A. This is very simple
and very formal, this law of irreversible process in valuation,
but it means much—it means that this irreversible character
is part of the "essentials of value as such."[2]

But Ostwald goes farther, and insists that all action would
be futile if this necessary law of valuation did not find itself
in harmony with a similar law of irreversible process in the

---

[1] Whether this irreversibility of the time process *is* the world's deepest fact
we shall consider later (p. 422). Here we are concerned merely with the argument
built by Ostwald on this assumption.
[2] Chapter X, pp. 336 ff.

world in which actions take place and values are realized. "And to recognize this from another side," he continues, "let us think for a moment that the law of dissipation of energy were not valid, that therefore the happenings did not have to take place in one way, in the sense of increasing dissipation, but permitted themselves to be turned about. In general it would be a matter of indifference what we did, since all could be or would be brought back to the earlier condition." Thus when Mephistopheles sees all his efforts in vain at the conclusion of *Faust*, he cries, "How much labour vainly employed!" But if the world processes were reversible, he would have merely to let the scene with the angels take place in the opposite direction in order to make good his stupidity. The entire world of ends and values disappears on the assumption of the reversible process.

Enough has been said, I think, to indicate why it has seemed, at least, possible to infer "the all-important opposite conclusion that the entire world of ends and values rises from the law of dissipation as its deepest source." But enough has also been said, I think, to suggest the doubts that must arise as to the satisfactoriness of the solution. Nietzsche, to be sure, far from finding the law of value incompatible with the reversed process, actually found in our ability to contemplate the eternal recurrence of our acts the ultimate criterion of their value. Perhaps the law of value lies deeper than any formulation of Ostwald's. But that is not the point that we wish to emphasize at the moment. It is rather an important question which Ostwald himself has apparently overlooked— namely, whether the increase and conservation of value possible in a world where the law of dissipation is the "deepest law" are the *same* as the increase and conservation postulated in the world of ends and values. This the most superficial reflection compels us to deny.

The law of dissipation, if we ascribe metaphysical significance to it, as Ostwald does, has two aspects. On the one hand, there is the law of irreversible process, as the deepest fact of nature and of life; on the other hand, there is the idea of a terminus to which the irreversible process leads. In a world in which the irreversible process is the deepest fact there is, indeed, an element of conservation. But what is it that is conserved? In the sphere of energy it means merely absence of change in quantity – a notion wholly compatible with change, and even loss, in qualities and values. The fact of irreversible process is no guarantee of conservation in this sphere. It is, indeed, rather possible to say that conservation in this latter sense is scarcely compatible with any philosophy that identifies becoming completely with being. It is customary to say that the past is conserved by being taken up and absorbed in the future. But this is in part, at least, merely words; for if change is the ultimate fact the past is largely dropped out and gone. Conservation as contemplated by Ostwald, we may say without hesitation, is far from identical with conservation as contemplated by the "law of value." More than this, the law of dissipation not only establishes a direction, a direction made possible by its irreversible character, but it also sets a terminus. It is this terminus which Ostwald entirely ignores. Intelligible progress implies a direction and a goal, but it also implies an imperishable goal. If dissipation is the deepest source of the world of ends and values, the goal of that world is a perishable goal.

VII

Now, it is precisely this aspect of the metaphysical interpretation of the law of dissipation that has attracted the attention of William James. Finding, as he does, the whole meaning of philosophical conceptions in their meliorism, he is committed to the belief that the ideal is in the future. Although, perhaps, not guilty of the futuristic fallacy that whatever comes next must be better, still the better must be found in the future or not at all. Moreover, although a pragmatist, he is not quite guilty of that kind of reasoning which sees in the problem merely the psychological question of how much time must be assured to man for progress to possess meaning and value. It is not surprising, therefore, that he found it necessary to try to turn the edge of the law of degradation, and that in his replies to Henry Adams, in which the attempt is made, a distinct note of irritation should appear.[1]

---

[1] Letter to Henry Adams, found in vol. ii of William James's *Letters*, p. 344.

The point of James's contention is that the second law of thermodynamics *is irrelevant to history save as it sets a terminus, and this fact of terminus makes no difference to the meaning and value of history and the truth of progress.*

As might be expected, James does not accept wholeheartedly the metaphysical character of this law, but he argues on the basis of its acceptance. "It is customary for gentlemen to pretend to believe one another, and until someone has a new and more revolutionary concept, which may be to-morrow, all physicists must play the game by holding religiously to the above doctrine. It involves, of course, the ultimate cessation of all perceptible happening and the end of human history. With this general conception . . . no one can find any fault—in the present state of scientific conventions and fashions." But granting its metaphysical character, he finds it necessary to protest against certain interpretations of the great statistical drift downwards of the great original high level of energy.

The second law is, he contends, wholly irrelevant to history, save as it sets a terminus, and all that the second law says is that, whatever the history is, it must invest itself between that initial *maximum* and the terminal *minimum* in energy level. Generalizing this, he proceeds to the conclusion: the second law is wholly irrelevant to the realm of values. "The clock of the universe is running down," let us suppose, "and by so doing makes the hands move. The energy absorbed by the hands and the mechanical work they do is the same day after day, no matter how far the weights have descended from the position they were originally wound up to. The history which the hands perpetuate has nothing to do with the quantity of the work, but follows the significance of the figures which they cover on the dial. If they move from o to 12, there is progress; if from 12 to o, there is decay. . . ." In other words, if we may be permitted to paraphrase, it is the irreversible order of value, itself not temporal, that gives meaning to history, not the temporal process of the statistical drift.

But now comes the point on which all hinges. In his peculiarly vivid way James proceeds: "Though the ultimate state of the universe may be its vital and physical extinction, there is nothing in physics to interfere with the hypothesis that the penultimate state might be the millennium—in other words, a state in which a *minimum* of difference of energy level might have its exchanges so skilfully canalized that a maximum of happy and virtuous conduct would be the only result. In short, the last expiring pulsation of the universe's life might be, 'I am so happy and perfect that I can stand it no longer.' You don't believe it, and I don't say I do, but I can find nothing in *Energetik* to conflict with its possibility."

It is doubtful, perhaps, whether this can be taken as more than an eloquent gesture, of a piece with those gestures which modernism in general is so fond of making. But if it is something more, the significance of this attempt to turn the edge of the law of dissipation—at least, for our purposes—scarcely allows of exaggeration. The drafts which meliorism makes upon the future can then be honoured, even if physical and vital extinction is the universe's doom. Provided the principle of the maximization of value is realized, it makes no difference whether the value is conserved or not. What, we may well ask, is the inner meaning of such a position as this? It means, I think, only one of two things. Either that conservation is not a necessary part of the meaning of progress, that realization and conservation can be separated in thought, or else it means that value is in some way independent of the temporal process.

The second of these alternatives we can scarcely suppose James seriously to have entertained. While it has much in common with the most exalted insights of traditional thought, it is hardly in tone with a pragmatical philosophy. It is suspiciously like those much berated philosophies that solve problems by escaping into the realm of timeless values. It is surely only the first alternative that James would consider.

This idea that conservation is not a necessary part of the idea of progress is but one aspect of a much deeper and more widespread feeling of our time—namely, that conservation is not a necessary part of the essentials of value. Value, it is said, is not absolutely dependent upon its own conservation. It is what it is. "That which we treasure as beautiful and good may retain its value, whatever fate be its lot and whatever shadows may darken its fall. A thought is not necessarily less true, nor a feeling less pure and noble, because it must pay its debt to time. Should it be the fate of the good and beautiful to perish, would it therefore be less good and beautiful?"

I do not wish to deny a certain nobility in such sentiments, but this does not prevent me from feeling that they are essentially unintelligible—a feeling which, I am sure, would be shared by the plain man and traditional philosophy alike. I seem to detect something of this feeling in James himself—the hidden cause, I rather think, of the obvious irritation with which he makes his answer to Henry Adams. Was it n t this same William James who called a like point of view, when proposed by another, a fantastic philosophy? "As if the world of values were independent of existence!" These are James's own words. "It is only," he continues, "as being that one thing is better than another. The idea of darkness is as good as that of light, as ideas. There is more of value in light's being."[1]

And *is* there not something fantastic in such a philosophy? It is impossible to escape the conviction that there is something axiologically unintelligible in this doctrine of irrelevance. As applied to progress it is essentially contradictory to separate progress from conservation—to say, for instance, that progress has taken place but come to an end. Whenever we say there *has been* progress, we always mean there *is* progress. If it stopped it would not be progress. That is, the stop, the end, in any ultimate metaphysical sense, changes the entire perspective in which the process is viewed. Permanence is a necessary mode in which to express value. Value is not "what it is" without the implication of eternity which by its very nature it seeks.

VIII

Neither an effort such as that of Ostwald, to show the compatibility of the law of dissipation with the law of value, nor, again, such an attempt as that of James, to show their irrelevance, has proved wholly satisfactory. Both fail at the crucial point. Both fall short of the demands made by the

[1] *Letters of William James*, vol. ii.

"essentials of value." The first attempts unsuccessfully to identify conservation with irreversibility; the other denies the necessity of conservation of value altogether.

There is, however, still another attitude, still another solution of the problem, that merits our consideration. For a philosophy that knows its business, Bosanquet maintains, the law of dissipation makes no difference.[1] On the premises of James's philosophy such a statement could, perhaps, be taken as little more than an eloquent gesture. But there is an interpretation of it which may conceivably be a great deal more. It might mean that ultimately time, and the time process, is irrelevant to value, because value can neither come into being nor pass out of being; that terminus as understood in the law of dissipation can have no application either to value or to being in any ultimate sense. This position is one which I believe to be not only intelligible and true in itself, but one that is implied in principle in all traditional thought. But let us first see what it is for philosophy to know its business in this connection.

To know one's business in philosophy is, first of all, to know the objective of philosophy—to know that its central problem is that of the relation of value to existence or reality. To know one's business in this special connection is to know what the essentials of value really are, and to know what are the real significance and implication of the laws of existence. As stated at the beginning of this chapter, our problem is twofold—to examine the law of entropy itself, its validity and its implications; and, secondly, to examine the relations of the essentials of value, on which finality and progress rest, to this "cosmic" law.

For Bosanquet, to know one's business here means first of all properly to interpret the essentials of value, to know what it is that the postulates of value really are and imply. For him, as we have seen, this means that we must give up entirely the notion that the ideal belongs to the future, and abandon all notion of the coincidence of termination and end.[2] If this interpretation of value were accepted, it is obvious that the law of dissipation would make no difference. For that in the law which does make a difference is precisely the idea of

[1] *The Value and Destiny of the Individual*, p. 320.   [2] Chapter X, p. 361.

a terminus; and if ends, and the values which ends presuppose, have nothing to do with temporal end, obviously irrelevance is the necessary conclusion. But a complete dissociation of terminus and end we found impossible. Not only must the purpose of our earthly life be realized if that life is to be intelligible, but there must be a *time* in which it shall be accomplished. We cannot abandon all notion of the connection of terminus and end and continue to speak an intelligible teleological language. But it is quite possible that further reflection may affect vitally our notion of the nature of this relevance.

The law of dissipation does set a terminus, but it is all-important to understand just what this terminus means—and of what it is the terminus. It is said to be "the vital and physical extinction of the universe" that this law contemplates. I think it may be said without hesitation that it contemplates nothing of the sort. The process of dissipation, devolution, can no more be applied to the universe than the process of evolution—and for the same general reasons. The law, therefore, does set a terminus, but to a particular process in the universe, not to the universe itself.

In developing this point we must first of all recall that *our* world is not identical with the *whole* world. The presumption that the life and motion of our world system will come to an end at some time or other does not justify us in believing that the life and motion of the countless world systems that make up the sum of existence will come to an end with it. For all we know, the action and reaction between the different world systems, which are probably at different stages of development, may draw a world whose motion has come to an end into the evolutionary processes of the rest of existence. But it really does not tell us that physical and vital extinction *of our own world* is its necessary doom. It does, indeed, tell us that changes that are visible and heterogeneous will be more and more diluted into changes that are invisible and homogeneous (provided always the assumptions on which the inference is made are valid), and it draws the conclusions that the instability to which we owe the richness and variety of changes taking place in our world will gradually give way to relative stability of elementary vibration continually and perpetually repeated.

But even this idea rests, as we have seen, on the dogmatic acceptance of certain assumptions that are by no means necessary. Even if this were not so, as regards the relation of life and mind to these processes, we have precisely the same problem here as in the case of the concept of evolution. As in the case of evolution, there is a sense in which life and mind do emerge and a sense in which they do not, so in the case of devolution there is a sense in which they may disappear and a sense in which they do not. So far, therefore, as the dilemma presented to us at the beginning of our study is concerned, we may say without hesitation that it is not cogent. We are not compelled either to extend the principle of degradation to life and mind, or to go over frankly to irrationalism and mysticism. It is part of reason itself to recognize the limited and provincial character of its own conceptions. For my own part, I have no objection to going over to mysticism, or trenching on the mystical when it is necessary, but this is not one of the places where it is necessary.

To pretend, therefore, to speak for the universe in terms of narrow and abstract predictions of physics and astronomy is, indeed, "to betray a bias of mind that is provincial." We may even go so far as to say that, although we may use the symbolism of the degradation of energy, we must not take it too seriously and degrade the world system as well. This world system does not begin with mere motions of mass particles and it does not end with heat—that is, movements distributed in a uniform way among such particles. All this I am myself ready to say. But I do not wish to base my argument solely upon this limitation of science and its method. I wish to strike a much deeper level of thought—that of philosophical intelligibility. On this level the whole idea of extinction of the universe is meaningless.

The "universe," we have repeatedly seen, cannot be spoken of intelligibly without including in it more than the actual. The identification of being with that which becomes, with processes of evolution or devolution, is impossible. The only subjects of temporal evolution or devolution are the concrete objects, organisms, individuals within the world—not the world or universe itself. As there is no evolution of being, so there is no devolution. Quite generally expressed, it is only to empirical individuals or forms that either of these concepts applies.

Thus the individual may conceivably perish—whatever "perish" may mean—but the species does not, in the same sense. The single species may pass away, but life, as a succession of individual organisms and species, does not. Life may, perhaps, become extinct in parts of the universe, but that of which life is the phenomenal expression, matter, energy, whatever we may choose to call it, does not. Finally, it is even conceivable that matter or energy, as special forms of being, may "pass away" (our assumption that they do not is simply an assumption for special purposes and based upon a special and limited field of experience), but being, of which they are manifestations, does not pass away and cannot. At least, our way of thinking, our forms of thought, permit nothing else. We can, I suppose, very well contemplate the idea that there should not have been any world at all—at least, there are those who claim to be able to do so. But if being is once given we can conceive its disappearance into nothing as little as its coming from nothing. We may speak of God as creating the world out of nothing, or, what is the same idea in a modern atheistic form, of the world creating itself gradually, but it is difficult to give these phrases any intelligible meaning. However poetically suggestive such concepts may be, they are absolutely impenetrable to our thought. *And no less so is the idea of being passing into nothing.* No finite determination of being can put a limit to our thinking. But if being is once assumed, then the fact that we describe by the abstract concept, being, must, for all clear thinking (at least for our thinking), inevitably be underivable and indestructible.

"There is," as Simmel says, "no such thing as entropy of being." But there is also, if the relation of value to being is properly understood, no such thing as entropy of value. Everything turns here on this relation, on the inseparability of the two for thought. Judgments of evolution and devolution themselves are impossible without evaluation, and the values acknowledged in such judgments are themselves not subject to these judgments. Otherwise expressed, the very values in terms of which we condemn the world as a meaningless alteration of processes of life and death, of evolution and decay, are themselves in the universe—are part of being. Our position here is, of course, that of Hegel put in a different form. Abstract being, being abstracted from all determinations, is equal to nothing. But all determinations and distinctions within being presuppose acknowledgment of value. Being and value are inseparable.

This line of thought is not only true in itself as axiological or metaphysical thinking; it is also, as I believe, the essence of traditional thought in these matters. The system of values in terms of which we judge evolution and progress cannot itself evolve. The system in terms of which we judge devolution cannot itself be subject to devolution. True enough, it will be said, *but these are not the values with which we are here concerned.* It is rather with the values that "emerge," that are "acquired" in time, with value defined as adaptation, with value as conditioned by organic life and experience. The fact that there is no entropy of being, no entropy of value in any ultimate sense, does not exclude the element of terminus to the time processes in which values are acquired and realized. This termination of time processes within the universe is significant for valuation and the "life of values," and it is this significance that we must determine. Terminus in this sense is *not* irrelevant to values.

This is doubtless true, and it is, in fact, precisely this relevance that I have insisted upon in our discussions of finality. Not only must the purpose of our earthly life be accomplished in some sense if there is to be intelligible teleology, but there must be a time in which it is accomplished. And if terminus is significant in this sense it must also be significant and relevant when it means an end in a dysteleological sense—when, in other words, it means the termination of a life process, of individuals, of societies, perhaps even of worlds.

Now, as a matter of fact terminus in this latter sense has always been conceived of as relevant and significant. In the case of the individual life terminus or death has always been felt to be part of the life form of values itself. This is true of the individual life. It is conceivable also that it is true of value movements of the historical process—of world movements. Rise and decline of civilizations, development and decay of worlds, may conceivably be as necessary for the significance of individual civilizations and worlds as birth and death for the individual life.

In developing this point I wish to recall again the fact that the sole metaphysical element in the law of dissipation (that alone which philosophy must take account of, the rest being abstract and symbolic) is the element of irreversible process and termination of the process, that element which we describe concretely as decay or death, and which we recognize when we describe the law of dissipation in such picturesque terms as "our dying world." From this point of view, and for axiological or metaphysical reflection, our problem is nothing more nor less than a cosmic application of the significance of death.

Now, nothing is more certain here than that "physical" death of the individual functions thus as a condition of realization of significance. It is precisely because of the span of life allotted to us that a life plan has any significance. Without it, life itself would fall apart into meaningless repetition, exfoliation of process. The terminus in time may, in fact, enhance the value of life because the death of the bearer of value may conduce to the perpetuation of the value. We do not consider Socrates' life a failure because he was compelled to drink the hemlock. Quite the contrary. The termination of his life in time becomes rather a symbol of unity of significance, and that unity is not possible without the termination.

It was in connection with the phenomena of individual death that the classical thinkers did their axiological thinking. It is not at all impossible that the same line of thought may, *mutatis mutandis*, be significant for what is called "cosmic death." In the case of the former the significant thing has always been that death is part of the form of life itself. The very meaning of life is determined by the limit set by death; the perspective of ends and values is determined by it. The notion of death determines our life--not first in the hour of death itself, but throughout the whole of life. Our evaluation of life depends upon our evaluation of death.

The technical way of stating this has always been, from Plato to Hegel, the dialectic. Death cannot be thought without life nor life without death. They are but terms in a higher synthesis, in a deeper conception of life. Death is a negation. But it is not pure nothingness. Were it so, it would be entirely devoid of sense. On the contrary, it is pregnant with meaning. It is, as we have said, a necessary part of the form of life. Let us now consider the affirmation of life. Can we conceive life without conceiving its negation? It is impossible. Life in any significant sense includes its opposite, and the two phenomenal categories of life and death are moments in a larger life.

From this has been inferred the "endlessness" of life and the "immortality of the soul." Whether such inferences follow depends obviously upon what meaning we read into these terms. The endlessness of biological life is not proved by such an argument. The temporal immortality of the soul of man— that is, its eternal survival after death—is also in no way guaranteed. But then it is also true that such assumptions or hypotheses as these would contribute little to the solution of the axiological problem with which we are here concerned. The mere endlessness of biological life would be no guarantee either of the realization or of the conservation of values.

The mere fact that mind or soul survived bodily death eternally, or a series of bodily deaths, would by itself not necessarily mean increase of significance of life. This the more profound thought of East and West alike has always seen. But immortality—the endless life—has always been recognized as a symbol for the conservation of value; it is in this sense, and in this sense only, that immortality may be said to be either a universal or a necessary postulate of morals, or, more generally, of values. Intelligible life must of necessity be a conception of life the form of which contains death as one of its moments.

Termination, in the sense of death, is a symbol of the unity of significance of life. There is no reason why similar lines of thought should not hold for the larger time processes of history, or, indeed, of the cosmos itself. There is no reason to suppose that termination of such processes may not be as much the condition of their significance as in the case of the individual life span.

As a matter of fact, the argument is all the other way. It

seems rather more than probable that one of the conditions of the cultural values of a people being conserved in unity of significance is that that culture should have come to a temporal end. The "death" of Greek culture is the condition of its immortality. Of cultures no less than of individuals it may be truly said, "Call no one happy until he is dead."

IX

The real significance of these reflections lies in the consideration of the consequences that flow from the complete identification of being with becoming. The incoherence and contradictions in the attitudes of both Ostwald and James arise from this identification, and with it the assumption of the irreversible character of time and reality. On such a view "conservation" must either be identified with irreversibility or its necessity denied altogether.

In both theories it is assumed, not only that time is necessarily irreversible, but that the essence of value demands that it shall be irreversible. Into the first assumption I do not propose to go at any length. It is the second assumption that we are particularly concerned with here. For my own part, I have never been convinced that it is in the nature of time to be irreversible. If the time we have been regarding as cosmic is really the local time that in some modern theories it is—"a time bound up with the motion of the earth, with as little claim to universality as that of a ship that does not alter its clocks in crossing the Atlantic"—then our outlook on this question would be greatly changed. If the time order is arbitrary, then there will be progress or regress, according to the convention adopted in measuring time. The reversible character of time would be a natural conception. But our problem is quite other. It is rather the question *whether value is compatible with this reversible process.*

The cinema has made us familiar with reversible processes. We can no longer say that they are either impossible or unimaginable. But no amount of familiarity can apparently do away with the irrationality or absurdity of the reversed process. Movement of the flower back to the seed, the reversal of the processes of diving or of eating, are apprehensible but not intelligible. The topsy-turvy world to which these processes introduce us is a world of nonsense and as such unreal.

Further reflection on these processes makes it clear that it is only of life processes, and practical actions connected with the life processes, of which this is true. In the inorganic world of physical and chemical processes, reversible series are not only familiar but intelligible. Now, time is just as real in the one process as in the other—in the sense that "it takes time" in both cases. It is in this sense just as real in the reversed process of diving as in the normal process. The reversed process is felt to be unreal, but it is unreal because it is unintelligible. The proposition that time, to be real, must be irreversible, resolves itself, I think, into the proposition that to be *meaningful, intelligible*, it must be irreversible. In other words, reversible process and value process are thought to be incompatible. All intrinsic intelligibility goes back to the "essentials of value" as such, and to will oriented towards value—and this essential is irreversibility.

With this we have come back to a reconsideration of the thesis of Ostwald, that irreversibility is the fundamental law of all valuation and values. I am inclined to believe that this is true within limits, but only within limits. We have, for instance, what may be called "value circles." The egg is there for the sake of the chicken, but the chicken also for the sake of the egg; the individual for the species or race, but also the race for the individual. Ethics is valuable for its relation to religion, but also *vice versa*; life for culture, and culture for life. This *circular* character of so much of teleological thinking seems to suggest at least that valuation is not wholly a one-direction process.

It is assumed, I say, that the reversible process is wholly incompatible with value. And yet I am not quite sure that this is so. There are certain laws of the "spirit," of the world of values and their realization, which on this assumption are, to say the least, mysterious. I refer to the necessities of unlearning as well as of learning. We are told, for instance, that we must become again as little children. And we naturally ask with Nicodemus, "Can a man enter again a second time into his mother's womb and be born?" Can the processes of time be turned back? It is not at all clear, however, that reversal of process may not be a part of realization of value. Certainly for all those philosophies in which significance is realized through freeing from the phenomenal, part of that realization must be through the process of unlearning.

There is, then, no intrinsic reason why value and reversible process may not be compatible. On the other hand, reversibility of process seems in some sense and to some degree actually demanded by the principle of conservation of value. It is quite common to say, in those philosophies that completely identify being with becoming, that the past is conserved by being taken up and absorbed by the future. But if change is the ultimate fact, the past is largely dropped out. Let the dead past bury its dead may be, within limits, a good motto for practice, but it is a very bad one for general theory. Unless we are the dupes of the illusion that whatever comes next must be better, it is precisely the temporally "past" that often has the greatest value and the deepest "reality." Novelty in art, for instance, it has been wisely said, is essentially the element of surprise, the essential function of which is "to startle us into a new sense of the world about us and to give us a glimpse of the world of reality underlying the world of appearance." But such novelty is novelty in the world of appearance, and its function is often really to start us on a reverse process into the past, by which we recover a deeper reality which always persists, but which we have for the time lost.

It is always possible to say, and with a certain justification, that such apparent reversal of values is *only* apparent. Reaction in history, for instance, is not a real going back, for what results is really a new synthesis of the old and the new, and both processes are but moments in one onward, irreversible movement. None the less, it behoves us to go slowly in asserting the incompatibility of value with the reversible process. It was, to be sure, one of Nietzsche's chief contentions that they are compatible, that valuation is not inconsistent even with the doctrine of eternal recurrence. It seems to many minds a paradoxical—and even a hysterical—idea that our willingness to have our deeds return again, far from being the essence of futility, is rather the ultimate criterion of value.

But deeper reflection seems to suggest that it is simply a way of saying that time is ultimately irrelevant to value. Now, I would not be misunderstood here. This is in no sense an argument for the irreversible character of time. That is a problem for itself, which I feel neither the obligation nor the competence to handle. My only object here is to contest the necessary relation which many think to exist between value and the irreversible process. As but a phase of the complete identification of being with becoming it is subject to the same difficulties and the same doubts.

X

The problem of human destiny, we said at the beginning, has again entered into the foreground of interest and reflection in the form of a magnificent dysteleology—the second law of thermodynamics. Our interest in this conception of destiny is twofold. On the one hand, there is the fact that the problem of destiny is inevitable in one form or another, and, secondly, the particular form which the modern conception takes. Thought inevitably reaches out before and after—to the beginning and end of all things. This reaching out towards the "last things" brings the modern man to the New *Götterdämmerung*.

But this movement of thought—to last things no less than to first things—has a double meaning, at once temporal and axiological or logical. It was one of our chief objects to distinguish these two problems. We are, it has been said, faced with a dilemma. Either we must make this law, with its dysteleology, absolute, or hand over life, mind, and values to the irrational and mystical. Now, I have no objections to the mystical as such, but only to its connection with the irrational. The outcome of this entire study is to deny the cogency of this dilemma. The conclusions of our axiological reflections are, for us, precisely the essence of reason.

It would be easy for the casual reader to identify these conclusions with the well-known "belief in the conservation of values" as formulated by Höffding. But that would be to miss my entire point. For it is precisely my contention that it is not merely a belief but an axiological necessity. In his *Philosophy of Religion* Höffding does, indeed, consider this belief and its relation to scientific facts and laws. He canvasses the whole field of scientific hypothesis, and comes to the conclusion that there is nothing in the latter to forbid the former. He considers, of course, the problem presented by the law of dissipation, and his conclusions here do not differ in principle from ours, or, indeed, from those of any but the most uncritical views of scientific law. But ours is a metaphysical statement of the problem, and as such has sought a metaphysical solution.

Our statement has had, above all, the heuristic significance of making transparent the structure (the *a priori* structure, if you will) of value and being in their necessary relations. We may, indeed, have a *belief* in the conservation of particular values—in immortality in the concrete sense of poet and religionist—but that belief is something different from that with which we have here been concerned. Even then, however, we must insist that these more concrete ideas and beliefs, with all their symbolic elements, have their motives and their foundations alike in the realm of that which is necessary and true.

But the conclusions of this chapter have a much wider philosophical significance than this. The discussion of this particular problem of the law of dissipation, and of the different attitudes towards it, has had the immediate interest of raising the problem of world destiny, but it has also served to focus our attention on the much more general problem of the relations of matter, life, and mind in a system of thought. The significance of this particular problem is that it raises the general cosmological problem in its most characteristic as well as its most acute form. It is precisely because the "law of dissipation" is the most metaphysical of all the laws of science—and cannot by its very nature be anything but metaphysical in its implications—that metaphysics cannot escape the problem it sets. Specifically we were concerned with the relation of history to nature, and of progress to degradation. But from a still wider point of view we are concerned with the question of the systematic relation of the principal philosophical concepts, and ultimately, therefore, with the system of reality.

The metaphysical position as such has been well defined as that of the absolute relevance of all questions. Questions that are wholly irrelevant for particular sciences cannot be so from this wider point of view. Certain scientific conclusions — such as the character of organic evolution, the view that the heavens are older than life and mind, the probable extinction of organic existence on this planet "in a few brief million years"—may, it is said, profoundly affect the philosophy of values. It is difficult to see how they can fail to affect such a philosophy in some way. The problem is to see just how they affect it. On the other hand, it is equally true that certain conclusions as to the essentials of value and of the relation of value to being may affect vitally our interpretation of scientific principles. If we accept at all the principle that existence and value cannot be ultimately separated without contradiction, or, in other terms, the "value character of the theoretical," it is difficult to see how it can be otherwise. The principle of absolute relevance of all questions follows from the relation of value to reality that we have been maintaining throughout. The principle of absolute relevance contains in it, moreover, the principle of necessary system in philosophy. The problem of system may be stated in still another way. We have been concerned throughout with the *conditions* and the *form* of philosophical intelligibility. We have studied in detail the elements or moments in this form— origin and destiny—together with the notions of cause, purpose, progress and regress, and in general with the question of the relation of values to time; in short, the entire value-charged scheme of thought as it functions in traditional philosophy. It is in attempting to bring these elements together that the essentials of philosophical system appear. To the examination of these essentials, therefore, we must now turn in the concluding chapter.

CHAPTER XIII

HEADLINING THE UNIVERSE: THE SYSTEM
OF PHILOSOPHY

They are called wise who put things in their right order and control them well.
St. Thomas

Lord, who are we to catalogue living!
From a Modern Poem

I

"I am not narrow enough for a system, not even my own system." In these characteristic words Nietzsche has embodied the whole tragical paradox of human thought. In the same breath that he cries out against the limitations of system-making he admits its inevitableness.

The revolt against order in life and thought is, perhaps, the deepest note of modernism; the longing for systemlessness the deepest passion of a world weary of mechanism. With Nietzsche men have come to distrust all system-builders, to conjecture that "they are descended from registrars and office secretaries whose whole business is to label things and put them in pigeon-holes." To build systems—is not that to leave out the best that exists? Is not actually the part of reality where we least succeed with our systems the part that is highest with us? Logic and mechanic are always applicable only to the superficial. "He is a thinker? Does that not mean merely that he understands how to take things more simply than they are?"

From this widespread distrust of all systematic thought few of us moderns can wholly escape. It is reinforced by all that is called "vital and original" in the art, the science, the politics, and the philosophy of the day. Sensitive, as never before perhaps, to the individual impression, to the inexhaustible wealth of transitions and half-lights in existence, we cry out with the poet, "Lord, who are we to catalogue living!" In short, vicious abstractionism is the one horror of the modern world. We are all more or less like the journalist in *The Professor's Progress.* It was only, he complains, as a cub reporter in the police courts that he was really in touch with life. The more he came to "headlining the universe" the farther from reality he got.

For the great systems of traditional philosophy we moderns have, accordingly, very little sense. For these, as for any system indeed, we feel ourselves not narrow enough. But few of us have also the saving grace to add with Nietzsche, "not even for my own system." For few have either sufficient humour or sufficient irony to understand that even in our very systemlessness we have taken up a systematic attitude towards reality and life, that in our very denial of system we affirm it.

"Life as it merely occurs is senseless," as Mr. Shaw says. If we wish to put any sense into it we shall make our own systems, even if it be merely that of the professional adventurer who makes out of the very systemlessness of his life a life system. Not otherwise is it with the spirit of adventure in philosophy, when it revels in the open doors of the future, when it finds more meaning in the parts than in the whole. These so-called "life philosophies" are either senseless or they also become systematic.

"Where system is lacking, there philosophy is lacking also." "This," says Oswald Spengler, "is the unconscious prejudice of all professional philosophers against the intuitive thinkers to whom they feel themselves vastly superior." It is always possible to say such things. All sorts of conceptions and definitions of philosophy are abstractly possible. But there is always still the question whether they are intelligible. Even an intuitive philosophy when it seeks to communicate its intuition becomes systematic. The very idea of communicable knowledge is inseparable from the idea of system.

II

Opposition to system in modernistic philosophy no longer concerns itself with particular systems, no longer merely exploits the "strife of systems"; it turns its attack rather on the very idea of system, on the innate systematic of the intelligence as such. It seeks to dig under this inborn systematic, and thus to bring the whole framework of perennial philosophy to the ground.

The entire significance of system lies in the idea that it is necessary to make the world intelligible. But, we are told, system makes the world not more but rather less intelligible. "Nature," in the words of Goethe, "has no system; she has, she is, life and movement, from an unknown centre to a non-cognizable end." Nay more, to seek to impose such system upon nature is but to falsify it, to make it really less intelligible. Every system made is itself a product of history, and thus becomes part of historical temporal reality. As such it but adds to the variety and multiplicity of the world. Every new simplification begets a new complexity, every new rationalization another irrationality. The absolutizing of the historical categories finds its extreme consequence in the statement that every increase of rationality is accompanied necessarily by a corresponding increase of historical chaos.[1]

Now, it may be admitted that if "the ends of the world" cannot be brought together in *any* sense, there can, of course, be no system of philosophy. If life, reality, is a river without source or end, if the world process is from an unknown centre to an uncognizable goal, there can be no system. But there can also be no intelligibility. The traditional form of philosophical intelligibility is precisely this bringing together of the ideas of origin and destiny in a more fundamental conception. But it is just this, the critics of system insist, that cannot be done. It is the fundamental falsity, not to say irrationality, of the assumption of the world as a completed whole that makes system impossible. Reality is incomplete, and an incomplete reality and system are essentially incompatible ideas.

It is thus maintained that we cannot avoid a fallacy necessarily involved in the idea of an all-embracing system. Such a system could not be enlarged, for it would already contain all that there is. If it can be enlarged, it cannot be all-embracing, cannot be what it claims to be. The very notion of system has, therefore, been rendered self-contradictory and fallacious by being made all-embracing. Neither can its claim to truth be absolute so long as it is possible to subject it to

---

[1] A very clear presentation of this position is given by F. Zaniecki in his book *Cultural Reality*, chapter vi, especially p. 343.

reinterpretation. An absolute system that is not final is a self-contradiction.

In reply to this objection it is frequently said that no philosophy supposes that reality is exhaustible, or that the universe is complete, in the sense that the beginning and end of things can be grasped in any single concept. What is meant by the whole of reality is every possible form of it. In other words, we may know the whole in its essential structure without knowing it in details or without predicting the future. To admit novelties in the universe one does not need to suppose such a t.ing as a novelty in kind. "All the sorts of being that reality presents may well be eternally present—in God's life and consciousness, or in some timeless order."

For my own part, I see nothing intrinsically unintelligible in this conception. On the other hand, as I have sought to show, it is only by assuming such a timeless order of values that intelligible interpretation and communication are possible. Incompleteness of detail is, then, no argument against system. All systems are necessarily incomplete. The objection goes deeper than this. It is that the contents of knowledge are always reacting on its fundamental principles or structure, so that "no philosophy can flatter itself that it will not be *altered out of all recognition as knowledge grows.*" The development of knowledge is not a process of adding new truths to old—nor even of developing a coherent whole of experience. It rather resembles the increase of some plastic body which, whenever it takes place, involves a readjustment of every part.

Here, obviously, the crux of the matter is to be found. If knowledge is of such a character as here described, then, indeed, it is idle to talk of system. But then it is also idle to talk of knowledge in any intelligible way. Alteration which is alteration out of all recognition is not alteration but complete self-alienation. As recognized continuity is the condition of any intelligible purpose, so acknowledged continuity is the condition of intelligible knowledge. If complete heterogeneity of ends is unintelligible in life, it is *a fortiori* so in knowledge. It is a contradiction in terms.[1]

So long, therefore, as an intelligible world is not demanded, no answer to the opponents of system is possible. But all

[1] Chapter X, pp. 349 ff.

intelligible communication, whether in the form of description, explanation, or interpretation, involves a cosmos in the sense of an ordered whole. Chaos, strictly speaking, is incommunicable.

III

System in philosophy is ordinarily connected exclusively with the intellectual side of man, with the mechanical, the geometrical, the abstract logical; wherefore the anti-intellectualist finds in it the object of his deepest scorn. This I believe is a fundamental error. Systems are, indeed, the product of thought, but of that

> fine, fiery speed of thought
> By which the ends of the world are brought
> Together. . . .

Not, indeed, "in a wish," as the poet continues, in an individual caprice, nor yet again in an "over-individual longing," but rather in an immitigable scale or system of values which, as we shall hope to see, represents the normal and fundamental way of seeing the world.

System we have maintained to be necessary for intelligibility and intelligible communication. Our conception of the nature of philosophic system reflects, therefore, the nature of philosophic intelligibility.

The term "system" is in general used to designate the orderly relation of parts within a significant whole. It differs from such terms as "aggregate" or "collection" in expressly conn ting the orderly, inherent bonds which bind together, from the standpoint of rational apprehension, explanation, or interpretation, the parts of a whole. A state of things may, indeed, in general be defined as a system only when the particular features in it are so necessarily connected that we cannot alter one without radical alteration of the others.

This general meaning will be found to apply to the most diverse uses of the concept, such as the post-office system, the credit system, the solar system, the evolutionary system, or, for instance, the system of Hegelian philosophy. System, as thus understood, differs again from mere classification in that it does not remain outside the facts as a merely mental scheme; while it differs from organism in expressly connoting that it is from the standpoint of thought that the parts are inter-dependent.

It is, however, the notion of a *significant whole* that is deter-minative. The significance of system may be practical or theoretical, its intelligibility instrumental or intrinsic. As dis-tinguished from the partial systems of practice and science, which are instrumental, philosophic system seeks intrinsic intelligibility.

The germ of system is present in merely descriptive classi-fications, although the notion of system inevitably and always connotes more than mere analysis and classification. It is the task of systematization to represent all the knowledge attained at a given time as a whole of which all the parts are connected in necessary relations. We speak of classificatory systems, and the beginning of system, whether practical, scientific, or philo-sophical, is always external description, implying, as we have seen in an earlier chapter, the mutual externality characteristic of the space-time order.[1] Yet an intelligible system, one that shall make the parts intelligible, does not stop with classi-fication. To be intelligible it must still further be explanatory.

The first element in explanatory system is the idea of purpose or end. Thus the divisions or integration of the post-office system or credit system are intelligible only as seen in the light of their purpose. The idea of system thus includes, nay, carries at its very heart, the idea of teleology. The Darwinian theory, with its concept of evolutionary system, is itself, as we have seen, the supreme proof of this conception of system. Its denial of fixed species, the very basis of purely external and descriptive systems, forces it to a basis of classification which is of necessity teleological. At first sight apparently diametrically opposed to the teleological principle, it proves in the end to be not only compatible with it, but actually to demand it. The forms about which the individuals of a species group themselves become intelligible only in terms of adaptation, utility, and survival. If we look backward from forms that have developed in this way, the whole complex of varying forms and the

[1] Chapter VII, pp. 238 ff.

struggle for existence among these forms appear inevitably as means towards the attainment of these ends. Any intelligible "system of animate nature," once the idea of fixed species is destroyed, is necessarily a teleological system.

System carries at its very heart, then, the idea of teleology. Even a mechanical system is thus teleological. For if there is a sense in which a radical finalism is a reversed mechanism, there is a no less significant sense in which a mechanism is a reversed teleology. In fact, all partial systems, whether practical or scientific, whether the post-office system or the solar system as we conceive it, are instrumental, and have merely instrumental intelligibility. All involve purposes and the acknowledgment of values which are presupposed.

But instrumental intelligibility must somewhere touch intrinsic, and it is toward the intrinsic intelligibility of philosophic system that all partial systems strive. Two characteristics of philosophic system immediately make themselves felt. In order to do justice to the manifold of reality such a system requires as many "points of view," as many "principles of selection," as are required by these purposes and values. Philosophical knowledge, in the words of Hegel, "is based on the acknowledgment of the content and form of *all* aspects of reality, the freeing of these from the one-sidedness of their forms, and the raising of them to an absolute form or system."[1]

Philosophic system must thus be all-inclusive. But it can be all-inclusive only by becoming a system of values and validities. It is not a system of entities or existences, as many suppose. For these very notions of entity or existence, as we have seen, involve some element of abstraction, and with it the ordering of reality from some partial and instrumental point of view. Every affirmation of existence is *ex parte*, in that it involves an ontological prejudice; in other words, every such affirmation of existence, whether material, organic, mental, or spiritual, takes place from a particular point of view, involves the acknowledgment of a particular order and a particular kind of validity. In the frame of this order every affirmation of existence or non-existence takes a particular place, and this place is its validity. Every such judgment involves the acknowledgment of a value which is inherently related by

[1] *Encyklopädie*, § 573, p. 478 (Kirchmann ed., 1870).

internal bonds of necessity to every other value. It is at this point that the metaphysical principle of "absolute relevance" embodies itself in the principle of philosophic system.

From whatever angle we may take up the task of philosophic interpretation, from the standpoint of fundamental distinctions within being, such as mind, matter, life, spirit; from the point of view of philosophic categories or concepts, such as origin and destiny, cause and purpose, development and progress; or, finally, from the point of view of ultimate values—in every case alike the relative importance of every element is immediately raised. We cannot change our concept of life without changing the meaning of the other concepts in the system or hierarchy in which its meaning and validity are found. We cannot change our concept of purpose or development without changing the whole system of meanings and values in which it is found. We cannot change our concept of a value, as, for instance, the æsthetic value, without changing all the other values, as Croce's theory of the æsthetic shows. Every philosophical concept is an abbreviation of system, and this fact is the deepest ground for those internal relations of concepts, categories, and values which we call philosophic system.

For this reason, then, it is true that there is scarcely a philosopher by whom an order of value has not been assumed either explicitly or implicitly. The great philosophers, it has been well said, are not primarily describers of the universe, but rather organizers of values, economists of the spirit; and, indeed, we may say without hesitation that all philosophies, except those that ultimately imply the denial of philosophy, presuppose system in this sense. We may even go so far as to say that everything depends upon system, and the scale of meanings and values connected with it. If every phenomenon has ultimately the same meaning and significance—if it is, so to say, as good as another—there can be no talk of interpretation and intelligibility. The idea of a scale of value, of an ascending series, of degrees of reality—in short, the hierarchical principle— is an essential part of intrinsic intelligibility and therefore of philosophic system.

But the ideal of philosophical intelligibility is not yet exhausted in this concept of system. We may succeed in ordering things according to some principle or scheme of classification, according to some idea or end that is realized in them, or, finally, according to an ascending series, degrees of meaning or reality, but there is still something left out without which genuine intelligibility is still to seek. The ordering of things from the point of view of types that are static, or of an end that is progressive, or an ascending series of degrees of reality, is still a *static* system. The ascending series is as motionless as the genera and species of logical classification, which simply lie side by side. Constitutions, said Carlyle, must be made to march. Of all practical systems it is demanded that they work. It is only in their movement that they become intrinsically intelligible. A philosophical system, if it is to be really interpretative, must be made to march also.

It is here that the essence of intrinsic intelligibility is finally reached. It is here, also, that a third type of thought, distinguished from the descriptive and explanatory alike, enters in—one in which we seek to understand, not merely classes and laws, but reality in its individual character; not only as a static order, but as a living, moving process. It is for this reason that, as we have seen, evolutionary philosophies seem to be the intelligible philosophies *par excellence*. It is for this reason that the postulate of progress in some sense is the necessary condition of mankind's knowledge of itself and of the communication of that knowledge in history. Evolution, with its idea of *nisus*, makes the orderly sequence of the phenomena of nature move. Progress, with its notion of destiny, makes of history a unique and individual whole. No intelligible concept of evolution is possible without the idea of system; no criterion of progress is possible which does not presuppose a scale or system of values. But no such system has intrinsic intelligibility unless it does march; and it does not march unless origin and destiny, beginning and end, are brought together in some more ultimate concept—unless the order of value and the order of existence are brought together in some concept of intelligible movement.

Thus it is that intrinsic intelligibility is found only in philosophic system, and philosophic system merges into the traditional form of philosophic intelligibility. We have, of course, a supreme example of this in Hegel's attempt at an interpretative system, to attain to a vision of the universe springing out of the unity of the *Idea* which develops itself and creates the conditions of its own progress. But this particular attempt at philosophic system is but a peculiarly ambitious expression of a motive in philosophy which is perennial. We may even say that modern evolutionism in all its forms, when it becomes interpretative, strives towards system in this sense. It is this very motive that, in a sense, underlies even the creative evolutionism of Bergson. His very attempt to show that there can be no such thing as disorder, only another kind of order— the life order—is but the inevitable homage error pays to truth. We may even go so far as to say that this notion of the Idea as system, and as including origin and end, is, however disguised, present in every intelligible concept of evolution.[1]

This, then, is the meaning of the ideal of philosophic system. It is the one form of system that has intrinsic intelligibility, that intelligibility which attaches alone to the "inherent impulse of the idea," the *nisus* of a something acting in the direction of meaning and value. Such an ideal, despite the fact that it is the only intelligible one, has, however, for most modern minds insuperable difficulties. Hegel expressed it in his famous dictum, "The true is the whole"; the whole, however, is only *"das durch seine Entwickelung sich vollendede Wesen."* But is such a conception intelligible? Can it be made intelligible? That remains to be seen. This much at least can be said at the present stage of our discussion. Unless it can be made intelligible there is no intelligible philosophic system, and ultimately no intelligible world.

IV

It is historically true that there is scarcely a philosopher, of whatever kind, by whom an order of value has not been assumed either explicitly or implicitly. Now, it is our contention, not only that the hierarchical principle is assumed in all intelligible philosophies, but that as soon as this principle is developed the order of reality tends to take on essentially the same form or structure for all. Such structure, which we shall presently describe, is above the distinctions of realism and

[1] Chapter IX, pp. 326 ff.

idealism, of naturalism and spiritualism, and thus belongs to the form of intelligibility as such, irrespective of ontological prejudices.

Such a hierarchical order is present explicitly in all idealisms. The name "idealism" is in general given to those systems which make the "spiritual content" of life chiefly or alone significant and valuable, and accordingly assume that the substance of things consists in spiritual reality. In these systems the value concept plays a determining rôle from the beginning. They start out with the assumption of a key value that determines the entire order from the beginning.

The concept of idea and the concept of end play the central rôles in the philosophies of Plato and Aristotle respectively. The idea is transcendent, but the end is immanent. The "idea," as the original of individual concepts, divides into an indefinite number of particulars which, although in themselves without order, are ultimately ordered by placing them under the supreme idea of the good. Purpose or end, on the contrary, is a universal concept, to which of themselves all the individual ends subordinate themselves. Since it is an immanental principle, these purposes are to be developed immediately out of experience. Accordingly, all appearance constitutes a hierarchy of ideals or purposes which begins with the most universal and comprehensive, and ends with the most individual. Within the latter, in the second place, there is a transition from the imperfect to the more perfect. As a consequence of this double hierarchy, from individual to universal, and from the less perfect to the more perfect, the concept of immanent purpose leads necessarily to the concept of development in which classical philosophy culminated.

This hierarchical conception, with its idea of development, is the framework of traditional thought. From this framework in its main outlines later philosophy has, on the whole, deviated little. In the philosophies of Leibniz and Hegel—to take those in which, perhaps, besides the philosophies of Aristotle and St. Thomas, men have, on the whole, found themselves most at home—we find the structural principles of system very little changed. They become, if anything, even more explicit.

According to Leibniz, our soul is the only point in the

universe at which we are able immediately, and in any genuine sense, to know reality; for all that we know of other things rests upon our presentations of them. The entire world is embraced in our ideas, and we are able to judge the nature of things only after the pattern of our own souls. The world is accordingly conceived as a kingdom of soul-like entities or monads. Moreover, the order or system of the monads—and this is the important point here—can be none other than that which we find in our own souls: a hierarchy of ideas, from the lowest to the highest degrees of meaning. On the basis of his two principles—analogy and continuity—the world is to be conceived as a series or hierarchy of innumerable *vorstellende Kräfte*. Of the hierarchical character of the Hegelian system we need not here speak. For him, as we have seen, "Nature must be regarded as a system of stages or degrees in which one necessarily proceeds out of the other—not, however, in such a way that one is necessarily produced out of the other, but in the inner idea that constitutes the ground of nature."[1]

All idealistic philosophies, then, explicitly assume an order of value, and it is out of this order that the "system" of philosophy develops. In the realistic systems, on the other hand, whether materialistic or neutral, the order of values assumed is implicit.

At first sight even an implicit assumption of an order of value seems doubtful. Is it not the very characteristic of naturalistic conceptions to consider antitheses of value popular and superficial—to reduce values to non-value terms, to look upon all forms of being as equally necessary, and therefore as equally significant? And yet the exclusion of the value moment is only apparent. Even for Spinoza an angel belongs to a higher order of being than a mouse. It is possible to deny a value order with our lips, but not with our minds. It is possible to pervert values, but some value order remains. This follows inevitably from the fact that the relation of higher and lower (in their non-spatial sense) is as much a necessary form of apprehending the world as the relations of over and under, of greater and less.[2]

It is not necessary to dwell upon the naïve way in which this appears in the cruder types of materialism—from Democritus

[1] Chapter VI, p. 224. [2] Chapter X, pp. 344–45.

to the present day. The distinction between coarser and finer kinds of atoms, between the simpler and the more complex, the homogeneous and the heterogeneous—from these all value connotation appears to be removed, but it is, in fact, merely disguised. So soon as such distinctions are used in interpretation their real character appears. It is rather the more subtle conceptions of evolutionary naturalism that interest us. These evolutionists, we have seen, are either reductionists and resolve the ethical and spiritual into the cosmic order, or, objecting to reduction, make of the mental and ethical, of life, mind, and value, more adequate and higher statements of the world process. In the latter case we have an explicit scale of values; in the former it is there implicitly. For *naturalistic* realism has succeeded in becoming a philosophy —that is, in including cultural realities in its system only by means of evolutionism and its doctrine of progress. The concept of progress can be thus used, however, as we have seen, only by bringing in surreptitiously the idea of a system of values.[1] Naturalism can become systematic only by assuming the principles of system which it ostensibly rejects.

It is, therefore, the selection of key values that determines the differences within these two great types of system, as well as in minor degrees the differences of "tonality" within the systems. But the principle of scale, the *hierarchical* principle, is always presupposed. With an amazing sureness they all fill out a certain fundamental scheme. Something draws them, drives them, along a predetermined course. It is possible to select values—even, as we have seen, to pervert them—but the principle of value order still remains. What is it that thus draws them, or drives them, along this predetermined course? It is nothing else than the need of making themselves intelligible.

There is then, as I believe, a certain structure of reality, a certain order of value, that forces itself on all speculative thinkers, entirely irrespective of their prejudices, realistic or idealistic, intellectualistic or voluntaristic, or what not. This structure, or order, is in part at least *a priori*, and tends to override those selections of key values which determine divergences

---

[1] Chapter XI, pp. 385 f.

in system. This dominating structure seems to me to be roughly as follows.[1]

It consists of many grades, of which each presupposes in some sense those lower than itself, and of which each finds its completion or development only in so far as it is "possessed" or "indwelt," also in *some sense*, by that which is above. The senses in which the higher presupposes the lower, and in which the lower grade is taken up by the higher, are differently conceived in different systems—and it is this difference that creates the fundamental oppositions of systems; but the principle of scale or grades is present in all.

Such a conception seems, at first sight, to involve an infinite regress, and to suggest, at least, an infinite progress; and these inferences have been drawn by many thinkers. Whether such inferences are, in fact, necessary, or whether there is a lowest and highest term in the scale of finite existences, are questions which may be left undetermined at this point. It is only after we have considered the relation of the order of value to the order of existence that they can be intelligibly answered. Here we are concerned with merely the structure of reality *as given*, with the distinctions within reality which must be acknowledged if there is to be intelligible communication and interpretation of reality.

From this point of view, however, there are certain broad divisions within the series, e.g. Matter, Life, Mind, Spirit. Without recognition of these divisions no intelligible philosophy can be written. From the present point of view it is indifferent what we call them: fundamental categories or empirical qualities; simple entities or complexes. The significant point is that each has sufficient *identity* in itself, or sufficient distinction from the others, to make it *integral* from the standpoint of intelligible communication: intelligibility depends upon their retention.

Exact definition of none of these terms may be possible. Rather is it characteristic of them all that they are, strictly speaking, indefinable. They are, therefore, intelligible to all, not so much because they can be accurately defined by other words and concepts as because, on the contrary, these words

---

[1] For a similar development of this "structure," see the article by Archbishop Temple, already referred to in Chapter V, p. 184.

signify fundamental concepts that make other ideas and concepts understandable.

Thus the term "matter" may be quite intelligibly taken to cover the substance, or modes of action and reaction, which are studied in the sciences of physics and chemistry. It is clear that these sciences fail to make intelligible the self-movement that is one of the characteristics of life, or the comprehension of things in space and time that is one of the characteristics of mind. But this is not all. The living organism has in its material constitution an integral character, a subtlety of co-ordination, a spontaneity of adaptation, that no knowledge of chemistry or physics would enable the spectator to anticipate. Matter itself becomes fully intelligible—reveals its full possibilities, *what it really is*, only when life supervenes upon it, when it expresses itself in life.

Similarly, life reveals what it really is only when mind supervenes upon it. No study of zoology or biology will enable one to predict the occurrence among living things of a Plato or a Shakespeare, a Beethoven or a Newton. Their employment of faculties, doubtless first used for mere survival, in the interest of ends that have nothing to do with survival, is intrinsically unintelligible where life is taken in its exclusively biological sense. Even in this sense Life is, as we have seen, understandable only when we accept its immediate and indubitable meaning —as a centre of values, values realized in the processes of growth and survival. It becomes really intelligible only when values become explicit in mind and consciousness.[1]

But now we come to the most significant point—the *key value*, so to speak, in the traditional structure of reality, in the traditional system of the intelligible world. Mind, too, *as intellect*, becomes intelligible to us, shows us what it can be and do, only when it is guided by mind as *Spirit*. Intellect, except as interpreted by this fourth level or category, only too easily appears as a mere instrument or means to life; and appears oriented towards space and matter. Yet the mere existence of science, to say nothing of art and morals, their absolute values and their absolute claims on life itself, is sufficient to refute this conception of intellect. The acknowledgment of these claims and the values to which they corre-

[1] Cf. Chapter V, p. 199.

spond, is the condition of a large part of mind being intelligible to us at all. A naturalistic reduction may, indeed, seek to narrow mind to a purely biological and instrumental conception. All things are possible; but not all things are allowed— that is, if we wish to continue to speak intelligibly. It is, indeed, possible so to distend the meaning of any term as to include things that it is not. As it is possible so to distend the meaning of the word "selfishness" as to say that a man is self-indulgent when he wants to be burned at the stake, so it is possible to extend the instrumental concept of mind to include the values of art and religion; but we have then left all real intelligibility behind.

The terms in which traditional systems have described these levels, and the principle by which the hierarchical order is determined, are enlightening. From Aristotle, on through Leibniz and Hegel, the same idea has found expression in varying terms; for all, the essence of reality has been activity, movement—for all "the more immanent this activity, the higher the life," the more developed the reality. The key value, in other words, is the immanent activity of Spirit—that intrinsic intelligibility of intellect directed towards the good or value. The lower levels are determined by defect or negation. From "lifeless" matter, through the plant and animal life, the practical intelligence of man, to the level of spirit itself, we have a progression from external motion to immanent activity, from potentiality to actuality. It is in such terms, and such terms alone, I have contended, that the meanings of reality can be described and communicated. It is the development of this language that gives rise to the "inborn" order and systematic of the human mind.

V

The increasing acknowledgment of this hierarchical character of reality—the presence of the concept of "metaphysical levels" in recent philosophical thought—has raised again the entire problem of philosophical system, its nature and principles, and is bound to constitute the preoccupation of much of our thinking in the immediate future. And, indeed, the presence of such levels raises questions that take us into the very heart of philosophical system. Reality so presents itself. But why does it so present itself? If it so presents itself, how must these levels be related if the structure itself is to be intelligible? It is in the answer to these two questions that the greatest divergence of modern from traditional thought appears.

In a certain sense, indeed, this structure may be said to be *a priori*, if we take pains to remember just what *a priori* means. That the principle of scale itself is *a priori* we have already seen—in the sense that "it is true, no matter what." Transvaluation of values may be possible indefinitely, but such transvaluation leaves the principle of order or scale untouched. Reality, as we live and know it, is our reality only as the stuff of experience is "formed" by this principle of value. We orient ourselves in the world by relations of over and under, right and left, before and after, etc., but no less necessarily by relations of higher and lower, better and worse, etc.[1] These levels, so the latest philosophies run, are empirical qualities which can be arranged in an order of complexity and development. In a sense, of course, this is true, but the principle of hierarchical order, of levels, is "innate" in intelligibility and intelligible communication *as such*.

The doctrine of levels again implies degrees—of higher and lower; and the entire question of an intelligible interpretation of this structure turns on this question of degrees. It is at this point that the divergence in systems and systematic thought is, perhaps, most pronounced. On one view, the traditional view, these degrees represent degrees of value and reality. On the other view, that of modern realism and certain forms of the new idealism, they do not represent more and less of reality and value, but merely degrees of complexity. This separation of the "order of value" from the "order of existence and perfection," to use Professor Alexander's terms, is, like the separation of value and reality in general, the crucial point of divergence of modernism from traditional thought.

The acknowledgment of higher and lower levels is common to all philosophies; "but we must ask," says Lloyd Morgan, who in general represents the point of view we are examining, "higher and lower in what sense? They may be higher and lower in more senses than one. What I here mean, however, as that on which the pyramidal conception of levels is in a large sense founded, is higher and lower in a special sense." This special sense, it becomes clear from many passages, is one which seeks to avoid the implications of greater reality and greater value, traditionally associated with the idea of higher. "When two or more kinds of events . . . coexist in one system," he writes, "in such wise that the C kind involves the coexistence of B, and B in like manner involves A, whereas the A kind does not involve the coexistence of B, nor B that of C, we may speak of C as in this sense higher than B, and B than A." Illustrations given are of conscious events which involve physiological events and physiological events which involve physico-chemical events.[1]

In this sense of the word "higher" two things are to be noted. Firstly, it differs from higher and lower in the value sense, in that the involvement here contemplated is a one-way involvement. B involves A, but A does not involve B. It is, however, characteristic of the higher and lower, in the value sense, that not only does the higher involve the lower, but the lower involves the higher also. Both are parts of the value scale which is non-temporal, the one being as necessary to the other as the other is to it. In the second place, such a conception eliminates the element of potentiality which, as we have seen, is inevitable when value and existence are inseparable.[2] Potentiality is a concept that faces both ways, forward and backward, because value, with which it is connected, faces both ways. Not only does each grade involve or presuppose those "lower" than itself, but each finds its completion and development only in so far as it is possessed or indwelt by that which is above.

It is, then, in this interpretation of higher and lower, of grades of being, that the modern conception differs so vitally from that of tradition—in this separation of the order of perfection and existence from the order of value. So much depends upon this question for our entire conception of philosophical system that the justification of this separation must be examined with the greatest care.

---

[1] *Emergent Evolution*, p. 15.
[2] Chapter VIII, pp. 279 ff. Also Chapter IX, p. 308.

Now, as a mere historic fact there has been scarcely a philosopher by whom an order of value has not been maintained either explicitly or implicitly, and for whom, we may even say, the concept of degrees of reality has not been a "metaphysical necessity." The compulsion to put things in their right order is inviolable. Not even the modern thinker can wholly escape this ancient compulsion; but he can, and does, attempt to divorce this order from the idea of the "good" or value, with which traditional thought has invariably connected it.

This separation of value and perfection is expressed most consciously and explicitly, perhaps, by Alexander, although it is, of course, implicit in all modern naturalism. It is impossible, we have seen, even for a purely naturalistic philosophy to make itself intelligible without orders of being and degrees of perfection or development; but it is conceivably possible to cut loose from the traditional identification of degrees of perfection with degrees of reality and degrees of value. This Alexander attempts to do.

Thus, recognizing the grades of being, matter, life, mind, and values (spirit), as "having a relative self-identity, and as related to each other in a systematic fashion," yet they do not, he holds, "represent degrees either of reality or value." "Life," he says, "is not more real than matter, but a fuller kind of reality," whatever that may mean. "Values acquire a fuller reality, but no greater reality." The full import of the position, as well as of the meaning of the distinction between perfection and value, appears in his statement that Deity belongs to the order of perfection and not to that of value. "Value," he tells us, "is contrasted with unvalue, goodness with evil. But perfection is a notion based upon the empirical fact that there are various types of good life, comparable to the various types of successful animals or plants which can be arranged in their order of complexity of development."[1]

The motives lying back of this attempt to separate "perfection" and "value" seem to be two. On the one hand, critics of traditional thought profess to find certain internal difficulties in the concept of an "order of value" itself, a certain meaninglessness in the very notion. On the other hand, certain

[1] *Space, Time and Deity*, 1920, vol. ii, chapter ix, section F. Also p. 410.

discrepancies between the world of existence and the world of values prevent, it is said, any identification of value and perfection. The latter is the more important reason, but the first is by no means to be neglected, for it underlies much of modern thinking, and involves one of the most fundamental problems of the theory of value.

I confess that I have never quite understood the point of this criticism of the concept of an "order of value." It seems to turn, however, on the idea that the predicates "higher" and "lower" (which are applicable to the order of being) are not applicable to the order of value in the sense of the "good." For what do we mean, it is asked, when we say that A is a higher good than B? What is the standard of comparison? It is not goodness, for by hypothesis both A and B are good. "To be good is to be good," as Alexander says. "There are no degrees of good." He concludes, then, "that no sense can be attached to the conception of an order of values so long as such conception involves the applicability of the terms 'higher' and 'lower,' 'better' and 'worse.'" I repeat that I do not really understand this, but so far as I do, it seems to be merely a consequence of that conception of value as a quality which we have already found untenable. To be good is to be good; as a quality *it is what it is*. To introduce the ideas of "better" and "worse" introduces the idea of "ought to be" and "ought not to be"—which, as we have seen, is incompatible with the idea of value as a quality. The fallacy in analysis of value here involved has, however, already been disclosed.[1]

On the other hand, to speak of an order of perfection which is not an order of value is for me absolutely meaningless. I am unable to conceive of a perfection which is not of goodness in some sense. To say that perfection is a notion based on the empirical fact that there are various types of existence that can be arranged in their order of complexity or development, is not only to give an untrue account of the origin of the conception, but involves also the begging of the question implied in all attempts to define value in terms of development— that *petitio principii* on which all modernistic notions of progress are based, and which leads to the unintelligibility to which they are all condemned.[2] It does not follow, of course, that

[1] Chapter IV, pp. 142 ff.   [2] Chapter IV, p. 137.

because perfection is inseparable from goodness in some sense, goodness in the metaphysical sense is to be identified exclusively with moral goodness. That "moral goodness or perfection is not to be confounded with metaphysical perfection or greatness," to make use of Leibniz's words, is not only the essence of traditional thought, but is also clear to anyone who is not still under the prejudice that identifies value exclusively with the a-logical values.

The separation of the idea of perfection from that of value is impossible because it is unintelligible. In other words, if we separate them there is no justification for the retention of the hierarchical or pyramidal structure of reality. The concepts of "higher" and "lower," as used in the "special sense" of evolutionary naturalism, are "weasel words" that have had all the meaning taken out of them. But perhaps this is precisely what this naturalism proposes to do—to use perfection in a wholly "*denatured*" sense, as a synonym for mere complexity. To use it in its natural sense involves, it is held, insuperable difficulties arising out of certain discrepancies between the order of value and the order of existence.

This second point is the well-known argument against the notion of degrees of reality. Perfection, we are told, belongs to the order of existence or reality. But the idea that one part of existence can have more reality than another can have no meaning because the notion of degrees of reality has meaning only if we connect the order of existence or reality with that of value, and against such relation there are reasons that are prohibitive. Value, we are told, is contrasted with unvalue, goodness with evil. The notion of perfection, on the other hand, is a notion based upon empirical facts which do not involve this contrast, but rather merely an order of complexity of development. In other words, in the order of existence there is no unvalue, there are no minus signs.

One way of stating this is that, while the existential standard is monistic, the value standard is dualistic. In the existential scheme "the lowest rung of the ladder" may be occupied by that which is almost "naught," but in the scale of values we have, as in our thermometers, to register temperatures far below the freezing-point. There are some happenings, as there are some existences, of which it must be said that it is better that they should not have come into existence at all. It is this difference which, above all others, makes it difficult to bring the scale of being into relation to the scale of value. For from the point of view of being such statements are nonsense.

To bring the "existential" scheme into correspondence with the "value" scheme has been one of the most constant efforts of metaphysics. This correspondence may conceivably be "forced," we are told, in one of two ways. One way is by making matter, the lowest grade of the existential order, an entity with negative characteristics and values, and then we have a metaphysical dualism; or we may retain the monistic conception of existence, and force our value judgments to conform to it by holding that evil is only a defect of goodness, the appearance of positive evil being valid only within the limited sphere of moral activity. According to this view the minus signs disappear when we contemplate the moral world under the form of eternity. Both of these solutions of the problem have had their exponents in traditional thought. It is, however, the conflict of the two motives that, as we shall see, has created the chief problems of philosophic system.

These difficulties—of bringing the order of value into relation with the order of existence—are obviously but a special case of the difficulties which attend the general problem of the relation of value to existence. The same duality of value and existence, the inalienable difference between the "ought" and the "is," which is the indispensable condition of volition, seems here to forbid that monism which makes the negative but appearance. On the other hand, the order of value is no stranger to the order of existence, and the same abstraction of value from existence that required us to think of value as an addendum has as its consequence here the demand that we shall unite in an external and arbitrary manner two orders which seem contradictory in their essence and structure.

One thing, at least, we may say, I think, without hesitation. The two orders of existence and value are so deeply involved in the constitution of our thought that it is impossible to separate them. The perceptual object, the æsthetic object, the historical happening—what are these objects when the value element is abstracted? Things do not need to be beautiful and good in order to "exist" in the narrow sense of the word employed by science, but things do have to be in the relations of value as well as in other kinds of relations to be things in the sense of concrete experience and intelligible discourse. It is, as we have repeatedly seen, practically impossible to confine ourselves to the purely existential aspect of the world: it is theoretically impossible also. This is the general standpoint from which our present problem must be approached. The peculiar difficulty—that which leads so much of modern thought to separate "perfection" from "value"—is that created by the minus signs in the order of value. It is necessary to consider the meaning of negation, or of the negative, in the two orders.

Now, strictly speaking, there is in existence neither positive nor negative. We speak of negative numbers, negative quantities, negative electricity, but negative here has a special meaning; it refers to a distinction among existences. Negative quantities and negative electricity are as much positive entities as positive numbers and positive electricity. In other words, existence or being as such does not allow itself to be divided into positive and negative. The negative of existence is non-existence, of being, non-being. But there is another meaning of negation, one which is often overlooked, but which has a special significance for metaphysical discourse and metaphysical system, and that is its *value* connotation.

We have already had occasion to consider this rôle of negation in metaphysical discourse.[1] It is now necessary to carry our study a step farther. Ordinary pragmatic discourse constantly makes use of these two meanings of negation. Let us, for example, take the words "human" and "inhuman," "natural" and "unnatural." Evidently the negatives here have two meanings. They can designate purely existential concepts, in which case inhuman is equivalent to non-human and unnatural to non-natural. In these cases the terms are without specific content or meaning. In the second case the use of the negative is quite different. Here the negation of human or natural gives negative values or the invalid. This second meaning can be neither apprehended nor communicated without a prior acknowledgment of a positive value of the human and the natural.

In the idiom of logic the terms "inhuman" and "unnatural" have an infinite signification when taken in the existential sense, and as such become meaningless. We may put a house in the class inhuman; the proposition is not untrue, but it is meaningless. It is only in a limited universe of discourse that negation is significant; but the boundaries of such a universe can be determined only by purpose and the acknowledgment of the values which the purpose presupposes. In sum, significant negation is, therefore, but a special case under the general principle that existence abstracted from value is meaningless. As the general question, What is the real? is futile, if being is abstracted from value, so the correlative "unreal" has no meaning except as it is distinguished from other forms of being; and this involves acknowledgment of purpose and value.

All this has a very definite bearing on our problem of the relation of the two orders of existence and value. In the first place, significant negation enters into the very formation of the concepts that mark the broad divisions or levels within the hierarchical series. It is impossible to give an intelligible meaning to matter without defining it as lacking something of the next higher level, of life, and the same holds of each of the higher levels of being. This is expressed in the fact that it is impossible that each level should reveal its full possibilities, what it really is, until the other supervenes upon it, until matter expresses itself in life, until life expresses itself in mind, and mind in that which is its possibility—namely, spirit. On the other hand, it is equally impossible to express the nature and meaning of a higher level without negation of something of the lower.

In the second place, because of these very facts of significant negation, because without it we cannot even form intelligible concepts of being, this negation expresses at once an axiological and an ontological meaning. The two orders of existence and value, we have already seen, are so deeply involved in our thought that it is impossible to separate them, and nowhere is that clearer than at this point. Of the two historic ways of "bringing together" the two orders, that which makes of matter, the lowest grade of the existential order, an entity with negative characteristics is accordingly the only one possible. By this I mean that the only ontological propositions about matter that are ultimately intelligible are also axiological propositions. All genuinely ontological propositions are axiological.[1]

From all which it follows—to return to our earlier problem—that no conception of levels of being, no hierarchical conception, can be intelligibly expressed without the idea of degrees of reality, without the concept of higher and lower in the value sense. But why not say, with Alexander and all those of his way of thinking, *fuller* reality and not *greater* reality, and thus at least save the face of those to whom to be is to be, to be real is to be real, and for whom there are ultimately no distinctions in being. For myself I must answer, first of all, that I do not understand what a fuller reality is as distinguished from a greater. But even if I did I should still have to insist that the proposition "to be real is to be real" is tautologous, and as such meaningless. If it is given any meaning, it is only by importing into the term "real," as used in the predicate, some value connotation. This involves either some *ex parte* ontological prejudice, or else some system of values and validities in which the meaning of "real" has a place. In short, "degrees of reality" is inseparable from an intelligible use of the ontological predicates.

VI

Thus the chief question at issue between traditional and modernistic systems is their divergent interpretations of the concepts of grades of being, of higher and lower. Both recognize that a hierarchical or pyramidal conception is necessary for intelligible description and interpretation of reality—it is forced upon us by the "facts" and the necessities of intelligible interpretation. The further question is how such an hierarchical conception itself may be made intelligible.

This problem appears in connection with a second question presented by the "structure" of reality, and it is at this point that the whole problem of intelligible system comes to a head.

The structure of reality as described seems to involve an infinite regress and to suggest an infinite progress, and these

[1] Chapter IV, p. 157.

inferences have been drawn by many thinkers. Indeed, it is one of the most common features of recent thinking to attempt to combine the hierarchical conception with this idea of endlessness in both directions. This, again, is one of the consequences, or in some cases one of the motives, of the attempt to separate the order of value from the order of existence, but this attempt has in this case, as in others, the same result. The idea of an infinite regress and an infinite progress makes the hierarchical or pyramidal conception unintelligible.

A pyramid without base and apex, a hierarchy without top or bottom, are obviously meaningless ideas. But why attempt to give more than a suggestive meaning to that which is obviously figure? Figurative in a certain sense these ideas are, but they are more than figure. The contradiction we here feel merely expresses one which we must also feel whenever we attempt to combine the idea of levels with the idea of infinite progress and infinite regress.

This contradiction has already appeared at a number of points, from our study of space and time straight through our examination of the problems of finality, progress, and degradation. Given the idea of a spatially or temporally endless universe, it is impossible that any one direction in the universe can be really distinguished from any other. Similarly, the concepts of purely immanent finality, of heterogeneity of ends, taken in any absolute sense, become unintelligible, for the reason that the very distinctions and degrees of value on which the conceptions of finality are built, and to which if they are to be intelligible they must be carried back, become meaningless. In other words, we may conclude that the doctrine of levels, with its hierarchical conception of reality, is incompatible with the complete identification of being with becoming. The difficulties which we became aware of in our study of the problems of origin and destiny now come to a head in the problem of philosophic system.

In an earlier connection I said, and attempted to show, that we can bring causality and finality together only by the postulation of a series of degrees, only if we postulate "a kind of metaphysical necessity in virtue of which the confronting of the all-perfect being with the zero, non-being, is equivalent to the affirmation of all the degrees of reality that measure the interval between them."[1] But it is also true that we cannot postulate the series of degrees without bringing causality and finality together in one non-temporal system. It is this latter point that I wish to emphasize here. What our contention means is briefly this. Granted that the hierarchical principle of metaphysical levels is necessary for intelligibility, and intelligible communication of the meanings of reality, then an intelligible hierarchical conception can be formed only by bringing the ideas of beginning and end together in a more ultimate concept. In other words, *an intelligible hierarchical conception of reality can be formed only within the bounds of the traditional form of philosophic intelligibility.*

Systematic interpretation of reality, such as this hierarchical or pyramidal conception of reality proposes to be, is, as Lloyd Morgan well says, "under a double restraint or requirement, that imposed by the constitutive structure of 'nature' itself, and that which is imposed by the regulative structure of the logical field as such."[2] It is this double requirement which we have sought to keep in mind in the preceding discussion.

The first requirement is the recognition that the two orders of value and being are so deeply involved that they cannot be separated—that distinctions of meaning and value are as much constitutive of "nature" as are the forms of intellect. Nature presents itself at the beginning as a series of degrees of meaning and value, and any intelligible description or interpretation of nature must presuppose their acknowledgment.

The second requirement—that imposed by the regulative structure of the logical field as such—is the demand that we also acknowledge the implications of this mutual involvement of the two orders—more particularly, a non-temporal order of value. In Lloyd Morgan's terms: "Just as at the naturalistic base of things there is involved a space-time frame, so too, as I conceive it, there is foundational in Spiritual Reality what I may perhaps call a value frame. And just as I acknowledge the space-time-event system as real quite independently of human knowledge thereof, so do I conceive the values to be real independently of the human folk who are influenced thereby. In other words, just as we do not make space-time

---

[1] Chapter VI, pp. 228 ff. [2] *Op. cit.*, p. 179.

events, though they go to our making, so too, as individual persons, we do not make values, but are made by them."[1]

Wherein, one may well ask, will this value frame, when it is thought out, differ from the degrees of reality and perfection with which traditional thought has always operated? I do not believe that it will differ in any significant way, for the constraint which here determines interpretation is precisely that which it has always been—the demand for an intelligible world, and for the intelligible communication of the meanings of that world.

VII

For those who have accepted our conception of philosophy, the great historic systems now take on a new meaning and a new form. In a sense these "little systems" have their day. They have their day, and in a sense also cease to be. They are but broken lights of *the* system of philosophy, and that, all large-minded philosophers recognize, is "more than they."

The traditional form of philosophic intelligibility, as we have described it, is at once the germ of all system in philosophy, and that to which all systems must return if they are to have intrinsic intelligibility. The concept of metaphysical levels is necessary for the intelligible communication of the meanings of existence, but the concept of levels itself can be made intelligible only by the principle of totality and system in its traditional form.

But the recognition of these facts serves only to introduce us to the last and most difficult problem of system; for over against this fundamental motive, or principle, of traditional systems there has been another conception or motive, only a little less powerful, that has constantly worked against it. This is the principle of *logical totality*, which, as we have seen, issues in a monism of being which seems to wipe out all distinctions, in a static conception of reality which makes movement and evolution impossible—in short, in a concept of system which is, in its very nature, self-contradictory.

[1] "The Philosophy of Evolution," in *Contemporary British Philosophy*, vol. i, p. 305.

For the opponents of system this is, in truth, what system in philosophy always is—the development of the logical motive. Our study of traditional systems has shown that for them this is not so. Yet it must be admitted that traditional systems have not been wholly unambiguous. They have been dominated throughout by two motives—the hierarchical, which may be described as the principle of subordination; and the logical, describable as that of co-ordination. In the two great historical types of system, the idealistic and the naturalistic, both of these two motives have been present in different degrees. In the idealistic systems, as studied in an earlier section, the hierarchical dominated, and was, indeed, the primal and essential motive of, systematization; but it was constantly crossed by the abstract logical. In the Greek systems the attempt was made to fuse the principle of a hierarchy of values with the principle of logical order, and in a system such as that of Hegel we have an attempt to identify degrees of meaning and value with degrees of logical totality or completeness. In place of a single hierarchical conception we have what was described as a *double hierarchy*.

This conflict of motives has constantly tended to disrupt systems; and it is, in fact, the consciousness of this conflict which is one of the chief, if sometimes hidden, sources of opposition to the whole idea of system in philosophy.[1] This conflict is but a special form of the incompatibility of the order of values with the order of being which we have just been considering. It is the same conflict that expresses itself in the two conflicting propositions: There are degrees and levels of reality; all things are equally real, there can be no degrees in being. Or, again, the order of values is dualistic, the order of being monistic, and these two orders can be brought together only either by carrying the dualism of value into being, or by sacrificing differences of value to a monism of being.

This conflict of motives is as old as philosophy itself. It appears, of course, at all the most critical points of philosophic

---

[1] The presence of these two motives has given rise to two meanings of system—a narrower, which we may call *logical*, and a broader, which we may call *axiological*. It is the latter conception that has really dominated traditional philosophy throughout its history, and it is for system in this sense that we shall argue throughout the remaining pages of this chapter.

thought; but in its most intense form, in the antagonism between the ethical and the logical consciousness.

A moral interpretation of the world, which is uniformly expressed in religious or religiously toned systems, rests upon the antithesis of good and evil, on a selection of the former and a rejection of the latter, on the assurance that the good is in some sense dominant. But if we try to make God something greater, something that includes both, if we try to conceive God as all in all, we simply abolish moral distinctions. So the "ordinary consciousness," to use Hegel's somewhat contemptuous terms. And the ordinary consciousness, so sensitive is it to this antagonism, will not hesitate even to accept a finite god and to talk of a "god in the making."

But the conflict, so intense at this point, really runs throughout the whole of philosophic thought. It is the essence of the conflict between the transcendental and purely immanental teleology—the former emphasizing the principle of scale; the latter the principle of co-ordination, of organic whole or totality. It is, as we have also seen, the root problem of an intelligible concept of progress. For many, any conception of totality, any monism of being, must make the treatment of finality, moral values and progress, all the concepts that imply value, equivocal. Such a procedure is for them impossible without sacrificing other values to the logical, without a panlogism that swallows up all distinctions of value.

The seriousness of this problem will not be denied by anyone at all aware of the true inwardness of modern thought. That there is a deep-seated incompatibility between these two motives of systematizing, organizing thought is patent. The only real attempt to solve it is that of which the fundamental principle was enunciated by Hegel.[1] That his attempt to

---

[1] In principle, his solution consisted in the identification of the principle of system, as logical totality, with the principle of value through the concept of individuality. It is true that it is only in the later developments, such as Bosanquet's, that this identification has been made completely explicit, but it was always implied in Hegel's thinking. On this theory the attempt is made to *retain* the hierarchical principle of scale or subordination within the concept of system by equating degrees of value with degrees of wholeness or individuality, and equating the latter with degrees of reality. But the attempt is also made to retain the principle of co-ordination by seeking to show that the principle of totality is *equally* realized in the different forms of consciousness and different types of values.

reconcile them has been wholly satisfactory few would be disposed to claim. But first let us consider the attempt more closely, preferably in the form chosen by one of the contemporary upholders of this view.

"If," says Sorley, "we are to compare values at all, we must give up the idea of scale for system," and system here means "the ordering of parts within a significant whole." There are only two ways, we are told, in which the values of things can be compared. Either we cling to the idea of scale, and with this idea assume definite qualities of an indefinite thing or quality we call good or value; or, on the other hand, we equate highest value with the all, totality, and comparison is made in terms of the relation of the part to the whole. In the latter we have really abandoned scale for "system," or, at least, so merged the former in the latter as to have sacrificed some of its meaning.[1]

Now, if equating value with the all means giving up the idea of scale, it means also the denial of the structural element in system as we have found it actually to exist. It involves the sacrifice of external finality for that purely internal finality which we have found to be unintelligible. The reduction of value to a relation of part to whole involves that sacrifice of other values to the logical values which logical monism necessitates. But let us see first what is really involved in this procedure.

Value is identified with the logical whole, and comparison of value is made in terms of the relation of the part to the whole. But how, it may be asked, can the whole of reality have a value? Is it not as meaningless to predicate value of the whole as it is to say that the totality of matter is heavy? And yet it is precisely this that we must say—that the whole of reality must have value and significance on its own account—if the parts are to get their value from their relation to the whole. It is precisely here that the hierarchical motive inherent in the texture of our understanding puts in its caveat. For our mind, the functions of which are bound up with primal differences in content, only that which is in some way different and contrasting can be the subject of significance and value. This principle of scale, we have repeatedly seen, is not merely

[1] *Moral Values and the Idea of God*, p. 52.

"psychological." Our empirical way of valuing things is bound up with an *a priori* form, with the idea that beyond the valued thing there is necessarily another thing that has another value.[1] The hierarchical motive rests upon an *a priori* principle of value as such, through which the distinctions within being, in the absolute sense, alone acquire any meaning. How, then, can being in this most general sense, as the absolutely universal, or being as a totality, have value? Even though it be absolute in the sense that it is not dependent upon any conception or purpose beyond it, yet it is hardly conceivable that any bit of reality can retain its value when every other bit possesses value in the same degree. Then this character falls within being, and the accentuation and distinction which come through the predicate "value" is lost.[2]

It is the immitigable feeling expressed in these last sentences which will always, if I mistake not, stand in the way of a complete reduction of the scale of value to logical relations, and of philosophical system, in the larger sense, to logical system or totality. This feeling, expressed in the view that such a logical monism necessarily makes the treatment of personality, moral distinctions, and progress to a degree at least equivocal, is not without its basis in fact. The complete identification of value and being, we have long since seen, is impossible by way of intellect alone. The deep-seated incompatibility between these two motives of organizing and systematizing thought is but an indication of this impossibility, and the incompatibility cannot be resolved in the fashion proposed.

But does the point of view here described really present the problem in quite the right way? Need we *give up* the principle of scale for system? May it not be that the principle of scale is the essence of philosophical system?—that system, in the narrower sense of logical totality and the type of co-ordinating thought which this involves, represents merely *one* value in a larger system of values? May it not be that the "presupposition of totality," as it is implied in all philosophical thinking and

[1] Chapter X, pp. 338 ff.
[2] Absolutists, such as Bosanquet, do not, it is true, ascribe value to the whole. For them the Whole is rather the ground of all value. In other words, the whole does not *have* value as a *quality*. But, as we have seen earlier (in Chapter III), the tendency is still to make logical consistency ultimate, and with it to make the notion of logical system final.

germinal in all philosophic system, is of another type—namely, that which we have described as axiological unity?

This is the answer to the question that we, at least, feel obliged to make. All our preceding studies justify us in this conclusion. Not only does a study of actual historic systems show that their dominant motive is axiological; an examination of the axiom or presupposition of totality also shows that metaphysical totality, totality as the presupposition of intelligible communication and interpretation, cannot be reduced to logical totality.[1]

Everything turns here on this concept of axiological totality; and this in turn is bound up with the question, In what sense may logic be said to be the essence of philosophy, in what sense is it necessarily related to intelligibility and intelligible communication? The world is not intelligible to us, we have seen, unless the concepts in which the world is apprehended and expressed are in logical connections. But it is not these connections that alone or ultimately make it intelligible. Logical propositions give us merely the scaffolding of the world. Of themselves they treat of nothing. Unity for logic means merely necessary thought synthesis. Metaphysical totality, and with it philosophical system, enters only with the notion of an *ens realissimum*. With this enters likewise the idea of "dominant unity"; and thus the hierarchical principle of subordination becomes necessarily the ultimate principle of metaphysical system.

All this may be put in a more popular and, perhaps, more convincing way. It is perfectly obvious that the underlying motive of philosophic system, as distinguished from the abstract and partial systems of science, is valuational. Men want to "put things in their right order" (and therefore, in so far as knowledge necessarily issues in practice, "to control them well"). It is obvious, also, that in order to construct with certainty such an order, we should also have to grasp with exactness a completed scale. The "existence" of such a completed scale is the presupposition of all intelligible concepts of evolution and progress. This completed scale, this significant whole, is the axiological unity which is the germ of all system. The transparently incomplete nature of our actual experience,

[1] Chapter II, pp. 53 ff.

makes it, of course, impossible to do this. We may feel reasonably certain, however, that any such completed experience must be established along the lines of our actual experience as hitherto developed. We may be equally sure that no such completed experience will contradict the principle of "dominant unity," the hierarchical principle, structural in organizing thought. For one thing, no such further experience will ever make it necessary, or even possible, to do otherwise than give a privileged position to something. For another, no such experience will conceivably modify in principle either the fundamental distinctions in levels of being or the fundamental forms of value that are constitutive of our experience. A completed scale is impossible. Yet it is reasonable to suppose that the scale of values that is structural in traditional philosophy is immitigable in the sense that it is the necessary condition of the intelligible communication of the meanings of reality. It is also reasonable to suppose that it is the essence of all philosophic system.[1]

---

[1] This general position regarding axiological unity may be illustrated by reference to a particular problem that has played a leading rôle in modern philosophy. One form in which the principle of co-ordination has been championed as against that of subordination is the doctrine of absolute values and the principle of the autonomy of values it seems to imply.

It appears to be almost a corollary of a doctrine of absolute values that these universal values, or their partial expressions and embodiments, are not intelligible in terms of each other. If knowledge and understanding of the separate kinds of activity of the spirit, such as the scientific, the economic, the ethical, the æsthetic, presupposes an individual value or system of values for each kind, obviously the values must remain as separate as the kinds of spiritual activity. However good a man's acts may be, it is a confusion to say that they are true, or to say that goodness and truth are the same. It is also only in a metaphorical sense, and even then in one that is dangerous to knowledge, that beautiful objects are said to be true, or moral acts and mathematical systems beautiful. It follows, also, that the subordination of one value to another, of ethical and æsthetic to truth values, etc., is questionable. Intelligibility of one in terms of the other, or subordination, means relativity and contradicts the idea of absolute values.

Now, there is a certain limited sense in which this principle of autonomy is valid. The "philosophy of distinct concepts," the corner-stone of Croce's philosophy, for instance, is the condition of true evaluation, as it is the condition of intelligible communication and interpretation. *Das Anerkennen* of the fundamental types of validity, and of values, is the condition, as Hegel says, of philosophical *Erkennen*. But pressed to an extreme it easily becomes unintelligible. A glaring illustration of this—one of many—is Croce's doctrine of the æsthetic. On his view, the category of the æsthetic must be kept absolutely distinct from that of logic and morals. Truth, for instance, belongs wholly to logic, and to apply it to the æsthetic is merely a sign of confusion of thought. But in his development

VIII

All this sounds well enough. But, after all, is not this whole conception of philosophic system, as a system of values and validities, and as distinguished from merely logical system, based upon very sophisticated, if not sophistical, distinctions? After all, you cannot get away from the essentially logical nature of system. The attempt to order values, whether in the form of subordination or co-ordination, is still essentially a logical process. Any system of philosophy must be a system of concepts; the values of experience must be put in conceptual form. The system must, therefore, be logical, and in so far as it is logical it must rest upon the absolute character of the logical values of non-contradiction and necessary connection. Even if philosophy declares that the ultimate reality of the world is value, its ultimate meaning a unity or system of values, must not this result of thought be fixated in concepts and expressed in judgments? By this very fixation and expression is not the co-ordination of values again sacrificed? Does not the whole again become the object of knowledge, and all other values subordinated to logical values? Not only must a privileged position be given to something, but that something must be logic.

of his doctrine of the æsthetic as expression he is unable to avoid the concept of truth—at least implicitly, and actually often explicitly. For it is *adequate* expression that determines the criterion of the æsthetic, and this adequacy can be thought of only as truthful or sincere expression, or as agreement of expression with that which is to be expressed. It is only with truth, in some narrowly defined logical sense, not with truth in the natural use of the conception, that the æsthetic has no commerce.

The fact is that truth, goodness, and beauty are bound by "a threefold cord not lightly broken." The nature of that cord is not easily described, but its existence is even less easily denied. Autonomy of ultimate values, in some limited sense, is the condition of true evaluation as it is of intelligible communication. On the other hand, it is equally certain that no such relative autonomy can be in contradiction with the scale of values which a completed experience would mean. We are accustomed to classify our ends and values as truth, goodness, and beauty. The synthesis of these, their arrangement in a scale, is as yet beyond us. All attempts to reduce them to a common term, as, for example, wholeness or a contradictionless whole of experience, leave an unresolved remander. All attempts to reduce them one to another have proved unsuccessful. We attempt at best to combine them by way of compromise and co-ordination, and we feel that in the final result each contributes to our understanding of reality. But this compromise and co-ordination we feel can be only relative. We feel that values are really a system, and in the last analysis this system of values is the system of philosophy. For reason, properly understood, is the system of values.

To such questions, it would *seem*, there can be only two possible answers. We may, on the one hand, admit this contention, accept the view that logic is the ultimate science of being, and identify philosophic system with logical system, with all the consequences it entails. Or we may, on the other hand, while recognizing the necessity of system for the theoretical, logical mind, also frankly recognize its limitations, and admit that life and reality are alogical and escape all system. These difficulties have all been summed up in what has been described by Bergson as the dilemma of all systematic philosophy—either logical dogmatism or logical scepticism.

We may, it is said, on the one hand "hypostatize the logical unity, logic and nature, in a being who is nothing since he does nothing, an ineffectual God who simply sums up all the given; or in an eternal matter from whose womb have been poured out the properties of things and laws of nature; or, again, in a pure form which endeavours to seize an unseizable multiplicity, and which is, as we will, the form of nature or the form of thought. All these philosophies in their different languages tell us that logic and science are right in treating reality as identical with logic." Or we may, on the other hand, still assuming that logic and system are identical, recognize the impossibility of system, *in this sense*, grasping life, reality, and change, admit that the latter are irrational, and accept the consequent scepticism and agnosticism.[1]

But there seems to me to be a third possible position—a way out of this dilemma by which philosophy may remain truly systematic and yet not accept either of these alternatives. That is to recognize *another principle of order*. Bergson, in his argument regarding the contrast of order and disorder, rightly denies any absolute character to disorder or chaos. To deny that reality is identical with logical order does not necessarily mean that it is without order. And he then speaks of the Vital Order. But can this concept—for it is a concept—be given any intelligible meaning? Only, I think, if this order is conceived as an order of values. It is unnecessary to recall again our discussions of the life concept—how that concept cannot even be intelligibly formed without reference to value and a scale of values, how evolutionary philosophies which make life the

[1] *Creative Evolution*, pp. 196, 197.

ultimate concept can escape ambiguity and unintelligibility only by a concept of life which is life-transcendent.[1] It must suffice here to draw the inevitable conclusion that the concept of a vital order, in so far, at least, as it is more than a mere negation of an order that is mechanical or static, in so far as it has any positive content, must be conceived as an order of values.

The point I am here seeking to make is a fundamental one. Life, as a *category*—and it is a category if we use it in thought at all—has in it already the germ of system. Every category implies system. What is life? Do you answer in biological terms? Immediately its unlimited, non-rational character has become limited and rational, and its place in a system of thought become inevitable. Do you answer it in terms that transcend the biological categories? Again the vague, the indefinite, the unlimited, that character of the term which made it inimical to system, becomes definite and limited, and again some system becomes inevitable. By this I mean that the term "life" then becomes meaningful only if you distinguish it from merely biological existence, while this distinction can be made only by the acknowledgment of values which have significance only within a system of values and validities. In other words, we have here but a special case of the general principle that in every theoretical, and therefore intelligible, denial of system, we affirm it. A vital order is still an order, and anyone who makes use of the term "order" in any meaningful way must use it with its necessary implications.

IX

But this so-called dilemma of all systematic philosophy still persists in the modern mind, and the point at which it is most cogent is naturally in connection with the ideas of evolution and progress, those forms in which the meaning of life and history finds conceptual embodiment. Traditional thought has always found system and development compatible. This combination of development with system is one, however, which the modern mind positively refuses to find intelligible. Systems

[1] Chapter IX, pp. 325 ff.

must be made to march, but they absolutely cannot be made to do so.

Space forbids any extensive treatment of this problem. It must suffice to consider it as merely a special case of the general dilemma. We shall content ourselves with suggesting two points of a general nature.

We may suggest, in the first place, that there cannot be any final and intrinsic incompatibility between the notions of progress and system. If there is any one thing that has emerged clearly from our study of progress it is that progress itself is essentially a systematic concept. It is impossible to form an intelligible concept of progress without a system of values. Wherein, then, lies the difficulty? It seems to arise from a certain ambiguity in the notion of progress itself. If we speak of progress as a fact, there seems to be no question that the fact can be determined only by reference to a scale or system of values. But we also speak of progress as an end or goal, and progress in this sense is assumed to be impossible without continuous change incompatible with any concept of system.

Now, we have already seen that progress as a goal is a treacherous, if not futile, idea. Progress as the aim of the historical life of man can be given no intelligible meaning. Progress that makes its goal as it goes, taken in any absolute sense, is a nonsense. This is peculiarly evident in connection with the idea of progress in knowledge. It was made quite clear, I think, that if progress in knowledge implies the idea that the contents of knowledge are always reacting on its fundamental structure so that no philosophy can flatter itself that it will not be altered out of all recognition as knowledge grows, then system and progress are incompatible. But then progress and genuine knowledge are also incompatible. If we have an evolving knowledge in any absolute sense, do we ever really know where we are, or do we know in what direction to turn in order to orient ourselves in the world? "It was only after the invention of the compass that Columbus ventured across the uncharted seas. And if he was mistaken in thinking that the land immediately west of Europe was India, he was, at least, correct in his basal assumption that made the voyage across the Atlantic a glorious adventure and not a mad prank." So a recent writer, and we may well ask with him, "What if we have no compass or even polar star?" Doubtless knowledge "grows from more to more," but there is no way of telling that it thus grows if the idea of knowledge itself is subject to absolute change.

But the dilemma of all systematic philosophy strikes deeper than this. System and evolution itself are said to be incompatible. Unless the whole evolves, change and evolution as aspects of the whole are reduced to illusion; but if the whole evolves there can be no system. The familiar contention of the modernist may be summarized thus. If the whole is real, then change and movement in any form that is equally real must be ruled out in advance. If, on the other hand, we accept the reality of change and movement, we are at once debarred from maintaining the existence of a true whole.

This is so common an assumption nowadays that it goes almost unchallenged. Quite the contrary is the case—as, indeed, all the systematic thinkers of the past have seen, for whom change and development were really intelligible only in an unchanging whole. An intelligible concept of evolution, no less than of progress, can be formed, we have already seen, only on the basis of a system of values.[1] Moreover, the moment we begin to talk about evolution of the whole in the sense that we talk about evolution of finite organisms, we are on the brink of the unmeaning. If we are to apply the ideas of development, movement, to the whole in any intelligible sense, we must give these ideas a new meaning. The only kind of development applicable to reality as a whole is development of the Idea.[2] Even in the physical sciences the opposition between totality and change seems to be disappearing as the necessary result of the most recent physical conceptions.[3]

[1] Chapter XI, pp. 385 ff.   [2] Chapter IX, pp. 326 ff.

[3] It is an interesting fact, as has recently been pointed out by a number of writers, that, while modernist philosophy makes this assumption, modern physical thinking is proceeding in the opposite direction. The method of dealing with time that is distinctive of the theory of relativity, instead of emphasizing, as we might expect, this opposition between wholeness and change, has made it possible, if indeed not necessary, to subsume change and development under a still profounder concept of the whole. As a result of the now familiar unity between the categories of space and time, the universe becomes one that may be surveyed as a whole in which past, present, and future are one. It is a four-dimensional unity. The particular point in this theory at which the union of totality and change appears is in the concept of the universe as physically finite

Evolution and development, therefore, cannot be ultimately incompatible with system. Our chief concern here, however, is with the contention that change and movement become *unreal* if system is real.

Here, again, we must insist, we are concerned with *intelligible* movement, just as we were concerned with intelligible progress and evolution as concepts which imply movement. We are not concerned with motion as an irrational brute fact, supposed to be apprehended in some mysterious way by brute perception or some mystical intuition, but as apprehended by thought. The mind grasps movement only by *notions*—the concepts, namely, of potency and actuality or realization. These concepts, we have maintained, are neither merely practical, nor are they intellectual dogmas forced on a resisting reality. They spring rather out of the fact that interpenetration and continuity, the very essence of duration and motion, are themselves intelligible only as successive states are held together by value. They are value concepts, and constitute the only way in which meaningful becoming and movement may be grasped.[1] Need it be pointed out that hierarchical system and intelligible movement are not only compatible but actually imply each other?

and the conception of gravitation within that universe. On this view all gravitational phenomena, changes within the system, are the effects of a universal and permanently distributed condition of stress throughout the finite universe. They are manifestations of an omnipresent, but locally variant, property of the omnipresent ether, such that every localized modification is instantaneously communicated at all other points.

That the physicist has no difficulty in thinking such conceptions is, of course, in itself no proof that they are metaphysically ultimately intelligible. To bring into our reckoning the phenomena of life, mind, and value might, indeed, bring to light difficulties in the combination of wholeness and change which do not here appear. But one thing may, at least, be said without hesitation. Any supposed *a priori* difficulties in the concept of change in an unchanging whole must be ruled out. For physical thinking at least, not only are these concepts compatible, but, paradoxical as it may seem, on this view, the physical system of reality, just because it is a system, just because it is unchangingly stressed, must contain within itself incessant change in the form of gravitational phenomena, change which is the direct result of the unchanging nature of the whole. Now, if physical thinking can find such concepts intelligible, it is entirely gratuitous to say that metaphysical thinking shall not. It is not *a priori* impossible to retain change in all its essentiality in a whole which itself, as a whole, does not change. The supposed contradiction between development and wholeness which is so continuously insisted upon as fundamental and irreducible need not be so.

[1] Chapter VII, p. 250.

The true is the whole, but the whole is *das durch seine Entwickelung sich vollendede Wesen*. In these terms we found Hegel seeking to express the ultimate conditions of an intelligible world—conditions which include both system and development. This idea of *dynamic system*, of a self-completing whole, is, I hold, not necessarily internally contradictory and unintelligible. That the complete rationalization of this idea, this fusion of totality and progress, is possible, I would be the last to affirm. It is no more possible than the complete rationalization of the ideas of the uncaused cause, the consummation of the end, the imperishable goal, or any other ultimate metaphysical ideas, no more possible than the complete fusion of value and being that underlies them all. An element of the mystical and ineffable can no more be excluded from this idea than from any of the great interpretative ideas. "Trenching on the mystical" is involved in any complete fusion of value and being, and a mystical element will necessarily appear in all metaphysical language that expresses that fusion. I do not say, then, that such notions can be made completely intelligible. I insist, merely, that these notions are necessary for intelligibility and intelligible communication; they are part of an intelligible world. Of such is the notion of philosophic system.

In any case, this much may be said with a certain confidence as the necessary outcome of the argument of this chapter. System is a necessary condition of philosophical intelligibility. The only intelligible conception of philosophic system, however, is one which views it as a system of values and validities—in short, the axiological concept of totality as we have developed it. Finally, the historical embodiment of this notion of system is found only in that *form* of philosophical intelligibility, that entire value-charged scheme of thought, which has functioned continually throughout traditional philosophy. From this all systems have derived, and to this all systems must, in one form or another, ultimately return.

X

Cui bono? What boots all this to those of us who still know in our hearts that we are not narrow enough for any system

to those of us who still find the world such a manifold of
transitions and half-lights that it is absurd to impress an order
upon them, to those of us for whom life, reality, is so full of
a number of things that we have no interest in trying to order
them? With all you have said, it is still headlining of the
universe you propose, and for ourselves we prefer it without
headlines.

All that you have said may be true enough. We must have
a system whether we will it or not. You may have shown its
inherent necessity in thought. It may even be granted that
the logical difficulties in the concept of system may be overcome, but what of it? For us it is all one gigantic *ignoratio
elenchi*. In fact, we have no common ground. You appeal to
"reason," whatever that may be; we appeal to impression:

> "Against a copper-pink, sunset sky
> Black laces of tree-tops peacefully lie.
> A robin, with unique art untold,
> Both light feet together, is tearing the mould:
> The sea roars with storms—is dimpled with calms;
> A child runs shouting to his father's arms;
> Lord, who are we to catalogue *living*!"

Now, in so far as all this is but expressive of a mood of the
Time-Spirit, there is, it must be repeated, no answer. Life is
moody, art may be, and even science often is, but philosophy
dare not be. To such impressionism there is no theoretical
answer, and an extra-theoretical position is no philosophical
position at all. But this very mood is itself often the expression
of a theoretical judgment, and, we have seen, based on grounds
of reason. In so far as it claims to be that, it may be brought
to the bar of intelligibility and reason.

Isn't it really more *intelligible*, so we may imagine those of
this way of thinking and feeling expressing themselves—isn't
it really more meaningful to conceive the world as systemless,
as not only incalculable but ultimately uninterpretable? Why
should not one, for instance, instead of thinking of the world
as will or the world as reason, as rational or irrational, think
of it as a "world of imagination," to which neither of the terms
of this dichotomy applies? Is not life and living just like that?
And to think life and the world that way, as limitless variety

and limitless creation, as we find it in our own imagination, is not that to make it intelligible in the only sense it can be made so?

Here at last—is it not perfectly evident?—we have followed modernism to its ultimate stronghold. Here we have the Time-Spirit in one of its franker moods. Is there any possible answer to be made to such a position?

Apparently not. If such a world appears intelligible there seems to be nothing further to say. Here we have, perhaps, merely a question of taste, even if from our point of view perverted taste, and all disputation is futile. And yet there is still something to say, and in trying to say it we come to the *last* word that can be said in philosophy. For, after all, we are all *thinking* here, irrespective of what we think. There are ultimately only three possible positions for thought to take, only three possible places where it can come to any kind of rest. Either all anchorage fails and we rest in scepticism, illusionism, nihilism. Or it may have some kind of hold on reality. If it has a hold at all, this must be found either in the limited or the unlimited. The former means system of some sort; the latter means that Life, in the indefinite, un-limited sense of the poem, is taken as ultimate; and the last word, then, is pure impressionism.

Pure impressionism is, however, in the last analysis, incom-municable. Even the language of poetry, that language by which man seeks to communicate his more integral experiences and more significant meanings, becomes intelligible only within a universe of discourse which itself presupposes a system of values and validities. Even the language of the mystics, that language in which men seek to communicate the incommuni-cable and the ineffable, itself presupposes such a system. As the great Christian mystics have in the main found it possible to express themselves only within the forms of dogmatic theology, so the great philosophical mystics have not only been at home within the traditional system of realities and values, but, in so far as they have sought to communicate their meanings, have found it possible to do so only in a language which implies that system. All intelligible communication thus involves a universe of discourse which is, in its very structure and essence, systematic.

It is, then, not a question of order or absence of order, of system or systemlessness; it is rather a question between orders. Into some order the things will inevitably fall if we try to talk about them at all; it is, therefore, a question of the right order. It is not a question whether a philosopher has or has not a system; for only through system does he become a philosopher. The real question is whether in that system we have a normal and fundamental way of seeing the world. Only if he has the right order will a philosopher become part of the Great Tradition in philosophy, only then, indeed, will his language be ultimately and permanently understood. In this last sentence is to be found the epitome of all that this book has attempted to say. Philosophy is intelligible discourse about the world, and the metaphysical idiom of the Great Tradition is the only language that is really intelligible.

POSTSCRIPT

IT is foolish to try to say everything at once, yet this is precisely what the philosopher, more than anyone else, is tempted to do. Convinced as he is of the absolute relevance of all questions, there remains always the feeling of having left important things unsaid. The present writer has not wholly escaped this temptation. In the manuscript of the book as prepared for publication, there was also a third part which, for various reasons, was not included in the printed form. It may not be amiss to state the titles of the three chapters which composed this part. They will, at least, serve to indicate the topics which, it was felt, an exhaustive treatment of the main theme would include, and to suggest that the writer is not unaware of certain problems which the reader of the book will inevitably raise.

A chapter entitled *The Language of Metaphysics* considers in detail the problems of the "philosophy of language" which have been raised at various points in the work. In general it attempts to make good the thesis that the Great Tradition alone speaks an intelligible language. A second chapter considers the general problem of *The Nature of Truth*, and more particularly "the truth of metaphysics." The object of this chapter is to develop more fully the relation of truth to intelligibility and to show that traditional philosophy has uniformly taught a liberalistic conception of truth in contrast to narrow and inadequate conceptions of modern thought. Finally, a third chapter, entitled *Trenching on the Mystical*, seeks to show the place of the mystical element in perennial philosophy, the relation of the language of mysticism to the language of metaphysics, and, in general, to uphold the validity of the mystical element by showing that there can be no adequate communication and interpretation of our experience without this trenching on the mystical.

The relation of this unpublished part to the present work needs no further comment. The development of these themes and their publication under the general title of *The Language of Metaphysics* would constitute a proper sequel to the present book.

INDEX